The Other World

SMITH COLLEGE STUDIES
IN MODERN LANGUAGES
· NEW SERIES ·

ESTABLISHED IN HONOR OF
THE SEVENTY-FIFTH ANNIVERSARY
OF THE OPENING OF
SMITH COLLEGE

I

The Other World

ACCORDING TO DESCRIPTIONS IN MEDIEVAL LITERATURE

HOWARD ROLLIN PATCH

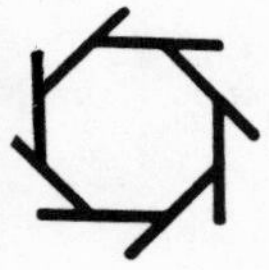

1970

OCTAGON BOOKS

New York

Reprinted 1970
by special arrangement with Harvard University Press

OCTAGON BOOKS
A DIVISION OF FARRAR, STRAUS & GIROUX, INC.
19 Union Square West
New York, N. Y. 10003

AM

LIBRARY OF CONGRESS CATALOG CARD NUMBER: 77-96164

Printed in U.S.A. by
TAYLOR PUBLISHING COMPANY
DALLAS, TEXAS

DEDICATED TO

MARY, PRISCILLA, ROBERT,
AND HOWARD

PREFACE

THE PRESENT VOLUME is offered as the fulfillment of a pledge made years ago to extend a preliminary study, the results of which the author had published in an article, beyond the limits then reached into something like a comprehensive survey of the whole field. It soon became apparent that no one could complete such a task alone. Only what might be called the prolegomena for the work might be presented with suggestions for method and some indication of the extent of the material. The author hopes that he has succeeded in clarifying certain preliminary questions and in offering a technique for the analysis of particular instances which may be applied fruitfully beyond the limits of the documents here examined.

It will be noticed that the method changes in the course of this specific investigation. In the early chapters the results of the work of other scholars are summarized, not, however, without consulting as often as reasonable space permitted the primary sources available. In the chapter on visions the narratives are outlined rather fully by name, but in the chapters after that the discussion becomes more cursory, especially where the material is better known. In the field of the romances the principle of organization has often been that of similarity of plot structure or of types of subject matter. It has seemed unnecessary to present here a detailed analysis of the plots of stories which have been so often worked over before, many times in connection with the same questions. Here certainly many of the conclusions proposed must be tentative, and at present one can hope to offer only a different approach perhaps or a little further light on the road to achievement. The author enters the lists of Arthurian romance with considerable trepidation in view of the blasting spells and beheading so often encountered there. As often as seemed possible he has tried to keep clear of special theories of mythological derivation where the battle of controversy is still on and to hold to the high road of what ideas, if any, seem to have been generally accepted.

Little could have been done in all this study without the previous researches of many scholars, and it is impossible to indicate fully the author's indebtedness to all those who have made his way easier. It is my happy obligation, however, to express my gratitude here to scholars who have assisted me in dealing with special phases of the work to which reference may not be pertinently made in the footnotes. Professor Agnes C. Vaughan read the section on classical material for me with helpful suggestions. Professor Eleanor S. Duckett went carefully over the chapter on the literature of visions. Professor Francis P. Magoun, Jr., of Harvard University, gave me advice on the chapter on Germanic literature; and Professor Kenneth Jackson and Professor Fred N. Robinson, both of Harvard, helped me with the discussion of Celtic documents. Professor Roger S. Loomis of Columbia University and Mrs. Loomis set me right at many points on the material of the romances. Professor Edna Williams of Smith College has given me the benefit of a detailed criticism of the method of presentation I have adopted, and I have nearly always made use of her suggestions. But by all odds my greatest debt is to Professor Archer Taylor of the University of California, folklorist extraordinary and friend incomparable, who read over almost the whole manuscript with care more than once and gave me the benefit of his learning and his wisdom at more points than I can now represent in any adequate way. But with him, as with all the rest, the author is bound to say that if there are merits in this book they are often those contributed by such assistance, and whatever blame there may be for faults is the author's alone.

Grateful acknowledgment must go to William Morrow & Company, Inc. for permission to use a brief excerpt from James Hilton's *Lost Horizon,* to the Johns Hopkins Press and the editors of the Kemp Malone volume for the right to use the substance of my own article in that book, and to Random House, Inc. for permission to quote the four lines from Auden's poetry. Henry Holt & Company has allowed me to quote various passages from *Ancient Irish Tales* by Cross and Slover, and from *Latin Writers of the Fifth Century* by Eleanor S. Duckett. The Columbia University Press permits me to use the translations in Hollander's *Old Norse*

Poems; and Professor Hollander himself, for the University of Texas, has granted me the same right for his *Poetic Edda*. I am also indebted to Professor Brodeur for permission to use his translation of the prose *Edda*. A special word must be added with regard to the generosity of the library at the University of California and of that at Harvard University, where every possible favor has been granted and work is made unusually pleasant. The interlibrary loan has also facilitated my task again and again, where I have had to consult books of some rarity, perhaps even more than once. The librarians of the Smith College Library have given me every assistance, and only students who have worked here can know fully of their unstinting kindness.

I take special pleasure too in thanking my former student, Mrs. Gordon Potter, who has followed me every step of the way in this undertaking, from the time she heard my first lectures on the subject in my seminar through the years when she has checked the footnotes in detail and from time to time brought me up short in the matter of accuracy or consistency. Now and then no doubt her patience has been tested by the impression that with me she has been embarked in a rudderless boat floating from one illusive shore to another, where the inhabitants stand jeering with the renewed cry, "It is they! It is they!"

Howard R. Patch

Northampton, Massachusetts

CONTENTS

THE OTHER WORLD

Subest fons uiuacis uene
adest cantus philomene
Naiadumque cantilene,
paradisus hic est pene,
non sunt loca, scio plene,
his iocundiora.

Carmina Burana

Beware. All those who follow me are led
Onto that Glassy Mountain where are no
Footholds for logic, to that Bridge of Dread
Where knowledge but increases vertigo.

W. H. Auden

INTRODUCTION

MAN SEEMS ALWAYS to have cherished, in vision or imagination, strange thoughts of a mysterious country to which he longs to go. Whether this takes the form of a supposed realm of delight which he may actually wish to visit, though the journey be difficult, or whether it is like a memory out of the past or a dream of the future, he has his ideas of a golden age in the perfect milieu, or of a utopia, or of a region he will attain to after death if he fares well and the gods are propitious. So whether as an escape from reality or as an instinctive resource, he has brought forth from his imagination, and perhaps from actual visions, and perhaps, too, the subconscious, all the many images of the Isles of the Blessed, the Earthly Paradise, the Pied Piper's country inside the mountain, the garden on the mountain top, the heavenly city in the skies, and the realm under the earth or under the sea. Descriptions of such places are found widely distributed in the literature of every nation.

When scenes like these appear, however, it is not always obvious that ultimately they derive from a mythological origin and in particular from the tradition of these accounts of the type of Other World which I have indicated. Parts of an earlier idea may be borrowed, certain elements in several descriptions taken over, until the precise channel of transmission is thoroughly obscured. Perhaps it is never quite safe to draw a definite conclusion about sources immediate or remote. But it is my intention in this study to examine various documents in the medieval field, with special reference to English, French, and Italian, in order to discover examples of the Other World as it appears in allegory, romance, and didactic treatises of one kind or another, and to see whether we can identify the chief outlines of their background in folklore.

This task is hardly new, for its importance has long been realized and many scholars have been busy with the enterprise.[1]

[1] For the classical field the encyclopedias of Roscher, Pauly and Wissowa, and others, offer much material. Nearer to our subject, Hastings' *Encyclo-*

But even with the suggestions from their work and the material now made available, it is still impossible to make an exhaustive collection; for new items have a way of turning up and what we have on hand, together with what may be expected, would require many further monographs on detailed problems and several volumes for a final publication. In view of the extent of the available material it has seemed wise to make a more general survey of what is known and of certain instances that hitherto have escaped notice, to see whether any dependable conclusions are beginning to emerge so that other investigators may have something of a guide to assist them from this point on.

Skeptics may still maintain that some examples of the Other World here referred to represent nothing more significant than coincidence with the well known features of familiar descriptions of the scene. A castle surrounded by a moat on a hill, as it is described in some romance, may involve uncanny adventure, and yet reflect nothing more remarkable than medieval castles in general. That, of course, may be true if the description offers nothing more. But a survey of this kind should be of some help in determining whether that is all there is to the particular case under consideration. After we have followed various journeys to the Otherworld realm and visited the land under the sea or inside the hill, we should be more competent to identify characteristic features. Thus there can be little doubt that after Launfal has crossed the river in the lay of Marie de France, or Chaucer has ascended in the clutches of the eagle to the towers of the House of Fame, we have traveled with each of them to the mysterious country now being discussed. Proof of this, if it were needed for argument, will be apparent in many other instances to be studied. Moreover, we may be enabled to offer something more than a shrewd guess at the ultimate source in mythology from which these elements were taken.

In visions and dreams and symbolic "figures of the true," man

---

paedia of Religion and Ethics, II, s.v. "Blest, Abode of the," offers much, together with Stith Thompson's *Motif-Index of Folk-Literature*, III, and various monographs and studies by Edoardo Coli, Arturo Graf, Alfred Nutt, G. L. Kittredge, A. C. L. Brown, W. A. Nitze, R. S. Loomis, T. P. Cross, L. C. Wimberly, and many others, to all of whom this present volume is indebted both specifically and in a general way.

has set forth his ideas of the Other World with certain fairly constant elements that recur in descriptions, as we shall see, suggesting that something more than psychological coincidence is necessary to explain their use. As we have observed, the approach to the region is sometimes underground, down a well perhaps, and sometimes under the sea. It may also be by a path through a desolate tract or by a flight up through the skies. Sometimes there is a water barrier, a river, perhaps, or the sea. The realm is usually located on an island in such a case, or a group of islands. Sometimes too it may be inside a hill or a mountain or on top of the mountain. Thus nearly every kind of conceivable barrier may be set to the traveler. The point here, however, is to observe whether approximately the same type of obstacle appears in various documents otherwise related so that they imply a channel of transmission to later literature, or whether the obstacle seems entirely determined by chance.

In the same way it is important to study the features of the realm itself. Here we usually find a garden with a fountain or several fountains, and one or more conspicuous trees laden with fruit. The perfume of the place is sometimes marked with peculiarity, and the birds are especially to be noticed for the quality of their song. Other familiar motifs include the pavilion or dwelling place, a castle or a palace, jewels in the garden or in the decoration of the palace, the music which is heard, the predominance of crystal in the building, the effect of eating the fruit there, and a mention of the abnormal passage of time — short or long — during the visit. Many of these features, it is true, are quite commonplace, although they sometimes carry a special earmark of their origin. It is their combination, over and over again, according to a sort of formula, that reveals with some certainty the property room from which they have come. Here the advantage of a large number of examples will be clear in showing the types of formulae that make plain the whole development. When we find one or another of these same ground plans, so to speak, in some older mythology, we may be justified in making the inference that there lay the beginnings of that particular kind of Other World. But it should be borne in mind, as I have said, that whatever value the study may have does not lie merely in such conclusions, which must remain tentative to a greater or less degree; it consists also, I hope, in showing the range and variety of the material, and in that way in helping to map out the whole terrain of similar or related documents.

The first chapters will contain some account of the most characteristic features of the Other World in the early mythologies — oriental, classical, Celtic, and Germanic. Against the background, then, of what is evident here, we shall consider the literature of a large part of medieval Europe with a view to studying these features in its development, and attempt to suggest their significance. Doubtless it will appear from time to time in going over this kind of writing, as so often in other matters, that there is nothing new under the sun, even in man's dreams and aspirations and the revelations granted to him. That, if true, would have its own meaning. But the fascination of at least part of the evidence as it comes to us is that there is something new after all, sometimes through the personality of the various authors and again through the genuine originality and creative power that mark different uses of the same motifs.

Thus the island is one thing to Tristram when he goes there and meets Iseult, and another to Arthur on his way to Avalon. Differences in mythological origin or means of transmission, in the parallel use of what is fundamentally the same motif, may also explain certain variations in description, as in the contrasting accounts of the mountain in Chaucer's *House of Fame* and Dante's *Purgatorio*. The latter derives, it would seem, from medieval notions of the Earthly Paradise and its location, while Chaucer's rock of ice is taken partly perhaps from Nicole de Margival but ultimately also from more generalized folklore regarding the holy mountain as it came down through various allegories. Both still carry some of the older and varied meanings, and both show important features of originality in concept.

It may now be observed that it is no part of my responsibility in this study to determine whether in its mythological origins the Other World is truly or validly or consistently portrayed, whether it is based on actual experience, whether it can be attained only after death, or even what its precise meaning was at any period. In the literary use of broken-down mythologies most meanings change, and the physical elements themselves remain constant only in a general way. I have, however, limited my investigations to the longed-for country or supposedly more or less desirable region, and have therefore excluded the places of torture or punishment unless for some special reason they come within my province. Hell furnishes a significant counterpart for some of my material. When it is found along with the Elysian Fields, as in the *Aeneid* in the journey underground, it may be mentioned; sometimes it becomes important for us, as in the episode of the *Purgatory of St. Patrick* where souls to escape it have to cross the Bridge of Judgment if they would reach Paradise. But for the most part it is left out of account because in general it has little to do with the mysterious, enchanted, or delightful regions we are examining in romance and allegory.

Finally I may say that I have not gone into developments of my subject in the modern period, where journeys to mythical realms show further complications and excitements with the coming of scientific inventions that make adventure possible not only a thousand leagues under the sea or up to the Moon, but through microscope and telescope to imaginary lands beyond the wildest dreams of medieval man. The stories that I do consider, however, whether of the voyage in a rudderless boat to fairyland or in a flying chariot to the heavenly city, or an exploration in search of the Earthly Paradise, may fairly be regarded as preparing the way for the later excursions, just as early travelers looking for the Fountain of Youth came at last to stand "Silent, upon a peak in Darien" with a new universe opening before their eyes.

I

MYTHOLOGICAL ORIGINS

ORIENTAL AND CLASSICAL

Oriental Mythology

BECAUSE OF THE MIGRATIONS and the western spread of culture it is obvious that for the ultimate sources of important elements in descriptions of the Other World one must look to the east. Many scholars have been aware of the fact, and studies like those of Becker, Coli, Cox, and Landau, have suggested specific points of almost certain indebtedness. These may be listed in the course of the present investigation without presenting the full argument all over again. Moreover, the numerous manuals and encyclopedias of mythology have made a thoroughly detailed review of this field unnecessary here. The chief thing to observe for our purposes is the particular stamp or quality of the elements, where that is possible, as they come before us.

The ascent to heaven, the water barrier, the river, the bridge, and the holy mountain, are found singly or in various combinations in Eastern lore. According to the *Rig Veda* the dead on their way to heaven fly with wings or travel by a car to the skies to dwell with the Fathers and Yama.[1] The use of a ladder is familiar in Egyptian and Hebrew lore.[2] Elijah ascended in a fiery chariot. Angels in the Jewish and Christian tradition come for the souls of the dead.

[1] A. B. Keith, *The Religion and Philosophy of the Veda and Upanishads*, 2nd half, pp. 406ff.; *Rig Veda*, ix, 113, 7ff. (cf. Ludwig, *Der Rigveda*, II, pp. 567ff., § 945, 7ff., and Hillebrandt, *Lieder des Ṛgveda*, p. 37); Nutt, in K. Meyer's *Voyage of Bran*, I, p. 321; *Atharva-Veda*, iv, 34, 4 (trans. Whitney, *Atharva-Veda*, 1st half, p. 206).

[2] Cf. versions of the story of Jacob's Ladder: W. Max Müller, *Mythology of All Races: Egyptian*, p. 175. The ladder is an important folklore motif of which instances will appear from time to time in this study.

The water barrier is a feature in some form or other common to almost all the accounts. The Persian *Avesta* tells of the sea Pûitika in the west and also the sea Vouru-Kasha. In the latter of these is the tree Gaokerena, which bears the white Haoma, food of immortality.[3] Other trees are there as well which bear the seed of all trees on earth, and the birds Amru and Kamru shake them and spread the seed abroad. Obviously Vouru-Kasha is an Other-world element serving partly as background for a representative of the Tree of Life. Especially since the exhumation of the boat found in the tomb of Tutankhamen everybody has known that with the Egyptians the soul goes at death on a voyage to Paradise. In this case the vessel has its ornate cabin amidships and a gilded pavilion on the forecastle.[4] In the Babylonian epic of Gilgamesh, the hero travels across the waters of death, said to be in the south-east, to reach the fields of the blessed.

A bridge by which souls reach heaven is an essential of the Persian accounts:

At the head of the *Kinvad* bridge, the holy bridge made by Mazda, they ask for their spirits and souls the reward for the worldly goods which they gave away here below.

Then comes the well-shapen, strong and tall-formed maid, with the dogs at her sides, one who can distinguish, who is graceful, who does what she wants, and is of high understanding.

She makes the soul of the righteous one go up above the Hara-berezaiti; above the *Kinvad* bridge she places it in the presence of the heavenly gods themselves.[5]

[3] For the relation to the Soma drink see Griswold, *The Religion of the Rigveda*, pp. 209f. and 217f.

[4] The journey is westward with the sun god, according to Maspero, *Dawn of Civilization*, pp. 196 and 199–200. Cf. Mackenzie, *Egyptian Myth and Legend*, pp. 96ff.; Tylor, *Primitive Culture*, II, p. 48.

[5] *The Zend-Avesta*, Part I, *Vendîdâd, Fargard* xix, 29–30 (trans. by Darmesteter, *Sacred Books of the East*, IV, pp. 212–213). Cf. *The Zend-Avesta*, Part II, *Yast* xxii, 7–9 (*Sacred Books of the East*, XXIII, pp. 315–316) for an interpretation of the maid, and for the sweet-scented wind. In the seventh century A.D. the bridge appears also in the *Book Ardâ Vîrâf*, chs. iv–v (where it widens for the virtuous man) and ch. xvii. See the edition and translation by Haug and West, pp. 154ff. and 162ff. See also Dillmann, *Genesis* IV, p. 109; Delitzsch, *Wo lag das Paradies?* pp. 112f. The bridge is at home in Shinto and Buddhism: cf. *The Literature of Japan, World's Great Classics Series*, I, *Oriental Literature*, p. 254; Griffis, *The Religions of Japan*, pp. 63 and 293, n. 7; Hastings, *Encyclopaedia of Religion and Ethics*, II, pp. 700ff.

Dogs guard the bridge:

nor will the dogs that keep the *Kinvad* bridge help his departing soul through the howls and pursuit in the other world.[6]

The wicked soul of course falls down into hell, but the holy man passes in safety.[7] The bridge "in the form of a blade" grows broader as the righteous advance, but narrower for the wicked man:

Moreover, the bridge becomes a broad bridge for the righteous, as much as the height of nine spears . . . — and the length of those which they carry is each separately three reeds — ; and it becomes a narrow bridge *for* the wicked, even unto a resemblance to the edge of a razor. And he who is of the righteous passes over the bridge, and a worldly similitude of the pleasantness of his path upon it is when thou shalt eagerly and unweariedly walk in the golden-coloured spring, and *with* the gallant . . . body and sweet-scented blossom in the pleasant skin of that maiden spirit, the price of goodness. He who is of the wicked, as he places a footstep *on* to the bridge, on account of affliction . . . and *its* sharpness, falls from the middle of the bridge, and rolls *over* head-foremost. And the unpleasantness of his path to hell is in similitude such as the worldly *one* in the midst of that stinking *and* dying existence . . .[8]

It may be characteristic also of the East Indian and Babylonian,[9] and it reappears in Moslem literature.[10] In the latter Abenarabi says:

[6] *The Zend-Avesta,* Part I, *Vendîdâd, Fargard* xiii, 9 (*Sacred Books of the East,* IV, p. 154).

[7] *The Zend-Avesta,* Part II, *Vîstâsp, Yast* xxiv, 42 (*Sacred Books of the East,* XXIII, p. 339).

[8] *Pahlavi Texts, Dâdistân-i Dînîk,* xxi, 5–8, (trans. E. W. West, *Sacred Books of the East,* XVIII, pp. 48–49). Cf. the Iranian *Bundahishn,* cited by Pavry, *The Zoroastrian Doctrine of a Future Life,* p. 91.

[9] Hopkins, *The Religions of India,* p. 145; cf. Scherman, *Materialen zur geschichte der indischen visions litteratur,* pp. 110–111; Keith, *The Religion and Philosophy of the Veda and Upanishads,* p. 406 (referring to the dog who guards at the Avestan bridge and scares away fiends). For a suspension bridge in the epic of Gilgamesh see Ungnad and Gressman, *Gilgamesch-Epos,* pp. 49, 138, 165, n. 1. There is some dispute about the meaning of the very obscure passage. Cf. with Ungnad, Jastrow, *The Religion of Babylonia and Assyria,* p. 492; *Assyrian and Babylonian Literature, Selected Translations,* intro. by R. F. Harper, pp. 347f.; and the trans. of W. E. Leonard, *Gilgamesh, Epic of Old Babylonia,* p. 55.

[10] For later Persian cf. "Chanyud Pul," the bridge "finer than a hair and

el *sirat* se alzará desde la tierra en línea recta hasta la superficie de la esfera de las estrellas, y que su término será una pradera, que se extiende al exterior de los muros del paraíso celestial, a la cual pradera, denominada paraíso de las delicias, es adonde entrarán primeramente los hombres.[11]

From some such source the bridge found its way into the *Arabian Nights*,[12] but it had in other ways a fairly easy access to the later literature of Europe.

The holy mountain, another and generally important motif, appears commonly in Vedic mythology, where it is sometimes deified and prayers offered to it.[13] In the Persian *Avesta* we are told that the water of life flows down on the summit of the Hara Berezaiti. The Pahlavi *Bundahis* says the *Kinvad* bridge extends over the "Peak of Judgment," which is Mount Harburz.[14] Four

---

sharper than a razor" found in the seventeenth-century Persian *Dabistan*: see D. Shea and A. Troyer, *The Dabistan of School of Manners*, I, pp. 285ff.; reprinted in *Oriental Literature, Universal Classics Library*, VI, pp. 144f. Note the accompanying angel guide, and then the fragrant gale out of which "issued forth a beautiful nymph-like form . . ." Note also the "black and gloomy river of fetid water," collected from the tears shed by relatives of the dead (*ibid.*., pp. 294 and 148). Cf. also Alger, *The Destiny of the Soul. A Critical History of the Doctrine of the Future Life*, pp. 136f.; Mills, *Avesta Eschatology Compared with the Books of Daniel and Revelations*, pp. 47, 48ff.; A. V. W. Jackson, *Zoroastrian Studies; The Iranian Religion and Various Monographs*, § 83, p. 146; Pavry, *The Zoroastrian Doctrine of a Future Life*, pp. 79ff. (note p. 80 regarding the bridge as spanning Mount Damavand); *Harvard Journal of Asiatic Studies*, VIII (1944), pp. 196ff.

[11] Miguel Asín Palacios, *La Escatologia Musulmana en la Divina Comedia*, p. 151 (*Fotuhat*, iii, 573). Asín Palacios speaks of the bridge as adopted from Persian eschatology, and says it assumed various forms: ". . . *un edificio altisimo, o puente abovedado, o viaducto . . . un puente natural o paso resbaladizo . . . una cuesta o rampa de dificil ascensión*," *ibid.*, p. 150. Wensinck, *The Muslim Creed*, p. 232, remarks, "It belongs to the same order of ideas as the balance or the books; it is rather a kind of ordeal, for the bridge (*sīrāt*), having a very thin ridge, the wicked will fall down into the pit of Hell, whereas the righteous will pass over it without falling." It seems to be almost generally characteristic of the oriental form that the bridge furnishes a test for souls.

[12] Trans. E. W. Lane, *The Thousand and One Nights*, II, p. 418.

[13] Hopkins, *The Religions of India*, pp. 137, 359, 532; Keith, *The Religion and Philosophy of the Veda and Upanishads*, pp. 187f. For examples of the motif of the mountain in the *Rāmāyaṇa*, see Lovejoy and Boas, *History of Primitivism*, p. 443; in the Mahābhārata, *ibid.*, pp. 445f.

[14] *Bundahis* xii, 7, trans. E. W. West, *Pahlavi Texts* (*Sacred Books of the*

mountains uphold the skies in the Egyptian arrangement of the cosmos, and these seem to be sacred.[15] Among the Chaldeans a mountain was a pillar that joins heaven and earth, and they also tell of a mountain on which the gods dwell, taking the dead into their company.[16] The Babylonians described the Mashu Mountains as reaching to heaven and having at their summit a paradise of trees and precious stones where the gods live, while the dead human beings go inside to Aralu, the underworld, through an entrance guarded by monsters. According to the epic, Gilgamesh enters the realm under a mountain at a place guarded by scorpion men of giant stature. After twenty-four hours of wandering in great darkness (76 „Zwölf Doppelstunden hin ist das Innere [des Gebirges]," 77 „dicht ist die Finsternis. . . .")[17] he steps forth into an enchanted garden, in which he is especially delighted by one divine tree ornate with precious stones. He then manages to get across the swiftly rushing waters of death,[18] comes to the fields of the blessed, is bathed in an enchanted fountain of healing powers, and partakes of the magic plant (growing invisibly down in the sea) that restores vigor.[19] Ishtar goes to the underworld in search of her husband.[20] The journey through the mountain tunnel to the Other World seems to have had a subsequent influence in Arabian and European literature.[21] With the Hebrews

---

East, V), p. 36. See Pavry, *op. cit.*, pp. 80 and 82. Cf. *Bundahis* xxx, 33 (pp. 129–130).

[15] Maspero, *Dawn of Civilization*, pp. 17f.

[16] Ragozin, *The Story of Chaldea*, p. 276.

[17] Ungnad and Gressman, *Das Gilgamesch-Epos*, p. 41.

[18] See above p. 9, n. 9.

[19] Ungnad and Gressman, *op. cit.*; Ungnad, *Gilgamesch-Epos und Odyssee*; Jeremias, *The Babylonian Conception of Heaven and Hell*, trans. Hutchinson, pp. 19ff.; Mackenzie, *Myths of Babylonia and Assyria*, pp. 177ff.; Jastrow, *The Religion of Babylonia and Assyria*, pp. 489ff. and 558; Delitzsch, *Wo lag das Paradies?* p. 120. For Gilgamesh as "lord of the lower world" and numbered as underworld deity see Langdon, *Mythology of All Races: Semitic*, p. 235; for Ishtar and her descent to Aralu as a sort of Proserpine, see *ibid.*, pp. 326ff. and Jastrow, *Hebrew and Babylonian Traditions*, pp. 206ff. For a relation between the epic of Gilgamesh and the legendary account of Alexander the Great, see Jastrow, *Religion of Babylonia and Assyria*, p. 469, n. 3, and *Romanic Review*, IX (1918), pp. 152f., n. 12.

[20] Jastrow, *Religion of Babylonia and Assyria*, pp. 563f. and (trans.) *Assyrian and Babylonian Literature, Selected Translations*, pp. lii–liii and 408ff.

[21] For later influence of the Gilgamesh epic, in the matter of the subter-

Mount Zion was a holy place, where the Deity manifested Himself, and they knew the mountain also as entrance to the lower world and the abode of the dead.[22] According to the Moslems Paradise lies "sobre la cima de la montaña del *Jacinto,* a la cual ninguno de los humanos puede ascender." [23]

In nearly all the Eastern accounts the garden of the blessed shows certain constant features: the trees bearing precious fruits, the rivers that water the meadows, the heavenly food or drink. With the Persians the ruler is Yima, who died first of mortals and corresponds to Adam (with his sister as Eve). As king of the golden age he sits with the gods under a tree entertained with songs and other music, drinking Soma, which is brought from heaven by an eagle.[24] In the description of the golden age a negative formula occurs that is repeatedly used in various narratives of the Other World:

> And the fair Yima replied unto me, O Zarathuṣtra, saying:
>
> "Yes! I will make thy worlds thrive, I will make thy worlds increase . . . . There shall be, while I am king, neither cold wind nor hot wind, neither disease nor death." [25]

> In the reign of Yima swift of motion was there neither cold nor heat, there was neither age nor death, nor envy demon-made . . .[26]

Birds appear in the Persian scene:

> Regarding Karsipt they say, that it knew how to speak words, *and*

---

raneous voyage to the Earthly Paradise, see A. H. Krappe, *Philological Quarterly,* XX (1941), pp. 119ff.

[22] Jastrow, *Hebrew and Babylonian Traditions,* p. 26; Toy, *Introduction to the History of Religions,* § 65; Delitzsch, *Wo lag das Paradies*? pp. 117 and 120. The Egyptian *Book of the Dead* refers to the abode of the blessed as located in a lower world: Mackenzie, *Egyptian Myth and Legend,* pp. 96ff. Cf. also MacCulloch, *The Harrowing of Hell,* pp. 4ff.

[23] So says the *Rasail,* an encyclopedia compiled by an heretical sect, ii, 151, translated by Asín Palacios, *La Escatologia Musulmana en la Divina Comedia,* p. 162.

[24] See Oldenberg, *Die Religion des Veda,* pp. 535ff. and Griswold, *The Religion of the Rigveda,* pp. 209ff. and 217f.

[25] *The Zend-Avesta,* Part I, *Vendîdâd, Fargard* ii, 5 (*Sacred Books of the East,* IV, p. 12).

[26] *The Zend-Avesta,* Part III, *Yasna* ix, 5 (translated by Mills, *Sacred Books of the East,* XXXI, p. 232).

brought the religion to the enclosure which Yim made, and circulated *it*; there they utter the Avesta in the language of birds.[27]

Just so, we meet the formula again and again: the blessed shall neither hunger nor thirst; no storms shall assail their country; and so on. The *Midrash Konen* of the Hebrews gives an elaborate picture of Gan 'Eden. It is a building with five chambers for the righteous: one of cedar with ceiling of transparent crystal; one of cedar with a ceiling of fine silver; one of silver and gold ornamented with pearls, where the Tree of Life grows – and this is a sort of ladder on which the souls of the righteous may ascend or descend – and where the entrance is guarded by a flaming sword (changing from intense heat to icy cold); one of olive wood; and one of precious stones, gold, and silver, in front of which flows the river Gihon bordered with aromatic shrubs, and furnished with a sumptuous settee and canopy. In other Hebrew accounts Paradise has seven sections. One provides a tall musical pillar that plays songs automatically. Another has two diamond gates. Luxury and gold and jewels mark them all. One has four rivulets of milk, wine, balsam, and honey.[28] Streams of milk and honey are found in the Other World in many descriptions from the garden of Yima on.

More influential in the west is the passage in Genesis ii regarding the realm "eastward in Eden" with the tree "pleasant to the sight and good for food," the Tree of Life, and the Tree of Knowledge of Good and Evil. The river that waters this garden was "parted and became into four heads" –

> 11. The name of the first is Pison: that is it which compasseth the whole land of Havilah, where there is gold;
>
> 12. And the gold of that land is good: there is bdellium and the onyx stone.
>
> 13. And the name of the second river is Gihon: the same is it that compasseth the whole land of Ethiopia.
>
> 14. And the name of the third river is Hiddekel: that is it which goeth toward the east of Assyria. And the fourth river is Euphrates.

These four rivers reappear in later literature, as we shall see. In the vision of the world to come in the Book of Enoch we are

[27] *Pahlavi Texts,* Part I, *Bundahis* xix, 16 (translated by West, *Sacred Books of the East,* V, p. 70).

[28] *Jewish Encyclopaedia, s.v.* Paradise, p. 516.

told that Enoch drew nigh to a wall "built of crystals and surrounded by tongues of fire . . ."; the house he finds there has walls "like a tesselated floor (made) of crystals, and its groundwork was of crystal." Fire forms a prominent part in the scene: "A flaming fire surrounded the walls, and its portals blazed with fire"; he beholds also another and larger house all of fire, of which he says, "its appearance was as crystal . . ." [29] He sees a great and high mountain of hard rock, "and there were four places in it, hollow, deep, and very smooth, three of them dark, and one light with a fountain of water in the midst of it. And I said 'How smooth these hollows are, and deep and dark to look at!' " Raphael replies that these are the gathering places for the souls of the dead.[30] Remarkable or holy mountains appear frequently in the narrative, including "seven mountains of magnificent stones." [31] He comes to a river of fire which empties into a western sea, and he too tells of the Tree of Life and the Tree of Knowledge.[32] In the Slavonic *Book of the Secrets of Enoch* from the roots of the Tree of Life go forth four streams "which pour honey and milk, oil and wine." [33]

In Revelation the new Jerusalem is seen "in the spirit" from a "great and high mountain." It has the glory of God:

xxi. 11. . . . and her light was like unto a stone most precious, even like a jasper stone, clear as crystal;

12. And had a wall great and high, and had twelve gates, and at the gates twelve angels, and names written thereon, which are the names of the twelve tribes of the children of Israel:

13. On the east three gates; on the north three gates; on the south three gates; and on the west three gates.

14. And the wall of the city had twelve foundations, and in them the names of the twelve apostles of the Lamb . . . .

[29] *Book of Enoch*, edited by R. H. Charles, ch. xiv, 9ff. Cf. also, *The Book of Enoch Translated from Professor Dillmann's Ethiopic Text*, edited by R. H. Charles, pp. 80–81. For influence on the *Book of Revelation* see *ibid.*, pp. 43ff.

[30] Book of Enoch, xxii; for translation and comment see F. Crawford Burkitt, *Jewish and Christian Apocalypses*. Cf. also, R. H. Charles, *The Book of Enoch Translated from Professor Dillmann's Ethiopic Text*, pp. 93–94.

[31] Book of Enoch, xviii, 6–7. Cf. also xvii, 2.

[32] The river of fire, xvii, 5; the Tree of Life, xxiv, 4ff. ("Its fruit shall be for food to the elect," xxv, 5); the Tree of Knowledge, xxxii, 3.

[33] *The Book of the Secrets of Enoch*, translated by W. R. Morfill, ed. R. H. Charles, viii, 5ff.

16. The city lieth foursquare, and the length is as large as the breadth: . . . twelve thousand furlongs. The length and the breadth and the height of it are equal . . .

18. And the building of the wall of it was of jasper: and the city was pure gold, like unto clear glass.

19. And the foundations of the wall of the city were garnished with all manner of precious stones. The first foundation was jasper; the second, sapphire; the third, a chalcedony; the fourth, an emerald; . . .

20. The fifth, sardonyx; the sixth, sardius; the seventh, chrysolite; the eighth, beryl; the ninth, a topaz; the tenth, a chrysoprasus; the eleventh, a jacinth; the twelfth, an amethyst.

21. And the twelve gates were twelve pearls; every several gate was of one pearl; and the street of the city was pure gold, as it were transparent glass.

22. And I saw no temple therein: for the Lord God Almighty and the Lamb are the temple of it.

23. And the city had no need of the sun, neither of the moon, to shine in it: for the glory of God did lighten it, and the Lamb is the light thereof . . .

xxii. 1. And he shewed me a pure river of water of life, clear as crystal, proceeding out of the throne of God and of the Lamb.

2. In the midst of the street of it, and on either side of the river, was there the tree of life, which bare twelve manner of fruits, and yielded her fruit every month: and the leaves of the tree were for the healing of the nations . . .

5. And there shall be no night there; and they need no candle, neither light of the sun; for the Lord God giveth them light: and they shall reign for ever and ever.

With Islam there are two gardens for the man who fears the Lord, both of which are furnished with branching trees and flowing streams, with two kinds of every fruit, with couches lined with brocade, and pleasant maidens of modest glances. Besides these there are also gardens twain with dark green foliage, two gushing streams, with the accompanying fruits and with maidens who recline on green cushions and beautiful carpets.[34] The maidens seem to be an essential to the next world of the Moslems, but they are there furnished chiefly as an entertainment for men.[35] Para-

[34] *Qur'an*, lv, 45ff.

[35] *Ibid.*, xxxviii, 50, and lvi, 20; also, D. B. MacDonald, *The Religious Attitude and Life in Islam*, p. 205.

dise, as we have observed, is supposed to be on a mountain.[36] Following the account in the *Rasail* we find that here

> la tierra de su suelo era aromática y su aire templado en invierno y verano, de día y de noche; regado estaba por abundantes ríos y poblado de verdes árboles; variados y dulces frutos abundaban en él, olorosas plantas, flores de varia especie, animales no dañinos, pájaros, en fin, de agradables voces que entonaban placenteros y armoniosos cantos . . . .[37]

The twelfth-century Shakir Benmóslém of Orihuela tells us that

> Alzanse a la puerta del paraíso dos árboles grandes: en el mundo no se ve cosa que se parezca al aroma de estos árboles, a su umbroso follaje, a la perfeccíon, belleza y elegancia de sus ramas; a la hormosura de sus flores, al perfume de sus frutes, al lustre de sus hojas, a la dulce armonía de los pájaros que sobre sus ramas gorjean, a la fresca brisa que a su sombra se respira . . . . Al pie de cada uno de ambos árboles corre una fuente de aguas dulces, frescas, puras, que formán dos ríos verdes, semejantes al cristal por su transparencia, cuyo lecho es de límpidos guijarros de perlas y rubíes, cuyas linfas son más traslúcidas que el berilo, más frescas que la nieve fundida, más blancas que la leche. . . .[38]

Gardens and trees laden with birds are on their banks. The traveler to heaven finds himself provided with a bride in the eternal mansion.

The Classical Tradition

THE WATER BARRIER is familiar also among the Greeks, for perhaps the commonest location of the Other World with them is on a blessed island or group of islands. Such seems to be the idea implicit in the *Odyssey*'s account of the Elysian Fields:

> As for yourself, heaven-favored Menelaus, it is not destined you shall die and meet your doom in grazing Argos; but to the Elysian plain and the earth's limits the immortal gods shall bring you, where fair-haired Rhadamanthus dwells. Here utterly at ease passes the life of men. No snow is here, no winter long, no rain, but the loud-blowing breezes of the west the Ocean-stream sends up to bring men coolness; for you have Helen and are counted son-in-law of Zeus.[39]

[36] Cf. MacDonald, *op. cit.*, p. 289, for the view that in original sin Adam fell literally from the top of the mountain.

[37] *Rasail,* ii, 151, trans. Asín Palacios, *La Escatologia Musulmana en la Divina Comedia*, p. 162.

[38] *Abenmajluf*, ii, 61, trans. Asín Palacios, *op. cit.*, pp. 166f.

[39] *Odyssey* iv, 561ff., translated by G. H. Palmer, p. 62.

A similar idea appears in Hesiod:

> And they live untouched by sorrow in the islands of the blessed along the shore of deep swirling Ocean, happy heroes for whom the grain-giving earth bears honey-sweet fruit flourishing thrice a year, far from the deathless gods, and Cronos rules over them . . . .[40]

The garden of the Hesperides is variously located by the Greeks,[41] but sometimes in such an island realm, and the apples there guarded by a dragon represent the Otherworld fruit. The isle Ogygia of Calypso (who offers Odysseus immortality) belongs in this class, as do also Atlantis, Leuke (the "white isle" whither Thetis carries the body of Achilles), and the Fortunate Isles.[42] Atlantis in the *Critias* of Plato is the model for numerous utopias. Worth special note here is its temple, and its two springs — one of hot water, one of cold. In romantic vein the story of the journey of Iambulus according to Diodorus Siculus[43] shows the hero forcibly put to sea (in what corresponds to the rudderless boat in medieval literature) and tells of his arriving at an island on which much is strange and all is desirable. Servius remarks that Elysium and the Fortunate Isles are the same according to the philosophers. In describing them Horace falls into the use of the negative formula we have already noted:

> Pluraque felices mirabimur, ut neque largis
> Aquosus Eurus arua radat imbribus,
> Pinguia nec siccis urantur semina glaebis,
> Utrumque rege temperante caelitum.
>
> * * * *
>
> Nulla nocent pecori contagia, nullius astri
> Gregem aestuosa torret impotentia.[44]

[40] *Works and Days*, 170ff., translated by Evelyn-White, *Hesiod: The Homeric Hymns and Homerica*, p. 15. Cf. Rohde, *Psyche*, I, pp. 68ff. and especially p. 104. Of islands of this type Rohde remarks: "Es ist ein idyllischer Wunsch, der sich in der Phantasie des elysischen Landes befriedigt." On Hesiod cf. Highbarger, *The Gates of Dreams*, 50ff.

[41] Cf. the summary in the commentary of Servius, I, *Aeneid* iv, 484.

[42] Cf. Servius, *Aeneid*, v, 735. For Leuke see Kinkel, *Epicorum Graecorum fragmenta*, I, p. 34. According to Rohde, *op. cit.*, II, pp. 369–370, the islands are located in the underworld in the later period of Greek culture. Pertinent passages are quoted in *Primitivism and Related Ideas in Antiquity*, Lovejoy and Boas, pp. 290ff. Note on p. 297 the description of the Fortunate Isles by Isidore of Seville (*Etym.*, XIV, vi, 8).

[43] *Bibl. Hist.*, ii, 55–60.

[44] *Epod.* xvi, 52ff. For the formula cf. p. 12 above.

Plutarch speaks of islands in the Atlantic which were supposed to be Elysian Fields and adds they were sought by Sertorius.[45]

The whole idea of the happy isle is satirized by Lucian in his *True History* (ii, 4ff.), from which I may quote a few typical passages:

At a distance and more to starboard were five islands, very large and high, from which much fire was blazing up. Dead ahead was one that was flat and low-lying, not less than five hundred furlongs off. When at length we were near it, a wonderful breeze blew about us, sweet and fragrant, like the one that, on the word of the historian Herodotus, breathes perfume from Araby the blest . . . .

The island looks delightful with many rivers and meads and trees filled with song birds:

They told us on the way that the island was the one that is called the Isle of the Blest, and that the ruler was the Cretan Rhadamanthus . . . . The city itself is all of gold and the wall around it of emerald. It has seven gates, all of single planks of cinnamon. The foundations of the city and the ground within its walls are ivory. There are temples of all the gods, built of beryl, and in them great monolithic altars of amethyst, on which they make their great burnt-offerings. Around the city runs a river of the finest myrrh, a hundred royal cubits wide and five deep, so that one can swim in it comfortably. For baths they have large houses of glass, warmed by burning cinnamon; instead of water there is hot dew in the tubs . . . . Nobody grows old, but stays the same age as on coming there. Again, it is neither night among them nor yet very bright day, but the light which is on the country is like the gray morning toward dawn . . . . It is always spring there and the only wind that blows there is Zephyr.

Needless to say, the country abounds in fruits and flowers and plants of all kinds.

In the neighborhood of the city there are three hundred and sixty-five springs of water, as many of honey, five hundred of myrrh — much smaller, however — seven rivers of milk and eight of wine . . . . Two springs are by the table, one of laughter and the other of enjoyment. They all drink from each of these when the revels begin . . . . They all have their wives in common and nobody is jealous of his neighbour . . . .

[45] *Plutarch's Lives,* ed. Perrin, VIII, pp. 20–23.

The other islands near by include the Islands of the Wicked, from which the smoke was rising, and the island of Calypso. Later they come to the Isle of Women, the inhabitants of which are savage creatures of the sea who feed upon those who visit them.[46]

It is not essential to inquire how far the islands thus represented by Lucian and others, seriously or satirically, were regarded as abodes of the dead or retreats from the demands of ordinary existence or scenes of a primitive golden age. The interpretations vary somewhat with the different authors. As for the idea of the underworld, which was also widespread and is found in Egyptian lore and elsewhere,[47] it is probably true that the conception sprang from the practice of burial and that it was universally taken as a provision for departed spirits. Thus the realm of Hades is depicted by Homer in the eleventh book of the *Odyssey*. It is reached by crossing the ocean, as Circe gives directions:

> High-born son of Läertes, ready Odysseus, let not the lack of pilot for your ship disturb you, but set the mast, spread the white sail aloft, and sit you down; the breath of Boreas shall bear her onward. When you have crossed by ship the Ocean-stream to where the shore is rough and the grove of Persephone stands, — tall poplars and seed-shedding willows, — there beach your ship by the deep eddies of the Ocean-stream, but go yourself to the mouldering house of Hades. There is a spot where into Acheron run Pyriphlegethon and Cocytus, a stream which is an offshoot of the waters of the Styx; a rock here forms the meeting-point of the two roaring rivers . . . .[48]

Here she bids him make his sacrifices before he can speak with the dead. Odysseus carries out her instructions, and thus describes his approach:

[46] The translation above quoted is that of Harmon in the Loeb Library ed. of *Lucian*, I, pp. 309ff. Cf. also Lovejoy and Boas, *Primitivism*, pp. 299–303. Note also the island of the Hyperboreans as described, e.g., in Diodorus Siculus, *Bibl. Hist.*, ii, 47–48 (Loeb Library ed. vol. II, pp. 37–43). The journey of Sindbad shows oriental parallels. For parodies of the idea see E. Rohde, *Der Griechische Roman und seine Vorläufer*, pp. 206ff., n. 4.

[47] For an elaborate study of the theme of descent to the lower world see Hastings, *Encyclopaedia*, IV, pp. 648ff. For Roman examples see also Cumont, *After Life in Roman Paganism*, 70ff.

[48] Palmer, p. 162. For ultimate relation to the adventure of Gilgamesh in the underworld, see Ungnad, *Gilgamesch-Epos und Odyssee*.

and all day long the sail of the running ship was stretched. Then the sun sank, and all the ways grew dark.

And now she reached earth's limits, the deep stream of the Ocean, where the Cimmerian people's land and city lie, wrapt in a fog and cloud. Never on them does the shining sun look down with his beams, as he goes up the starry sky or as again toward earth he turns back from the sky, but deadly night is spread abroad over these hapless men. On coming here, we beached our ship . . . .[49]

The journey thus taken seems to be westward for any voyager in the Mediterranean.

Plato represents Socrates in the *Phaedo* as describing the underworld in some detail. The approach is complicated:

And the journey is not as Telephus says in the play of Aeschylus; for he says a simple path leads to the lower world, but I think the path is neither simple nor single, for if it were, there would be no need of guides, since no one could miss the way to any place if there were only one road. But really there seem to be many forks of the road and many windings; this I infer from the rites and ceremonies practised here on earth . . . . (107E–108A) [50]

All this is somewhat ironic, I fear, but the symbolism of the approach is still here. Socrates is very specific about Hades:

One of the chasms of the earth is greater than the rest, and is bored right through the whole earth; this is the one which Homer . . . and many other poets have called Tartarus. For all the rivers flow together into this chasm and flow out of it again, and they have each the nature of the earth through which they flow. (111E–112A) [51]

The streams are: Oceanus, which flows round in a circle; Acheron, flowing in the opposite direction (going through desert places and coming to the Acherusian lake); Pyriphlegethon, flowing out between the two through a burning region and into a lake; the Stygian river Cocytus, issuing into a "wild and awful place, which is all of a dark blue colour, like lapis lazuli" and making a lake called the Styx. Here the dead receive their penalty or recompense for their lives.

[49] *Ibid.*, p. 165.

[50] *Plato, Euthyphro, Apology*, etc., trans. H. N. Fowler, p. 370 (Loeb Library).

[51] *Ibid.*, p. 382.

Even with the idea of an underworld the water barrier is decidedly present. And the country reached is not one to impress the reader with its attractions. Erebus, where Hades and Persephone hold their court, is a place from which the daughter of Demeter would gladly escape. It is clearly underground,[52] and sometimes it is encircled by a river over which Charon has to ferry the spirits, while the dog Cerberus watches at the main entrance. Thus it is described in the sixth book of the *Aeneid,* where Aeneas enters by a cave, passing through the empty halls of Dis and following a road to the waters of "Tartarean Acheron":

> Here, thick with mire and of fathomless flood, a whirlpool seethes and belches into Cocytus all its sand. A grim warden guards these waters and streams, terrible in his squalor — Charon . . . .[53]

Here too should be cited the imitative passage regarding the underworld in Statius's *Thebaid* (viii, 1–126), referred to as Avernus, Tartarus, and Elysium (cf. viii, 15) as well as Erebus. Here too is the river barrier (with Charon) and also Cocytus, Phlegethon, and Styx. The work was widely known in the Middle Ages and adapted in the Old French *Roman de Thèbes.*

The scene in Virgil is too familiar to need quoting or even to compare in detail with Dante's use of it in the *Inferno.* According to the *Aeneid* the river Styx imprisons the region "with his ninefold circles." Minos shakes the urn that decides the lot of each who enters. The region of the Mourning Fields is assigned to those whom love has consumed, and the most remote part is where the souls of those renowned in war may dwell. The place of torment for the wicked is "under a cliff" — a broad castle "girt with a triple wall and encircled with a rushing flood of torrent flames — Tartarean Phlegethon, that rolls along thundering rocks." Here are Tisiphone, who scourges the guilty, and Rhadamanthus, "who holds his iron sway," chastising the wicked and extorting confession from them. At length Aeneas comes to the land of the blessed, where "an ampler ether clothes the meads with roseate light, and they know their own sun, and stars of

[52] See for example Hesiod, *Theogony,* 669, trans. Evelyn-White, *Hesiod: The Homeric Hymns and Homerica,* p. 127.

[53] 295ff., trans. Fairclough, *Virgil,* I, p. 527. On the two gates see Highbarger, *The Gates of Dreams.*

their own": this is the place for those who "suffered wounds fighting for the fatherland." In the lower world too is Lethe, the river from which spirits that are to return to human life may drink forgetfulness. At length Aeneas passes through the ivory gate of sleep and hastens to his ship. There are two gates, we learn: one of horn, whereby "an easy outlet is given to true shades," and the other of ivory, "but false are the dreams sent out by the spirits to the world above." The hero had previously made a voyage to the shrine of the Cumaean Sibyl, from which he made his way to the entrance of Avernus. So there is a general parallelism here, of course, to the voyage of Odysseus and his visit to the lower world.

Accounts differ in classical literature regarding the relation of the underworld rivers one to another and their location, but the most widely known plan is Virgil's. Some attempt was made by Italian natives to identify the place where the entrance to Erebus could be found. On the other hand, the whole conception of the lower world was treated in satiric vein by Aristophanes, by Pherecrates, and by Lucian. Lucian uses the setting in the *Menippus*, in *The Downward Journey*, and in the *Charon*. Pherecrates (fl. c. 438 B.C.) describes a land of Cockaigne which seems to be underground. Among the many delicacies on which people there feast are "roast thrushes, dressed for a *réchauffé*," which "flew round our mouths entreating us to swallow them." Pluto's realm is also a sort of "maidenland," for girls "in silk shawls, just reaching the flower of youth, and shorn of the hair on their bodies, drew through a funnel full cups of red wine . . . ." "Rivers of black broth . . . flow from the springs of Plutus all ready to be ladled up." [54]

The idea of a realm above the earth was, on the other hand, used by Plato in the famous vision of Er in the tenth book of the *Republic*. After the soul of Er issued from his body it "journeyed with a great company" and came to "a mysterious region where there were two openings side by side in the earth, and above and over against them in the heaven two others." [55] Here the judges

[54] Quoted by Athenaeus in *The Deipnosophists*, vi, 268, trans. Gulick, III, pp. 207ff. (Loeb Library). Cf. also Lovejoy and Boas, *Primitivism*, pp. 38–39, and Paul u. Braune's *Beiträge*, V, (1878), pp. 389ff. for the whole idea.

[55] Trans. Paul Shorey, *Plato: the Republic*, II, Loeb Library, pp. 493ff.

bid the righteous to go to the right and upwards through the heaven, while the unjust have to go to the left and downward. Thus through one of the openings of the earth souls were departing, and through the other came up souls "full of squalor and dust." Similarly, good souls were going up through one of the openings to heaven and others "clean and pure" were returning from the second. From the two groups of souls who have returned Er learns of the punishment of the wicked in Tartarus below and the joys of the blessed in Heaven above. At length the souls move to a place where they see a "straight light like a pillar," the very girdle itself of the heavens, from whose extremities stretches the spindle of Necessity. We need not follow further this disclosure of how the universe is constituted. But we do learn that the man who loves wisdom will not take the underground journey; he will instead find his course "smooth and through the heavens." After the souls have chosen their lots from Lachesis they are sent to the Plain of Oblivion through a terrible and stifling heat, "for it was bare of trees and all plants, and there they camped at eventide by the River of Forgetfulness, whose waters no vessel can contain."

The vision of Er is explicitly recalled by Cicero in the sixth book of his *Republic* in the introduction to the *Somnium Scipionis*. Scipio's dream, moreover, represents a kind of parallel to Er's experience. The younger Scipio is led in his vision on the very journey through the heavens that is suggested by Plato. He learns too of the arrangement of the spheres and of the blending of their music, which cannot be perceived by human ears. He looks back at the earth and finds it small and in a sense insignificant. Here above, he is told, eminent and excellent men find their true reward:

> And the best tasks are those undertaken in defence of your native land; a spirit occupied and trained in such activities will have a swifter flight to this, its proper home and permanent abode. And this flight will be still more rapid if, while still confined in the body, it looks abroad, and, by contemplating what lies outside itself, detaches itself as much as may be from the body. For the spirits of those who are given over to sensual pleasures and have become their slaves, as it were, and who violate the laws of gods and men at the instigation of those desires which are subservient to pleasure — their spirits, after leaving their bodies, fly about

close to the earth, and do not return to this place except after many ages of torture.[56]

The *Somnium Scipionis* influenced Lucan in his account of the flight of Pompey's soul in the *Pharsalia* (ix, 1ff.), Prudentius in his similar passage regarding Saint Agnes (*Peristeph.* xiv, 91ff.), Boccaccio in his *Teseida* regarding Arcite (xi, 1–3), and Chaucer in his account of Troilus (*Troilus,* v, 1808ff.). Chaucer gives a paraphrase of the work in his *Parliament of Fowls* (23ff.).

Flights of various kinds into heaven are not uncommon in oriental and classical literature. Most pertinent here perhaps is the account Lucian gives early in his *True History* of his journey into the region of the moon in the company of the vulture dragoons, with his glimpse of Cloudcuckootown. Ganymede was snatched up by the eagle, to be conveyed to the gods as cupbearer. Sindbad tied himself to the legs of the Rukh and was thus carried to "the highest region of the sky" only to be landed at last on a high hill above a valley full of jewels.[57] More striking, however, than any of these stories is that of the flight of Alexander the Great. It is found interpolated, apparently rather late, in the Pseudo-Callisthenes, but since it is reflected in the Archpresbyter Leo's *De proeliis* it must have been available at least by the tenth century.[58] According to the first of these, when Alexander

[56] Trans. Keyes, *Cicero: De re publica, De legibus,* Loeb, p. 283. For the idea of flight among the Stoics and also the Pythagoreans see Cumont, *After Life in Roman Paganism*, 96ff.

[57] "The Second Voyage," *The Thousand and One Nights,* trans. Lane, III, pp. 16f. Cf. the notes on oriental parallels, *ibid.*, pp. 86–89; also *Publ. Mod. Lang. Assoc.*, XXIII (1908), pp. 563ff.

[58] It appears in Müller's C type of MS (the γ tradition) in his edition of the Pseudo-Callisthenes appended to Fr. Dübner's edition of *Arrian,* p. 91. (*Pseudo-Callisth.*, ii, 39). For the literary history of the idea see G. Millet, "L'Ascension d'Alexandre," *Syria: Revue D'Art Oriental,* IV (1923), 85–113. The Latin ABC poem (pp. 102–103), which has been often referred to, would indicate that the story was known at least by the ninth century. Note the indication of oriental sources, *ibid.*, 111ff. Cf. also E. Rohde, *Der Griechische Roman und seine Vorläufer*, pp. 191–192 and notes; p. 206, n. 4. For the motif in art see Francis Bond, *Woodcarvings in English Churches*, p. 78; the *Burlington Magazine*, XXXII (1918), 136–140 and 177–185. Further bibliography for the cycle may conveniently be found in the introduction to F. P. Magoun's *The Gests of King Alexander of Macedon*, especially p. 41, n. 3. Cf. also R. M. Dawkins, "Alexander and the Water of Life," *Medium Ævum*, VI (1937), pp. 173ff.

reached the land of darkness on the way to the land of the blest and had found the well of the water of life, he wished to press on further. He also found some large tame birds which were lingering near, apparently to feed on the bodies of dead horses, and which therefore seem to have been vultures. Two of them he ordered to be harnessed with a pole on which was suspended some liver. As the birds pursued the meat, Alexander soared with them up into the sky. A winged creature of human shape appeared to him, and, asking if he who understood not earthly things could hope to grasp heavenly matters, bade the monarch to look down. Struck with fear Alexander looked down and saw the ocean coiled like a snake round the earth, which appeared like a threshing floor. Then he returned to earth again.

Substantially the same episode appears in the *De proeliis*. Even the griffons here may represent vultures.[59] Alexander's car or chariot, it is true, is chained to the griffons, and no winged monster arrives to furnish comment; but we are told: "quod uidebatur Alexandro orbis terrarum sicut area, in qua conduntur fruges. Mare uero ita uidebatur tortuosum in circuitu orbis sicut draco."[60] Then we read, "subito quidem uirtus diuina obumbrauit easdem grifes et deiecit eas ad terram in loco campestri longius ab exercitu suo iter dierum decem nullamque lesionem sustinuit in ipsis cancellis ferreis . . . ." In the Greek he is seven days' journey away.[61] Bellerophon, we remember, was also thwarted in his attempt to ascend to heaven on the back of Pegasus.

The holy mountain too is familiar in Greek mythology, especially in Olympus as the home of the gods. The *Odyssey* describes it with the usual negative formula:

> Saying this, clear-eyed Athene passed away, off to Olympus, where they say the dwelling of the gods stands fast forever. Never with winds

[59] Cf. *Oxford English Dictionary, s.v.* griffon, 2.

[60] I have used a text of O. Zingerle, *Die Quellen zum Alexander des Rudolf von Ems, Germanistische Abhandlungen*, iv, § 115. Cf. also F. Pfister, *Der Alexanderroman des Archipresbyters Leo*, p. 126, ll. 7ff.

[61] A reflection of the subterraneous voyage, in a tunnel through a mountain, as found in the Gilgamesh epic, also appears in one of the interpolations of the Alexander romance: see Krappe, *Philological Quarterly*, XX (1941), 119ff.

is it disturbed, nor by the rain made wet, nor does the snow come near; but everywhere the upper air spreads cloudless, and a bright radiance plays over all; and there the blessed gods are happy all their days. . . .[62]

Parnassus shows a similar idea as the home of the Muses.

From the foregoing account it is evident that nearly all possible forms of Otherworld description are utilized in oriental and classical literature. The journey to the skies is found in East Indian, Hebrew, and classical documents; crossing the sea is in the Persian, Egyptian, and classical literature, and the islands are referred to in Greek and Latin; the river is found in the Greek underworld as well as the Latin, and with the bridge it appears in Persian and Moslem. The mountain is common in Babylonian, Indian, Hebrew, and classical works, with the desired country or heaven or the home of the gods at the top; but a few times in Babylonian, Hebrew, and Greek, the region is inside instead. The tree with the fruit of life and the garden too are well known, and maidens are furnished for the delight of men in the Moslem paradise.

[62] Trans. Palmer, p. 89 (vi, 41ff.). In modern Thessaly the people still tell wonderful stories about happenings on the top of Olympus. See L. Heuzey, *Le Mont Olympe et l'Acarnanie*, pp. 138f. For the idea of the souls of the dead going to Olympus see Rohde, *Psyche*, trans. W. B. Hillis, ch. XIV, ii, n. 135 (p. 572). For the idea of gods dwelling within the mountains, see *ibid.*, ch. III, i, (pp. 95ff.).

II

AMONG THE CELTS

THERE ARE MANY POINTS of similarity between the classical ideas of the Other World and those of the Celts. Here too we find the Isles of the Blessed to be reached by a long voyage, the holy mountain, and a lower world. But all these are marked with strong differences from the equivalents in Greek and Roman mythology, and show with intensity that play of the Celtic fantasy which gives their accounts highly individualized characteristics. Whether these accounts refer to a place of the dead or an abode of the gods or an earthly Elysium, it is unnecessary to consider here, or how far these three conceptions are intermingled, or what the special origin of each idea may have been. "Many races," observes MacCulloch, "have imagined a happy Other-World, but no other race has so filled it with magic beauty, or so persistently recurred to it as the Celts." [1] The Other World of the Celts was in any case located on this earth,[2] often in the west,[3] and sometimes took the form of the Isles of the Blessed, the Land-beneath-the-Waves, the hollow hill, or the land beyond the mist, or varying combinations of these. Its names are many: Mag Mór (great plain), Mag Mell (plain of delights), Tír na n-Óg (Land of the Young), Annwfn (abyss), Tír nam Béo (Land of the Living), and so on. To this country went mortals summoned by the gods or by dignified Otherworld inhabitants; thither too departed the seekers after Elysium, and thither perhaps went the souls of the dead.[4]

[1] *The Religion of the Ancient Celts,* p. 390.

[2] Cf. Salomon Reinach, *Revue celtique,* XXII (1901), pp. 447ff.; G. Dottin, *Manuel pour servir á l'Étude de l'Antiquité celtique,* p. 353. For comparison with the Greek and East Indian, see Nutt, *Voy. Bran,* I, pp. 258ff.; D'Arbois de Jubainville, *Le Cycle mythologique Irlandais,* pp. 16ff.

[3] E. Hull, *Folk-Lore,* XVIII (1907), p. 158.

[4] But cf. Loomis, *Publ. Mod. Lang. Assoc.,* LVI (1941), pp. 895ff.; Brown, *Speculum,* XV (1940), pp. 3ff.; Krappe, *Rev. celtique,* XLVIII (1931), pp. 94ff.; Brown, *Origin of the Grail Legend,* pp. 339ff.

The most common form perhaps is that of the fortunate island or islands. Speaking of the island of "Brittia," Procopius remarks that it was regarded as the abode of the dead:

> They say, then, that the souls of men who die are always conveyed to this place. . . .
>
> The men of this place [on the coast opposite] say that the conduct of souls is laid upon them in turn. . . . And at a late hour of the night they are conscious of a knocking at their doors and hear an indistinct voice calling them together for their task. And they with no hesitation rise from their beds and walk to the shore, not understanding what necessity leads them to do this, but compelled nevertheless. There they see skiffs in readiness with no man at all in them, not their own skiffs, however, but a different kind, in which they embark and lay hold of the oars. And they are aware that the boats are burdened with a large number of passengers and are wet by the waves to the edge of the planks and the oarlocks, having not so much as one finger's breadth above the water; they themselves, however, see no one, but after rowing a single hour they put in at Brittia. And yet when they make the voyage in their own skiffs, not using sails but rowing, they with difficulty make this passage in a night and a day. Then when they have reached the island and have been relieved of their burden, they depart with all speed, their boats now becoming suddenly light and rising above the waves, for they sink no further in the water than the keel itself.
>
> And they, for their part, neither see any man either sitting in the boat with them or departing from the boat, but they say that they hear a kind of voice from the island which seems to make announcement to those who take the souls in charge as each name is called of the passengers who have come over with them . . . .[5]

Earlier in talking of the island Procopius had said that here "the men of ancient times built a long wall, cutting off a large part of it."[6] The climate on the two sides is different: on one side many people live as other men live, trees abound in fruits, there are many springs of water. On the other side "everything is the re-

[5] Procopius, *History of the Wars,* VIII, xx, 48–56 (*The Gothic War,* iv, 20), *Procopius,* trans. Dewing, V, pp. 267–271, Loeb. The story is cited by Tzetzes in the twelfth century (*ad Lycophron,* 1204): see E. Scheer, *Lycophronis Alexandra,* II, p. 346, scholia on 1200; and Zwicker, *Fontes historiae relig. Celticae,* III, p. 272.

[6] Dewing, *Procopius, Hist. of the Wars,* VIII, xx, 42–45 (Loeb, V, p. 265).

verse of this": no man can survive there even a half hour but snakes and serpents and other wild creatures hold it.

The story of the boat that ferries the dead is often cited; but where exactly is Brittia? Is it the Île de Bretagne [7] or is it Denmark? [8] Procopius says that it lies about two hundred "stades" from the coast and opposite the mouth of the Rhine "between the islands of Britain and Thule," [9] and one may suspect that he has gathered the story by hearsay or from a learned source rather than that he has consulted a map.[10] The classical idea of the region of the dead lying far in the west as reflected in Claudian (*In Ruf.*, i, 123) may be involved in the reminiscence. But Claudian puts the location in the extreme part of Gaul and one may reasonably guess that in both cases a bit of Celtic folklore has emerged. Certainly the word itself would seem to mean Britain.

The commonest form in which the island motif is employed is that of the *imram* or voyage to scattered islands, narrated by a survivor in such a way as to emphasize the element of the marvelous. Here we need not inquire whether the story began entirely in the field of fiction, or represents fantastic yarns recounted by sailors who had actual journeys to their credit, or shows a primitive missionary excursion much disguised by borrowings from paganism.[11] Doubtless there was told in early days many a story

[7] Cf. P. Sébillot, *Folk-Lore de France*, II (*La Mer et les Eaux Douces*), pp. 148ff.; A. Le Braz, *La Légende de la Mort chez les Bretons Armoricains*, I, pp. xviff.; D'Arbois de Jubainville, *Cycle Mythol. Irl.*, p. 231. MacCulloch, *The Religion of the Ancient Celts*, p. 87, notes that the Isle of Man was regarded by the Goidels as the island Elysium under its name of Isle of Falga. "Man," he suggests, comes from Manannán; but the latter may be derived from "Man." Cf. also Nutt, *Voy. of Bran*, I, p. 213.

[8] Dewing, *Procopius*, Loeb, V, p. 253, n. 1.

[9] Dewing, *Procopius*, Loeb, V, p. 253.

[10] That he may have got it from Plutarch's commentary on Hesiod is suggested in the note of Tzetzes on the same Greek writer, printed by J. Zwicker, *Fontes historiae religionis Celticae*, III, p. 271. Cf. MacCulloch, *The Religion of the Ancient Celts*, p. 342, and Brown, *Origin of the Grail Legend*, pp. 340–341. Miss Eleanor Hull comments that the dismal isle of spirits in Procopius and Plutarch is not representative of the joyous Irish Mag Mell (*Folk-Lore*, XVIII [1907], pp. 121–165); see also J. Grimm, *Deutsche Myth.*, II, pp. 694ff. (Stallybrass trans. II, pp. 832ff. and notes, IV, p. 1550); *Zeits. f. französische Sprache*, XXVIII (1905), pp. 66f.; and Brown, *op. cit.*, 340ff.

[11] The problem is discussed by W. F. Thrall in "Clerical Sea Pilgrimages and the *Imrama*," *Manly Anniversary Studies*, pp. 276–283.

that included accounts of visits to the Orkneys or Hebrides or Shetland Islands. Certain it is, however, that whatever element of truth may be included in the *imrama,* a considerable part is based on a fiction derived from early Celtic mythology. Probably the earliest of these tales that survive is that of Bran, son of Febal, usually ascribed to the eighth century.[12]

The *Voyage of Bran* tells how one day the hero heard sweet music. Overcome by its sweetness, he fell asleep and on waking found near by a branch of silver with white blossoms. He took the branch to his royal house and there saw a woman in strange raiment who sang fifty quatrains to him about the distant isle upheld by four pillars. She had brought a branch from the "apple tree" of Emain. In this distant land there was an ancient tree in blossom on which the birds sang the canonical hours. Joy "ranked around music" was known in the southern White-Silver Plain. "Unknown is wailing or treachery";

> There is nothing rough or harsh,
> But sweet music striking on the ear.
>
> Without grief, without sorrow, without death,
> Without any sickness, without debility,
> That is the sign of Emain —
> Uncommon is an equal marvel.

In Silvery Land "dragon stones and crystals drop." Here were music, wine, chariots of silver and gold, golden steeds, and many thousands of "variegated women." Here too was "the conspicuous stone" from which came a hundred strains. The woman listed the various delights and said:

> There are thrice fifty distant isles
> In the ocean to the west of us;
> Larger than Erin twice
> Is each of them, or thrice.

Here will come a great birth of a ruler, born of a woman "whose mate will not be known," and who is the Creator Himself come to heal sicknesses.

[12] Meyer, *The Voyage of Bran,* pp. 2–35; van Hamel, *Immrama,* pp. 1ff.; Cross and Slover, *Ancient Irish Tales,* pp. 588ff. Cf. Zimmer *Zeits. f. d. Alter-*

Bran goes in search of the island. And at sea he finds a man in a chariot riding toward him over the waves. This is Manannán son of Ler, the sea god, who sings thirty quatrains to him. He tells him of the Land-beneath-the-Waves, a place of all beauties and delights:

> Bran deems it a marvellous beauty
> In his coracle across the clear sea:
> While to me in my chariot from afar
> It is a flowery plain on which he rows about.

Here is a wood with blossom and fruit, a "wood without decay, without defect" on which the leaves are golden. Here the people are sinless.

Finally Bran sets forth again and sees the Island of Laughter and then the Island of Women. On the latter he and his men land and stay for many years, though it "seemed a year to them that they were there." When they returned home, one of the men sprang ashore: ". . . forthwith he was a heap of ashes, as though he had been in the earth for many hundred years." Bran told of his wanderings, bade the people of Ireland farewell, and departed: "And from that hour his wanderings are not known."

In this narrative several elements are clear: the fairy mistress who sought Bran to summon him to the Other World; the voyage and the islands; the Land-beneath-the-Waves; the Island of Maidens; the apple tree and the fruit-bearing wood; the use of crystal (common, as we have seen, in Otherworld descriptions); the musical stone; the birds singing the hours; the indication of the swift passage of time.

A similar story is the *Voyage of Maeldúin*,[13] dated by some scholars as early as the first half of the ninth century, by others as late as the beginning of the eleventh. According to this, omitting the framework it gives regarding the hero, we may note simply

---

thum, XXXIII (1889), 258; St. John D. Seymour, *Irish Visions of the Other-World*, pp. 62ff.; Brown, *op. cit.*, 271ff.

[13] Whitley Stokes, *Rev. celtique*, IX (1888), pp. 447–495; X (1889), pp. 50–95; van Hamel, *Immrama*, pp. 20ff.; Seymour, *Irish Visions*, pp. 69ff.; Boswell, *Irish Precursor of Dante*, pp. 150ff. For the date see Meyer in the *Zeits. f. celt. Phil.*, XI (1917), p. 148; with comment by Thurneysen, XII (1918), pp. 278ff. Cf. Tennyson's *Voyage of Maeldune* for a modern derivative.

that Maeldúin builds a boat and sets forth in search of his father's murderers. After various adventures he and his crew come to many islands including the following: (vi) an island with a house, in which beds are prepared "and food for three before every bed, and a vessel of glass with good liquor before every bed, and a cup of glass on every vessel"; (vii) an island surrounded by a great cliff, with a long narrow wood therein "and great was its length and its narrowness"; (x) an island with trees bearing golden apples; (xii) an island divided by a brazen palisade, with black flocks of sheep on one side and white flocks on the other; (xiii) an island with a mountain on it, from which the men are cut off by a great river — "Into this river Germán dipt the handle of his spear, and at once it was consumed as if fire had burnt it"; (xvi) an island divided into four parts by fences: a fence of gold, one of silver, one of brass, and one of crystal; kings in one part, queens in another, and maidens in the last — one of the maidens serves the travelers food and intoxicating liquor; (xvii) an island with the fortress with a brazen door, to which leads a bridge of glass — "When they used to go up on the bridge they would fall down backwards"; (xviii) a mountainous island, full of birds "shouting and speaking loudly"; (xx) an island with a golden rampart, on which is a fountain: it gives water on Wednesdays and Fridays, milk on Sundays and feasts of martyrs; on the feasts of the Apostles, of Mary and John the Baptist, and on the hightides of the year, it gives ale and wine; (xxiii) they voyage over a sea "like a cloud" and behold underneath it "roofed strongholds and a beautiful country" with herds and a huge beast and an armed man; (xxiv) an island surrounded by vast cliffs of water — the people shout "It is they! It is they!" (xxvi) they find a great silver column, with a silver net hanging from its top, a voice speaks from the summit; (xxvii) an island standing on a single pedestal with no entrance;[14] (xxviii) an island with a great plain on it, and on this a great tableland; a fortress there contains a house, in which are seventeen maidens ready to bathe the strangers, the queen has the gift of bestowing eternal life; (xxix) an island with marvelous fruit trees; (xxx) an island with a huge bird carrying

[14] Cf. *Zeits. f. celt. Phil.*, I (1897), 27–28, for belief that the world is based on columns.

an enormous branch of a tree on which are berries; (xxxii) an island with a revolving fiery rampart, in which is a doorway; through this doorway the travelers see the whole island and observe its inhabitants feasting with golden vessels.

In the riches of this vast collection we find not merely the island motif, but also the Land-under-the-Waves (xxiii), and the revolving rampart. In one or another of the accounts there is mention of food, liquor, fruit trees, and fruit, and the attendant maidens who offer entertainment. Notable is the silver column with the net hanging from the top (xxvi) and the empty banquet hall (vi).

In the *Voyage of Snedgus*[15] of the ninth or tenth century, the travelers come to an island where they find a stream tasting like new milk (14); another with a fence of silver over the midst and a fish-weir [over or on?] which is a plank of silver (15); another with warriors headed like cats (16); another with a great tree with beautiful birds — on top is a great bird with head of gold and wings of silver, telling of creation and Christ and the last judgment; the birds beat their sides with their wings so that showers of blood drop down from them for dread of the signs of Doom, and they sing psalms and canticles praising the Lord, "For they were the birds of the Plain of Heaven, and neither trunk nor leaf of that tree decays" (17–18); another with men headed like hounds, with manes of cattle on them (19); another with men headed like swine; another with a multitude of men and women — the women sing a "sianán" and the travelers are welcomed to the house of the king of the island (21ff.). Enoch and Elijah dwell here on the island, and there are two lakes, one of water and one of fire; another island great and lofty with a noble dwelling, in which are a hundred doors with an altar at every door (24ff.). In this account we note especially the tree with the singing birds. The Christian influence is so obvious, however, that Zimmer sees the story as a poetic description of a throng of Irish priests driven into the Gulf Stream from their course and landing at the Faroes.

[15] Whitley Stokes, *Rev. celtique*, ix (1888), 14ff.; van Hamel, *Immrama*, pp. 78ff.; Thurneysen, *Zwei Versionen der mittelirischen Legende von Snedgus und MacRiagla*, prose version B; Zimmer, *Zeits. f. d. Alt.*, XXXIII (1889), p. 212; Seymour, *Irish Visions*, pp. 79ff.

With this journey Stokes associates the *Adventure of Saint Columba's Clerics,* "based," he says, "on the same event" and probably to be dated in the tenth century.[16] It describes again the voyage of Snedgus and Mac Riagla, and refers to the same islands. It also incorporates and thus transmits a large section of the *Fís Adamnáin.* This work I shall consider in another section. For purposes of comparison, however, I may summarize the description, as follows: first, there is a "wondrous realm facing them on the southeast, with a veil of crystal between them and it" (17ff.); to the south is a golden porch, through which they see the "household of heaven"; a fiery circle is about the land "and thereinto and thereout [fares] every one, and it doth no hurt to the righteous"; the music of the birds enrapturing the blessed is mentioned; in the household of heaven is the throne of the king – a canopied chair with four columns of precious stone, and three birds on the throne who "celebrate the eight choice canonical hours"; the city wherein is the throne is surrounded with seven crystal ramparts, and the platform and base of the city are crystal; crystal again appears in the chancel-rail between the choirs of angels – "three precious stones, too, with a soft melodious sound, with the sweetness of music at every two choirs"; a veil of fire and a veil of ice in the chief gateway "and they a-clashing top against top for ever and ever." To get to the throne one must climb the seven heavens, and there are six "gates of guardianship" up to the kingdom guarded by archangels. Before the gate of the second heaven is a fiery river with a great flame (29). All the material in this part is, as I have said, taken verbatim from the *Vision of Adamnán,* including even the bridge (35) as follows:

> Now this is the first land to which he came: a land black and burnt, bare and seared, without any torture therein. A glen full of fire on the hither side of it, a vast flame there which comes over its border on every side. Black is its lower part, red its middle and its upper part. Eight monsters there, with their eyes like fiery gledes. And a vast bridge there is over the glen wherein those sinners are punished. It stretches from one brink to the other: its ends are low and its middle is high. Three hosts are preparing to wend across it, and not all pass. For a host of them broad is the bridge from beginning to end. For another host . . .

[16] Whitley Stokes, *Rev. celtique,* XXVI (1905), pp. 130ff. Cf. Zimmer, *Zeits. f. d. Alt.,* XXXIII, p. 211.

it is narrow at the beginning and broad at the end; and for the third it is broad at the beginning and narrow at the end so that they fall into the valley. Thus early is the oriental bridge introduced into Celtic literature.

The *Voyage of the Huí Corra,* probably of the eleventh century or shortly thereafter,[17] tells of islands that again remind us of those in the *Voyage of Maeldúin.* Before the journey Lochan has a dream of heaven and hell: (14) "So I saw the four rivers of Hell, even a river of toads and a river of serpents, a river of fire and a river of snow . . . . Thereafter I perceived that I was borne away to gaze at Heaven, and I beheld the Lord Himself on His throne, and a birdflock of angels making music to Him. Then I saw a bright bird, and sweeter was his singing than every melody. Now this was Michael in the form of a bird in the presence of the Creator." On the pilgrimage the brothers sail westward and come upon the islands: (44) first one "full of men agrieving and lamenting" – after this episode the jester dies on board and reappears in the form of a bird; (47) an island with a grove of apple trees and a beautiful river of wine (which keeps the men from perceiving wound or disease in them); (48) an island divided in four parts: in one the sedate folk, in another royal lords, champions in the third part, servants in the fourth; (49) an island supported by a pedestal which lifts it high over the sea: here are men whose converse can be heard;[18] (50) a marvelous river in the form of a rainbow which rises up into the sky – at times it has the taste of honey: (51) an island which is a silver pillar, four-cornered with a silver and bronze fishnet from its summit down to the deep "and Maeldúin beheld the same thing"; (52) an island with bright bird flocks, and with red flowers the size of tables; (53) an island with dead men in one part and living men in another, a fiery sea torments them from time to time; (54) an island surrounded by a brazen palisade and a brazen net spread on its spikes, the wind makes music on the nets which puts the men to sleep for three days and three nights; a woman feeds the travelers a food like soft cheeses and

[17] Ed. Whitley Stokes, *Rev. celtique,* XIV (1893), pp. 22ff.; van Hamel, *Immrama,* pp. 93ff. Cf. Zimmer, *Zeits. f. d. Alt.,* XXXIII, pp. 198 and 183ff.; Seymour, *Irish Visions,* pp. 74ff.

[18] Cf. *Maeldúin,* § xxvii.

gives them water from the well – "and there was no savour that they did not find therein"; (55–56) they see a bird which is the soul of a woman – it speaks to them of a bird flock, saying "The birds that ye see are the souls that come on Sunday out of hell"; (57) the travelers see three wondrous rivers – one of otters, one of eels, and one of black swans; (60) they see an island with shining grass and purple flowers, here is an abundance of birds and "ever-lovely bees"; (63) they see a horseman on the waves, he is suffering punishment for riding on Sunday; (64) they see an island full of men lamenting because they are tormented by jet-black birds; (67) an island bright and beautiful with a smooth wood full of honey, a heath, and a lake; an island with two springs, one turbid and one clear and bright (68ff.), the clear one gives water that puts the men to sleep; (71) a wondrous island with fair churches and bright altars, beautiful green grass, bees, and birds; (72) another beautiful island with a church, a bird greets them; (73) an island with a cell and a church, where dwells one of the disciples. In the allusions to torments this *imram* gives clear evidence of a reflection of the visions of heaven and hell. It shows the usual Otherworld features in the rivers, the well, the two springs, the food, and the singing birds which are souls.

Related in some way to voyages to blessed islands the *Adventure of Cian's son Teigue* [19] has a less mechanical procedure and seems to be indebted to the type rather than based on it. Teigue builds a boat to go in pursuit of his enemies. He and his men set forth, and see many sights: "they heard about them a concert of multifarious unknown birds and hoarse booming of the main; salmons, iridescent, white-bellied, throwing themselves all around the currach; in their wake huge bull seals, thick and dark . . . ." After twenty days they land on a shore, where they rest and where they find flocks of huge sheep; one gigantic ram in particular had nine horns. Again they light on a pair of "most peculiar islands" where they find birds of the bulk of eagles or cranes, red in color with green heads, laying eggs of blue and crimson. When some of the travelers eat of the eggs, feathers sprout all over them and disappear only when they bathe. A storm falls upon them at sea, and at length they come to a pleasing land with salmon in its

[19] O'Grady, *Silva Gadelica*, II, pp. 385ff.

harbor, delicate woods with empurpled treetops on its shores. Here they feel no need of food or fire: "the perfume of that region's fragrant crimsoned branches being by way of meat and satisfying aliment all-sufficient for them." They find an orchard of red-laden apples, leafy oaks, yellow hazels, purple berries bigger than a man's head. On the berries feed beautiful birds: "As they fed they warbled music and minstrelsy that was melodious and superlative, to which patients of every kind and the repeatedly wounded would have fallen asleep . . ."

Here they proceed to a wide smooth plain clad in flowering clover all bedewed with honey, with three prominent hills on each of which is a fortress. At the first hill Teigue sees the fair white-bodied lady, Gothnia's daughter. From her he learns of the "fortalice upon the high hill's face, with round about it a bulwark of white marble." The island itself is "loch island." Teigue moves on to the middle fort, which is of golden color, and speaks with a queen of gracious form draped in golden vesture. Here, she tells him, she bides in "everlasting life." This island, she says, is named "red loch island" because of a red loch in it, containing an island surrounded with a palisade of gold, "its name being *inis Patmos,* in which are all saints and righteous that have served God." She says this is "the Earth's fourth paradise; the others being *inis Daleb* in the world's southern, and *inis Escandra* in its boreal part (to the northward of 'the black watery isle'), Adam's paradise, and this island in which ye are now: the fourth land, I say, in which Adam's seed dwell — such of them as are righteous." On the third hill is a habitation of great beauty with a silver rampart, where appear a golden-haired couple with vesture of green. The lady is Veniusa, daughter to Adam. The youth by her side, who is eating a golden apple, is Connla. Teigue goes to the palace and enters, passing "the arched doorway with its wide valves and portal-capitals of burnished gold" on to the pavement tesselated of pure white, blue, and crimson marble. The house has four golden doors; crystal and carbuncle in patterns are set in the walls. Across the palace is a wide-spreading apple tree with both blossoms and fruit. Three birds enter ("a blue one, with crimson head; a crimson, with head of green; a pied one having on his head a color of gold") and eat an apple apiece, and warble "melody sweet and harmonized, such that the sick would sleep to it." The apples sustain the people of this isle. Here Cleena Fairhead gives Teigue an emerald cup that has great powers — it can change water into wine. To the travelers this whole visit seems to have taken "but one single day." Cleena however tells them "for an entire twelvemonth ye are in it; during which time ye have had neither meat nor drink nor, how long soever ye should be here, would cold or thirst or hunger assail you." The travelers depart over the sea. The "birds struck up their chorus for them" and by their music they are cheered. But as they go a magic veil incontinently obscures the land.[20]

After one has examined the *imrama* and the stories of this type, the material incorporated in the widely spread narratives regarding Saint Brendan becomes easy to understand.[21] Whichever came first, *imram* or saint's legend, in the development of this type of literature, the *Navigatio Sancti Brendani* with its derivatives in various languages certainly does not belong to the primitive form which related simply the voyage of a missionary. Fantasy and Otherworld material have here made their contribution in the earliest examples of the story we can discover. Saint Brendan himself belongs to the fifth and sixth centuries and the Latin prose *Navigatio* cannot be later than the tenth; but here

[20] A more literary invention, perhaps as old as the fourteenth century, is the *Adventures of the Children of the King of Norway* (ed. Douglas Hyde, *Irish Texts Soc.* I, pp. 50ff.) with the voyage and an isle of birds, an encounter with a horseman riding over the waves, an island with fruit trees and mansion with a wondrous cat, an island with a flower-bordered mansion and a damsel, an island with a giant, an island with half-black and half-white sheep. The most extraordinary features, however, are the Forest of Wonders (121ff.), the City of the Red Stream round which three chief flaming rivers flow (163ff.), and the Bridge (179ff.). The red lake of fire and fiery rivers (cf. p. 173) and the Bridge suggest a foreign importation.

[21] For the legend see G. Schirmer, *Zur Brendanus-Legende* and J. Dunn in the *Catholic Historical Review*, VI (1920–1921), pp. 395ff. For medieval versions see Zimmer, *Zeits. f. d. Alt.*, XXXIII, pp. 129ff.; Schulze, *Zeits. romanische Phil.*, XXX (1906), pp. 257ff.; Plummer, *Zeits. f. celt. Phil.*, V, (1905), pp. 124ff. Cf. C. Steinweg, *Die handschriftliche Gestaltungen des lateinischen Navigatio Brendani, Romanische Forschungen*, VII (Erlangen, 1893), pp. 2ff.; C. Wahlund, *Die Altfranz. Prosaübersetzungen von Brendans Meerfahrt*; E. G. R. Waters, *The Anglo-Norman Voyage of St. Brendan by Benedeit*; Seymour, *Irish Visions*, pp. 83ff. An Old Norse fragment is printed in C. R. Unger's *Heilagra Manna Søgur*, I, pp. 272–275.

we once more have the series of extraordinary islands and the familiar motifs.

Irish accounts of the life of Saint Brendan begin the story with an episode in which he climbs a mountain and sees the distant island which is the Land of Promise.[22] Various minor details distinguish the Latin *Navigatio,* the Irish lives, the Anglo-Norman version, the Flemish, Middle English, and other forms of the story from one another, but we cannot deal with them here. It is enough to summarize significant points in the description of the islands visited by the saint in a typical narrative, and for this I take the first Irish life as translated by Plummer.[23] Brendan sees the island full of furry mice as large as cats, the jester in the boat receives the Sacrament and dies and his body is thrown to the mice (xvii); a lofty island on which there is a house "with many chased vessels and gold-mounted bridles" (xix); an island with goodly streams full of fish and with herds of large sheep (xx); the island which is the Paradise of Birds, with many excellent fruits and marvelous birds "discoursing joyously from the tops of their trees," with streams flowing full of wondrous jewels, with a monastery and many churches, and with lights before the altars in the monastery which burn without ever being consumed (xxi); the island with a river whose waters intoxicate them into a sleep and torpor (xxii); the whale on whose back the travelers celebrate Easter (xxv); an island, to which they are not admitted, on which is a noble church (xxix); [on the second voyage] the island of dwarfs and leprechauns with faces as black as coal (xxxiii); the island whose brink is "of an appalling height, so that they could scarcely see [the top of] it, and it appeared full of firebrands and red sparks, and was as steep as a wall" (xxxiv); the rock on which Judas sits having his Sunday respite (xxxv),[24] the steep and rocky isle of Paul, the hermit (xxxvi); the great column "all of the colour of crystal from top to bottom, and there was the likeness of an enclosure round it on

[22] C. Plummer, *Lives of Irish Saints,* II, pp. 51ff.; *Zeits. f. celt. Phil.,* V (1904), 125f.; Zimmer, *Zeits. f. d. Alt.,* XXXIII, pp. 134f.

[23] Plummer, *op. cit.,* II, pp. 52ff.

[24] Cf. Matthew Arnold's poem, *Saint Brandan.* See too the article by P. F. Baum on "Judas's Sunday Rest," *Mod. Lang. Review,* XVIII (1923), pp. 168–182.

all sides of the colour of silver or glass . . . . everything could be seen through it . . . and it was full of great doors . . . . they found a Mass chalice on a bench in the side of the column" (xxxviii); the island of the demon smithy (xxxix); the island of great beauty full of "roots and fragrant herbs" with a fountain "fair of hue" in the middle (xli); the island with plain level surface all of white, where they receive the purple "scalts" (xlii); the radiant bird with a branch containing fruit like crab apples, which alights on the prow of their ship (xlii); the island of fruitful trees (xliii); the pleasant isle of the fishermen, near which they are pursued by the sea-cat (xlvi); the Land of Promise, which is Paradise — "where will be found health without sickness, pleasure without contention, union without quarrel, dominion without interruption, attendance of angels, feasting without diminution, meadows sweet in scent as fair blessed flowers" — and where they find an elder whose body is covered "with a white down like a dove or sea-mew" (xlvii). In this narrative the usual elements appear: the islands, the mountain, the fountain, the fruit trees — even the branch bearing apples of a sort, and — most interestingly perhaps of all — the crystal column. Also the elder whose body suggests the down of a dove or sea-mew may carry a reminiscence of bird-souls. Another and related legend, *The Twelve Apostles of Ireland* [25] tells of the coming of "an indescribably large flower" as a "token of the Land of Promise." Here is included a vision of hell which the devil shows to Brendan: "the hard dark prison" with flame and filth and "currents of ever-blazing streams."

It is clear that these voyages have elements from time to time of another conception than that merely of the island. The idea of the Land-beneath-the-Waves appears in the *Voyage of Bran* and the *Voyage of Maeldúin* (§ xxiii). Something like the Holy Mountain is found in the *Voyage of Maeldúin* (e.g. § xiii) and elsewhere. On the other hand the idea of a voyage to what presumably is the Isle of the Blessed appears in stories which do not belong to the *imram* type. An example of this is the story of Connla the Fair (found in the *Book of the Dun Cow* and else-

[25] Plummer, II, 93ff.

where),[26] in which the fairy mound or *síd* appears, but the fairy mistress herself in journeying to her "Land of the Living" uses a crystal boat.

So too Conn's love in the *Adventures of Art Son of Conn* travels from the Land of Promise in a coracle.[27] Later Conn takes a coracle and arrives at "a strange isle." Here he finds fair fragrant apple trees with many wells of wine, a bright wood with clustering hazel trees, bees humming over the fruits, "which were dropping their blossoms and their leaves into the wells" (§ 9, p. 157). Near by he saw a "shapely hostel thatched with birds' wings, white, and yellow, and blue." It had doorposts of bronze and doors of crystal. Here too is a throne of crystal. On a bed Conn is ministered to and his feet washed. Then he is fed with varied meats and drink which are given to him by he knows not whom. Again in a later voyage Conn sails in a coracle to a "fair, strange island" (§ 18, p. 165), where again he finds the house "thatched with birds' wings, white and purple." Here he finds a company of women and he sees a "crystal bower" ("with its doors of crystal and its inexhaustible vats, for, though everything be emptied out of them, they are ever full again," § 19, p. 165). So much of this recalls the *imrama*. But the later journey over the great and dark ocean, past the dense and thorny wood by the mountain, and over the icy river with its narrow bridge, all this is something else again and must be discussed separately. In the *Second Battle of Moytura* Eri beholds the sea "in perfect calm as if it were a level board. And as she was there she saw somewhat. A vessel of silver was revealed to her on the sea" and in it is the handsome youth Elatha, King of the Fomorians.[28]

The voyage also comes into *Serglige Conculaind* ("The Sick-Bed of Cú Chulainn"),[29] where we are told that Fann lives on an

[26] Translated in *Ancient Irish Tales*, ed. T. P. Cross and C. H. Slover, pp. 488–489; in Irish in *Leabhar na h-Uidhre* (*The Book of the Dun Cow*), 120[a]; critical edition by Pokorny, *Zeits. f. celt. Phil.*, XVII (1928), pp. 193ff. See *Zeits. f. vergleich. Sprachf.*, XXVIII (1887), pp. 417ff.; cf. O'Grady, *Silva Gadelica*, II, ix; R. I. Best and Osborn Bergin, *Lebor na Huidre, Book of the Dun Cow*. See also the Welsh *Spoils of Annwn*, translated by Loomis, *Publ. Mod. Lang. Assoc.*, LVI (1941), pp. 887ff.

[27] *Ériu*, III (1907), p. 153.

[28] *Rev. celtique*, XII (1891), p. 61.

[29] E. Windisch, *Irische Texte*, I, pp. 197ff.; *Serglige con Culainn*, ed. Myles

island. She appears to Cú Chulainn to win his love, and he goes to Mag Mell ("The Plain of Delights") by crossing in a bronze skiff. On this island is a palace containing thrice fifty couches and thrice fifty women on the couches – a sufficiently clear example of the Celtic idea of the Other World as a maiden land. Again we are told by LiBán that the Other World is "over a pure lake" where "troops of women congregate." Labraid's house (Labraid is a fairy king, husband of LiBán) is upheld by columns of crystal and silver. It has two kings, fifty beds on the right and fifty on the left, a warrior on each, and the beds have gold-adorned columns. One door is toward the west; and one is toward the east, where in the tree tops a flock of birds sing a "sweetly drawn-out song." Here too is a tree of silver, from whose branches comes beautiful music. There are thrice fifty trees each of which feeds three hundred people with abundant food, and there is a well "in that noble palace of the fairy mound," and a caldron of invigorating mead. Here are beautiful women and delightful music. In this land Cú Chulainn is entertained by the lovely Fann and stays for a month of joy. The confusion in the story between the island motif and reference to the Fairy Mound is again worth noting.

A storm on the voyage to the Other World comes into the story included in the *Colloquy with the Ancients.*[30] Ciabhán sets forth in "a high-prowed currach having a narrow stern of copper," in which are two other young men. "Now rose at them white and billowing waves, insomuch that each huge ocean billow of them equalled a mountain; and that the beautiful variegated salmon wont to hug bottom sand and shingle touched the currach's very sides. . . ." They are rescued by a warrior driving a dark gray horse reined with a golden bridle. They arrive at the "land of promise" and go to the fort of Manannán, where they

Dillon; *Anc. Ir. Tales,* Cross and Slover, pp. 176ff.; A. H. Leahy, *Heroic Romances of Ireland,* I, pp. 53ff.; cf. also the eighteenth-century journey of Oisín to the Land of Youth ("The Lay of Oisín," by Michael Comyn, Cross and Slover, pp. 439ff.); P. W. Joyce, *Old Celtic Romances,* pp. 385ff. Also cf. the Mongan story, *Zeits. f. celt. Phil.,* II (1899), pp. 316f.

[30] O'Grady, *Silva Gadelica,* II, pp. 198ff. Cf. other versions cited in Nutt's *Voy. Bran,* I, pp. 196–197.

are entertained with music and drink and juggling. Here they have love affairs with three girls and elope with them.

The Land-under-the-Waves is found, in combination with the *síd* motif, in a story of Loegaire [31] and how he helped Fiachna recover his wife, who has been abducted. He and his men dive into a loch, and they find a wonderful land by so doing, where Loegaire and his men enjoy the love of Fiachna's daughter and fifty other women for a year. Fiachna warns the men (when they start at length for home) not to dismount from their horses or they will be unable to return to the Plain of Delights. The same warning is given to Oisín in the eighteenth-century *Lay*, but in vain. Oisín is thrown from his horse by accident:

At once I lost the sight of my eyes,
My youth's bloom died, lean age began,
And I was left of strength bereft,
A helpless, hopeless, blind old man! [32]

Another example appears in the *Lad of the Ferule*,[33] according to which Murough hires the services of the lad whose only demand is that Murough will give him what he asks for at the end of a year. When the time is up the boy asks for a ferule to fit his stick and the only one that will serve is at the bottom of a lake. To this lake goes Murough, and at the bottom he finds the ferule, a caldron of marvelous powers, and a serpent. Murough kills the serpent, gets the caldron and the ferule. But he has to recover the caldron again, and he finds at the bottom of the lake the Tír na n-Óg or the country of the ever-young. After slaying a giant and freeing the country he sees the lad of the ferule (who is of course a supernatural being) enthroned in the Under-wave-Land "in a gold-overlaid chair, and a silver cushion beneath his feet, his three billets of yew in front of him, burning for him." Murough thinks he has been in the country for a week or two, but the lad of the ferule tells him it is for a year and a day.

The Land-under-the-Waves is also found in a story containing

[31] In the fifteenth-century Book of Lismore. O'Grady, *Silva Gadelica*, II, pp. 290–291.

[32] Cross and Slover, *Ancient Irish Tales*, p. 456.

[33] Ed. Douglas Hyde, *Irish Texts Society*, I.

the voyage motif — *The Pursuit of the Gilla Decair*,[34] where Dermot after encountering the wizard-champion at the well leaps with him into its depths. Here he finds a lovely country, a city of great tall houses, and a royal palace, and the adventures continue. At length the hero comes to a towering fortress where thrice fifty knights and as many beautiful ladies are assembled, and where Dermot is entertained. The country, he is told, is "Tír-fó-thuinn" ("country beneath the wave") and the champion is the "Wizard of the Well." Because of its interest as an entrance to the Other World we quote the description of the well:

> From east and west, from south and north, Duibhne's grandson traversed the plain and, as he looked abroad, was aware of a vast tree with interlacing boughs and thickly furnished; hard by which was a great mass of stone furnished on its very apex with an ornamented pointed drinking-horn, and having at its base a fair well of water in all its purity.[35]

The similarity of this scene and the plot that follows recalls strikingly the *Yvain* of Chrétien de Troyes and its related versions.[36]

Another form of the water barrier is the mist motif, as we have it in *Cormac's Adventures in the Land of Promise* [37] (found

[34] O'Grady, *Silva Gadelica*, II, pp. 292ff., especially 301ff.; cf. P. W. Joyce, *Old Celtic Romances*, pp. 245ff. Cf. Jaufre reaching the Other World through a spring in the thirteenth-century romance, *Jaufre*, ed. H. Breuer, ll. 8378ff. *(Gesells. f. roman. Lit.*, 46).

[35] O'Grady, *op. cit.*, II, p. 301; cf. Joyce, pp. 247–248. The well is found also in another story: Windisch, *Irische Texte*, III, 2, p. 209. For other examples of underwater realms and an Irish lost Atlantis "O-Brazila," note the many references cited in *Proceedings of the Royal Irish Acad.*, XXX (1912–1913), Section C, Arch. Ling. Lit., pp. 223ff., and in *Mod. Philol.*, XII (1914–1915), 599ff.; cf. also *Mod. Philol.*, XIII (1915–1916), pp. 731ff. (with the mist and the *sid*); Rhŷs, *Celtic Folklore*, I, pp. 170ff. and II, pp. 401ff.; J. Hardiman, *Irish Minstrelsy or Bardic Remains of Ireland*, I, pp. 367ff.; P. Sébillot, *Le Folk-Lore de la France*, I, *Le Ciel et la Terre*, p. 422; *Le Folk-Lore de la France*, II, pp. 56ff.; MacCulloch, *Relig. of the Ancient Celts*, pp. 151, 366, 371f.; Rhŷs, *Arthurian Legend*, chap. xv; W. Y. Evans Wentz, *The Fairy-Faith in Celtic Countries*, pp. 333–334; Le Braz, *Légende de la Mort*, I, pp. 381ff.

[36] Cf. A. C. L. Brown, "Iwain, a Study," [*Harvard*] *Studies and Notes*, VIII, p. 105, and *Romanic Review*, III (1912), pp. 143ff. — note especially 167, n. 36 and pp. 170f., n. 40.

[37] Ed. in W. Stokes and E. Windisch, *Irische Texte*, etc. III, 1, pp. 183ff.; Cross and Slover, *Ancient Irish Tales*, pp. 503ff. Cf. Zimmer, *Zeits. f. d. Alt.*, XXXIII, pp. 264ff.

in several manuscripts of the fourteenth and fifteenth centuries). Cormac sees a gray-haired warrior coming toward him clad in a purple, fringed mantle, with a ribbed, gold-threaded shirt, and two blunt shoes of white bronze. On his shoulder is a branch of silver with three golden apples which make such music when the branch is shaken that the wounded and sick are lulled to sleep thereby. This stranger eventually carries off Cormac's daughter, son, and wife to the Other World, "wherein is nought save truth, and there is neither age nor decay nor gloom nor sadness nor envy nor jealousy nor hatred nor haughtiness" (§ 27). The loss of his wife Cormac cannot endure, and he follows the stranger:

> A great mist was brought upon them in the midst of the plain of the wall. Cormac found himself on a great plain alone. There was a large fortress in the midst of the plain with a wall of bronze around it. In the fortress was a house of white silver, and it was half-thatched with the wings of white birds. A fairy host of horsemen [was] haunting the house, with lapfuls of the wings of white birds in their bosoms to thatch the house. . . . (§ 32).

He sees another fortress and another wall of bronze; within is a palace with beams of bronze, wattling of silver, and thatch of the wings of white birds. Outside in the yard is a fountain with five streams flowing out of it. "Nine hazels of Buan grow over the well," dropping their nuts into it, which five salmon despoil of their husks. In this story the traces of the idea of the bird Paradise, or the belief that human souls appear after death in the form of birds, are curiously evident in the motif of the birds' wings which resembles details in the story of the *Adventures of Art Son of Conn*. Also there is a similarity to certain details in the *imrama*: the branch of silver recalls the branch of the apple tree of Emain in the *Voyage of Bran*; the bronze walls and bronze beams are something like items in the *Voyage of Maeldúin* (§§ xii and xvi). The sleep-inducing music is familiar in other Celtic stories.[38] Druidical mist, which may perhaps be regarded as dis-

[38] See *Rev. celtique,* XVI (1895), p. 32 (*Rennes Dindšenchas*), mermaid's melody; Nutt, *Voy. Bran,* I, p. 198; *Voy. of the Huí Corra,* ed. *Rev. celtique,* XIV (1893), pp. 46–47, § 54; Leahy, *Heroic Romances,* I, p. 59; Child, *Ballads,* Index, V, p. 489, s.v. Music; Schofield, *Mythical Bards,* pp. 74ff., 310ff.; *Rev. celtique,* XII (1891), pp. 81, 109 (*The Second Battle of Moytura*); Hyde, *Children of the King of Norway,* p. 169; Campbell, *Pop. Tales,* II, pp. 65–66; D. MacInnes, *Folk and Hero Tales,* (F.L.S. xxv), pp. 63–65, 273; Boswell,

tinctively Celtic although its equivalent is found in Norse literature, appears in other stories – for example in the *Feast of Bricriu* and *Manawyddan*.[39]

One of the commonest types of Celtic Other World, however – almost as familiar indeed as the island motif – is that of the *síd* Elysium or fairy mound, to which references are almost innumerable. As MacCulloch describes them, "The *síd* were marvelous underground palaces, full of strange things, and thither favoured mortals might go for a time or for ever. In this they correspond exactly to the oversea Elysium, the divine land." [40] These fairy hills seem not to have been conspicuous for height or magnificence. The most familiar example is in the *Wooing of Étaín*.[41] The heroine herself, of whom the Egerton version gives a marvelous description,[42] is a creature from a fairy mound. Mider invites her to his *síd*

to dwell
In the marvellous land of the musical spell,
Where the crowns of all heads are, as primroses, bright,
And from head to the heel all men's bodies snow-white.

In that land of no 'mine' nor of 'thine' is there speech,
But there teeth flashing white and dark eyebrows hath each;
In all eyes shine our hosts, as reflected they swarm,
And each cheek with the pink of the foxglove is warm.

Irish Prec. of Dante, p. 30; J. R. Caldwell, *Eger and Grime*, pp. 131ff.; Paton, *Studies in the Fairy Mythol.*, pp. 31; 211, n. 5, etc.

[39] See §§ 36, 39, 40, *Fled Bricrend, The Feast of Bricriu*, ed. George Henderson, (Irish Texts Soc. II). See also the *Champion's Ecstasy*, Nutt, *Voy. Bran*, I, pp. 186ff.; MacCulloch, *Relig. of the Anc. Celts*, p. 367; Loth, *Mabinogion*, I, p. 101. For other tales see the *Scott. Celt. Rev.*, I, (1881), p. 70 (a shower); Campbell, *Pop. Tales*, II, p. 212; II, p. 451 (a shower); Maynadier, *The Wife of Bath's Tale*, pp. 26ff.

[40] *Relig. Anc. Celts*, p. 65; cf. also p. 39. He compares the parallel history of the Scandinavian elf and the elf house, p. 66, n. 5. The mounds were associated with the Tuatha Dé Danann. Cf. the story in *Zeits. f. celt. Phil.*, XIX (1931–1933), pp. 55ff.; also that in *Silva Gadelica*, II, pp. 247ff. In a study showing the indebtedness of *Sir Orfeo* to Celtic lore, Kittredge reviews allied material in *Am. J. Philol.*, VII (1886), pp. 194ff. On the underworld as Hades, the land of the dead, cf. Eleanor Hull, *Folk-Lore*, XVIII (1907), pp. 121ff., and MacCulloch, *Relig. Anc. Celts*, p. 341.

[41] *Irische Texte*, III, 1, pp. 113ff.; trans. A. H. Leahy, *Heroic Romances of Ireland*, I, pp. 11ff.

[42] Leahy *op. cit.*, I, pp. 12f.; Cross and Slover, *Ancient Irish Tales*, pp. 83f.

And so on. The ale is stronger there; streams, smooth and luscious, flow there, and wine and mead abound. "There are men without blemish, and love without sin." Mider finally takes Étaín away from her husband, and, as he carries her off "through the skylight of the house," people see two swans circling around Tara "and the way that they took was the way to the elf-mound of Femun." Eochaid digs up each of the elf mounds but he has many difficulties before he regains his wife. In the *Adventures of Nera*[43] the hero (after a strange exploit with a corpse that with the evil power of the dead blasts its enemy) enters a *síd* and there is instructed by a woman. When he asks her how he can pass on the information to his friends, she tells him his friends are sitting around the same caldron and fire as when he left them. "Yet it had seemed to him three days and three nights since he had been in the *síd*." Later we are told ". . . the fairy-mounds of Erinn are always opened about Halloween." Describing his visit Nera says: "I was in fair lands . . . with great treasures and precious things, with plenty of garments and food, and of wonderful treasures."[44]

In the stories so far referred to we find evidence of the Celtic belief in an Other World located on an island; within a fairy mound (*síd*); under the waves (to be reached sometimes by a *loch* or sometimes by a well); or through the mist. There is hardly a trace, except perhaps in some of the islands of the *imrama*, of evidence for the idea of a holy mountain. In so far as scholars have assembled material of that sort, it is exceedingly slight.[45] There are, however, at least two stories that describe an approach to the Other World which is very different from the examples so far considered, and which show a significant type of barrier. The

[43] *Revue celtique*, X (1889), pp. 214ff.

[44] *Ibid.*, p. 225.

[45] See MacCulloch, *Relig. of the Ancient Celts*, pp. 39 and 228; H. Gaidoz, *Zeits. f. celt. Phil.* I (1897), pp. 27–28. Cf. the "lovely hill . . . higher than every hill, with hosts thereon. A shining tree like gold stood on the hill: because of its height it would reach to the clouds. In its leaves was every melody; and its fruits, when the wind touched it, specked the ground." From the *Rennes Dindšenchas*, *Rev. celtique*, XV (1894), p. 430. Cf. also *Maxen Wledig's Dream* in the *Mabinogion*, Loth, I, p. 158 (see *Speculum*, XXII [1947], pp. 520ff.); and *Rev. celtique*, XVI (1895), p. 52 (the *Rennes Dindšenchas*).

first is *The Adventures of Art Son of Conn,*[46] part of which we have already considered. According to this story after a fortnight and a month in the island where he was entertained by Creide Fíralaind, he goes forth in his boat warned that "the way is bad" which he now must take with a dark wood and a "luckless gulf" of the sea by the wood; then a mountain and a great forest near it. He meets all these obstacles. In the "hapless sea" he finds strange beasts that rise around his coracle and he slays them. Here we may be reminded of the storm in the *Adventure of Cian's Son Teigue.* In the forest wild, which is "traversed as though there were spear-points of battle under one's feet," he is tormented by strange hags. And at length he comes to "the venomous icy mountain; and the forked glen . . . full of toads, which were lying in wait for whoever came there. And he passed thence to Sliabh Saeb beyond, wherein were full many lions with long manes lying in wait for the beasts of the whole world." And "After that he came to the icy river, with its slender narrow bridge, and a warrior giant with a pillar-stone, and he grinding his teeth on it, namely Curnan Cliabhsalach." He wrestles with the giant, whose "head came off the back of his neck." He forces the giant's wife to show him the way to Morgan's stronghold, and the Land of Wonders. A "fair palisade of bronze was round about it." It had an "ingenious, bright, shining bower set on one pillar over the stead, on the very top, where that maiden [the daughter] was. She had a green cloak . . . with a gold pin in it over her breast." Morgan's wife put to death all that came to woo her daughter, and it was she who contrived all the barriers – the bridge and forest and mountain. The suitors who fail are beheaded and their heads placed on the stakes round the palisade of bronze (where now there is one vacant stake). Art does battle with Morgan's wife, and it is her head that goes on the stake while he wins the maiden.

Another story with similar deviations from the common type is *The Wooing of Emer*[47] (as found in a late manuscript, Book

[46] *Ériu,* III (1907), pp. 165ff. (§§ 20ff.).

[47] Meyer, *Archaeological Review,* I (1888), No. 1–4, pp. 681ff.; E. Hull, *The Cuchullin Saga,* pp. 57–84; Cross and Slover, *Anc. Irish Tales,* pp. 153ff.; Meyer, *Rev. celtique,* XI (1890), 433ff.; Meyer, *Zeits. f. celt. Phil.,* III (1901),

of Fermoy, fifteenth century), where in the later version[48] we have the account of Cú Chulainn's approach to the stronghold island of Scáthach. At first he goes astray, and then a "terrible great beast like a lion" comes towards him, "which kept regarding him, nor did him any harm. Whatever way he went, the beast went before him, and moreover it turned its side towards him. Then he took a leap and was on its neck. He did not guide it then, but went wherever the beast liked." Four days he traveled and came to an island where lads, rowing on a loch, laughed at the spectacle. Here as instructed by a youth, he goes across the Plain of Ill-luck. "On the hither half of the plain the feet of men would stick fast. On the further half the grass would rise and hold them fast on the points of its blades." For half the distance Cú Chulainn follows the track of a wheel the youth gave him; and then the rest of the way an apple which was another gift. Beyond the plain is a "large glen" and "a single narrow path through it which was full of monsters that had been sent by Forgall to destroy him, and that was his road to the house of Scáthach across terrible high strong districts." Cú Chulainn next has to cross the "Bridge of the Cliff," which had "two low heads and the mid space, and whenever anybody would leap on its one head, the other head would lift itself up and throw him on his back." Three times the hero makes the attempt and fails. The men near by jeer at him. At last in a frenzy he makes the salmon-leap to the middle before the other end has raised itself, and he lands safely on the island. In the earliest form of the story the hero goes across the Plain of Ill-luck: "On the hither half of the plain men would freeze fast. On the other half they would be raised on the grass. He took a wheel with him that he might reach like that wheel across one half of the plain, so that he would not freeze fast. [The youth] also gave him an apple that he might follow the ground as that apple would follow it. Thus he escaped across the plain. . . ." He passes over a glen: "One

---

pp. 229ff. Meyer refers to his translation published in the *Archaeological Review,* as "often erroneous." See R. Thurneysen, *Die irische Helden- und Königsage bis zum siebzehnten Jahrundert,* I–II, pp. 377ff., especially 396ff. (Kap. 32), and Brown, *Publ. Mod. Lang. Assoc.,* XX (1905), pp. 688ff.

[48] See Zimmer, *Zeits. f. d. Alt.,* XXXII (1888), pp. 196ff. Cf. *Rev. celtique,* XI (1890), 435; *Publ. Mod. Lang. Assoc.,* XX (1905), 688, n. 2.

narrow path across it, yet that was his way to the house of Scáthach. Across a terrible stony height besides." [49] The salmon-leap is included further along, but not the bridge.[50] It appears, then, that the bridge may not belong to the earliest form of the story at all. And here we may note that the *Adventures of Art*, where the barriers are similar, occurs only in a fifteenth-century manuscript. Perhaps these dark valleys with forbidding woods and wild animals and the dangerous bridge (at least of the "slender narrow" type) are not proper to early Celtic folklore.[51]

The icy mountain in the *Adventures of Art* is certainly unique; the three hills with their strongholds in the *Adventure of Cian's Son Teigue* are in no way similar as barriers. Here we may note merely that, according to the somewhat dated theory of Zimmer, in some of the Irish stories (including the *Wooing of Emer*) a distinction is apparent between pre-Norse and post-Norse versions, and that Meyer regarded this point as proved.[52] On those terms the clue then for the solution of the problem would be in some foreign influence; and the possibility of this is suggested by a glance at the borrowed material in *Saint Columba's Clerics* outlined above. It will be the more apparent

[49] *Rev. celtique*, XI (1890), p. 447.

[50] On the bridge of the *Wooing of Emer* note the interesting suggestion by Miss Dunn of some relationship to the bridge of Chrétien's *Conte del Graal*, ll. 3356–83 (ed. G. Baist), and ll. 3402ff. (ed. Hilka), *Mod. Lang. Notes*, XXXIII (1918), pp. 399–405. This is not entirely disposed of by A. H. Krappe, *Balor with the Evil Eye*, pp. 106ff. Cf., however, *Publ. Mod. Lang. Assoc.*, XX (1905), p. 690, n. 3, for another parallel, and see Loomis, *Arthurian Tradition and Chrétien de Troyes*, pp. 384–385.

[51] Cf. however, in the *Feast of Bricriu*, "the Plain-of-the-Two-Forks, the Gap-of-the-Watch," etc. to the "slope of Bregia," where the mist overtakes Loegaire (*Irish Texts Soc.* II, 45, § 36), followed by the fight with the giant; the plain of *Cormac's Adventure*, Windisch, *Irische Texte*, III, 1, p. 213; the valley and the mountain in *Les Mabinogion* (*Maxen Wledig's Dream*), Loth, I, pp. 214–215, where the island motif also appears (but cf. *Speculum*, XXII [1947], pp. 520ff.); the valley of "purest streams, woods, and soil," *Trans. Ossianic Soc.* VI (1861 for 1858), p. 167; and L. A. Paton, *Studies in Fairy Mythol.*, pp. 87f. Cf. also the woods or valley in *Trans. Ossianic Soc.* II (1855), pp. 131f., and *Rev. celtique*, VII (1886), pp. 289ff., which have been suggested; the "Forest of Wonders" in the literary piece *The Adventures of the Children of Norway*, ed. D. Hyde, pp. 121ff.; Le Braz, *Légende de la Mort*, II, p. 340. For toads and monsters as obstacles see the verses translated in *Publ. Mod. Lang. Assoc.*, XX (1905), 689, n. 2.

[52] *Rev. celtique*, XI (1890), p. 435.

when in the chapter on visions we consider a group of stories – the *Vision of Adamnán*, the *Vision of Fursa*, the *Vision of Tundale*, and *Saint Patrick's Purgatory*, which, though early and associated with Irish lore, unquestionably derive from other sources.

As with the Greek, the Irish journey to the Other World was satirized. In the *Vision of MacConglinne* (from a fourteenth- and a sixteenth-century manuscript but at least as old as the twelfth century) [53] the leading character recounts his vision which "an angel manifested to him." [54] He went in

A lardy coracle all of lard
Within a port of New-milk Loch,
Up on the World's smooth sea.

They go over the "ocean's heaving waves":

The fort we reached was beautiful,
With works of custards thick,
    Beyond the loch.
New butter was the bridge in front,
The rubble dyke was wheaten white,
    Bacon the palisade.

The door was dry meat, the threshold bare bread, cheese-curds the sides, pillars were of old cheese, and so on and so on.

Behind was a wine well,
Beer and bragget in streams,
    Each full pool to the taste.

There were a "loch of pottage fat" and hedges of butter around the wall outside; a row of fragrant apple trees, an orchard, a forest of leeks, onions, and carrots. The chief and his wife sat within. These details furnish obvious parallels to the Irish Otherworld journeys.[55] Perhaps a similar reflection is found when MacConglinne goes to the well and sees the phantom there, a monster with a "very broad four-edged belly," like a caricature of some of the giants in the other stories.

[53] Ed. Kuno Meyer, *Aislinge Meic Conglinne*; *The Vision of MacConglinne, A Middle-Irish Wonder Tale*, with an Introduction by W. Wollner, pp. viiff.; also Cross and Slover, *Anc. Irish Tales*, pp. 551ff.

[54] Meyer, *op. cit.*, pp. 34ff. Cf. also 66ff.

[55] See Nutt, *Voy. Bran* I, pp. 207f.; II, p. 180, n. 1.

In all these Celtic descriptions occur certain elements that by frequent use become familiar motifs. The coracle of bronze or silver or crystal that carries the traveler is one that we have often noticed.[56] Sometimes it is propelled by the oars of the voyager as in the story of Bran; sometimes it is guided by the fairy mistress as in the *Adventures of Connla the Fair.* The guiding animal is another common feature: like the lion in the *Wooing of Emer,* on which Cú Chulainn rode on his way to the fortress of Scáthach.[57] The bridge that conveys the traveler to the Other World is found, as we have seen, in the *Adventures of Art* (where, however, it appears to be part of a borrowing from Latin vision literature,) and the *Wooing of Emer.* It is rarely referred to in ancient Celtic.[58] There is Mongan's bridge which falls beneath the traveler; and there is the bridge of glass in the *Voyage of Maeldúin* (§ xvii): those who attempted to cross fell down backwards. If the Celts originally had a bridge of their own it was probably of this fantastic type. It does not seem to fit into their voyage across the sea or journey inside the hill.

The fruit trees in the Otherworld garden and the fruit (usually an apple) are mentioned in the *Adventures of Connla the Fair,* the *Voyage of Bran, Cormac's Adventures in the Land of Promise,* and other stories, where occasionally the branch from

[56] On the rudderless boat see E. Hull, *Folk-Lore,* XVIII (1907), p. 162; Paton, *Fairy Mythol.,* p. 16, n. 1.

[57] Cf. Brown, *Publ. Mod. Lang. Assoc.,* XX, 690ff.; Caldwell, *Eger and Grime,* pp. 120ff. and p. 172, n. 146; Campbell, *Pop. Tales,* I, 4f., 84, 169, 209f.; Campbell, *Superstitions of The Highlands and Islands of Scotland,* Glasgow, 1900, pp. 208–218; cf. Cross, *Mod. Philol.,* XII (1914–15), p. 606 and pp. 632ff.; *Y Cymmrodor,* V (1882), p. 89; G. Henderson, *Survivals in Belief among the Celts,* pp. 137ff.; Kittredge, *Gawain and the Green Knight,* pp. 231ff.; W. Larminie, *West Irish Folk-Tales and Romances,* pp. 211–218; Loth, *Les Mabinogion,* I, pp. 261ff. (*Kulhwch and Olwen*); Duncan MacInnes, *Folk and Hero Tales,* pp. 87ff., 151ff.; *Silva Gadelica,* II, pp. 198ff., 297ff.; C. Plummer, *Vitae sanctorum Hiberniae,* I, p. cxxxii, n. 8.; Rhŷs, *Celtic Folklore,* I, pp. 234ff. and II, p. 434.

[58] For Mongan's bridge see *Zeits. f. d. Alt.,* XXXIII, p. 160, and Meyer, *Voy. Bran,* I, p. 77; see *Zeits. f. celt. Phil.,* I (1897), p. 27; *Irische Texte,* I, 1, p. 50; see also the example in the literary *Children of the King of Norway,* ed. D. Hyde, pp. 178ff., ("a great bridge over a sea river that was between two islands, and many bodies and corpses with many wounds upon them on each side of that bridge, and many heads of heroes on forks and on spits on each side of it, above the margin of that bridge.") Also, *ibid.,* 193–195, note

the tree reminds us of the Virgilian golden bough.[59] The well or fountain in the garden is found frequently in the *imrama*: in the *Voyage of Maeldúin* (§ xviii) is a fountain which gives water on Wednesdays and Fridays, milk on Sundays and feasts of martyrs, ale and wine on special feasts; in the *Voyage of the Huí Corra* we have an island with two springs – one turbid and one clear and bright (68ff.),[60] the water of the clear one puts men to sleep; in the *Voyage of Saint Brendan* (§ xxii) is another sleep-giving river. In the *Adventures of Art Son of Conn* we find a well into which the fruit trees drop their leaves and blossoms.[61] In stories of the

the serpent "lying in its midst." MacCulloch (*Relig. Anc. Celts*, p. 346) referring to the bridge in the *Adventures of St. Columba's Clerics* says: "But here it may be borrowed from Scandinavian sources, or from such Christian writings as the *Dialogues* of St. Gregory the Great." But here it comes from the Fís Adamnáin. The bridge of whale bone in *Maxen Wledig's Dream* (*Mabinogion*, Loth, I, p. 158) occurs in an episode that looks like an importation (cf. *Speculum*, XXII [1947], p. 520ff.) A modern Breton instance is noted by Le Braz, *Légende de la Mort*, II, p. 359; cf. also the instance mentioned in *Folk-Lore*, VI (1895), p. 170 (the *Superstitions of the Lewis*: "on the bridge . . . that led to heaven . . . a one-eyed dog kept watch on one side and a one-eyed cat . . . on the other . . . and allowed no one to pass to heaven who was unkind or cruel to cats and dogs on earth"). See also *Publ. Mod. Lang. Assoc.*, XXXIII (1918), pp. 635ff.; Paton, *Fairy Mythol.*, pp. 85–86; and *Romanic Review*, IV (1913), pp. 166ff. Finally a theosophical study may be cited, *The Bridge of the Gods*, by E. F. Pinchin, concluding: "There never is any 'objectified' bridge in this Gaelic Mythology. . . ." p. 90.

59 On the branch of silver in Celtic see D'Arbois de Jubainville, *Cycle mythol. Irl.*, pp. 274f.; Hull, *Folk-Lore* XII (1901), pp. 431ff. See the branch of berries in the *Voyage of Maeldúin* (§ xxx); the huge purple berries in the *Adventures of Cian's Son Teigue* and the apples that sustain the people of the isle; cf. also *Voy. Bran* (xliii). Note the silver tree in the *Sick-Bed of Cú Chulainn*; the tree by the well in the *Pursuit of the Gilla Decair*; the trees bearing golden apples in the *Voy. of Maeldúin* (viii); the Tree of Virtues in the *Children of the King of Norway*, pp. 123 and 145, (with "heavy-broad branches" and various colors and wondrous fruits). Cf. MacCulloch, *Relig. Anc. Celts*, pp. 79, 162f. ("the divine tree became the mystic tree of Elysium, with gold and silver branches and marvellous fruits"), pp. 198ff.; Cook in *Folk-Lore*, XVIII (1907), pp. 24ff.

60 For such use of contrast cf. *Maeldúin* (§ xii) island of white and black sheep; *Snedgus*, (21) two lakes, one of water, one of fire; for contrasts cf. *Voyage of the Huí Corra* (53) an island with dead men in one part and living men in another tormented by a fiery sea; two wells, of falsehood and truth, *Trans. Ossianic Soc.* II (1855), pp. 151, 155.

61 In *Cormac's Adventures* is a similar well out of which five streams flow; cf. also the *Rennes Dindšenchas*, *Rev. celtique*, XV (1894), p. 457, where also are found the hazels of wisdom and the seven streams. For Celtic worship of river and wells see MacCulloch, *Relig. Anc. Celts*, pp. 181ff.

type of the *Gilla Decair* the well is the entrance to the Other World. This is sometimes guarded by a champion or a monster, like the hag in the *Adventures of the Sons of Eochaid*[62] and the Wizard of the Well in the *Pursuit of the Gilla Decair*. It is sometimes active:

Bóand wife of Nechtán son of Labraid went to the secret well which was in the green of Síd Nechtaín. Whoever went to it would not come from it without his two eyes bursting . . . . Once upon a time Bóand went through pride to test the well's power, and declared that it had no secret force which could shatter her form, and thrice she walked withershins round the well. [Whereupon] three waves from the well break over her and deprive her of a thigh and one of her hands and one of her eyes.[63]

In some stories the well or fountain is in the background when the fairy mistress first appears and serves perhaps to identify her. A striking example of this is found in the *Courtship of Étaín*: "And Eochaid came to that place to take the maiden thence, and this was the way that he took; for as he crossed over the ground where men hold the assembly of Bri Leith, he saw the maiden at the brink of the spring. A clear comb of silver was held in her hand, the comb was adorned with gold; and near her, as for washing, was a bason of silver whereon four birds had been chased . . . ."[64]

Birds and their conduct and their songs form an enormously important collection of motifs. In the *Voyage of Bran* is an ancient tree in blossom on which the birds sing the canonical hours; in the *Voyage of Snedgus* (17–18) is a tree with beautiful birds — on top is a great bird that tells of creation and Christ and the last

[62] *Rev. celtique*, XXIV (1903), pp. 197ff.; another version, *Ériu*, IV (1910), pp. 101ff.; cf. Cross and Slover, *Ancient Irish Tales*, pp. 510–511.

[63] *Rev. celtique*, XV (1894), p. 315.

[64] Leahy, *Heroic Romances of Ireland*, I, p. 12. This is somewhat parallel to the scene where a hero meets the fairy mistress at a ford: as in the *Cattle Raid of Cooley*, § xivB (trans. J. Dunn, *The Ancient Irish Epic Tale Táin Bó Cúalnge*, etc., pp. 161ff.). Cf. the shorter *Fled Bricrend*, Windisch, *Irische Texte*, II (Leipzig, 1884), pp. 188–189; *Silva Gadelica*, II, pp. 220f. For the whole subject of the fée at the well see the masterly essay by Cross on the *Lanval* story, *Mod. Philol.*, XII (1914–1915), especially pp. 599ff. citing many examples and also [*Kittredge*] *Anniv. Papers*, pp. 380ff. For sacred lochs and wells see G. Henderson, *Survivals in Belief among the Celts*, pp. 315ff.

judgment, and the birds sing psalms and canticles in praise of the Lord; the *Voyage of the Huí Corra* gives us a "bird-flock of angels" making music to the Lord, Michael in the form of a bird, the jester who dies and reappears as a bird, the song bird who is Michael (44), the bird which is a woman's soul (55–56). The *Adventures of Cian's Son Teigue* tells of the birds that lay eggs of blue and crimson which have had effects on those men that eat them; also of birds that feed on berries and sing songs that put sufferers to sleep.[65] The *Voyage of Saint Brendan* (xxi) tells of the island which is a Paradise of Birds, where the birds discourse joyously from the tops of trees. The bird carrying a branch from the Otherworld fruit tree is found here too (xlii). In the *Sick-Bed of Cú Chulainn* the birds sing a "sweetly drawn-out song" in the treetops. In the *Adventures of Cormac* the house of white silver and the house of bronze are thatched with the wings of white birds. No doubt the idea behind all this is what is indicated in the *Voyage of the Huí Corra* (55–56) where the soul of the woman says: "The birds that ye see are the souls that come on Sunday out of hell" – in all cases the birds are souls, and that is why they sing the hours. Something else again, however, is found in the *Wooing of Étaín* where Mider and Étaín are transformed into swans.[66]

The fortress or palace or splendid house we have frequently seen in the Otherworld accounts, and aside from their lavish adornment there is nothing steadily characteristic about most of

[65] See pp. 45–46, n. 38 above. Cf. also *Irische Texte,* IV, 1, pp. 744ff.; *Silva Gadelica,* II, pp. 119f.

[66] Dechtire and her maidens "came then in the form of a bird-flock" – see *Irische Texte,* I, pp. 134f. (*The Birth of Cú Chulainn*); cf. *Rev. celtique,* III (1876–1878), pp. 349f.; XXI (1900), p. 377 (Elijah preaching to the birds); XXVIII (1907), pp. 299ff.; the *Fís Adamnáin,* § 7 (*Irish Precursor of Dante,* p. 32 — three stately birds that celebrate the eight canonical hours accompanied by the Archangels); MacCulloch, *Relig. Anc. Celts,* pp. 348ff., who notes (360), "The bird form of the soul after death is still a current belief in the Hebrides": A. Le Braz, *Légende de la Mort chez les Bretons,* I, pp. 342, 350; II, pp. 34f., 40f. (n. 2). See parallel material cited in *Rev. celtique,* XXXI (1910), pp. 430ff.; *Mod. Philol.,* XII (1914–1915), pp. 616ff.; [*N. Car.*] *Studies in Philol.,* XI (1913), pp. 33ff.; *Cath. Histor. Review,* VI (1920–1921), p. 422. Cf. *Children of the King of Norway,* pp. 98ff.; E. Ingersoll, *Birds in Legend, Fable, and Folklore,* p. 165. Professor Kenneth Jackson tells me of the modern Cornish belief that sea gulls are the souls of sailors.

them. They are built of precious metal perhaps, and the use of silver or crystal is noteworthy in these scenes.[67] More striking still is the revolving castle, like the fiery rampart in the *Voyage of Maeldúin* (§ xxxii), in which is a doorway through which the travelers see the whole island and observe its inhabitants at their feast. In the *Feast of Bricriu* the citadel of Cú Roí is a turning fortress: "In what airt soever of the globe Cú Roí should happen to be, every night o'er the fort he chaunted a spell, till the fort revolved as swiftly as a mill-stone. The entrance was never to be found after sunset." [68] Associated too with the Otherworld dwelling or domain are vessels of various types, such as the cup of gold and the caldrons of truth in the *Adventures of Cormac*, and the inexhaustible vats in the *Adventures of Art*.[69] Of this, the caldron of plenty, there seem to be four chief examples: the caldron of

[67] "Glass must have appealed to the imagination of Celt, Teuton, and Slav . . . ." MacCulloch, *Relig. Anc. Celts*, p. 370. A house of silver appears in *Cormac's Adventures*, where the branch of silver with three golden apples may also be noted; a silver rampart is in the *Adventures of Cian's Son Teigue*; a fence and plank of silver, *Voy. Snedgus* (15); cf. *Maeldúin* (§ xvi); a silver tree is in the *Sick-Bed of Cú Chulainn*; a silver column is in the *Voy. Maeldúin* (§ xxvi); cf. *Voy. Huí Corra* (51); *Voy. St. Brendan* (xxxviii). A crystal bower is in the *Adventures of Art, Ériu*, III, p. 165; a palace with crystal throne is in *The Colloquy, Silva Gadelica*, II, pp. 222f.; a vessel of crystal in a fairy mound, *Cormac's Adventures, Irische Texte*, III, 2, p. 209; a crystal boat, *Connla the Fair*. Cf. also *Romanic Rev.*, III (1912), p. 158, n. 28. Columns of crystal and silver uphold Labraid's house in the *Sick-Bed of Cú Chulainn*. Gems light the palace in this and other stories: see *Rev. celtique*, XXXI (1910), pp. 462f., n. 1.

[68] *Fled Bricrend*, ed. G. Henderson, p. 103 (§ 80). In the *Book of Taliesin*, Caer Sidi has been interpreted as "turning fort": W. F. Skene, *The Four Ancient Books of Wales*, I, pp. 264 and 276; Nutt, *Voy. Bran*, II, p. 89. For a better rendering as "fort of the Fairies" see Rhŷs, *Celtic Folklore, Welsh and Manx*, II, pp. 678–679; cf. Nitze and collab., *Perlesvaus*, II, pp. 151ff.; and see *Publ. Mod. Lang. Assoc.*, LVI (1941), pp. 901ff. Note, however, "Caer Pedryvan, four its revolutions," Skene, *op. cit.*, I, p. 264, and cf. *Publ. Mod. Lang. Assoc.*, LVI, pp. 890ff. For the revolving castle see also Brown, *Iwain*, pp. 76ff.; *Origin of the Grail Legend*, pp. 356ff.; Kittredge, *Gawain and the Green Knight*, pp. 42 and 244f.; Loomis, *Celtic Myth and Arthurian Romance*, pp. 113 and 175f.; and pp. 278ff., 312 (n. 252), and 290ff. below. Note the turning mountain in the *Marvels of Britain*: *Auctores Antiquissimi*, XIII, ed. T. Mommsen (*M.G.H.*), p. 218 ("mons qui gyratur tribus uicibus in anno").

[69] *Irische Texte*, III, pp. 209–210 and 215–216; *Ériu*, III (1907), p. 165. Cf. also *Children of the King of Norway*, p. 111; the caldron of the chief of Annwfn, Skene, *Four Anc. Books*, I, 264 f. ("It will not boil the food of a coward").

Dagda – "no company ever went from it unthankful"; the caldron of Gerg; that of Cú Roí; and that of Cormac.[70] Of Cú Roí's we are told:

> There was a caldron in the fort:
> The calf of the three cows,
> Thirty cows within its gullet,
> That was its portion.
>
> They used to resort to that caldron,
> Delightful was the struggle,
> Nor did they come away from it again
> Until they left it full.
>
> There was much gold and silver in it,
> 'Twas a goodly find.
> I carried off that caldron
> With the daughter of the King.

Of the last of these we are told:

> This, then, was the solution which Cormac invented, namely, to place on the fire the Five-fist Caldron which was in Tara . . . and to put into it swine and beeves, and to sing over it an incantation of lords and poets and wizards (§ 9). It was a caldron of this kind that used to be of old in every hostel of the royal hostels of Erin. And this is why it was called *coire aisic* 'caldron of restitution,' because it used to return and to deliver to every company their suitable food.

No food spoiled therein, and the king and the poet received from it a thigh, the literary sage got a chine, young lords got a shinbone, and so on.

The inhabitants of the Other World include the ruler or god,[71] and the fairy mistress,[72] of whom we have seen examples

[70] *Rev. celtique,* XII (1891), p. 59 (§ 6); *Irische Texte,* III, p. 517; *Ériu,* II (1905), pp. 21f.; *Irische Texte,* III, pp. 205–206. For these and others considered in a thoroughgoing survey see Brown's paper in the [*Kittredge*] *Anniv. Papers,* pp. 235ff., and note (p. 249) that there seems to be a "persistent association between Celtic magic cauldrons and the Land-beneath-the-Waves." See also MacCulloch, *Relig. Anc. Celts,* pp. 381ff.

[71] Manannán, see MacCulloch, *Relig. Anc. Celts,* pp. 87ff.

[72] See [*Kittredge*] *Anniv. Papers,* pp. 380ff.; the types listed in *Mod. Philol.,* XII (1914–1915), pp. 599ff.; cf. *Rev. celtique,* III (1876–1878), pp.

in the stories of *Connla the Fair,* the *Sick-Bed of Cú Chulainn,* the *Adventures of Art,* and elsewhere. The joys of love are freely shared in this happy realm, which is noted for its beautiful women and is sometimes called Maiden Land: in the *Voyage of Bran* the traveler sees the "island of women"; seventeen maidens and their queen welcome the strangers in the *Voyage of Maeldúin* (§ xxvii); in the story of *Connla the Fair* we read:

> That is the land which rejoices
> The heart of everyone who wanders therein;
> No other sex lives there
> Save women and maidens.[73]

"Out of the Land of Lasses in the West" one fairy mistress says she has come and she also refers to the Land of Men.[74] The inhabitants of this region are often to be identified by their use of certain colors: green is a favorite among them, and red is also used.[75] Silence must be observed regarding the names of these creatures.[76] Time spent in their domain almost always seems shorter than it really is: Bran's visit to the island of women lasted many years but it seemed to the men "only a year." When the travelers returned home, one of the men sprang ashore; "forthwith he was a heap of ashes." In the *Adventures of Cian's Son Teigue* the period seems but one day and yet was actually a twelvemonth during which they had no food or drink. In the *Lay of Oisín in the Land of Youth,* after falling from his steed Oisín loses the sight of his eyes and the bloom of his youth.[77] But the reverse of all this is found in the *Adventures of Nera,* where to

---

344ff.; Brown, *Origin of the Grail Legend*, pp. 30, 37, and *passim*. Cf. also for Maiden Land, MacCulloch, *Relig. Anc. Celts,* pp. 385f.; *Silva Gadelica,* II, p. 238; Brown, *op. cit.*, p. 284, and *passim*. For the fairy lover as a type see *Rev. celtique,* XXXI (1910), pp. 430ff.; [*N. Car.*] *St. Philol.,* XI (1913), pp. 29ff.; Paton, *Fairy Mythol., passim.*

[73] Cross and Slover, *Anc. Irish Tales,* p. 490.

[74] *Silva Gadelica,* II, pp. 238f.; Nutt, *Voy. Bran,* I, pp. 199ff.

[75] Green: *Silva Gadelica,* II, p. 221; Leahy, *Heroic Romances of Ireland,* I, p. 59; etc. — for green and red cf. *Mod. Philol.,* XII (1914–1915), p. 595, n. 3.

[76] *Mod. Philol.,* XII (1914–1915), p. 622; Brown, *Iwain,* pp. 31ff.; *The Debility of the Ultonian Warriors,* (Hull, *Cuchullin Saga,* pp. 97ff.).

[77] Cross and Slover, *Ancient Irish Tales,* pp. 455–456; Joyce, *Old Celtic Romances,* pp. 398–399. Cf. also Le Braz, *Légende de la Mort,* II, p. 360.

the hero it seems "three days and three nights since he had been in the *síd*" and yet actually on his return he finds his people around the same caldron at which they were sitting when he left.[78]

[78] *Rev. celtique,* X (1889), p. 221. On the whole subject of the Celtic Other World and its location see also T. F. O'Rahilly, *Early Irish History and Mythology* (Dublin, 1946), pp. 481ff. and *passim.*

III

GERMANIC MYTHOLOGY

THE COSMIC PLAN according to the early Teutons seems a little clearer in its details than that which we can infer from Celtic ideas on the subject – perhaps even a little more consistent.[1] We can be sure of an underworld for the dead, the realm of the goddess *Hel,* to which even Baldr goes; and also we know, at least from the Viking period on, of a heavenlike place, *Valhalla,* to which go heroes who have fallen in battle – not only these, but other distinguished dead.[2] Once perhaps Valhalla too was an underworld realm, but later placed in the skies.[3] The dwelling of the gods is *Asgard,* located on high. Otherworld realms also include *Jǫtunheim,* realm of the giants, whose approach is "over moist mountains" in darkness,[4] and *Muspellsheim,* realm of fire, whose barrier is the forest *Myrkwood.* A world tree that unites the whole frame of things is *Yggdrasil the Ash,* with one of its roots near the fountain *Urd* where the fates (Norns) meet in deliberation. In its tops sits a wise eagle; at its roots gnaws the serpent *Nídhǫgg* close to the well *Hvergelmir;* [5] and always between the two creatures runs the squirrel *Ratatosk.* Another tree is *Laerad;* the goat *Heidrun* crops the leaves and her udders produce mead. The gates of the underworld realm close fast on the heels of him who enters.[6] Around *Hel's* kingdom (or the lower world) runs

[1] Cf., however, Chantepie de la Saussaye, *The Religion of the Teutons,* trans. B. J. Vos, pp. 345f.

[2] On the Valhalla idea see Schullerus in Paul u. Braune's *Beiträge,* XII (1887), 221ff.

[3] De Vries, *Altgermanische Religionsgeschichte,* II, § 326, 401f.

[4] *Skírnismál,* 10, trans. Hollander, *The Poetic Edda,* p. 78, st. 11.

[5] To the world-tree the idea of *Irminsul,* or huge pillar, may be somehow related. See Chantepie de la Saussaye, *op. cit.,* 124f.; MacCulloch, *Mythol. of All Races,* II, *Eddic,* 335ff.; Mannhardt, *Baumkultus,* 303ff.

[6] Cf. *Sigurtharkvitha in Skamma,* st. 69; (*Edda,* ed. Neckel, I, p. 212; trans. Hollander, *Poetic Edda,* p. 306, st. 67); de Vries, *Altgerm. Relig.,* II, p. 400 (§ 325). See also the *Sólarlióth,* 39 (trans. Hollander, *Old Norse Poems,* p. 108;

the river *Gjoll* (the roaring, resounding one), across which we find a bridge; [7] and up to the heavens also extends the bridge *Bilrost* or *Bifrost,* over which *Heimdallr* (whose dwelling is the mount of heaven *Himinbjǫrg*) watches as guardian. The conception of islands of the blessed, says de Vries, is found only after Celtic influence has had a chance to exert itself in the sagas.[8] The idea of a world of the dead across the sea, however, is implied in the custom of putting the dead in burning ships and sending them out over the waves, and perhaps implied also in that of burying boats in the mounds with the dead.[9]

Northward seems the characteristic direction of the soul's journey.[10] The descent to *Hel* is not only underground but across

---

Old Norse original in F. Jónsson's *Den Norsk-Islandske Skjaldedightning,* I, A, pp. 628ff.; B, pp. 635ff.). In later German folklore cf. the iron door in the folktale cited by Siuts, *Jenseitsmotive im deutschen Volksmärchen,* p. 70, § 187.

[7] Of which de Vries (*op. cit.,* II, 400, §325) remarks: "die Gjallarbrú, die vielleicht durch mehrere Zwischenstufen auf die persische Zinvatbrücke zurückgeht, aber doch so beschrieben wird, dass einheimische Elemente dabei zutage treten: sie ist nicht messerscharf wie die Brücken der mittelalterlichen Visionen, sondern breit und mit glitzerndem Golde beschlagen." See also de Vries in *Tijdschrift voor nederlandsche Taal en Letter Kunde,* LIV (1935), pp. 77–81; Hastings, *Encycl. Relig. and Ethics,* XI, pp. 475–476. For the bridge in later folklore cf. Siuts, *op. cit.,* pp. 41–42; Strömback, "Om Draumkvædet," *ARV,* 1946, pp. 35ff. Milton's bridge is of this character: *Par. Lost* ii, 1027–1030.

[8] De Vries, *Altgerm. Relig.,* II, p. 398 (§ 324); Sophus Bugge, *The Home of the Eddic Poems,* (trans. W. H. Schofield) pp. 315f. Cf. Ch. de la Saussaye, *Relig. of the Teutons,* p. 290.

[9] See Ch. de la Saussaye, *op. cit.,* pp. 81 and 91; de Vries, II, p. 28 (§ 30); K. Stjerna, *Essays on Questions Connected with the Old Eng. Poem of Beowulf,* trans. J. R. Clark Hall, pp. 97ff. The burial of the boat with the dead, of course, may imply merely the provision of one of his treasures or of a useful object for the departed spirit in his new life. See also F. B. Grummere, *Founders of England,* with supplementary notes by F. P. Magoun, pp. 322ff. (cf. p. 326, "For just as burial in the earth brought about belief in that shadowy land, the 'under-world,' so perhaps these old boat-burials made men think of a spirit-world oversea."). Cf. the instance at Sutton Hoo, C. W. Phillips, *The National Geographic Magazine,* LXXIX (1941), pp. 247ff. Cf. J. Grimm, *Deutsche Mythologie,* II, pp. 692ff. (trans. J. S. Stallybrass, II, pp. 830ff.; and notes, IV, pp. 1549f.). On burning corpses on ships, see *The First Nine Books of the Danish History of Saxo Gramm.,* trans. O. Elton, with introd. by F. Y. Powell, (*Publ. Folk-Lore Soc.,* XXXIII), Book III, 74 (cf. pp. lxvif.). For the "death journey by ship" cf. also A. Olrik, *The Heroic Legends of Denmark,* pp. 400ff.; Siuts, *op. cit.,* pp. 38ff.

[10] See Vǫluspá, st. 37 (*Edda,* ed. Neckel, I, p. 9; trans. Hollander, *Poetic Edda,* p. 9, st. 30); *Sturlunga Saga,* II, 243, ed. K. Kålund, Copenhagen, 1906–11; *Gylfaginning, Edda* etc., ed. Jónsson, p. 93; de Vries, *op. cit.,* II, p. 399,

water. In the *Vǫluspá* (if rather violent emendations may be trusted) [11] we read:

> Sails a ship from the north with shades from Hel;
> o'er the ocean stream steers it Loki . . .

A rather late account (probably of the twelfth century) of a voyage to an island where a meeting of the gods is held appears in the *Víkar saga* inserted in the *Gautreks saga,* where we are told how Horsehair Grani wakened Starkad in the middle of the night and with him rowed in a small boat to an island. There in a clearing in the midst of a forest they found a meeting of the Allthing. Eleven men sat there in chairs; a twelfth chair was empty. This Horsehair Grani took for himself, and they all hailed him as Odin. With Thor he then debated the destiny of Starkad.[12] A characteristic barrier of the Other World seems to be a river; Valhalla has *Thund* (*Grimnismál,* st. 21); we find the land of the giants so bounded; the division is thus marked between the abode of the gods and the giants (*Vafthruthnismál,* st. 16, "Ifing," that never froze over); round Asgard flows a river on which, according to Rydberg, "floats a dark, shining, ignitible mist." [13]

Most important evidence for this general plan of the universe is the *Vǫluspá* (*Elder Edda*), where we learn of the Ash Yggdrasil:

> An ash I know hight Yggdrasil,
> the mighty tree moist with white dews;
> thence come the floods that fall a-down;
> evergreen stands at Urth's well this tree.
>
> Thence wise maidens three betake them —
> under spreading boughs their bower stands . . .

§ 324, ("Dass wir hier mit uralten Vorstellungen zu tun haben, wird durch mehrere Umstände bewiesen. . . "); I, p. 102 (§ 49).

[11] St. 51 (trans. Hollander, *Poetic Edda*, p. 13, st. 43). For *north* MSS read *east*: for *Hel* MSS have *Muspel.* But the changes here indicated by Hollander are those almost universally adopted by editors (cf. also the *Gylfaginning,* trans. A. G. Brodeur, *The Prose Edda*, pp. 79–80).

[12] *Die Gautrekssaga,* ed. W. Ranisch (*Palaestra,* XI), pp. 28–29. For the date see pp. lxxxiiiff.

[13] *Teutonic Mythol.,* I, pp. 238ff. He refers to Thjǫdolf's poem (see Brodeur, *The Prose Edda,* p. 133). For the river in later German folklore cf. Siuts, *op. cit.*, pp. 39–40.

and the poem goes on to list the three Norns (Fates).[14] Later Heimdall the watchman is referred to; the well of Mímir; the river Slith filled "with swords and knives";[15] Nídhǫgg; the realm of Hel. A hall is described in Nástrond ("Corpse-strand") as follows:

> A hall standeth, from the sun so far,
> On Ná-strond's shore: turn north its doors;
> drops of poison drip through the louver,
> its walls are clad with coiling snakes.[16]

The obviously great antiquity of much of the material in the *Vǫluspá* gives this poem in the *Edda* a special authority for our knowledge of Germanic heathendom.

In the *Grimnismál* we have reference to Himinbjǫrg (with implications certainly of a holy mountain) where Heimdallr "O'er men holds sway . . ."[17] Of Valhall we read it has "Five hundred doors and forty" and "Eight hundred warriors through one door hie them . . . to fight the Wolf."[18] It is "gold-bright"; its rafters are spears, it is roofed with shields, and its benches are strewn with breastplates.[19] Here too is the great caldron Eldhrimnir (st. 18), in which the flesh of the boar is miraculously renewed each day to be cooked afresh. It is surrounded by the river Thund:

> Thund roars loudly; sports Thióthvitnir's
> fish in the foaming flood;
> the strong stream seems too stiff to wade
> for warriors to Valholl bent.[20]

[14] *The Poetic Edda*, trans. Hollander, stanzas 11–12 (pp. 4–5).

[15] Cf. Saxo, *Hist. Dan.*, I, 31. De Vries finds this river "eine jüngere von christlicher Visionsliteratur beeinflusste Vorstellung" (*Altgerm. Relig.*, II, § 325, p. 400).

[16] Hollander, *Poetic Edda*, p. 10, st. 31.

[17] St. 13, Hollander, p. 65. Cf. de Vries, with reference to eastern conceptions (e.g. the Hara-berezaiti, p. 409): "Es ist deshalb gewiss nicht ohne Bedeutung, dass Heimdallr, dessen Beziehung zur Weltsäule wir schon erkannt haben . . . in Himinbjǫrg wohnt." Cf. Ch. de la Saussaye, *Relig. of the Teutons*, p. 225; Munch, *Norse Mythol.*, p. 17.

[18] St. 23, Hollander, p. 67. Cf. Munch, *Norse Mythology*, p. 5.

[19] St. 9, Bellows, *The Poetic Edda*, p. 89.

[20] St. 21, Hollander, p. 66.

Heidrun the goat is mentioned biting the branches of Laerad and furnishing mead. The hart Eikthyrnir is there too:

> on the hall that stands,
> eateth off Laerath's limbs;
> drops from his horns in Hvergelmir fall,
> thence wend all the waters their way.[21]

The bridge Bifrost is referred to as burning always – presumably on the last days.[22] Yggdrasil with its three roots; Ratatosk, the squirrel; the eagle and Nídhǫgg are here too; and the river Gjoll.

The *Skírnismál* tells of the journey of Skírnir to win a bride in the Otherworld realm of Jǫtunheim. He calls for a steed to assist him, saying to Frey:

> "Thy steed then lend me to lift me o'er weird
> ring of flickering flame,
> the sword also that swings itself
> against the tribe of trolls."[23]

He says it is night and he must "fare over moist mountains." From this story we may perhaps infer the motif of a barrier of fire; and one remembers too the circle of fire which surrounded Brynhild, the supernatural flames about the barrows of the dead, and the mysterious fire in the *Saga of Grettir the Strong*.[24] The fact is, however, that there is no clear case in early Norse literature of a real wall of fire as we find it in the Greek and Latin visions, and what we do discover of this sort may only be sporadic or an importation.

[21] St. 26, Hollander, p. 67.

[22] St. 29, Hollander, p. 68. According to the *Fafnismál* (st. 15) and also *Gylfaginning* (trans. Brodeur, *Prose Edda*, p. 79) it breaks. Cf. *Grimnismál*, st. 44: also *Helgakvitha Hundingsbana*, st. 49 (Hollander, p. 237). See Ch. de la Saussaye, *Relig. Teut.* pp. 286, 344. Another interpretation (Munch, *Norse Mythol.*, p. 5) is that the fire burns to prevent the giants from crossing the bridge.

[23] St. 9, Hollander, p. 77.

[24] *The Saga of Grettir the Strong*, ch. xviii, trans. G. A. Hight. For these and other instances with interesting discussion see Ellis, *The Road to Hel*, pp. 174ff. Cf. the fire over the whole island of the mounds in the *Hervarer saga ok Heidreks*, ed. Bugge, pp. 315–316, 318, and 320; *Eddica Minora*, ed. Heusler and Ranisch, pp. 15ff. I have not seen the edition of Jón Helgason. Cf. the translation in Hollander's *Old Norse Poems*, pp. 30–35.

The journey down to Hel appears in *Baldrs Draumar*:

> Up rose Óthin, oldest of gods,
> and on Sleipnir the saddle laid:
> to the nether world rode, to Niflhel dark.
> A hound he met which from Hel did come.

Odin rides to the eastern door "to the haunted howe of the hoary seeress," and her spirit rising speaks in death:

> "What man is this, to me unknown,
> who maketh me fare such fear-fraught ways?
> Was I buried in snow and beaten by rain
> and drenched with dew, dead was I long." [25]

From this it would seem that the spirit has journeyed through the realm of Hel and found it thus. In the *Helreith Brynhildar* where Brynhild went in a wagon down the road there is no detail offered except that regarding the rocky house of the giantess along the way. The *Vǫluspá* tells us (st. 46), "In fear quake all who on Hel-roads are." [26]

In the *Gylfaginning* of Snorri Sturlasson, which is less reliable for its mythological material,[27] we read of Valhall again that there was "a hall so high that [King Gylfi] could not easily make out the top of it: its thatching was laid with golden shields after the fashion of a shingled roof." [28] Within are three "high-seats," one above another, and three men sat thereon. According to this work "evil men go to Hel and thence down to the Misty Hel": [29] but here is undoubted evidence of Christian contamination. The well Hvergelmir is mentioned with its various rivers. Múspell is described as "light and hot." Much is said also of Bifrost, the bridge "from earth to heaven," ("it may be that ye call it 'rainbow'"): "It is of three colors, and very strong, and made with cunning and with more magic art than other works of craftsmanship. But strong as it is, yet must it be broken, when the sons of Múspell shall go forth harrying and ride it, and swim

[25] Sts. 2 and 5, Hollander, pp. 136, 137.

[26] Bellows, *Poetic Edda*, p. 20.

[27] See Ch. de la Saussaye, *Relig. Teutons*, pp. 208f.; V. Rydberg, *Teutonic Mythol.*, pp. 395ff.

[28] *Prose Edda*, trans. Brodeur, p. 14.

[29] *Ibid.*, p. 16. For a description see p. 42.

their horses over great rivers . . . ." [30] Yggdrasil is the "greatest of all trees and best: its limbs spread out over all the world and stand above heaven." The three roots and their location are described. Mímir drinks of the well under one of its roots and uses the Gjallar Horn to drink with. The eagle, the squirrel, and the serpent Nídhǫggr are listed. Many serpents indeed are here. Heimdallr is referred to as dwelling in Himinbjǫrg "hard by Bífrost: he is the warder of the gods and sits there by heaven's end to guard the bridge from the Hill Giants." He has the "trumpet . . . called the Gjallar-Horn." Hermódr "rode nine nights through dark dales and deep, so that he saw not before he was come to the river Gjöll and rode onto the Gjöll-Bridge; which bridge is thatched with glittering gold" (p. 73). The guardian of the bridge is the maiden Módgudr. Hermódr is riding on Helway to seek out Baldr, and as he comes to Hel-gate he spurs his steed so that the steed "leaped so hard over the gate that he came nowise near to it" (p. 74). Of Nástrond we read it "is a great hall and evil, and its doors face to the north: it is all woven of serpent-backs like a wattle-house; and all the snake-heads turn into the house and blow venom, so that along the hall run rivers of venom; and they who have broken oaths, and murderers, wade these rivers. . . ." (p. 82).

The Eddic poems and Snorri's treatise offer evidence of the mythological scheme that prevailed at least among these writers and early Germanic poets. In Saxo's *Danish History* we have, however, some accounts of journeys to the Other World that show how these ideas appeared in actual operation, so to speak. First in the well-known story of King Hadding,[31] the hero was once at supper when a woman bearing hemlocks was "seen to raise her head beside the brazier." The king wants to know where such fresh herbs have grown in winter. The woman wraps him in her mantle and takes him to the nether regions. "So they first pierced through a certain dark misty cloud" and then went along a path to sunny regions. "Going further, they came on a swift and tumbling river of leaden waters, whirling down on its rapid

[30] *Ibid.*, pp. 24ff. Bifrost is burning to keep out the Hill-Giants ("That which thou seest to be red in the bow is burning fire." Page 28).

[31] *Dan. Hist.*, I, 31 (trans. Elton and Powell, pp. 37f.).

current divers sorts of missiles, and likewise made passable by a bridge." On the other side are two armies encountering. Then comes a wall hard to climb. The woman cannot leap it, but she throws over it a cock, whose neck she has wrung, and there the cock comes to life again. The story in general seems a fair reflection of a visit to an early Scandinavian Hel, with a trip across the river Slith.

Another tale is that of Gorm,[32] who makes a voyage to seek the realm of Geirrod noted for its treasures. "For those who had tried it declared that it was needful to sail over the Ocean that goes round the lands, to leave the sun and stars behind, to journey down into chaos, and at last to pass into a land where no light was and where darkness reigned eternally." Thorkill is chosen as guide and they set off, reaching at last a "precipitous island." They climb the rocky heights and find cattle – but monsters led by one huger than the rest make them repay for taking cattle by yielding up three men. They sail on to farther "Permland" – a "region of eternal cold, covered with very deep snows, and not sensible to the force even of the summer heats; full of pathless forests . . . ." Here they land and "as twilight approached" they are greeted by an enormous man, brother of Geirrod and named Gudmund, who invites them to be his guests. They go forth in his carriages. "As they went forward, they saw a river which could be crossed by a bridge of gold." They want to pass over but are restrained by Gudmund. Finally they arrive at Gudmund's dwelling, but here they are warned by Thorkill "to abstain from the food of the stranger . . . and to seek a seat apart from the natives, and have no contact with any of them." There are other taboos. Round the table are the twelve noble sons and twelve noble daughters of Gudmund. Noticing that the king barely tastes what is set before him, Gudmund reproaches Gorm. But Thorkill gets them out without difficulty. Next the temptation of the daughters is offered to the guests. Four of the Danes succumb and are maddened thereby. Then Gudmund, seeing that most have escaped, takes them to the other side of the river to continue their journey.

[32] *Ibid.*, VIII, 286 (trans. Powell, pp. 344ff.). Cf. Rydberg, I, pp. 312ff.; de Vries, *Altgerm. Relig.* II, pp. 379f. (§ 312).

The travelers then cross the river to Geirrod's land and find his town an abode of filth and horrors. The battlements show stakes with severed heads of warriors. Inside the town is everything foul and loathsome. They do find some treasures and touch them covetously, whereupon they are assailed in various ways. Geirrod and his daughters, it seems, are suffering a punishment here inflicted on them by Thor. The travelers return, ferried across the river by Gudmund. One of the men, Buchi, embraces a daughter of Gudmund's but "his brain suddenly began to whirl, and he lost his recollection." This story shows the old pagan conception of Hel obviously contaminated by Christian notions. It is a place of punishment. Furthermore another confusion seems to be in some reflection of Jǫtunheim, and yet the Gjallar Bridge is here. The voyage at the beginning of the story suggests something of the Irish journeys. A similar motif follows immediately in the voyage of Thorkill (VIII, 293f.), where, again, everything in the underworld is foul and corrupt – with serpents, noisome smells, venom, and disease. First Thorkill comes to a "sunless land, which knew not the stars, was void of daylight," and there he is greeted in a cavern by giants who speak of "his attempt to explore with curious search an untrodden region beyond the world." After four days' voyage more, he comes to "a land where an aspect of unbroken night checked the vicissitude of light and darkness." He goes through this cavernous realm, and sees "a number of iron seats among a swarm of gliding serpents." Next he sees a "sluggish mass of water gently flowing over a sandy bottom." He crosses this and at length comes to a gloomy room where Utgarda-Loki is found laden hand and foot with enormous chains. Thorkill plucks a hair from his chin, and a great stench comes forth. The travelers are spattered with the poison of the snakes, and only five at last escape with their leader.[33]

All these accounts include some suggestion of the darkness of the lower world, and, no doubt under Christian influence, the

[33] Another voyage similar in some respects to these outlined is that of Eric the Speech-wise (V, 127ff.), which Powell (pp. lxxvif.) thinks is based on the archetype of an Otherworld journey. Notice the river and the bridge (135). Cf. also *Thorsteins Saga Bœjarmagns* (outlined in Schlauch, *Romance in Iceland*, pp. 30–31) with the barrier of the cold river.

realm seems to have become rather undesirable or even positively horrible. The river barrier is always found (marked in the Hadding story by the presence of missiles whirled along in the current), and also the motif of the bridge. These items, as we have seen, are included in the mythology of the poets. Another reminiscence of a journey to Hel, however, is also included in the account of Helgi Thoreson,[34] who, we are told, went north to Finmark for trading, and got overtaken by the dark in a forest so that he was separated from his companions and did not get back to his ship. His experience was rather pleasanter, it appears.

As night deepened, he saw twelve women dressed in red ride out of the forest on red horses with trappings that glowed like gold. Chief of the maidens was Ingeborg, daughter of Gudmund of the Glittering Plains. The ladies set up a fine tent and furnished it all with gold and silver. Then Ingeborg invited Helgi to eat and drink with them, and eventually offers to let him sleep with her. He stays for three nights, and she gives him two chests – one of silver, one of gold. He is to tell no man whence these have come. Then he goes to his ship. His men ask him where he got these treasures, but he does not tell. Next Yule, when Helgi is down at the harbor, two strange men come and carry him off. His brother reports the event to the sorrowing father Thor, who tells King Olaf. A year later Helgi and the two strangers appear before Olaf and give him two horns plated with gold as a present from Gudmund. Olaf has them filled with good drink, and, letting the bishop bless them, offers them to the men. The strangers cast the horns down, confusion follows, three of Olaf's men are killed, and the strangers depart. Next Yule at Mass three men again appear to King Olaf and one is Helgi, who is now blind. He has been blinded by Ingeborg so that he will attract no ladies of Norway. He says he has been happy with Ingeborg but Olaf's prayers have made it difficult for Gudmund to retain him. Here, in what has become almost a fairy story, we see the forest barrier, the element of darkness, the taboo of

[34] See Rydberg, I, pp. 310ff.; Saxo, trans. Elton, p. lxviii. For the saga itself, occurring in the *Saga of Ólaf Tryggvason*, see *Fornmanna Sögur eptir gömlum Handritum*, etc., III, pp. 135–141.

speech. But the realm of the Glittering Plains (*Glæsisvellir*—[35] "erum við sendir of Guðmundi a Glæsisvöllum . . ." *Fornmanna Sögur*, III, p. 138) shows delights only in part, suggested by Saxo's story of Gorm.

A brief episode undoubtedly related in material is that in Saxo regarding Hother, who "chanced, while hunting, to be led astray by a mist, and he came on a certain lodge in which were wood-maidens." He asks them who they are: "They declared that it was their guidance and government that mainly determined the fortunes of war. For they often invisibly took part in battles . . . ." They warn Hother that Baldr has seen his foster sister while she bathed and has developed a passion for her, but Hother is not to attack this "demigod."

When Hother had heard this, the place melted away and left him shelterless, and he found himself standing in the open and out in the midst of the fields, without a vestige of shade. Most of all he marveled at the swift flight of the maidens, the shifting of the place, and the delusive semblance of the building. For he knew not that all that had passed around him had been a mere mockery and an unreal trick of the arts of magic.[36]

The mist motif also occurs in the story of Hadding.

The journey to Valhalla is the theme of the *Lay of Eric* and the related *Lay of Hákon*. Neither gives us much of a description of this heavenly region. In the first of these Odin prepares for the coming of Eric:

"What dreams be these, now? Methought that ere daybreak
I got Valholl ready to make room for warriors;
I waked the einheriar [fallen warriors], asked them
to rise up,
to put straw on benches, and to rinse the beer-jugs;
and the valkyries, to deal wine out as though a
warrior drew nigh." [37]

[35] On the word see de Vries, *Altgerm. Relig.*, II, p. 380 (§ 312). Cf. Rydberg, I, p. 310.

[36] Elton and Powell, trans., Saxo, III, § 70 (p. 84). L. A. Paton, *Fairy Mythology*, p. 161, draws attention to this passage. Cf. Chaucer, *Wife of Bath's Tale*, D, 989ff., and *Mod. Lang. Notes*, L (1935), pp. 85ff.

[37] *Old Norse Poems, etc.*, trans. Lee M. Hollander, p. 64, st. 1. For the *Lay*

A journey to a Christianized Hell and the Christian Heaven with pagan reminiscences is found in the twelfth- or perhaps thirteenth-century *Sun Song* (*Sólarlióth*): [38]

> Full long I sate, in sickness drooping —
> much then me listed to live;
> but he prevailed who had more power:
> was I doomed to suffer death.
>
> The ropes of hell held me fast,
> when slung about my sides;
> tear them would I, but tough they were;
> unbound, one freely fares.
>
> I alone knew in all ways how
> sorrows were heaped on my head:
> a world of honor those maids of hell
> did show me every eve.
>
> The sun I saw, the day-star in sooth,
> droop in the world of din;
> but Hel's gate heard I on the other hand
> grate with grinding.[39]

He sat for nine days "On the norns' settle," fared "through seven seats of victory" (the seven spheres beyond the earth?), saw birds "with singed wings" fly to the "world of pain," saw the tortures of Hell, and then the bliss of the redeemed ("was their resting place on rays of heaven") — "high wains fare the heavens along" to the Lord. The ropes of Hell probably mean the bonds of sickness. The maids of Hell are simply those emissaries that seem to foretell the pains awaiting him. An ancient touch is found, however, in the reference to the grinding of Hel's gate. Later the snakes used for torture — "poison-fanged snakes pierced these knaves, thrusting through their breasts" [40] may recall for us the serpents in the voyage of Thorkill and anticipate those in Dante's *Inferno*.

---

of Hákon, see *ibid.*, pp. 66ff. For the Old Norse see F. Jónsson's *Den Norsk-Islandske Skjaldedigtning*, [I], A, 174–175; B, 164–166.

[38] Trans. Hollander, *Old Norse Poems*, pp. 101ff.; Old Norse, F. Jónsson, *op. cit.*, [I], A, 628ff.; B, 635ff.

[39] Hollander, *op. cit.*, p. 108, sts. 36–39.

[40] Hollander, *op. cit.*, pp. 112ff., sts. 64ff.

A story often referred to but one that is obviously later than most of the material considered (it is in the fourteenth-century *Fláteyjarbók*) is that of Erik the Far Traveler (*Eiríks saga viðförla*).[41] According to this narrative, Erik, son of King Thránd of Norway, set out to seek Odainsaker and in company with a Danish prince went to Constantinople, where the king converted the hero to Christianity. It is he who tells Erik how God made Heaven (a bright hall) and earth and Hell (a pit for the heathen and for Christian renegades). He goes on to say that Odainsaker is identical with Paradise ("Paradisum köllum vér svá eðr jörð lifandi") and lies in the east beyond India. No one can get there because it is surrounded by a fiery wall reaching to heaven. Erik and the Danish prince, with other companions, however, keep on, pass through Syria and India, and come to a dark country where the stars are seen by day as by night. Here they find a great golden cup. They go through the forests and come to a river, over which is a stone bridge ("steinbogi"), and the other side of which is a fragrant plain. Erik thinks this river is the Pison. On the bridge is a dragon, and Erik with one of the men rushes at it, sword in hand, only to be swallowed up. (His Danish companion gives him up for lost and departs.) In this process Erik and his man thought they were surrounded with smoke (akin to mist?), but suddenly as it cleared found themselves in a great plain where there were abundant blossoms and sweet fragrance, where rivers of honey flowed, and where it was never dark and objects cast no shadow (". . . sólskin var þar svá, at aldri var þar myrkt ok aldri bar skugga á"). The land seemed empty of people; but Erik comes to a tower, suspended in the air and without foundation, to which a ladder conducts him. In this tower there is a luxurious room, where food (all kinds of dainties and a gem-laden tankard of wine) is served, and beds wait for the weary. Here they eat and sleep. At this time Erik's guardian angel appears to tell him that Odainsaker (or the Land of Living Men) is *not* the same as Paradise (since only spirits come to

[41] C. C. Rafn, ed., *Fornaldarsögur Norðrlanda,* III, pp. 661–674; V. Ásmundarson, *Fornaldarsögur,* III, pp. 515–527 (the text used in the present summary); Vigfússon and Unger, *Fláteyjarbók,* I, pp. 29–36. See also Rydberg, *Teutonic Mythol.,* I, pp. 306ff., and Schlauch, *Romance in Iceland,* 49ff.

Paradise), but the two regions border each other. Here we still have the darkness, the forest, the river, and the bridge, but the story has clearly been affected by outside influences – in particular in the name of Pison.

A very early story, on the other hand, once current among the Lombards, is the rather famous one recounted by Paulus Diaconus in the eighth century regarding King Gunthram. I quote: [42]

This Gunthram indeed of whom we have spoken was a peaceful king and eminent in every good quality. Of him we may briefly insert in this history of ours one very remarkable occurrence, especially since we know that it is not at all contained in the history of the Franks. When he went once upon a time into the woods to hunt, and, as often happens, his companions scattered hither and thither, and he remained with only one, a very faithful friend of his, he was oppressed with heavy slumber and laying his head upon the knees of this same faithful companion, he fell asleep. From his mouth a little animal in the shape of a reptile came forth and began to bustle about seeking to cross a slender brook which flowed near by. Then he in whose lap (the king) was resting laid his sword, which he had drawn from its scabbard, over this brook and upon it that reptile of which we have spoken passed over to the other side. And when it had entered into a certain hole in the mountain not far off, and having returned after a little time, had crossed the aforesaid brook upon the same sword, it again went into the mouth of Gunthram from which it had come forth. When Gunthram was afterwards awakened from sleep he said he had seen a wonderful vision. For he related that it had seemed to him in his slumbers that he had passed over a certain river by an iron bridge and had gone in under a certain mountain where he had gazed upon a great mass of gold. The man however, on whose lap he had held his head while he was sleeping, related to him in order what he had seen of it. Why say more? That place was dug up and countless treasures were discovered which had been put there of old. . . .

[42] *Hist. of the Langobards*, trans. W. D. Foulke, III, 34 (pp. 147f.); for the Latin see *Scriptores Rerum Langobardicarum et Italicarum s. vi–ix*, ed. L. Bethmann and G. Waitz, pp. 112f. For an analogue from India see Hans Naumann, *Primitive Gemeinschaftskultur*, pp. 63ff.; and for the transmission of Gunthram's story by medieval writers, S. P. Cowardin, Jr., *On an Episode in the Mid. Eng. Metrical Romance of Guy of Warwick*, and *Romanic Review*, IV (1913), p. 189.

Here again are forest, river, and bridge. In the latter item there is a suggestion of the narrowness so essential to the oriental motif. We may also note the obvious reminiscence of the paradise within a mountain.[43]

All these ideas are in striking contrast to what we regularly find in Celtic lore. In the German documents the darkness, the desolate forest, the river, and the bridge seem familiar elements and entirely in harmony with a Germanic background. Theoretically, at least, the bridge *may* have been derived from oriental sources.[44] The *Dialogues* of Saint Gregory were known and indeed translated into Old Norse, and here in the famous description of the Bridge of Death we read: "En hann sagþi sva, at hann sa ǫ́ micla þa es brú vas yvir, oc ór þeiri ǫ́ up lagþi þoco svarta oc illan da*un*. En oþrom megin arennar voro fagrir staþir oc vellir blomgaþir ollom enom fegrstom grosom, oc vas þar ilmr dvrligr oc fiólþi liosa manna." [45] It is a fairly close translation; and with the description of the house of gold on the other bank, it would all fit into Norse mythology and may have influenced it. But Bifrost and the Gjallar Bridge are older than the period of this Norse translation and seem uninfluenced by it. Some common ancestor would seem to offer a more likely hy-

[43] For Wotan's abode within a mountain in popular German belief, see Ch. de la Saussaye, *Relig. Teutons*, pp. 225f.; the abode of souls in mountains (Barbarossa in the Kyffhäuser, Siegfried in Geroldsek, etc.,) *ibid.*, 290f. For ideas of a mountain ridge, as a watershed of the lower world, see Rydberg II, p. 417. But here Rydberg is trying to make Teutonic mythology more consistent with itself than the evidence will allow. On this tendency cf. Powell, *Saxo*, p. cxvi. And on the holy mountain motif, such as we have in Himinbjǫrg, see also Munch (trans. Hustvedt), *Norse Mythology*, p. 270; Ellis, *The Road to Hel*, pp. 87ff.; *Mythology of all Races*, II, J. A. MacCulloch, *Eddic*, p. 316 (Charlemagne's army enter the hill). So too Grimm, *Deutsche Mythol.*, II, pp. 780ff.; trans. Stallybrass, III (1883), pp. 935 and 953ff.; W. Golther, *Handbuch germ. Mythol.*, pp. 288f.; E. Mogk, *Reallexikon der german. Altertumskunde*, ed. J. Hoops, I, pp. 225f.; W. von Unwerth, *Untersuchungen über Totenkult und Ódinnverehrung bei Nordgermanen und Lappen*, etc., pp. 7ff.; Siuts, *Jenseitsmotive*, pp. 42–43, 57–58. For the underworld in folklore, cf. also F. Panzer, *Studien zur germ. Sagengeschichte*, I, 116 and 120; Siuts, *op. cit.*, pp. 50, 53–54, 55ff.; Reidar T. Christiansen, *The Dead and the Living*, (*Studia Norvegica*, I, No. 2) , pp. 89ff.

[44] See above page 61, n. 7.

[45] *Dial. Greg.* iv, 36. C. R. Unger, *Heilagra Manna Søgur*, I, p. 250. Cf. Liestøl, *Draumkvæde*, p. 54.

pothesis. The forest, whether derived from Myrkwood or another source, appears in harmony with the widespread Teutonic tree worship and sacred groves.[46] The paradise within a mountain is not clearly found in the religion of the Eddas, but the underworld realm is reflected in the Second Lay of Helgi Hundingsbane. Here, after Helgi's death, one of Sigrun's maidens visits his burial hill and sees that Helgi rides to the hill "with many men." She holds converse with him (stanzas 40ff.),[47] and at length goes home and sends Sigrun to speak with him. "Sigrún went into the mound to Helgi," and makes a bed for him. Thus Helgi speaks:

"No wonder, ween I, will unwonted seem,
sooner or later, at Seva Fells,
since lies with lifeless leader's body
in the howe, Hogni's white-armed daughter —
with the dead the quick, the queenly woman." [48]

But apparently at dawn Helgi must leave for Valhalla:

"Along reddening roads to ride I hie me,
on fallow steed aery paths to fly:
to the West shall I of Windhelm's bridge . . ." [49]

The bridge, of course, is Bifrost. In the *Eyrbyggja saga* we read of Holy Fell or Mountain on Thorsness, which Thorolf "held in such worship that he laid down that no man unwashed should turn his eyes thither, and that nought should be done to death on the fell, either man or beast, until it went therefrom of its own will." [50] Now Thorolf's son, Thorstein Codbiter, went out to fish and was drowned; that same evening a shepherd of Thorstein's saw into the fell on the north side and there beheld

mighty fires, and heard huge clamour therein, and the clank of drinking-horns; and when he hearkened if perchance he might hear any words

[46] Ch. de la Saussaye, *Relig. of the Teutons*, pp. 355f. See also *ibid.*, pp. 297f., for trees as the abode of souls; and Mannhardt, *Baumkultus*. The forest as barrier appears in German folktales: cf. Siuts, *op. cit.*, pp. 30ff.

[47] Hollander, *Poetic Edda*, pp. 234ff. Cf. also Hervǫr seeking the buried Angantýr, *Hervarar saga ok Heidreks*, ed. Bugge, pp. 314ff.

[48] St. 48, Hollander, p. 236.

[49] St. 49, Hollander, pp. 236–237.

[50] *Eyrbyggja saga*, chap. 4; trans. *The Story of the Ere-Dwellers*, W. Morris and E. Magnússon, *The Saga Library*, II, p. 9.

clear of others, he heard that there was welcomed Thorstein Codbiter and his crew, and he was bidden to sit in the high-seat over against his father. . . . That foretoken the shepherd told in the evening to Thora, Thorstein's wife; she spake little thereon, and said that might be a foreboding of greater tidings.

And the news came of Thorstein's death the morning after.[51] In the *Landnámabók* the pagan followers of Authr believed that at death they would enter the hill on which she had a cross erected (called Cross-Hill). It was consecrated as a place of sacrifice.[52] In *The Saga of Burnt Njal*

tidings were heard from the north and Bearfirth, how Swan had rowed out to fish in the spring, and a great storm came down on him from the east, and how he was driven ashore at Fishless, and he and his men were there lost. But the fishermen who were at Kalback thought they saw Swan go into the fell at Kalbackshorn, and that he was greeted well; but some spoke against that story, and said there was nothing in it.[53]

An even more striking story in the same saga is that of Flosi's dream: [54] Flosi "stood below Loom-nip," and he "looked up to the Nip, and all at once it opened, and a man came out of the Nip, and he was clad in goat skins, and had an iron staff in his hand. He called, as he walked, on many of my men, some sooner and some later, and named them by name. First he called Grim the Red . . . ." After this stranger had called many in this fashion, "I asked him for his name, but he called himself Irongrim." The stranger says he is going to the Althing, sings a song prophesying battle, gives a mighty shout, throws down his staff with a mighty crash — "Then he went back into the fell, but fear clung to me." " 'It is my foreboding,' says Kettle, 'that all those who were called must be 'fey.' It seems to me good counsel that we tell this dream to no man just now.' "

[51] *Ibid.*, chap. xi; Morris and Magnússon, p. 19.

[52] *Landnámabók*, II, 16, ("trúðu þeir því, þat þeir dœi í hólana," ed. Ásmundarson, p. 83). Cf. II, 12, where pretty much the same thing is said of Thórólf's followers and Helgafell: "þat var trúa þeira þórólfs frænda, at þeir dœi allir í fjallit," p. 74; II, 5 ("þeir Selþórir frændr enir heiðnu dó í þórisbjörg") *ibid.*, p. 62; and III, 7 ("hann kaus at deyja í Mælifell"), *ibid.*, p. 141.

[53] Chapter 14 (*The Story of Burnt Njal*, etc. trans. G. W. Dasent, I, p. 51).

[54] Chapter 132 (trans. II, pp. 198f.).

Another pertinent episode is that of the burial of Gunnar: "They cast a cairn over Gunnar, and made him sit upright in the cairn." [55] Later we read:

Now those two, Skarphedinn and Hogni, were out of doors one evening by Gunnar's cairn on the south side. The moon and stars were shining clear and bright, but every now and then the clouds drove over them. Then all at once they thought they saw the cairn standing open, and lo! Gunnar had turned himself in the cairn and looked at the moon. They thought they saw four lights burning in the cairn, and none of them threw a shadow. They saw that Gunnar was merry, and he wore a joyful face. He sang a song, and so loud, that it might have been heard though they had been further off . . . . After that the cairn was shut up again.[56]

Another description of an interior is in the *Tale of Thorstan Oxfoot*.[57] Here Thorstan dreams he sees a barrow or grave-hill open, and there appears from it a man clad in red. The man gives his name, Bryniar, and says he lives in the barrow: "Now wilt thou come with me and see my house?" They go in together and "it was fairly bedecked." On the right hand were eleven men all clad in red "and not so ill to see." On the other side were twelve, all clad in black, and one – the biggest – was very ugly to look on. This is Ord, brother to Thorstan's guide Bryniar. He has a ring that restores speech. They all sit in silence for a time. Occasionally a man rises and gives Ord a treasure. At length, after Ord grows more and more ungracious, fighting begins. The blows the black-clad men deal one another heal at once. But the blows the red-clad men deal behave naturally, and at length Ord and his men are killed. Bryniar takes the ring from the dead Ord, bestows it and money on Thorstan, saying, "we brothers are earth-dwellers or ghosts." Finally Bryniar leads Thorstan out of the cave, and Thorstan wakes, with the ring Bryniar gave him and the purse.

[55] Ch. 77 (trans. Dasent, I, p. 249.)

[56] *Ibid.*, chap. 1, pp. 250–251. For the antiquity of this episode and Gunnar's song see von Unwerth, *Untersuchungen über Totenkult*, p. 21. Cf. the verses quoted from a similar episode, A. Heusler and W. Ranisch, *Eddica Minora*, p. 93, (C); also *Landnámabók*, ii, 7, *Íslendingabók . . . og Landnámabók*, ed. V. Ásmundarson, p. 64.

[57] *Fornmanna Sögur*, III, pp. 115–119; trans. G. Vigfússon and F. York Powell, *Origines Islandicae*, II, pp. 585–586.

The external appearance of these holy mountains was doubtless affected by Icelandic or Scandinavian scenery. Of Norway Saxo tells us, "Craggy and barren, it is beset all around by cliffs, and the huge desolate boulders give it the aspect of a rugged and a gloomy land." And of Iceland he says, "In this island there is likewise a mountain, whose floods of incessant fire make it look like a glowing rock, and which, by belching out flames keeps its crest in an everlasting blaze. This thing awakens our wonder as much as those aforesaid . . . ." [58] The idea that Mount Hecla in Iceland, which was volcanic, contained a realm of torture,[59] conceivably might have assisted the idea of the localization there and in other mountains of the ancient German underworld. We have seen that Valhalla was originally an underworld, as well as mountainous; Jǫtunheim too was of this sort.

But as far as interior details are concerned, these stories of the realm within the Holy Fell and grave mound quite possibly might be derived from those of the Celtic fairy mounds or the *síd.* If the idea of sea journeys to the Other World was Celtic, that of the Other World within the Fell or barrow may have come without difficulty from that same influence.[60] Even so, the external character of the scene would probably reveal the channel of transmission; the fairy mound is vastly different from the craggy mountain.

And von Unwerth maintains that with the Germanic burial custom of putting the dead into a barrow or hill, the accounts of the violation and robbing of these hills almost always include a representation that the dead live therein.[61] The struggle of Grettir with the howe-dweller Karr in the *Saga of Grettir the Strong* (ch. xviii) is a case in point. Grettir invades Karr's grave

[58] Saxo, *Preface,* (trans. Elton, pp. 9–11). Cf. de Vries, *Altgerm. Relig.*, II, § 324 (p. 398): "Für die Norweger ist aber das hohe Gebirge im Osten und das arktische Gebiet im Norden der eigentlohe Útgarðr"; Maurer, "Die Hölle auf Island," *Zeitschrift des Vereins für Volkskunde,* IV (1894), pp. 256ff.; *Speculum Regale,* ed. O. Brenner, chs. 13–14, pp. 30ff. (trans. L. M. Larson, *The King's Mirror,* pp. 126ff.).

[59] Maurer, *op. cit.*, pp. 267ff.

[60] For Celtic influence cf. (on the mist motif) Sophus Bugge, *The Home of the Eddic Poems* (trans. W. H. Schofield), pp. 320–321; on the journey to a happy isle, *ibid.*, pp. 289–290.

[61] W. von Unwerth, *Untersuchungen über Totenkult etc.*, pp. 23ff. Cf. Ellis, *The Road to Hel,* p. 83, and Schlauch, *Romance in Iceland,* 171–172.

and sees him sitting on a throne. As the hero begins to steal the treasure, he feels his hand seized and the battle begins, from which Grettir escapes after he cuts off the head of his opponent. More striking still perhaps is the story in Saxo [62] of the time some men attempted to rob the barrow of Aswid. Asmund has been buried alive with him (to fulfill a childish vow of friendship). Aswid has come to life at night and struggled with him. And now Asmund's ghastly body comes up in the basket with which the others expect to draw up treasures. Asmund reproaches the men: "By some strange enterprise of the power of hell the spirit of Aswid was sent up from the nether world, and with cruel tooth eats the fleet-footed [horse], and has given his dog to his abominable jaws. Not sated with devouring the horse or hound, he soon turned his swift nails upon me . . . ." In Aswid's return to life there is, it would seem, a clear reflection of the conception that the dead live on in these regions. Whether outside influence then has contributed anything or not, these hollow hill stories are based on German custom and (certainly to some extent) belief.[63] And perhaps we have here the beginning of the development that, through stories of Frederick Barbarossa and Charlemagne and others enjoying immortality within their mountains, lead on also to Arthur's court within the mountain or volcano [64] and the idea too of the paradisial realm such as appears in the Venusberg.[65]

Distinguishing features then of the Germanic Other World may be listed as follows: (1) again and again it is described as surrounded by a river barrier; (2) the river is fiercely dangerous – Slith flows with "swords and daggers" and Thund is a "torrent wild"; (3) the bridge is a steady feature – Bifrost and the Gjallar Bridge; (4) the road to the Other World (being an underworld) is through a dark forest; (5) when the Other World is underground it is often in a rocky fell or craggy mountain. Other familiar and somewhat typical features are the voyage motif, the mist barrier, the mead drink, the fountains or wells, the world tree, and the realm within the barrow or hill.

[62] Trans. Elton, pp. 200ff.

[63] Cf. von Unwerth, *op. cit.*, pp. 25f.

[64] See pp. 231ff. below.

[65] See Barto's *Tannhäuser and the Mountain of Venus*, pp. 18ff.

IV

THE LITERATURE OF VISIONS

THE LITERATURE WHICH PURPORTS to describe actual visions during the Middle Ages is vast, and only that part of it is here considered which deals with some sort of representation of the realm which man enters after death. Whether these accounts are genuine or not is of no present concern. Experiences which men have had or which they have only thought they have had, accounts which are set down in good faith or consciously as fiction or as forgeries, and narratives written in the mood of burlesque or satire, are all grist to our mill. They all offer elements that show the tradition of Otherworld motifs, and nearly always they may have served to make a contribution in this way to literary works of a wholly different type. Moreover, they may also contain details that come ultimately from ancient sources. Even if the vision in question was an actual experience, it may have derived at least in part from subconscious memories of what had been read or heard before. On the other hand, what may be merely coincidences in such experience have a meaning of their own as well.

Material available for these narratives of invasion into the next life is found in the mythologies described in the preceding survey. Much of the detail of our study of the older religions comes from documents which were written after faith had departed and the significant features retained only an imaginative or poetic value for the writer who set them down. As with any collection of motifs here is a literary property room. Or if real belief was still suggested in any of them, so much the more potent would be their force for a reader whose attention was turned toward adventures after death. Much of this wealth of description was not confined to what was written — that is to say, to the documents that have survived — but was floating in the medieval air of faith and credulity and artistic interest, and was transmitted by the channels of folktale and even popular rumor based on avid memory and long, long thoughts. Thus oriental culture, the religious life of Greece and Rome, the Jewish tradition, the Celtic and the Norse, could furnish details of the Other World even for writers who could hardly recognize their own indebtedness. Plato's Vision of Er and Cicero's Dream of Scipio as well as the ascent of Elijah were ready at hand, directly or indirectly, for those who were thinking of a journey to the skies. The Vision of Er especially might have suggested a pattern for the medieval documents; for here we have an account narrated after the soul of Er returned to its body and men had thought he was really dead.

More striking than any of these, however, because it involves much of the precise framework later found in medieval stories is the Vision of Thespesius in Plutarch's *Moralia* in the essay *Concerning Such Whom God is Slow to Punish*. Here we read of a sinful man, Thespesius, injured by a fall and thought to be dead, but rescued from the grave so that he could tell of his experiences received in the period when his soul seemed to have left his body. He found himself in something like the midst of the sea but really among the stars where the souls of the dead were ascending like bubbles. Here he learned about divine justice. At length he was borne on the rays of light to see a great bottomless chasm, which was fringed within with "pleasing verdure of various herbs and plants" with all sorts of flowers and strong perfume.[1] Later he came upon a "prodigious standing goblet, into which several rivers discharged themselves." These rivers were of different colors, white and purple. Demons were here mixing the rivers. Also, he saw various lakes, one of boiling gold, one of cold lead, and one of iron "very scaly and rugged." At the end he was whirled away "with a strong and violent wind, forced as it were through a pipe" to his own body.

Another vision described by Plutarch, also apropos, is that of Timarchus, which comes into the *Discourse concerning Socrates' Daemon*. Timarchus went down into the cave consecrated to

[1] For the translation, see *Plutarch's Morals*, ed. W. W. Goodwin, IV, (essay trans. John Philips,) pp. 176ff. On this vision and its possible influence see E. J. Becker, *Medieval Visions of Heaven and Hell*, pp. 27ff., 79, 85, 93, and 98.

Trophonius and there "performed all the ceremonies that were requisite to gain an oracle." [2] He stayed two nights and one day. When he entered he was in thick darkness, and "not certain whether awake or in a dream" he felt a stroke on his head and with the parting of the sutures of his skull his soul "fled out." Joyous with the sense of purer air, his soul was "very jocund" and heard a small noise "very sweet and ravishing"; looking up, it saw no earth but islands shining with "gentle fire" and changing colors. "These whirling, it is likely, agitated the ether, and made that sound . . . ." About the islands was a sea of varied color in which they floated, being carried hither and yon or tossed and whirled. Into the sea came two fiery rivers spreading fiery white over it; down below was a dark chasm from which howls and bellowing issued. An "invisible thing" interpreted the scene to the soul and it saw the daemons of men like stars "leaping about the hollow, some darting into it, and some darting out of it again." Eventually the soul returned to the body of Timarchus and he came back to consciousness. The whole experience rather strikingly resembles the *Legend of Saint Patrick's Purgatory* of many centuries later.

Another extraordinary parallel, but considerably later – dating probably from the seventh century A.D. – and less accessible to European literature, may be found in the Pahlavî *Book of Ardâ Vîraf*,[3] which tells of a Persian who under the influence of narcotics enjoyed the privilege of having his soul take a journey to the "Chinvat" (*K*inva*d*) Bridge. There he met the soul of a pious man, whose good thoughts and deeds appear as a beautiful virgin. He then passes the bridge and sees the paradises: one in the star track, one in the moon track, and one in the radiance of

[2] *Plutarch's Morals*, ed. Goodwin, II, (essay trans. Thomas Creech,) pp. 207ff. The cave and the "requisite ceremonies" are described by Pausanias: see *Pausanias's Description of Greece*, trans. with commentary, J. G. Frazer, V, 200ff. and for the original, *Pausaniae Descriptio Graeciae*, ed. J. H. C. Schubart, II, pp. 258ff. (IX, xxxix). A vision that should also be cited perhaps is that in the pseudo-Virgilian *Culex*, 210ff.

[3] *The Book of Ardâ Vîraf, The Pahlavî Text*, ed. and trans. by Martin Haug and E. W. West. A medieval East Indian document describes the difficult road to Hell: see *Roman. Forsch.* V (1890), 546ff. The journey is rough with thorns, anthills, sharp stones, and flames. See *A Prose English Translation of Markandeya Purana*, Manmatha Nath Dutt, 57ff.

the sun. Later he returns to the bridge, where he finds a wicked man whose evil nature appears in an ugly damsel, and after this experience he sees Hell and its tortures. Once more he comes back, and this time to the mountain below which the bridge is located and to a desert. He now beholds the hell which is on earth:

and I was carried on to Chakât-i-Dâîtîh, below the Chinvat bridge, into a desert; and was shown hell in the earth of the middle of that desert, below the Chinvat bridge.[4]

Notable in this account is the departure of the soul from the body with the help of the narcotic, its eventual return, and the vision of the bridge, the mountain, and the desert. In one scene of the first hell is a great river "gloomy as dreadful hell," which some souls cross easily, some with difficulty, and some cannot cross at all.[5] Here one may think of the graded punishments in the river of fire in the *Visio Sancti Pauli* later to be discussed.

There was, moreover, a considerable literature on which I have not so far touched, much of it in the same vein, which played an important part in the formation of this type of description. I refer to certain Jewish and Christian revelations, and writings based on Gnosticism and the religious ideas familiar in Neoplatonism. The Gnostic universe was made up of a succession of spheres or realms including the "highest lightworld," the higher lightworld, the lower lightworld, cosmos, and the underworld. The myth of the fall of Sophia to the lower world (somewhat like the Babylonian story of the descent of Ishtar to the abyss where she is prisoner, and perhaps related to it) together with her deliverance by the Soter or Christus, furnishes parallels to the legend of the Harrowing of Hell. One Apocalypse (of the first or second century A.D., an Egyptian production usually called the *Apocalypse of Zephaniah*) tells of an ascent with the guidance of an angel that, although definitely not related in any way, might quite well be derived from the description of Scipio's Dream so far as the similarity of the details regarding the flight itself is concerned:

[4] *Book of Ardâ Vîraf,* ch. liii, 2–3 (p. 183).

[5] *Ibid.*, ch. xvi, 3 (p. 165). For graded punishments cf. pp. 92–93, 101, and 107–108 below.

"I, however, went with the angel of the Lord, and he led me above my whole town. No one appeared to me. I saw the whole earth . . . . below me like a drop of water . . . which came up from a spring." Here was neither darkness nor night, but all is light in this realm, so the angel says. "He led me now above the mountain Seïr and showed me three men, with whom two angels were walking . . . ." He comes to some iron gates, which open at once before the angel. He sees iron doors that scatter fire almost fifty stades, and he beholds a great sea of fire.[6]

The mountain is a little curious here, perhaps, and may be an importation.

A fragment of an eighth- or ninth-century Gnostic document, showing possible contact with Celtic culture, gives the account of a soul's ascent through seven heavens: specific material on the first two is not included, but in the third is a fiery furnace; in the fourth is a wall and fiery river; in the sixth is a burning wheel; and in the seventh the throne of the Lord, which too gives forth flames and light. Hell is described as a city with walls of redhot iron and twelve towers.[7]

Like the apocalyptic books, but prophetic in form, the *Sibylline Oracles* in Greek (which originated with the Jewish Christians as early as the second century) offer considerable material for the vision literature of a later time. In the second book

[6] This is my summary and rendering of the German translation by Steindorff in the series of Oscar von Gebhardt and Adolf Harnack, *Texte und Untersuchungen zur Geschichte der Altchristlichen Literatur, neue folge II*, 3, pp. 149ff. The revelation is called by some the *Apocalypse of Zephaniah*. See James, *The Apocryphal New Testament*, p. 525 (n. 2), and p. 530 (n. 3); also T. Silverstein, *Visio Sancti Pauli*, p. 92, (n. 3). For the cosmology of Gnosticism, see Carl Schmidt on *The Book of Jeû*, in *Texte und Untersuchungen*, VIII, pp. 345ff.; and further, J. A. MacCulloch, *Early Christian Visions*, pp. 43ff.; Hastings' *Encyclopaedia*, VI, pp. 233f.; and Carl Schmidt, *Koptisch-Gnostische Schriften*, I, *Die Pistis Sophia — Die Beiden Bücher des Jeû Unbekanntes Altgnostisches Werk.*

[7] Printed in the *Revue Bénédictine*, XXIV (1907), pp. 323–324; the Celtic connection is discussed by M. R. James, *Journal of Theological Studies*, XX (1919), pp. 15f.; Seymour points to evidence that some form of this apocalypse was known to the author of the *Vision of Adamnán, Irish Visions of the Other-World*, pp. 112ff. The description of the river and the wall is worth special notice: "Tunc uenit angelus, baiulat illius usque ad quartum celum qui uocatur iothiam, ubi habitat flumini igneo & muro flumini; altitudo flumini XII milia cubitis & fluctus eius exalatur usque ad quintum celum & ubi peccatoris morantur XII annis in medio fluminis."

of this collection we are told of the punishment reserved in the next world for sinners:

all these will the wrath
Of the immortal God cause to approach
The pillar, where around a circle flows
The river inexhaustible of fire.
Then will the angels of the immortal God,
Who ever liveth, direly punish them
With flaming scourges and with fiery flames,
Bound from above with ever-during bonds.
Then in Gehenna, in the midnight gloom,
Will they be to Tartarean monsters cast,
Many and fierce, where darkness is supreme.
But when all punishments have been entailed
On all whose hearts were evil, then straightway
From the great river will a fiery wheel
Circle them round, pressed down with wicked works . . . .

They shall burn "Amid the darkening shades of Tartarus," but the righteous souls God will send to "light and life exempt from care," to a land where there is abundant fruit and "fountains three, of honey, wine, and milk." Here the land "divided not" is common to all:

For there no longer will be poor nor rich,
Tyrant nor slave, nor great, nor small, nor kings,
Nor chieftains, but all share a common life.
No more will any say the night has come,
Or morrow comes, or yesterday has been.
They have no trouble about many days.
Spring, summer, autumn, winter will not be
. . . . .
For he will make it one long, lasting day.

God will pluck the steadfast from the "flame that rests not" and send them on

Unto another and eternal life,
In fields Elysian, where are the great waves
Of the deep-bosomed Acheronian lake.[8]

[8] Milton S. Terry, *The Sibylline Oracles, Translated from the Greek into*

Here the combination of Greek, Jewish, and Christian elements, for which Egyptian Jews may be responsible, is obvious enough, and also the negative prophetic formula which is found in the Gnostic passage as well.

Closer still to our present subject are the Jewish revelations set down in the early Christian period, like the *Apocalypse of Baruch* of the first century or the beginning of the second. Here the angel takes Baruch "into the heavenly firmament, and it was the first heaven, and in that heaven there are very great doors . . . ." The journey takes fifty days. "And we saw a great field, and there were men living in it; they had the faces of oxen, and the horns of stags and the feet of goats, and the bellies of sheep." The doors, says the angel, are "as great as the expanse from the East to the West." In the second heaven is a great house with living creatures in it with faces like dogs, feet like those of stags, and horns like those of goats. They are people "who built a tower wishing to get into heaven." Baruch takes a journey of thirty-two days and sees a great field in which "there was a very great mountain, and on it lay a serpent as from the East to the West, and it bent down drinking from the sea every day a cubit and ate the earth like grass." Later he also sees the chariot with four horses that carries the sun, and the Phoenix flying above it.[9] This Slavonic version is somewhat abridged and shorter than the Greek, which interestingly gives the following account of the approach to the first heaven: "And taking me he led me where the heaven is fastened, and where there was a river which no one can cross . . . ."[10] But how Baruch got across is not precisely indicated.

English Blank Verse, pp. 65ff. (ii, 342ff.). For the Greek see J. H. Friedlieb, *Oracula Sibyllina*, pp. 44ff. and J. Geffcken, *Oracula Sibyllina*. For the date see Friedlieb, *op. cit.*, pp. xix–xxii. Cf. Lovejoy and Boas, *Primitivism*, pp. 85ff.

[9] Trans. of the Slavonic text, W. R. Morfill, pp. 96ff. in *The Apocalypse of Baruch, Texts and Studies*, ed. J. Armitage Robinson, V, *Apocrypha anecdota*, second series, M. R. James. For the Greek text see *ibid.*, pp. 84ff. Cf. also Bruno Violet and H. Gressmann, *Die Apokalypsen des Esra und des Baruch in Deutscher Gestalt*, pp. xcii–xciii, for the use here of the *Apocalypse of Ezra*. The Syriac text is different in some respects — see R. H. Charles, *The Apocalypse of Baruch*. With such revelations one may also compare the story of the Harrowing of Hell in the apocryphal *Gospel of Nicodemus*, on which see, for example, MacCulloch, *The Harrowing of Hell*.

[10] James, *Apocrypha anecdota*, p. 85 (§ 2).

Written at about the same time and widely influential, the *Apocalypse of Ezra* shows a slightly different arrangement of the barrier to the Other World:

6. [Hear] again another thing: There is a city that is built and set in a large place of the valley, and that city is full of many good things; 7. and its entrance is narrow and set on a height, so that there is fire on the right hand, and on the left deep waters; 8. and a single path is set between these two, between the fire and the waters, so that that path only sufficeth for a man's footstep alone.[11]

Strait and narrow is the way that leadeth to eternal life, and steep also. Much is implied here. It is significant, I think, that in a much later period a fragmentary *Visio Esdrae* develops the hints received: the valley is now Hell and the fiery river is the barrier over which there is a bridge:

Seven angels carry Esdras to Hell over seventy steps. He sees the fiery gates and before them are two lions whose mouths and nostrils and eyes exhale fire. A fiery river is ahead and over it a great bridge, which the righteous joyfully cross. But for the wicked the bridge becomes as fine as thread and they fall from it into the river confessing their sins.[12]

The author of the version of which this is a fragment, however, did not invent these new points; almost certainly they were already familiar in other documents by the time it was written.

The *Apocalypse of Peter*, of the second or perhaps even the

[11] G. H. Box, *The Apocalypse of Ezra . . . . Translated from the Syriac Text*, p. 48 (vii, 6–8). For the Latin see Bruno Violet, *Die Esra-Apocalypse*, Part I, pp. 128–129. For the date see Violet and Gressmann, *Die Apokalypsen des Esra und des Baruch*, p. xlix. Cf. also Box, *The Ezra-Apocalypse*, and R. L. Bensly and M. R. James, *The Fourth Book of Ezra, Texts and Studies*, III, No. 2. In the writings of Reiner of Liège, there is a vision in which an island of the usual Paradise type is reached only by a very narrow path through a turbulent sea (Migne, *Patr. Lat.*, CCIV, cols. 160–161).

[12] This is my paraphrase of the important features. For the whole account see Vienna *Sitzungsberichte*, 67, pp. 202–206, A. Mussafia, "Sulla visione di Tundalo." I cannot discover any indication here of the date of this fragment. For the Latin see p. 204: "et pons iste reuertebatur in subtilitatem ut filum staminis et cadebant in hoc flumen confitentes peccata sua . . . ." For scriptural authority for the strait and narrow way see Matthew vii:14 and Luke xiii:24. Cf. the "two ways" in Jeremiah xxi:8, in the *Didache*, and elsewhere, and note the Pythagorean Y symbol for the roads, Cumont, *After Life in Roman Paganism*, pp. 150ff.

first century, offers other details: the holy mountain, the hazardous cliff, and the fiery floods.

"And my Lord Jesus Christ our King said unto me: Let us go unto the holy mountain. And his disciples went with him praying." The disciples ask to see one of the blessed to learn how they live. Two men shining like the sun suddenly appear with bodies whiter than snow and ruddier than the rose. The Lord shows them a very great country "outside of this world" exceeding bright "and the air there lighted with the rays of the sun, and the earth itself blooming with unfading flowers and full of spices and plants, fair flowering and incorruptible . . . ." Perfume from this pleasant region is borne on the air.

The wicked, however, are punished in floods of fire and in a river of fire where men and women are hung on fiery wheels; and in Hell is a burning lake with a cliff down which sinners are hurled and forced to climb up again.[13]

The *Testament of Abraham,* originating probably in the second century in Egypt but assuming its present form in the ninth or tenth century, is almost a medieval narrative of vision, partly no doubt because of the influence it shows of other vision literature of the later period. For our purposes I may summarize it as follows:

The Archangel Michael is sent to consult with Abraham concerning his death. He finds the patriarch near the oak of Mamre, sitting beside yokes of oxen ready for plowing. As they leave the field they pass a cypress tree which with "human voice" praises the Lord with the *tersanctus.*[14] They proceed to Abraham's house, where all has been set in readiness for gracious hospitality. There at length the time of Abraham's death is revealed to him. (Section x) "And the archangel Michael went down and took Abraham upon a chariot of the cherubim, and exalted him into the air of heaven, and led him upon the cloud together with sixty angels, and Abraham ascended upon the chariot

[13] For Hell see M. R. James, *The Apocryphal New Testament*, pp. 510, 513, 517; and for Heaven, p. 518. Also cf. A. Menzies, *Ante-Nicene Fathers,* IX, pp. 141 and 146; J. A. MacCulloch, *Early Christian Visions,* pp. 10ff. A river of fire with souls immersed at various depths appears in the *Apocalypse of the Virgin,* James, *op. cit.* p. 563.

[14] On the speaking tree here see M. R. James, *Testament of Abraham, Texts and Studies,* II, 2, pp. 59ff., with parallel instances, in particular of the trees of Paradise, urging that it is a Moslem idea that the trees of Paradise continually sing.

over all the earth. And Abraham saw the world as it was in that day, some ploughing, others driving wains . . . ." He would destroy the sinners he sees, but the Lord is merciful and diverts him from the idea. So he is next taken to the first gate of Heaven. Here he sees two ways — one narrow and constricted, the other broad and spacious. Two gates there also are, one narrow and one broad. Outside is a man with terrible appearance even like the Lord himself. Many enter the narrow way and few the broad. The scene of judgment follows.[15]

Most of the features of this account show little novelty and their scriptural origin is easily identified; but it may serve as an easy transition to the actual narratives of vision.

THE SHEPHERD OF HERMAS. Written in Greek about the middle of the second century, the *Shepherd of Hermas* is a document that might also be classified with the transition because of its element of didacticism, although it is ostensibly based on a real vision. The purpose of teaching, however, and often by symbolism, is fairly constant in all the literature of this type, early and late, inasmuch as the framework of these stories implies that the vision itself is granted primarily as an exhortation, a warning, or an encouragement to others to whom it may be described. Here we have the river, the thorny path, and the mountain:

When walking on a journey to Cumae, Hermas became sleepy. A spirit seized him and took him away through a certain pathless district, where the ground was precipitous and "broken up by the streams of water." So he "crossed that river, and came to the level ground and knelt down and began to pray to the Lord." The heavens opened and the vision of Rhoda appeared speaking from Heaven.[16]

Later he sees a great tower being built on the water with shining square stones. This is to be the dwelling of the righteous. It is foursquare, with stones so fastened their joints cannot be seen. An allegorical interpretation is added, in which we learn that these foundation stones are the apostles, bishops, teachers, and the like,

[15] *Ante-Nicene Fathers,* IX, pp. 183ff. For the date see James, *Texts and Studies,* II, 2, p. 76, who edits the Greek.

[16] *The Shepherd of Hermas,* etc. in *The Apostolic Fathers,* Kirsopp Lake, II, (Loeb), *Vis.,* I, i, 3 (pp. 7–8). For the river in the Greek (I, i, 3, p. 8): "διαβὰς οὖν τὸν ποταμὸν ἐκεῖνον ἦλθον εἰς τὰ ὁμαλὰ . . . ."

who serve God; some, which come from the depths of the sea, are those martyrs who have suffered for the name of the Lord; some, however, are cast away as worthless, or fall into the fire.

"The Shepherd of Punishment" puts the wicked sheep in "a certain place precipitous and thorny and full of thistles so that the sheep [can] not disentangle themselves from the thorns and thistles, but [are] caught." [17]

The shepherd, the angel of repentance, takes Hermas to Arcadia to a breast-shaped mountain, from the top of which he sees a great plain with twelve mountains. Each has a different appearance: one is black as pitch; one bare without herbs; one full of thorns and thistles; one with half-dried herbage; one with green herbs is steep; one is full of cracks; one has vigorous herbage; one is full of springs; one is a desert; one has huge trees; one has trees with abundant fruits; one is all white and very beautiful. In the midst of the plain is a great white rock higher than the hills, in which is a glistening door with twelve maidens round about. Here men come to build a great tower. The Lord of the tower comes and smites the stones, some of which turn black. The rock is interpreted as the Son of God. The tower is the Church; and the mountains are also explained.[18]

THE VISION OF PERPETUA. Whatever be the truth about other documents, the *Vision of Perpetua* (from the first years of the third century as set down by its redactor Tertullian) seems to be based on a genuine experience. The symbolism, however, is partly traditional:

Perpetua sees a narrow ladder of gold stretching toward heaven, at the foot of which is a huge dragon, and round the steps of which are cruel hooks and knives. In the name of Christ she mounts the ladder and gains the top, after she has watched Saturus climb in safety. Later, Saturus, in a vision with which he is favored, is taken by four angels to the east, where he sees a spacious place with rose trees and every kind of flower. The leaves of the rose trees sing unceasingly. He crosses a violet-covered plain and meets the martyrs.[19]

[17] *Ibid., Sim.*, VI, ii, 6 (pp. 175–176). For the tower see *Vis.* III, ii, 4ff. (pp. 31–33).

[18] *Ibid., Sim.*, IX, i, 4ff. (pp. 219ff.)

[19] J. A. Robinson, *Texts and Studies*, I, part 2, *Passio S. Perpetuae*, pp. 61ff. For the Latin see p. 66 (iv, 8ff.): "uideo scalam aeream mirae magnitudinis pertingentem usque ad caelum, et angustam, per quam nonnisi singuli ascen-

The reminiscence here of Jacob's Ladder seems to be likely, but this symbolism calls for further examination with reference to other examples. Singing trees we have already encountered in the *Testament of Abraham.*

THE VISION OF SAINT PAUL. The *Vision of Saint Paul,* from as early perhaps as the third century in its Greek form, had an enormously wide influence in the centuries that followed. It was condemned by Saint Augustine, was utilized by Dante, and was known to Chaucer. At least by the beginning of the sixth century it appeared in a long Latin version, of which redactions were made from the ninth century on. Of these, Redaction IV was most popular and survives in at least twenty-seven codices. Versions of the story as a whole appeared in many European languages, of which there are at least eight in Middle English. Some of its material, borrowed in what has been called its "English-Irish pendant," the *Purgatory of Saint Patrick,* spread more widely still.

The story, according to the long Latin version in an eighth-century manuscript, runs as follows:

Caught up in body as well as spirit into the third heaven Saint Paul sees an angel host. His angelic guide bids him look down upon the earth: "And I looked down from heaven upon the earth and beheld the whole world, and it was as nothing in my sight; and I saw the children of men

---

dere possent: et in lateribus scalae omne genus ferramentorum infixum. erant ibi gladii, lanceae, hami, macherae: ut si quis neglegenter aut non sursum adtendens ascenderet, laniaretur et carnes eius inhaererent ferramentis. et erat sub ipsa scala draco cubans mirae magnitudinis . . . ."

Of Saturus, pp. 78ff. (xi, 14ff.): "Passi, inquit, eramus et exiuimus de carne, et coepimus ferri a quattuor angelis in orientem, quorum manus nos non tangebat. ibamus autem non supini sursum uersi, sed quasi mollem cliuum ascendentes. et liberato primo mundo uidimus lucem immensam . . . et dum gestamur ab ipsis quattuor angelis, factum est nobis spatium grande, quod tale fuit quasi uiridarium, arbores habens rosae et omne genus flores. altitudo arborum erat in modum cypressi, quarum folia canebant sine cessatione . . . ." For the influence of the *Shepherd of Hermas,* see pp. 26ff., and for that of the *Apocalypse of Peter,* pp. 37ff. Note "A Coptic Counterpart to a Vision in the Acts of Perpetua and Felicitas," Johannes Quasten, *Byzantion,* XV (1940–1941), pp. 1ff. Cf. also MacCulloch, *Early Christian Visions,* pp. 18ff. On the ladder note, for example, the oriental instances mentioned by Cumont, *After Life in Roman Paganism,* pp. 153–154. Cf. the steps to heaven in the *Vision of Gunthelm,* Migne, *Patr. Lat.,* CCXII, col. 1061.

as though they were nought, and failing utterly . . . ." After various experiences, observing a soul brought to the judgment of God, he comes to the second heaven. Here at the beginning of the foundation was "a river that watereth all the earth." "This," says the angel, "is the Ocean." He sees the river flowing with milk and honey, trees full of fruits, and by the Lake Acherusa the city of Christ with its twelve gates of great beauty and the four rivers that compass it about — the river of honey, the Phison; the river of milk, the Euphrates; the river of oil, Geon; the river of wine, Tigris.

He goes to witness the punishment of sinners and all the ungodly, and comes upon a river of fire burning with heat, in which the sinners are sunk up to their knees or navels or lips or hair according to their culpability. After the spectacle of the sinners and their torments he is led to Paradise, where he sees the four rivers and a tree from which the waters flow forth and the Tree of the Knowledge of Good and Evil and the Tree of Life.[20]

At the point where the river of fire appears, Redaction IV (of the ninth century) introduces the wheel of fire and the bridge. The detail of the bridge was almost certainly taken from the *Dialogues* of Gregory, where we shall examine it presently; wheels of fire appear in the *Apocalypse of Peter* and the *Sibylline Oracles.* Here the Latin will be useful for later comparison:

Saint Paul sees a river with beasts that devour sinners. "Et desuper illud flumen est pons, per quem transeunt anime iuste sine ulla dubitacione, et multe peccatrices anime merguntur unaqueque secundum meritum suum. Ibi sunt multe bestie dyabolice multeque mansiones male preparate . . . . Tantum uero potest quisque per pontem illum ire quantum

[20] Trans. in M. R. James's *The Apocryphal New Testament,* etc., pp. 526ff. Cf. the version in the *Ante-Nicene Fathers,* IX, pp. 149 ff. For the Latin see James, *Texts and Studies,* II, 3, pp. 1–42. Cf. also C. Tischendorf, *Apocalypses apocryphae,* pp. 34–69. On the date and the redactions see the masterly study by T. Silverstein, *Visio Sancti Pauli,* where he holds that the detail of the bridge was taken from Gregory. Further material appears in H. Brandes, *Visio Sancti Pauli, Ein Beitrag zur Visionsliteratur* etc.; *Romania,* XXIV (1895), pp. 357ff., "La descente de saint Paul en enfer," etc., by P. Meyer; *Romanische Forschungen,* II (1886), pp. 256ff., "Die lateinischen Visionen des Mittelalters," by C. Fritzsche. The chief sources are apparently the Apocalypses of Peter, Elias, and Zephaniah, according to Silverstein, *op. cit.,* p. 3. On this and the other visions see also Landau, *Hölle und Fegfeuer in Volksglaube* etc.; E. Willson, *Middle Eng. Legends of Visits to the Other World;* MacCulloch, *Early Christian Visions of the Other-World;* and August Rüegg, *Die Jenseitsvorstellungen vor Dante.*

habet meritum."[21] Here too sinners are immersed in the river up to their knees, navels, lips, or eyebrows. Later in an icy place he sees sinners tormented in half of their body by heat and in half by cold.

Much of this narrative represents Hebrew and Christian tradition, including the ascent, the rivers, and the Tree of Life. But the river of fire, the wheel of fire, and the bridge are ultimately of another derivation.

THE NARRATIVE OF ZOSIMUS. *The Narrative of Zosimus concerning the Life of the Blessed* goes back at least to the time of Commodian (c. 250 A.D.), who refers to it; but in its present form it is not so ancient. It has special interest in showing a number of variations on familiar themes:

Zosimus has fasted forty years in the desert and prays that he may see the way of life of the blessed. An angel tells him of God's promise that he shall journey to the blessed but shall not dwell with them. Issuing from his cave he travels forty days until, exhausted, he sits down and spends three days in prayer. A camel arrives, places its knees on the ground, receives him on its back and takes him to a spot where it deposits him. "There there was much howling of wild beasts, and gnashing of teeth, and deadly poison." Zosimus again prays, and a great earthquake shakes the land: ". . . and a storm of wind blew me and lifted me from the earth, and exalted me on its wing, and I was praying and journeying till it set me upon a place beside a river, and the name of the river is Eumĕles. And behold when I desired to cross the river, some one cried as if from the water, saying, Zosimus, man of God, thou canst not pass through me, for no man can divide my waters . . . ." And a "wall of cloud" stretches from the waters to the heaven. Zosimus prays

[21] Edition of H. Brandes in *Englische Studien*, VII (1884), p. 45 (reprinted by Brandes in his *Visio Sancti Pauli*, 75–80). Cf. Silverstein, *Visio Sancti Pauli*, pp. 52ff., and for the bridge, *ibid.*, pp. 77ff. and p. 123, n. 85, where he suggests that the idea of a bridge is already found in IV *Ezra*, vii. Cf. above page 87. He notes also that the vernacular renderings emphasize its narrowness and slipperiness (p. 77). This fact suggests an interesting return to what were certainly its original characteristics in Gregory and the oriental accounts. For the bridge in Redactions V and VIII, see Silverstein, *op. cit.*, pp. 198 and 209 respectively. On oriental influence for the bridge, see Ward, *Catalogue of Romances*, II, p. 399. For the wheel of fire here and in the Gnostic fragments, see Silverstein, *op. cit.*, pp. 76f. For the Motif of graduated immersions, see *Mod. Lang. Notes*, LI (1936), pp. 450–451. On later influence of Redaction IV cf. Voigt in *Palaestra* 146 (1924), pp. 10ff.

and ". . . behold two trees sprang up out of the earth, fair and beautiful, laden with fragrant fruits. And the tree on this side bent down and received me on its top, and was lifted up exceedingly above the middle of the river, and the other tree met me and received me in its branches and bending down set me on the ground; and both trees were lifted up and set me away from the river on the other side. In that place I rested three days . . . ."[22]

Here the mode of ascent is unusual (if it is indeed actual ascent), and also what seems to be the equivalent of the bridge is certainly unique. The barrier of cloud beside the river may perhaps suggest something analogous to the Celtic mist. Finally, it is worth noting that Zosimus began having his experiences in a desert. In the matter of further details of importance we are later told that "the breadth of the river is about thirty thousand paces, and the cloud reaches to heaven, and the depth of the river to the abyss." In the land of the blessed "there was no mountain, but the place was level and flowery . . . ." Zosimus is led to a cave and eats food under a tree; "water came out from the root of the tree sweeter than honey."

The blessed say, "God placed us in this land, for we are holy but not immortal." They have "no vine, nor ploughed field, nor works of wood or iron, nor have [they] any house or building, nor fire nor sword, nor iron wrought or unwrought, nor silver nor gold, nor air too heavy or too keen." They have wives only long enough to beget two children, and after that they withdraw from one another's society and live in chastity, not knowing that they ever shared the intercourse of marriage. The one child is destined for marriage and the other for virginity. "And there is no count of time, neither weeks nor months nor years, for all our day is one day. . . The fruit of the tree falls of itself for food at the sixth hour." "But when the time of forty days comes, all the trees cease from their fruits, and the manna that [God] gave to our fathers rains down from heaven . . . ." The blessed die at length in

[22] Translation in the *Ante-Nicene Fathers,* ed. A. Menzies, IX, pp. 219ff. For the Greek text see M. R. James, *Texts and Studies,* II, 3, *Apocrypha anecdota,* pp. 96ff., edited by J. Armitage Robinson. With the wall of cloud cf. the "nebula tenebrosa" as a wall for Paradise, Migne, *Patr. Lat.,* LXXXVII, col. 432.

peace and patience and love, "for we have no torment nor disease nor pain in our bodies, nor exhaustion nor weakness . . . ."

Zosimus returns as he came. The trees bend down and receive him and set him on the other side of the river. The storm again gathers him up in its wings, and the camel once more takes him on its back to his original station.

THE LIFE OF SAINT PACHOMIUS. Translated from the works of an unknown Greek author, the life of Saint Pachomius is included in the *Vitae patrum* of Herbert Rosweyd that gave impulse to the compilation of the *Acta sanctorum*. This life almost certainly goes back to the period of roughly the fourth to the sixth century. Here we find the story of a monk who wanted to be vouchsafed the vision of the estate of monks in general after death. Being ever constant in prayer, he was rewarded with the sight of a throng of monks in a deep rocky valley, from which some wanted to escape and could not, while some lay at the bottom of its depth and darkness tearful and wretched and others with the greatest toil managed to climb to the light.[23] It is a scene that anticipates vividly "the deep and awful ravine" with sulphurous vapor where, according to Caesarius of Heisterbach, the Abbot of Morimond was plunged and his soul tossed by demons from one side to the other through the mist. We are later informed that "that valley was a part of Hell." [24]

THE DIALOGUES OF GREGORY THE GREAT. The *Dialogues* of Saint Gregory were enormously influential in the Middle Ages from the late sixth century, when they were written, until at least the end of the period.[25] Here indeed is to be found what for this chapter may be called the classic instance of the bridge:

[23] Migne, *Patr. Lat.*, LXXIII, col. 262: "Uidit ergo, sicut ipse narrauit, multitudinem monachorum in ualle quadam profunda satis atque caliginosa consistere, et alios exinde uelle conscendere, nec ualere, quia occurrebant ex aduerso sibi . . . ."

[24] *The Dialogue on Miracles, Caesarius of Heisterbach,* trans. H. von E. Scott and C. C. Swinton Bland, with an introduction by G. G. Coulton, vol. I, p. 41 (I, xxxii).

[25] See above the study of Germanic literature, pp. 74f.; the literature of visions, p. 92. A significant reference may be noted in the *Dialogue* of Caesarius of Heisterbach, XII, xxi (trans. Scott and Bland, vol. II, p. 308).

Stephen, a resident of Constantinople, actually died and lay unburied all the following night. His soul was carried to the dungeon of Hell, but the devil objected that he had "commanded not this man to be present but Stephen the Smith." The unwanted soul was returned to the body and Stephen the Smith died at that same hour. Three years later a certain soldier was brought to the point of death, his soul was taken from his body and then afterward put back, and he was able to tell of his experiences. He narrates how "he saw a bridge, under which a black and smoky river did run, that had a filthy and intolerable smell: but upon the further side thereof there were pleasant green meadows full of sweet flowers, in which also there were divers companies of men apparelled in white . . . ." Here was the delicate savor of Heaven, and divers particular mansions shining with brightness and light, and one especially magnificent, sumptuous house made of bricks of gold, "but whose it was, that he knew not."

On the bank of the river were certain houses, some touched by the stinking odor of the river and some not. "Now those that desired to pass over the foresaid bridge, were subject to this manner of trial: if any that was wicked attempted to go over, down he fell into that dark and stinking river; but those that were just and not hindered by sin, securely and easily passed over to those pleasant and delicate places." He observes a priest pass over in safety. "Likewise, upon the same bridge he said that he did see this Stephen . . ." whose foot slips and lets half his body hang over the edge. Stephen is now finally dead, but while certain terrible men try to pull him down into the river, white and beautiful persons draw him up. The bridge teaches us that that path is "strait" which leads to everlasting life, and the stinking river is the corruption of vice.[26]

It seems to be generally assumed that this account was derived, directly or indirectly, from oriental sources.[27] While certain

[26] *Dialogues of Saint Gregory*, ed. E. G. Gardner, pp. 224ff. (iv, 36); Migne *Patr. Lat.*, LXXVII, cols. 384ff. (§§ 432ff.) For the Latin see Migne, col. 384 (§ 432f.): "quia pons erat, sub quo niger atque caliginosus foetoris intolerabilis nebulam exhalans fluuius decurrebat. Transacto autem ponte, amoena erant prata atque uirentia, odoriferis herbarum floribus exornata, in quibus albatorum hominum conuenticula esse uidebantur."

[27] So Gardner, *op. cit.*, p. 274, and Fritzsche, *Roman. Forsch.*, II (1886), p. 267. The narrowness of the bridge is barely suggested in Gregory's version, although he does have it in mind as we can see from his interpretation (Migne, *Patr. Lat.*, LXXVII, col. 388: "Per pontem quippe ad amoena loca transire iustos aspexit: *Quia angusta ualde est semita quae ducit ad uitam* (Matth. VII:14)."

features seem to be lacking, such as the emphasis on the narrowness of the oriental bridge, and while there is not much here that could not be invented (granted the idea of the narrowness of the path that leads to eternal life, and the further need of an obstacle), we should accept this explanation, I am sure, rather than appeal to the force of coincidence. Perhaps some manuscript of Gregory we now lack contained a reference to the narrowness, which at any rate appears later in vernacular accounts that derive from the *Dialogues* through the *Vision of Saint Paul.*[28] But the fact that it is missing here and also in Redaction IV of the *Vision of Saint Paul* makes it possible that the tradition of the motif had a fresh contact later with some other document showing influence from the East.[29]

THE VISION OF SAINT SALVIUS. In the *Historia Francorum* of about the same period Gregory of Tours tells of the vision Saint Salvius enjoyed of the heavenly city:

Supposedly dead and already prepared for burial, Salvius returned to life on the very morning of his own funeral. As he opened his eyes he complained that he had come back to the shades of this earthly habitation. For three days thereupon he fasted and the third day he told his story.

Four days before, he says, when his fellows saw him die, he was taken by two angels to the highest heaven so that not only the filthy earth but the sun, moon, clouds and stars, seemed to be under his feet. Thence by a shining gate he was led to a dwelling paved with gold and silver, where shone an ineffable light and there was a multitude of people, men and women. The angels opened a path for him through the throng, and he came to a spot where there was a cloud more shining than any light: no sun, no moon or star was there, but this shone more than all the stars, and from the clouds came a voice like that of many waters. Sweet perfume filled him so that he had no need to eat or drink. But he is told that he must return to the earth for the sake of the Church. As he returns to consciousness and when he tells of the mystery of this perfume, it is taken away from him and his tongue is covered with grievous wounds and is swollen.[30]

[28] See above p. 93, note 21.

[29] Silverstein (*Visio Sancti Pauli*, p. 77) compares a Moslem version. See discussion above in the present study, chapter I, pp. 8ff.

[30] *Grégoire de Tours, Histoire des Francs*, ed. H. Omont and G. Collon,

This account shows some indication of being based on a genuine experience, however much it is conditioned by details in the Book of Revelation and Saint Paul's own reference to being caught up into the third heaven. But the ascent is interesting as a parallel to the tradition of the *Somnium Scipionis.*

THE VISION OF SUNNIULF. From Gregory of Tours comes also the account of what is a vision or dream of Sunniulf, Abbot of Randau, which is included in one of the chapters added later to the *Historia*:

Sunniulf was led to a certain fiery river at the shore of which people were gathering like bees at a beehive, and some were submerged to the waist, some to the armpits, and some to the chin. Over the river was a bridge so narrow that there was scarcely room for one foot on it. On the other side was a large white house. Sunniulf asks the meaning of all this and is told that those religious who are careless of the discipline of their flock fall from the bridge and those who are strict pass over in safety to the house.[31]

Here we find primitive elements that have been omitted in the *Dialogues* of Gregory the Great. The river in the *Dialogues* may

---

new ed. by R. Poupardin, pp. 254–255; Migne, *Patr. Lat.*, LXXI, cols. 416–418; *Mon. Germ. Hist.*, *Scriptores rerum Merovingicarum*, I, *Hist. Franc.*, ed. W. Arndt, pp. 290–291; *History of the Franks by Gregory Bishop of Tours, Selections, Translated with Notes,* by Ernest Brehaut, pp. 168–171. Passages of special importance in the original may be quoted as follows: "ita ut non solum hunc squalidum seculum, uerum etiam solem ac lunam, nubes ac sidera sub pedibus habere putarem" (ed. Poupardin, p. 254; cf. Arndt, p. 290); "in quo superpendebat nubes omne luce lucidior, in quo non sol, non luna, non astrum cerni poterat, sed super his omnibus naturali luce splendidius effulgebatur, et uox procedebat e nubi, tamquam uox aquarum multarum" (ed. Poupardin, p. 254; cf. Arndt, pp. 290–291). Cf. also O. M. Dalton, *The History of the Franks by Gregory of Tours,* II, pp. 285ff.

[31] Poupardin, *Gregoire de Tours,* p. 133 (*Hist. Franc.*, iv, 33). For the adding of the chapter see *ibid.*, p. vi. The Latin runs as follows: "ductum se per uisum ad quoddam flumen igneum, in quo ab una parte litoris concurrentes populi ceu apes ad aluearia mergebantur; et erant alii usque ad cingulum, alii uero usque ascellas, nonnulli usque mentum, clamantes cum fletu se uehementer aduri. Erat enim et pons super fluuium positus angustus, ut uix unius uestigii latitudinem recipere possit. Apparebat autem et in alia parte litoris domus magna extrinsecus dealbata. Tunc his qui cum eo erant, quid sibi haec uelint, interrogat."

be fiery by implication and that feature suggests early material; but here we have the narrowness of the bridge emphasized and the detail of the submerging of the sinners. It seems clear then that the writer of Redaction IV of the *Vision of Saint Paul* could have had access not only to the account furnished by Saint Gregory (with the mansions of Hell and the grouping of sinners) but also to another like that known to Gregory of Tours and Sunniulf. Or there may have been a common source for both containing all these elements.

THE VISION OF FURSA. According to Bede's *Ecclesiastical History* when Fursa was sick he had a vision: "from evening until cockcrow being out of the body he was thought worthy to behold the sight of the angelical company . . . ."

The angels carry him away once, but are sent back. On another night and within three days, three angels took him heavenward again, and looking down he saw a dark valley beneath him. This we may infer is Hell.[32] In the air he observes four fires – one for liars, one for the covetous, one for strife, and one for pitilessness. They are joined together in one big flame, which the angels part for him to go through. Beyond he sees the heavenly company. Eventually Fursa is burned a little when a devil snatches up one of the sinners tormented in the flames and hurls the victim at him. The angel explains: "That thou hast kindled hath burned in thee." On returning to the flesh Fursa carries the scar of this experience.[33]

Here the flight to heaven and the dark valley are significant in what again seems to be part of a real experience.

[32] So says Fritzsche, *Rom. Forsch.* II (1886), p. 269, but the text says merely, "Respice mundum."

[33] *Baedae opera historica,* J. E. King, Loeb Library, I, pp. 415ff.: *Ven. Bedae Historiam Ecclesiasticam*, ed. Charles Plummer, I, pp. 164ff. Cf. also *Acta sanctorum Bolland.*, 16 January, II, pp. 401–403 and 411–412; Fritzsche, *Rom. Forsch.*, II, pp. 268f.; and Arnold B. van Os, *Religious Visions*, pp. 27ff. The vision is also recounted in Aelfric's homilies: see Benjamin Thorpe, *The Homilies of the Anglo-Saxon Church*, II, pp. 332ff. For an Irish version, see *Revue celtique,* XXV (1904), pp. 385ff. According to the *Acta sanctorum* hands under the snowy feathers of the angels support Fursa in his flight, and in Heaven he sees the towers of the angels and the saints. For the story transferred to a monk of Canterbury see Wright, *Saint Patrick's Purgatory*, pp. 10f., note.

THE VISION OF DRYTHELM. Bede also tells of the vision of one Drythelm, who died and returned to life with a narrative of what he saw in the next world. With a guide of shining countenance and bright apparel he went toward the east:

". . . and as we walked, we came to a great broad and deep valley, so long that no man could measure it; and this lay on the left hand as we went, and shewed one side exceeding terrible with flaming fire, the other no less unendurable with vehement hail and chilly snow beating and drifting into every corner. And both places were full of men's souls . . ." The souls leap in their torture from one side to the other. Further along he finds "every corner full of darkness. And as we entered into it, within a little space it became so thick that I saw nothing but the darkness, saving only the bright glow and coat of him which did guide me." Flames of fire here and there appear, with souls like sparks ascending and descending, and the stench of the place was great. They come again to clear light and then to a solid wall. "When then we had come to the wall, I cannot tell by what means, we were straightway upon the top. And behold there was there a very broad and pleasant field, so full of the fragrance of fresh flourishing flowers, that by and by the marvelous sweetness of their scent drove away all the stench of the dark furnace . . . ." Here is a fair light, gatherings of men in white garments, and the melodious noise of musicians. This is the valley where souls are examined and tried.[34]

The dark valley here is a familiar feature, and also the pleasant plain. Rather striking is the division of the first of these into regions of fire and snow.

THE VISION OF BARONTUS. From the period near the end of the seventh century comes the story of the vision Barontus had, when he was thought to be really dead. He saw devils and angels battling for his soul; but the archangel Raphael successfully defended him and conveyed him with great rapidity up to Heaven. At the

[34] Bede, *Eccles. Hist.*, V, xii (*Baedae opera historica*, Loeb, II, pp. 253ff. Cf. also *Romanische Forschungen* VIII (1896), p. 361. For Aelfric's version in his homilies see Thorpe, *op. cit.*, II, 348ff. It is also found in the *Liber visionum* of Othlo, Migne, *Patr. Lat.*, CXLVI, cols. 380ff. and see also Helinandus for most of the details, Migne, CCXII 1059f. Cf. van Os, *Religious Visions*, pp. 29ff. On Bede's account of the vision as compared with Stephen's experience described by Gregory the Great see *Speculum*, XXI (1946), p. 409.

first gate of Paradise he recognized former brothers of his monastery. At the second gate he saw innumerable thousands of children in white and virgins praising God. At the third gate, which was like glass ("habebat similitudinem uitri"), was a multitude of saints with crowns and shining countenances residing in the mansion there. He saw other mansions being prepared for others yet to come, and he saw the martyrs there. At the fourth gate was splendor and light on all sides. Next he was led to see the tortures of Hell and the mansions which are there too, with darkness and murky vapors. At length with other experiences he returned to the body.[35] This heavenly vision is of special interest because of the four gates it describes.

THE VISION OF THE MONK OF WENLOCK. Sometime before 717 A.D., according to the tenth epistle of Saint Boniface, occurred the rather elaborate vision of which he wrote to Eadburga, Abbess of Thanet:

Angels took the Monk of Wenlock and bore him up into the air until he was able to see the whole earth surrounded with a burning fire. The angel made the sign of the cross and the flames diminished. He then beheld a throng of evil spirits and a great chorus of angels, which seem to represent the way in which he is accused by his own sins and defended by his virtues. He sees fiery pits vomiting flames, and souls in the form of black birds suffering in the flames, pleading and howling and crying with human voices ("in similitudine nigrarum auium per flammam plorantes et ululantes et uerbis et uoce humana stridentes . . . .") He sees a pitchy river boiling and flaming, over which was placed a piece of timber for a bridge. Over this the holy and glorious souls strove to pass. Some went securely, others slipped and fell into the Tartarean stream. Some were wholly submerged in the flood, others to the knees, some to the middle of the body, and some to the ankles. All eventually came out of the fire rendered bright and clean to ascend the other shore. Beyond the river were walls shining with splendor great in length and height — the heavenly Jerusalem. Evil spirits were plunged into the fiery pits.[36]

[35] *Acta sanctorum Bolland.*, 16 March, pp. 568ff. Note the reference to the *Dialogues* of Gregory, p. 569.

[36] *Die Briefe des heiligen Bonifatius und Lullus,* ed. Tangl, (*M.G.H. Epistolae selectae*, I), pp. 7ff. Also see *Bibliotheca rerum Germanicarum*, ed. P. Jaffé, III, *Monumenta Moguntina* pp. 53–61. Also Migne, *Patr. Lat.*, LXXXIX, Ep. XX, cols. 713ff. and *M.G.H.*, *Epist.* III (*Epistolae Meroving-*

The souls in the form of birds recalls a Celtic motif but is, I suspect, independent of that tradition.[37] Here again we find the bridge and the submerging of victims at various levels in the stream, as in the *Vision of Sunniulf* according to Gregory of Tours and Redaction IV of the *Vision of Saint Paul.*

Another letter of Saint Boniface (CXII), which is fragmentary, also seems to have contained a reference to the bridge, but all we have is the account of how sinners were submerged in a river to the ankles or to the neck, while the fiery stream went clear over the head of some. All are eventually released from the punishment, and so here too the scene is purgatorial. Beyond lies a land of rejoicing with a celestial turn to the bridge motif: the road goes to the first heaven in the form of a heavenly bow ("in specie arcus caeli"), another to the second, and from the second to the third.[38]

THE LEGEND OF SAINT BARLAAM AND SAINT JOSAPHAT. In the middle of the eighth century, John of Damascus or some other ecclesiast

---

ici et Karolini, I, Berlin, 1892), 252ff. The letter was translated into Old English (see *Mod. Lang. Review* XVIII [1923], pp. 253ff.), and also for a modern rendering see *The English Correspondence of Saint Boniface,* E. Kylie, London, (*The King's Classics*), pp. 78ff. (reprinted in *The Letters of Saint Boniface,* Ephraim Emerton, [*Records of Civiliz.,* XXXI] pp. 25ff.). The bridge is described in the Latin as follows (ed. Tangl, pp. 11–12): "Nec non et igneum piceumque flumen bulliens et ardens mirae formidinis et teterrimę uisionis cernebat. Super quod lignum pontis uice positum erat. Ad quod sanctae gloriosęque animę, ab illo secendentes conuentu properabant desiderio alterius ripę transire cupientes. Et quaedam non titubantes constanter transiebant, quaedam uero labefactę de ligno cadebant in Tartareum flumen, et aliae tinguebantur pene quasi toto corpore mersae; aliae autem ex parte quadam, ueluti quedam usque ad genua, quaedam usque ad medium, quaedam uero usque ad ascellas . . . ." Cf. also Tangl, *Die Briefe des heiligen Bonifatius* in *Die Geschichtschreifer der deutschen Vorzeit,* vol. XCII.

[37] Cf. the vision in the *Historia Lausiaca* of Palladius, Migne, *Patrologia Graeca,* XXXIV, col. 1076 B–C (ψυχὰς ἀνιπταμένας ὡς ὄρνεα). The souls flying like birds over the black giant are judged by whether they get safely over or are struck by his hands.

[38] Ed. Jaffé, pp. 274f. Cf. p. 275: "Deinde ab ipsa terra tramitem usque ad caelum primum in specie arcus caeli, inde alium ad secundum, a secundo ad tertium; et albatorum conuenticula uiuorum et mortuorum; et superius celum semper pulchrius inferiori aspexisse, ferebat."

wrote the story of Barlaam and Josaphat, clearly for purposes of instruction in the midst of the iconoclastic controversy, borrowing from an Indian legend of Buddha and somewhat from the *Apocalypse of Peter*. After the original Greek, numerous other versions appeared in various languages; for the story was popular and influential, and found its way into the *Legenda aurea* and the *Speculum historiale* of Vincent of Beauvais, and later even into the drama of Lope de Vega. The vision that concerns us is the one enjoyed by Josaphat (or Ioasaph) for his enlightenment about good and evil:

After a long prayer he falls asleep, and sees himself carried off by "certain dread men" through places he has never seen before. At last he stands in a great plain filled with flowers and fruits; the trees stir a breeze and their leaves rustling send out a gracious perfume. Golden thrones are here all set with precious stones; here too are settles and couches. Near by are running waters, clear and delightful. He sees a radiant city surrounded by walls of gold, her streets filled with light, and winged squadrons to make melody such as mortal ear never heard. This is "the rest of the righteous." Taken back across the plain again (protesting he would like to stay), he is carried to regions of darkness filled with every kind of woe. Here is a glowing furnace of fire, and the worm of torment. This, he learns, is the place for sinners. His tears fall copiously and he is prostrate with longing for the good and fear of the evil.[39]

The plain, the flowers, fruits, and trees, are conventional – and even the golden city. The use of music here is more interesting, and something like a coincidence with a Celtic motif is found in the rustling of the trees, which, according to the Greek, makes a "sweet sound" (*τά τε φύλλα τῶν δένδρων λιγυρὸν ὑπήχει αὔρᾳ τινὶ λεπτοτάτῃ*, § 281, p. 468), an idea preserved in Caxton's version of

[39] *Saint John Damascene, Barlaam and Ioasaph,* G. R. Woodward and H. Mattingly, Loeb Library, pp. 468ff. Cf. "Barlaam und Joasaph," in Bavarian Akademie *Abhandlungen* (*Philos.-Philol. Classe*), XX (1897), pp. 1–88, Ernst Kuhn; *Harvard Theol. Review,* XXXII (1939), pp. 131ff.; and *Barlaam and Josaphat, English Lives of Buddha,* Joseph Jacobs, p. x, for the later versions, and pp. xcvii ff. for sources; also *The Story of Barlaam and Joasaph, Buddhism and Christianity,* K. S. MacDonald and J. Morrison. For the influence of the *Apoc. of Peter* on the vision see J. A. Robinson, *Texts and Studies,* I, 2, pp. 37ff.

the *Legenda aurea* where he says that "the leuys of the trees demened a swete sounde which came by a wynde agreable." [40]

THE VISION OF ROTCHARIUS. The heavenly mansions are described in the *Vision of Rotcharius,* from the beginning of the ninth century. An angel leads the way "per amoenitatis uiam," and three houses appear: the first not of wood and stone, but constructed like a throne, and here live the saints; the second, the most splendid, contains the majesty of the Lord; the third, in an inferior place, "tota deformitate repletam," contains clerics and laymen, who are being purged of sin by standing in fire up to their chests while warm water is being poured over their heads.[41]

THE VISION OF THE POOR WOMAN. From the same period comes the vision of a poor woman, who, guided by a man in monkish garb, saw the place of rest for the saints and of punishment for the wicked. Here she found many famous people, some in great torture, some in glory. For example here was Picho, friend of Charlemagne, into whose mouth two demons poured liquid gold. She also saw here a great wall reaching to Heaven and after that another inscribed with gold characters. Beyond, she is told, is the Earthly Paradise.[42]

THE VISION OF WETTIN. From the early ninth century too comes the vision which Hetto wrote in Latin prose about Wettin, Abbot of Reichenau, and which Walafrid Strabo put into Latin verse at the age of fifteen:

The devil appeared to Wettin, and other demons besieged him, but an angel in radiant garments came to his assistance. On awakening from this experience Wettin asked the brothers to pray for him and to read the *Dialogues* of Gregory to him. Once again in his sleep an angel

[40] Jacobs, *op. cit.,* p. 30. Cf. the tree of silver in the *Serglige Conculaind,* above, p. 42; the singing rose trees in the *Vision of Perpetua,* above, p. 90; and also cf. p. 88, n. 14, for the suggestion of Moslem influence.

[41] *Anzeiger für Kunde der deutschen Vorzeit,* XXII (1875), cols. 72–74, ed. W. Wattenbach. Fritzsche in *Rom. Forsch.,* II, p. 277, finds resemblance here to the Book of Enoch.

[42] W. Wattenbach, *Deutschlands Geschichtsquellen im Mittelalter bis zur Mitte des Dreizehnten Jahrhunderts,* I, pp. 260f., n. 3.

appears to him, praising him for becoming strengthened by the *Dialogues,* and then taking him, leads him "per uiam amoenitatis immensae praeclaram." Two mountains of great height and incredible loveliness as if made of marble came into view, round which flowed a great fiery stream where a multitude of the damned were in torture. Others were punished in other places, and there was a sort of castle of wood and stone reserved for the purgation of monks, sending up smoky vapor. A mountain also appeared on the summit of which was an abbot exposed to the wind and the rain for his cleansing. Wettin is led later to a magnificent structure of great size and incredible beauty where dwell the saints.[43]

The pleasant path is here, as in the *Vision of Rotcharius,* and also an interesting use of the mountains, apparently as barriers. The fiery stream doubtless reflects the story in Gregory.

THE VISION OF BERNOLDUS. At the end of the ninth century Bernoldus dictated his vision of the realm of purgatory where he saw various bishops who invited prayers for their relief. He came, he says, to a dark place ("locum tenebrosum"), to which light was shining from a beautiful and fragrant region (the realm of the saints); and in the darkness he saw a rock:

Et uidi iuxta illam petram magnam et altam, profundam uallem, et puteum teterrimum, et aquam nigram quasi pix esset, et interrogaui illum hominem qui se Jesse nominauit, quid esset ille puteus . . . .

The pit, he learns, is Hell, and from it issue flames and smoke. Here, of course, are demons and a throng of tortured souls. The dark and deep valley we have met before.[44] The black water may recall Gregory's river, and there is something like it too in the *Vision of Adamnán,* which is perhaps earlier.

THE VISION OF SAINT ANSCAR. Toward the end of the ninth century too a vision came to Saint Anscar, then a child of five. He found

[43] *MGH, Poetae Latini aeui Carolini,* ed. E. Dümmler, II, pp. 268ff.; Strabo's rendering, pp. 301ff. Cf. Fritzsche, *Rom. Forsch.,* III (1887), pp. 337–338.

[44] This vision has been assigned to Hincmar of Rheims. See Migne, *Patr. Lat.,* CXXV, cols. 1115–1119. For a reference to the *Dialogues* of Gregory see col. 1118. Cf. Fritzsche, *Rom. Forsch.,* III (1887), pp. 340–342, who classifies it with political visions.

himself in a certain filthy and slippery place from which he could not emerge. Opposite, however, was a fair path: "secus illum uero locum esse uiam amoenissimam, in qua uidebat procedentem quandam quasi dominam omni ornatu et honestate praeclaram . . . ." This beautiful lady, with several others in white in her train, is the Virgin Mary, who comes to assist him out of the slippery region. In another vision he sees purgatory: "Ubi cum multa passus esset, praecipue tamen tenebras densissimas pressurasque immanissimas et suffocationes uisus est tolerasse . . . ." In still another he sees the saints.[45] The dark region and the pleasant path are familiar motifs.

THE VISION OF CHARLES THE FAT. The vision enjoyed by Charles the Fat about 885 is told in William of Malmesbury's *De rebus gestis Anglorum.* A figure of light, holding a shining ball of thread like a comet, appeared to him and, making him bind an end on his right thumb, he led him "in labyrintheas infernorum poenas." Charles saw "profundissimas ualles et igneas," all full of burning pitch and sulphur and lead. Here are familiar souls in torture. Demons try to tear the thread from his finger, but his guide comes to his protection. Together they ascend very high fiery mountains "de quibus oriebantur paludes et flumina feruentia, et omnia metallorum genera bullientia . . . ." Furnaces of pitch and sulphur are on the banks. Dragons attack him, but his guide intervenes:

Et descendimus in unam uallem, quae erat ex una parte tenebrosa, ardens uelut clibanus ignis; ex alia uero parte tam amoenissima et splendidissima ut nulla ratione dicere ualeam.

Here he sees two fountains, one tepid, one hot, signifying different degrees of punishment. On the dark side of the valley many people are suffering; and the two fountains, he is told, are awaiting him too unless he repents him of his ways. At last he is led "ad dextram luculentissimae uallis paradisi." [46] In this account

[45] *MGH,* Scriptores, II, 690ff., ed. D. C. F. Dahlmann. Cf. Fritzsche, *Rom. Forsch.,* III, pp. 342ff.

[46] William of Malmesbury, *De gestis regum Anglorum,* ed. William Stubbs, I, pp. 112–116; *MGH, Scriptores,* X, 458, ed. D. G. Waitz. Cf. Fritzsche, *Rom.*

the deep and fiery valley, the mountains with burning rivers, and the divided valley (one part dark, another delightful) with the two fountains, represent interesting variations on themes already long familiar. This vision is clearly a political document, with references to specific figures — Lewis, father of Charles, Lothar, his uncle, and Lewis, his cousin.

THE VISION OF ADAMNÁN. An Irish vision of Saint Adamnán, found in the Book of the Dun Cow (eleventh century) and in the Speckled Book (fourteenth century) but perhaps going back to the ninth century, shows material of the same general tradition as the other documents considered in this chapter, however much it is elaborated by the Celtic fantasy. The *Fís Adamnáin* tells of the soul's being taken up to heaven by an angel. There we see much that might be based on a Gnostic view of the heavens and on the Book of Revelation: a crystal veil, seven crystal walls of various hues, the floor and base of the city of crystal with the sun's countenance upon it, six guarded doors, rivers of fire (§§ 16–18), and also — and here, of course, is a notably Celtic touch — the "three stately birds" perched on the throne of the Lord singing the eight canonical hours. Moreover "Six thousand thousands, in guise of horses and of birds, surround the fiery chair, which still burns on, without end or term" (§ 8). The fiery rivers are barriers to the third, fourth, and fifth heavens.

Adamnán is taken to see the realm of torture, even to the nethermost hell, a glen "filled with fire" with huge flames, serpents, and other creatures. Here an "enormous bridge spans the glen, reaching from one bank to the other; high the middle of it, but lower its two extremities" (§ 22). "Three companies seek to pass over it, but not all succeed. One company find the bridge to be of ample width, from beginning to end, until they win across the fiery glen, safe and sound . . . ." The second company "find it narrow at first, but broad afterwards." For the last group

---

Forsch., III, pp. 344–345; MacCulloch, *Medieval Faith and Fable*, pp. 190–191. For influence on Dante see *Mod. Lang. Notes*, LI (1936), pp. 449ff., with an interesting account of the development of the story from before the time of William of Malmesbury. Cf. also Collin de Plancy, *Légendes de L'Autre Monde*, pp. 72ff.

the bridge is broad at first but strait afterward and narrow until they fall from it into the glen. Here too is a fiery sea and a silver wall, a black lake and a black river, and a fiery wall. This is the land of pain: "For this is the nature of it: Mountains, caverns, and thorny brakes; plains, bare and parched, with stagnant, serpent-haunted lochs. The soil is rough and sandy, very rugged, ice-bound. Broad fiery flagstones bestrew the plain. Great seas are there, with horrible abysses, wherein is the Devil's constant habitation and abiding-place. Four mighty rivers cross the middle of it: a river of fire, a river of snow, a river of poison, a river of black, murky water" (§ 30). After seeing all this, the saint returns to the land of the redeemed and there finds the Tree of Life and "the souls of the righteous in the form of white birds."[47]

However much richer in detail, this vision is similar in substance to the others we have been studying, with the ascent to heaven, the scene of the realm of the blessed and that of those in torment, and with familiar material such as the fiery rivers, the glen, and the bridge, which, we note, can hardly come from Saint Gregory in its present form. The Celtic element may be found in the shift in the arrangement here and there, and in the birds singing the hours and also the bird souls.

THE VISION OF LAISRÉN. Also an Irish account going back to the early tenth century or even the ninth, the *Vision of Laisrén*, shows something of the same material based, it would seem, on the same tradition:

[47] C. S. Boswell, *An Irish Precursor of Dante*; Windisch, *Irische Texte*, I, pp. 167ff. It is also found in a MS in the Bibliothèque Nationale. Boswell notes the bridge in oriental lore (p. 71) and the birds on the sacred tree in Persian (p. 85). His argument for direct oriental influence furnishes some useful material, but he adds that the manner in which the bridge appears here suggests that the "source of inspiration was one of the ecclesiastical legends, though we find the usual difficulty of assigning any given item to some one specific source" (p. 197). He regards Gregory's version as a connecting link between the East and the Irish school, and points out that the bridge in the *Wooing of Emer* is different (p. 131). Cf. further, Seymour, *Irish Visions of the Other World*, pp. 94ff., and similarities in such works as the Book of Enoch, the *Vision of Esdras*, the *Shepherd of Hermas*, and the *Apocalypse of Peter*. For startling parallels to a Gnostic document see p. 84 above, and Seymour, *op. cit.*, pp. 112ff. For the section incorporated in the *Adventure of Saint Columba's Clerics* see above, pp. 34f. Cf. *Beiträge zur engl. Philol.*, XXX, Leipzig, 1935.

At the end of a thrice-three-day fast, sleep overpowered Laisrén in church, and a voice said to him "Arise." He saw a shining figure bidding him approach. He then observed his own soul hovering over the crown of his head. Two angels took it and rose to a place where the church was now opened toward Heaven. Angels and demons came to dispute over it, and the soul was granted a vision of Hell —

"Thereupon he is let down northward into a great glen. It seemed as long to him as if he saw from the rising of the sun to its setting. He sees a great pit as it were the mouth of a cave between two mountains, which they entered above. For a long time they went along the cave, until they came to a great high black mountain before them at the mouth of Hell, and a large glen in the upper part of that mountain. This was the nature of that glen: it was broad below, narrow above. That cave was the door of Hell, and its porch." Here he finds a sea of fire with "an unspeakable storm and unspeakable waves upon it," and souls in torment.[48]

The northern location of this Hell is significant. The mountain barriers are not unusual: we may contrast the two beautiful mountains in the *Vision of Wettin* above. A new element in this tradition is the approach along the cave, and possibly such an underground route may carry a distant reminiscence of the idea of the hollow mountain, but not in the Celtic style.[49] The glen and pit are constant features, as is also the sea of fire.

THE VISION OF ANSELLUS SCHOLASTICUS. The darkness of Hell is reflected in some lines of a vision written in verse by Ansellus (of the school of Fleury in the tenth century) at the command of his abbot, Odo. A brother at Rheims, he says, asleep in his dormitory there, seemed to see the Lord descend from the cross and lead him down to Hell:

[48] *Otia Merseiana,* I, pp. 113ff., ed. Kuno Meyer from a fifteenth-century manuscript (p. 113). Cf. Seymour, *Irish Visions,* pp. 20ff.

[49] Cf. the tunnel and the pit in Guibert Nogent's account of his mother's dream (eleventh century): her soul issued from her body and seemed to go along a narrow passage to emerge by a great pit from which souls were coming forth. Her husband Evrardus was there: "Cumque ueluti per quamdam porticum duceretur tandem inde emergens ad ora cuiusdam putei coeperat propinquare" — Migne, *Patr. Lat.,* CLVI, cols. 876–877. The valley as hell appears in the visions of Flodilda (mid-tenth century), J.-J. Ampère, *Hist. Litt.,* III, p. 283; Fritzsche, *Rom. Forsch.,* III, p. 346, referring to Du Chesne, *Script. rer. Franc.,* II, p. 624.

Tunc tenebrarum principes
Ac pallidae mortis duces,
Tortoresque saeuissimi
Peruasoresque rapidi
Diffugiunt citissime . . . .[50]

Here is an obvious offshoot of the story of the Harrowing of Hell.

THE VISION OF HERIGER. The well-known satiric vision recounted by a prophet to Heriger, Archbishop of Mainz, according to the eleventh-century Latin poem, refers to Hell as surrounded by dense woods:

Inde cum multas referret causas,
subiunxit totum esse infernum
accinctum densis undique syluis.[51]

The poem goes on to describe the visit to Heaven, where the saints serve a rich feast to the redeemed. John the Baptist is cup-bearer, Peter is head of the cooks.

THE VISION OF ALBERIC. A twelfth-century vision, famous for its similarities to details in the *Divine Comedy*, is that of Alberic, who was taken up by a dove, and, with the guidance of Saint Peter and two angels, visited Hell and Paradise:

Alberic, monk of Montecassino, wishes to give the correct version of the story of his vision, which has already become known. For nine nights and nine days he lay as if dead. A bird like a dove approached him and seemed to draw his soul from his mouth. He was transported on high above the earth, whereupon Saint Peter and two angels appeared and

[50] E. du Méril, *Poésies populaires latines antérieures au douzième siècle*, pp. 200ff. Note references to the visions of Ezechiel and Daniel, p. 203. On the Harrowing of Hell, for other descents, see J. A. MacCulloch's book of that title, p. 36, and *passim*.

[51] Du Méril, *op. cit.*, pp. 298ff.; Karl Breul, *The Cambridge Songs*, No. 26, pp. 59f.; S. Gaselee, *Oxford Book of Medieval Latin Verse*, pp. 66ff.; translated in Helen Waddell's *Medieval Latin Lyrics*, pp. 148ff.; also in P. S. Allen and H. M. Jones, *The Romanesque Lyric*, pp. 278–279. MacCulloch, *Medieval Faith and Fable*, p. 200, suggests that "The forests of Hell and the sensuous feasts of Heaven in this vision may be taken from the *Edda* — the dark valleys through which Hermod rode to Hel, and the banquets of Valhalla." Any direct connection, however, seems doubtful.

led him to see the places of torture of the inferno. He travels along a path through a wood "plenum subtilissimis arboribus quarum omnium capita ac si sudes acutissima erant, et spinosa," and he comes to a terrible valley where sinners are submerged in ice, some to the knees or flanks, some to the chest. He visits another valley, all full of thorny trees, where women are tortured. He sees a ladder of iron of great length, filled with teeth emitting sparks, with a great vat of boiling oil and pitch at its foot. While sinners climb, their feet are burned by the flames from the vat, and sometimes they fall down into it. Further along Alberic sees a valley with a lake of red molten metal, and then a river of burning pitch, over which is an iron bridge. This the righteous find broad enough for easy passage; but for sinners it becomes as narrow as a thread in the middle and they fall from it.

Later comes another great valley with dense, thorny trees, and, near by, a field of healing with lilies and roses and a wonderful fragrance where Paradise is located. Paradise is on a high plain close to Heaven and guarded by cherubim. Here is the Tree of Life. Led by the dove, Alberic visits the seven heavens, and is taken to a high wall — but what he sees beyond that he cannot reveal.[52]

The ladder here may remind us of the ladder with knives in the *Vision of Perpetua.* The visit to the seven heavens may be a reminiscence, like that in the *Vision of Adamnán,* of the scheme in the revelations of Gnosticism. Most striking, however, is the path through the thorny wood, and the valley of thorny trees shows the same motif. While the iron bridge over the burning river of pitch is somewhat like that in Gregory, it adds the detail of becoming narrow for sinners. The detail of sinners submerged in ice is an interesting variant of the motif as it is found in the *Vision of Saint Paul,* describing those who are plunged into the river of fire.

[52] Francesco Cancellieri, *Osservazione intorno alla questione promossa dal Vannozzi dal Mazzocchi dal Boltari especialmente dal P. Abate D. Giuseppe Giustino di Costanzo sopra l'Originalità della Divina Commedia di Dante,* pp. 132–207. Doves convey the soul in the *Vision of Bonellus,* in Migne, *Patr. Lat.* LXXXVII, col. 435. Cf. A. d'Ancona, *Scritti Danteschi,* pp. 59ff.; Fritzsche, *Rom. Forsch.,* III, pp. 354ff. The account of the bridge is as follows (Cancellieri, *op. cit.,* p. 168): ". . . in cuius medio pons erat ferreus multam habens latitudinem per quem pontem iustorum anime tam facilius, tamque uelocius transeunt, quam immunes inueniuntur a delictis: peccatorum autem ponderibus grauati cum ad medium eius uenerint, tam efficitur subtilis, ut ad fili quantitatem eius latitudo uideatur redigi. Qua illi difficultate prepediti, in eundem flumen corruunt: rursumque assurgentes, ac denuo recidentes, tamdiu ibidem cruciantur . . . ." The bridge is here purgatorial.

THE VISION OF THE BOY WILLIAM. In the twelfth century, we are told, occurred the vision of the boy named William which Vincent of Beauvais describes in his *Speculum historiale.* The boy, led by a man of noble mien, first comes to a dark valley with fire on one side and cold water on the other. He sees the pit of Tartarus and the devil. He comes to a high wall with no perceptible openings, but he gets by and sees a round house with armed men in it. In a great field he finds souls rejoicing in glory.[53] Here the divided valley of cold and heat recalls the *Vision of Drythelm.*

THE VISION OF TUNDALE. From the middle of the twelfth century comes the *Vision of Tundale,* one of the most widely known, found in numerous manuscripts, originally perhaps in Latin, but retold in Italian, German, Dutch, English, and other languages, including a modern use in the poem by Matthew Arnold.

Brother Mark tells the story, saying that he has turned it out of Irish into Latin.[54] A certain nobleman named Tundale fell ill and lay as if dead for three days. On his return to life he recounted what he had seen. His soul, having left his body, followed his guardian angel to a dark and terrible valley ("ad uallem ualde terribilem ac tenebrosam et mortis caligine coopertam. Erat enim ualde profunda et carbonibus ardentibus plena . . .") Here he found souls roasted on the burning coals. After that he came to a vast mountain over which was a narrow road, on the one side of which was fire and on the other ice and snow ("Erat namque ex una parte illius itineris ignis putridus, sulphureus atque tenebrosus, ex altera autem parte nix glacialis ey cum grandine uentus horribilis.") Then they came to a valley too deep to see to the bottom, but across it lay a very long plank in the manner of a bridge. Here none but the elect could cross. Many tried to get over it, but only a priest bearing the palm of his pilgrimage could succeed. However, an angel helped Tundale to pass safely.

They had various other experiences and then they saw another bridge longer and narrower than the first, and fixed with sharp iron

[53] Vincent of Beauvais, *Spec. Hist.,* Venice, 1591, xxvii, caps. 84–85, p. 1126; Seymour, *Irish Visions,* pp. 159f.; van Os, *Religious Visions,* pp. 67f. Cf. the vision of Boso by Simeon of Durham, *Opera omnia,* Rolls Series LXXV, I, pp. 130ff.

[54] For an Irish version see V. H. Friedel and Kuno Meyer, *La Vision de Tondale.* For one in Old Norse see Liestøl, *Draumkvæde,* pp. 83ff.

nails. Here were monsters gathered to seize the sinners as they fell from it into the stormy lake below. Here a soul bearing a sheaf of grain was crossing and blocked Tundale's passage, as he was compelled to lead after him a cow he had once stolen. The two souls stood facing each other and weeping for a while until Tundale suddenly found himself on the other side.

At length he came to the field of joy and the fountain of life. Here was a door that opened of its own accord, and within was a beautiful meadow filled with flowers and sweet odors, in which was a great multitude of souls. Tundale saw a silver wall, within which was a throng in white rejoicing and praising God. No night nor any sadness was found there. Further along he came to a wall of pure gold, and seats covered with gold and precious stones, where sat the continent and the martyrs. He saw also a vast tree covered with fruits and flowers and birds of every kind. Underneath sat men and women rejoicing and praising God. The tree, we are told, was Holy Church. Here too was a high wall of various precious stones, and beyond this wall, which they climbed, they saw the nine orders of angels.[55]

Here the influence of the *Dialogues* of Gregory on the passages regarding the bridges is fairly clear [56] in the figure of the priest; but the narrowness of the bridge is curiously emphasized, recalling the *Vision of Sunniulf*, and the detail of the iron nails in one instance is added. The monsters, ready to devour sinners, recall the later form of the *Vision of Saint Paul*. The path with heat and

[55] A. Wagner, *Visio Tnugdali Lateinisch und Altdeutsch*. Cf. A. Mussafia, Vienna *Sitzungsberichte*, 67 (1871), pp. 157ff.; Ward, *Catalogue of Romances* II, pp. 416ff.; and V. H. Friedel and Kuno Meyer, *Versions inédites de la Vision de Tondale*; Seymour, *Irish Visions*, pp. 124ff.; Becker, *Medieval Visions of Heaven and Hell*, pp. 81ff. The vision is also described by Helinandus, Migne, *Patr. Lat.*, CCXII, cols. 1038ff.

[56] Such is also Seymour's opinion, *Irish Visions*, pp. 157ff., who thinks that the sevenfold division of the Other World here (with other details) derives from the *Vision of Adamnán* (p. 152). The descriptions of the bridges run as follows: "Tabula autem longissima ab uno monte in alium in modum pontis se super uallem extenderat, qui mille passus in longitudine, in latitudine uero unius pedis mensuram habebat. Quem pontem transire nisi electus nemo poterat. De quo uidit multos cadere, neminem autem preter presbiterum unum illesum pertransire. Erat autem ille presbiter peregrinus, portans palmam et indutus sclauinio et ante omnes intrepidus pertransibat primus," ed. Wagner, p. 15. For the other, Tundale sees "stagnum amplum ualde et tempestuosum, cuius fluctus astantes non permittebat cernere celum . . . Per latum uero eius pons multum angustus erat et longus, cuius longitudo quasi per duo miliaria tendebatur; talis enim erat latitudo stagni. Latitudo uero

cold reminds one of the *Vision of the Boy William* and the *Vision of Drythelm*. And the terrible and dark valley continues a familiar theme.

THE LEGEND OF SAINT PATRICK'S PURGATORY. Another exceedingly widespread story is that of the visit of the Knight Owen to the cave in the island of Saint Patrick's Purgatory (or Station Island, County Donegal) in Ireland. Owen was supposed to have visited the cave in 1153, and to have told of his experiences to Gilbert of Louth, who in turn narrated them to Henry of Saltrey. Versions of the account in Latin appear in a large number of manuscripts; it is introduced into the *Flores historiarum* of Roger of Wendover, into the *Legenda aurea*, into Vincent of Beauvais's *Speculum historiale*, in Middle English into the *South English Legendary*, and elsewhere. It was retold by Marie de France and used for a play by Calderón. "Let him who has his doubts about purgatory, go to Ireland and enter the purgatory of S. Patrick," says the monk in the *Dialogue* of Caesarius of Heisterbach.[57] Froissart when he was in England asked if there were any foundation in truth for the marvelous things that were said to be seen in the cave, and a knight who had been there said that there was.[58] There is hardly a detail of the story, however, which cannot be paralleled in other visions of this type:

After fifteen days of fasting and prayer Owen is put into the cave. At first it is quite dark, and then gets lighter ("Ingrauescentibus magis ac magis tenebris, lucem amittit tocius claritatis. Tandem ex aduerso lux paruula cepit"). He proceeds until he comes to an open plain in which is a building like a cloister, where monks warn him of the coming temptations of demons. The demons arrive and lead him through a wilderness where the earth is black and swept by an icy wind ("Nigra

---

ipsius pontis quasi unius palme mensura. Longior namque et angustior erat, quam pons ille, de quo superius diximus. Erat etiam ista tabula inserta clauis ferreis acutissimis . . . ." *ibid.*, p. 19.

[57] *The Dialogue of Miracles*, trans. Scott and Bland, vol. II, p. 327 (xii, 38). For the Latin see *Dialogus*, ed. Strange, II, p. 347. Cf. also p. 348 (dist. XII, cap. xxxix).

[58] John Froissart, *Chronicles of England, France, Spain*, etc., trans. T. Johnes, pp. 565–566 (IV, lxii). Cf., however, the skepticism of William Caxton regarding the spot (*Mirrour of the World*, ed. O. H. Prior, p. 99, *EETS:ES*, 110).

erat terra et tenebrosa . . . ."). Various plains of punishment appear to him and a bath house filled with pits of sulphur and molten metal into which sinners are immersed at various depths. He is led to the top of a high mountain, where naked people suffer from a tempest that hurls them into a river of icy water ("in flumine fetido ac frigidissimo"). He sees a deep fiery pit, and a broad fiery river filled with demons (". . . . ad flumen unum latissimum et fetidum peruenerunt. Erat autem flumen illud totum flamma quasi sulphurei incendii coopertum atque demonum multitudine plenum . . . .") over which is a slippery bridge so narrow that one could not stand on it and so high it made one dizzy to look downwards. Owen, however, calls on the Holy Name, and the bridge becomes broader as he passes over it. At length he reaches Paradise, which is surrounded by a high wall, one gate of which is adorned with precious stones and metals. The gate opens and a great flood of fragrant air rushes towards him as if the whole world were turned to perfume. Here he is met by a procession led by two archbishops. Here too are meadows with flowers and fruit trees, and a great throng of people. This is the Earthly Paradise. Later he gets a glimpse of Heaven as well.[59]

Here we find almost direct reminiscences of other accounts, and reference to Gregory the Great is included in the text.[60] The broadening bridge, however, is more like that in the *Vision of Adamnán*.[61] The dark path, the underground approach, the dark

[59] C. M. Van der Zanden, *Étude sur le Purgatoire de Saint Patrice*. Cf. T. A. Jenkins, *The Espurgatoire Saint Patriz of Marie de France* (*Investigations Representing the Departments of Romance Languages, etc.*, 1st series, vol. VII, Decennial Publ.), pp. 235ff.; Philippe de Felice, *L'Autre Monde, Mythes et Légendes, Le Purgatoire de Saint Patrice*; Liestøl, *Draumkvæde*, pp. 105–106 (referring to an Old Swedish version); G. P. Krapp, *The Legend of Saint Patrick's Purgatory, Its Later Literary History*; Seymour, *Irish Visions*, pp. 168–187; Thomas Wright, *Saint Patrick's Purgatory*, etc.; H. L. D. Ward, *Catalogue of Romances*, II, pp. 435ff. On Marie's version see also Foulet in *Rom. Forsch.*, XXII (1908), pp. 599ff. On the manuscripts and later versions see Van der Zanden, *op. cit.*, pp. 76ff. and 148ff.; Jenkins, *op. cit.*, pp. 235ff.; Mall, *Rom. Forsch.*, VI (1891), pp. 139ff.; Koelbing in *Eng. Stud.*, I (1877), pp. 57ff.; Max Voigt in *Palaestra* 146, pp. 121ff. (for the bridge, sharp as a knife and trembling like a poplar leaf but getting firm and broad, see pp. 167ff.; and another, of wonderful height and length, pp. 235f.). For letters of safe-conduct to the Purgatory and the visit of William Staunton (and others) see Krapp, *op. cit.*, pp. 31ff. and 54ff.

[60] Van der Zanden, *op. cit.*, pp. 6 and 161; cf. Jenkins, *op. cit.*, pp. 242, 280, and 310; and Becker, *Medieval Visions of Heaven and Hell*, pp. 92–93.

[61] Cf. the description here (*Van der Zanden, op. cit.*, p. 17, cf. 170): "Et ecce in ponte illo erant tria transeuntibus ualde dubitanda: primum, quod ita lubri-

wilderness, the mountain, and the fiery river and fiery pit, are all familiar features in these visions, as are also the meadows with fruit trees and flowers and perfumed air. The icy river is simply a variant of the river of fire.

ELIZABETH OF SCHÖNAU. From 1156, according to the author of the *Libri Viarum Dei,* comes the account of the visions of the mountain of God which were granted to Elizabeth of Schönau. Almost on the Feast of Pentecost, as Elizabeth herself described her experience, she saw in a vision of her spirit ("in uisione spiritus mei") a "very high mountain" shining with an abundance of light on its summit:

> To the top led three roads. The middle one had the color of a stone of hyacinth; the right one was of green; and the left one of purple. At the top of the mountain stood a Man garbed in tunic of hyacinth color and girded with white, with face shining as the sun, eyes radiant as stars, hair like whitest wool, and in His mouth a sharp sword. In another vision, on Pentecost, more roads appeared: one delightful except for the fact it was full of brambles until halfway up; another narrow but full of flowers; a third broader and, as it were, paved with red sides and very dangerous. In another vision of the same scene on the octave of Pentecost, four other roads were visible: one was bordered with brambles; another was arid and difficult to ascend because of huge lumps; the other two were open and delightful. Elizabeth then expounded the meaning of all these details: "Mons excelsus, altitudo coelestis beatitudinis est; lux in uertice montis, claritas est uitae aeternae . . ."[62]

The influence here of the Book of Revelation is self-evident, especially in the description of the Man at the top of the mountain. The various roads with their symbolic interpretation represent something new. Here it may be appropriate to note the frequent appearance of the mountain in the apocalyptic visions of another

---

cus erat ut, si eciam latus esset, nullus aut uix quis in eo pedem figere posset; aliud, quod ita strictus erat quod fere intransibilis; tertium, quod ita altus erat quod horrendum esset deorsum aspicere." Cf. Jenkins, *op. cit.*, pp., 277–278 and 317. The width of the bridge here indicated recalls the similar detail in the *Vision of Tundale* and the *Vision of Sunniulf.* For influence also of the *Vision of Saint Paul* and that of Thurkel cf. Seymour, *op. cit.*, pp. 181ff.

[62] Migne, *Patr. Lat.*, CXCV, cols. 164ff.

twelfth-century lady, Hildegard of Bingen, such as the iron-colored mountain in the *Scivias* with windows in the sides in which human heads were visible. The mountain, we are told, signifies the strength and stability of God's kingdom.[63] Also she describes for us the mountain of hard white stone with shining mirror at its top,[64] and again in the *Scivias* the mountain on which is located the four-sided edifice surrounded by a double wall. The corners are directed to the four points of the compass.[65] The elaborate interpretation of the meaning of all this need not concern us here, except to note that the corners of the edifice designate Adam (the south corner), Noah (the eastern), Abraham and Moses (northern), and the Trinity (the western).

THE VISION OF GUNTHELM. According to Helinandus a novice lying on his pallet (in 1161), apparently more dead than alive, had a vision in which Saint Benedict appeared to him and guided him on a journey to the next world. Against the blows of demons they made their way up some steps until they came to a region of great light and pure air.

There they found a chapel suspended in the air, and in it a throng at whose center sat the Mother of Mercy like the sun among the stars. Next Saint Benedict led the novice to a flowery and delightful region where there were monks and novices. One of this company addresses the novice by name as Gunthelm, and sends a message by him to the abbot. After this experience Saint Raphael guides him through Paradise, where he sees the golden city, the beautiful gate, the garden of herbs and beautiful trees and singing birds. Here under a tree is a limpid fountain whose stream courses through the city, and here too is a tree of great height and beauty at the top of which is a man of great stature and beauty dressed in a costume of many colors. This is Adam, first father of mankind. The novice is next conducted to the region of darkness where he sees towers of smoke and flame, and later Raphael takes him to see Hell itself with its huge wheel of torture and the punishment of Judas. Finally Saint Raphael orders him to return to his body, and to tell nobody of his vision except the abbot. This injunction the novice disobeys by at once reporting what he has

[63] Migne, *Patr. Lat.*, CXCVII, cols. 385ff.
[64] *Ibid.*, col. 955.
[65] *Ibid.*, col. 577, and elsewhere in Book III.

seen, and he is then disciplined by Saint Benedict, who reappears for the purpose.[66]

In this narrative there is little of special originality. The journey up the steps is found elsewhere, for example in the ladder mounted by Saint Perpetua. The tree with Adam at the top is like the World Tree in general, as for example in the story of the tree in the Garden of Eden which Seth was allowed to behold. The chapel suspended in the air is, however, worthy of notice.

THE MONK OF EYNSHAM. The twelfth-century vision which was the privilege of a young monk at Eynsham (often confused with Evesham) is fairly well known in the Middle Ages:

A youth in the monastery at Eynsham (near Oxford), who had been ill a long time, and was found as if dead, had a vision of which he told on his return to consciousness. He was led, so he said, by a venerable old man who turned out to be Saint Nicholas, to a region of torments located in a marshy spot. "Thenne went we yestewarde [eastward] by a pleyn weye in a right path til we came to a certen regyon. that was ful wyde and brode and ouer horabulle and gastfull in sight. fowle and myry of thicke cley" where were a great number of people in torment.[67] They go on to a second place, a deep dark valley beyond a mountain: "we came to the seconde place of purgatorye and tormentys in the whyche was an hye hylle vppe al mooste to the clowdys and was deuyded fro the forseyde fyrste place of purgatorye. And thenne lyghtely and swyftely we wente on thys same hye hylle. And there was vndyr the farthyr syde of thys hylle a full depe valeye and a derke . . . ."[68] girt about with projecting ridges of rock. Here was a black

[66] Migne, *Patr. Lat.*, CCXII, cols. 1060–1063. On a Norse version see Liestøl, *Draumkvæde*, pp. 87ff., and for influence in Old Norse, see below, p. 122. On the colors of Adam's costume see p. 120 below.

[67] Caxton's rendering, *The Revelation to the Monk of Evesham*, ed. Edward Arber, p. 36. According to the Latin (*Romanische Forschungen*, XVI [1904], p. 661) "Ibamus igitur per uiam orientis tramite scilicet planam, quousque peruenimus ad regionem quandam spatiosam nimis, uisu horrendam, palustri situ et luto induritiem inspissato deformem." Cf. also *Analecta Bollandiana*, XXII (1903), p. 254.

[68] Caxton, *op. cit.*, p. 40. In the Latin (*Roman. Forsch.* XVI, p. 664): "Erat itaque sub remoto illius montis latere uallis profundissima et tenebrosa, altrinsecus iugis rupium eminentissimis cincta, cuius longitudinem nullius perstringeret aspectus. Ima eiusdem uallis, fluuium dixerim an stagnum nescio, tenebat, amplitudine latissimum, teterrimo latice horrendum, quod nebula foetoris indicibilis iugiter exhalabat." Cf. *Analecta Bollandiana*, XXII, p. 258.

pond with a foul mist over it. One side of the mountain gave forth fire; the other was cold with snow and hailstorms. Both sides of the mountain and the valley too were full of souls as hives swarm with bees. Some were drowned in the pond and from thence were taken up and cast into the fire and carried up like sparks to the other side of the mountain into the cold storms. This cycle was repeated.[69] The third place of torture was another large field full of sinners amid sulphurous smoke, foul mist, flame, and pitch.

Finally the monk saw Paradise. Here was a great crystalline wall, whose height no man could see, and whose length no man could measure. Here was a bright and shining gate marked with a cross, which rose to admit the blessed. Within all was bright with a glorious shining light. From the ground up to the top of the wall were steps, and the righteous who came in at the gate ascended these. There was no difficulty or toil for them in ascending, but the higher they went the more eager they became. And above was visible the Lord on His throne, and about Him five hundred souls who worshipped and thanked Him for His great mercy.[70] In Paradise was the marvelous sweet music of bells.[71]

The dark valley, which is fairly typical, the mountain of heat and cold, and the wall of Paradise, recall the *Vision of Tundale.* The somewhat ladderlike ascent to Heaven may recall the *Vision of Perpetua* but almost certainly is independent of it, belonging rather to a general tradition of the idea of Jacob's ladder.

THE VISION OF GODESCHALC. A twelfth-century vision is that recorded of the hermit Godeschalc. Here the only important fea-

[69] Cf. the version in Huber's text: P. M. Huber, *Beitrag zur Visionsliteratur und Siebenschläferlegende des Mittelalters,* I, p. 9, xiii. For souls ascending like sparks, cf. Plutarch's *Vision of Timarchus,* the *Vision of Drythelm,* and Migne, *Patr. Lat.,* CCXII, col. 1059.

[70] "Erant quoque ab imo usque ad summitatem eius gradus mira pulchritudine dispositi per quos ascendebant agmina letantium, mox ut fuissent per ianuam introgressi. Nullus fuit ascendentium labor, difficultas nulla, non quelibet in ascendendo mora, superior semper alacrius quam inferior scandebatur gradus. In plano itaque deorsum consistens deducebam longo oculorum intuitu per hos gradus in sublime ascendentes . . . ." *Analecta Bollandiana,* XXII, p. 315.

[71] For the whole vision and its date see Ward, *Catalogue of Romances,* II, pp. 493ff.; Becker, *Medieval Visions of Heaven and Hell,* pp. 93ff.; *Analecta Bollandiana,* XXII, pp. 225ff.; *Roger of Wendover, Chronica,* etc. ed. H. O. Coxe, III, pp. 97ff.; van Os, *Religious Visions,* pp. 68ff.

tures for us are: first, that he must cross a tract filled with thorns ("terra spinas et tribulos germinabat"), and secondly, that led by two angels on his tour, he sees a river filled with steel knives which he must get over on some boards. Sinners were cut by these knives, which makes one think of a similar river referred to in Saxo Grammaticus.[72]

THE VISION OF THURKEL. Early in the thirteenth century, Roger of Wendover tells us, Thurkel had his vision of being led by Saint Julian to a spacious church. In the middle of this, from what appeared to be a font, rose a great flame illuminating the whole edifice. Near the wall, on the outside, was the pit of Hell. On the eastern side, between two walls, was a purgatorial fire, and beyond was a large, cold salt lake, over which was a great bridge filled with nails and sharp stakes ("Deinde restabat pons magnus aculeis et sudibus per totum affixus quem pertransire quemlibet oportebat antequam ad montem gaudii perueniret. . . .") Here some souls went quickly and easily, but some slowly with great suffering from the stakes and the nails. Some were immersed to various heights in the lake. On the slopes of the Mountain of Joy was a great church, with a meadow near by in which were fragrant flowers and fruit trees and a fountain that gave source to four rivers of varied liquid and color. Over this fountain was a tree of great size bearing the choicest fruits and having the odor of spices. Here in this Earthly Paradise was Adam with one weeping and one laughing eye and a garment of various colors. The garden has a jewelled gate and a golden temple.[73]

The bridge in this account recalls that filled with nails in the

[72] For the vision see excerpts in *Scriptores rerum Brunsvicensium*, etc., G. W. Leibniz, I, pp. 870ff.: For the river, p. 872: ". . . fluuius erat ferreis aciebus repletus, quem transire oportebat . . ." and "ligna natantia sponte ad littus appulsa eos recipiebant et transuehebant, atque inter eos Godeschalcum." As for the sinners, "Hos flumen transituros acies illae conscindebant et carne priuabant." For a full summary cf. Liestøl, *Draumkvœde*, pp. 91ff. The reference in Saxo will be found above, pp. 66–67. The river may be Slith in the *Edda* (*Voluspá* st. 36) : cf. above p. 63.

[73] *Roger of Wendover, Chronica, siue Flores historiarum*, ed. H. O. Coxe, vol. III, pp. 190ff.; *Roger of Wendover's Flowers of History*, etc., trans. J. A. Giles, II, pp. 221ff.; ed. by H. L. D. Ward in the *Journal of the British Archeological Assoc.*, XXXI (1875), pp. 420ff. For the bridge see Ward *op. cit.*, p. 446, as quoted. For the beautiful mountain cf. Migne, *Patr. Lat.*, LXXXVII,

Vision of Tundale. The fire and the cold lake represent, it would seem, a use of the motif of heat and cold we have already found in the *Vision of Tundale* and other documents. The pleasant field on the Mountain of Joy is noteworthy, and also the borrowing of the four rivers from the Eden of the traditional Earthly Paradise. Probably from this source too comes the great fruit-bearing tree.

THE VISION OF OLAV ÅSTESON. In the Norse *Draumkvæde* from the early thirteenth century the story is told of the dream of Olav Åsteson, in which he visited the Other World in his long sleep which lasted from Christmas Eve until Epiphany. The poem has been described as "probably the most widely known and most fully discussed of the Norwegian popular ballads." [74] Ballad though it is, the piece offers a typical vision of the sort we have been considering in this chapter and indeed is in part clearly derived from works of that kind. It is especially interesting, therefore, as showing one striking bit of evidence of how far this material pervaded the popular mind and how far it traveled by oral and written tradition.[75] Sitting in the church porch,

---

col. 436. The Paradise is described, Ward, p. 458: ". . . loco amoenissimo et splendido herbarum et florum uarietate, arborum et fructuumque redolantia referto . . ." For the fountain: "Super hunc fontem extitit arbor pulcherrima mirae magnitudinis, immensae proceritatis, quae omnigenum fructuum abundantia ac specierum redolentia ubertim affluebat." Cf. also Seymour, *Irish Visions,* pp. 182–183, for the influence of Saint Patrick's Purgatory here; Becker, *Medieval Visions of Heaven and Hell,* pp. 96ff.; and van Os, *Religious Visions,* 74ff. Thurkel's vision seems to be reflected in the *Grande Chanson des Pèlerins de S. Jacques*: cf. G. G. King, *The Way of Saint James,* III, p. 271 and pp. 541–542; and an article by the same writer in *Romanic Review,* X (1919), pp. 38ff. On Spanish influence see also Ward, *Catalogue of Romances,* II, p. 510; and on Adam's robe as in the *Vision of Gunthelm* according to Helinandus, *ibid.*, II, pp. 510–511, and Migne, *Patr. Lat.,* CCXII, col. 1062. Cf. above, p. 117, and Becker, *Medieval Visions of Heaven and Hell,* p. 99.

[74] Knut Liestøl, *Draumkvæde,* p. 17. For the versions see *ibid.*, pp. 26ff., and for the date, pp. 128ff. Liestøl presents the two most important versions in Old Norse, pp. 134ff., and a translation, pp. 7ff. His study includes a thorough-going analysis of the vision motifs in the poem and the probable sources. He finds it "in the main based on three visions: Tundal's, Gundelin's [Gunthelm's], and, last but not least, Thurkill's," (p. 117). I quote from his translation.

[75] *Ibid.,* pp. 112ff. Cf. too, Dag Strömbäck, "Om Draumkvædet och dess Källor," *ARV,* 1946, pp. 35ff.

according to the *Draumkvæde,* Olav gives an account of his dream:

He has been up to the clouds and down to the sea and "fared over holy water and over the valleys low." He did not see the waters "for under the earth they flow." With his horse, accompanied by his dog, he went "through briar and thorn," and his scarlet cloak was damaged and the nails torn from his feet. His soul was drawn forth from his body through a narrow ring; the scarlet cloak again suffered and the nails were torn from his fingers. He came to the Gjallar Bridge "so high up in the air" decked all with red gold and gold pinnacles. A serpent, a dog, and a bull were there "fierce and wroth" to prevent passing over. Olav, however, went across the bridge and also waded a "miry marsh, where never a foot finds hold." The bridge, he tells us, was fitted with "sharp hooks in a row," and the marsh was stinking. He then came to the lonely lakes where "the glittering ice burns blue," and next over "lovely lands" where he saw "the shining Paradise." He saw too "the pilgrims' church" where he knew only his "blest godmother" with gold on her fingers, and hosts came riding from the north and the south. Saint Michael, leading that from the south, blows his trumpet for the judgment of every living soul. Olav now beholds the punishment of sinners and in the manner of the Beatitudes learns the reward for good deeds. Who gives shoes to the needy will not have to walk on the thorny moor; who gives a poor man a cow will not "trip or swoon" on the Gjallar Bridge; who gives the poor man bread will have no fear of the fierce dog's bark; who gives the poor man corn need not fear the bull's horn; who gives clothes to the needy will not be afraid of the glacier.

The resemblances here to other visions are obvious and hardly need much exposition. The identification of the ordinary bridge, familiar from the time of Gregory the Great in vision literature, with the Gjallarbrú of Old Norse shows the kind of combination of traditions we constantly meet, whether or not originally the idea of such a bridge came into Old Norse from the East or from Saint Gregory.[76] The thorny moor we have seen elsewhere, in the visions of Alberic and Godeschalc, for example. The miry marsh is familiar in the *Vision of the Monk of Eynsham.* The sharp hooks in the bridge recall the nails in the bridge seen by Tundale

[76] Cf. Liestøl, *op. cit.,* pp. 54 and 64ff., and Strömbäck, *op. cit.,* pp. 53ff.

and the nails and sharp stakes in that in Thurkel's vision.[77] The whole poem throws a curious light on the well-known *Lyke-Wake Dirge*, of a later time, but also popular in origin, where we find the thorns in the "Whinny-muir," and the bridge known as the "Brig o' Dread." In fact that production seems almost like a derivative from the last part of the *Draumkvæde*.

ÉTIENNE DE BOURBON. Also in the thirteenth century a vision was described to Étienne de Bourbon by a certain reliable man (*probus homo*), who said it came to his own father.[78] The man had been found cold in apparent death, but was restored to life with warm baths and other treatment. Thereupon he said that, when he had lain there as if dead, a voice summoned him and he was led to a field of great size:

> There he heard a great throng of dark and horrible spirits uttering terrible cries. After various experiences and pursued by the demons he came to the shore of a broad and foul river ("litus cujusdam fluuii et latissimi") which was full of fire, sulphur, horrible beasts, dragons, and serpents. Here he saw[79] a very narrow and very long bridge which seemed hardly half a foot in breadth and reached to Heaven. This he had to ascend with the demons after him; the ascent grew easier and easier until at the top he was greeted by the Virgin Mary, who led him back to his own chamber.

Here then is what we might describe as the orthodox account of the bridge, recalling Gregory the Great and Gregory of Tours.

GONZALO DE BERCEO. In the same period Gonzalo de Berceo describes a vision in his *Vida de Santo Domingo de Silos* in which

[77] With the serpent on the bridge cf. the dragon in the story of Erik the Far Traveler, p. 72 above.

[78] Étienne de Bourbon, *Anecdotes Historiques, Légendes et Apologues*. A. Lecoy de la Marche, pp. 38ff. In this case we seem to have the name of the very man who narrated the vision; for, according to the editor, Étienne has added a marginal note saying that the story was told him by Stephanus de Marusiaco "qui non est defunctus" (p. 39, n. 1).

[79] ". . . respiciens uidit pontem artissimum et longissimum, qui uix uidebatur dimidii pedis latitudinis et pertingere uidebatur uersus celum. Cum autem, necessitate compulsus, pontem ascenderet et leuius magis ac magis ascenderet, et demones post eum, sed uix et cadendo, postquam uenit ad summum, deficit ei pons . . . ." (p. 41).

we see a terrible river, mighty as the sea, fearful to cross, and a bridge of glass. The passage is unique enough to quote:

> Vedia me ensueños en vn fiero logar,
> oriella de vn flumen tan fuerte com̃o mar,
> qualquier abria mjedo pora el se plegar,
> ca era pauoroso e brauo de passar.
> Ixien delli dos rios, dos aguas muy cabdales,
> rios eran muy fondos, non pocos regaiales,
> blanco era el vno com̃o piedras christales,
> el otro mas vermeio que ujno de parrales.
> Vedia vna puente enna madre primera,
> auia palmo e medio ca mas ancha non era,
> de ujdrio era toda, non de otra madera,
> era, por non mentiruos, pauorosa carrera.[80]

At the end of the bridge he is met by two "barones" who honor him with crowns. In this account the river and the bridge belong without question to the oriental tradition; but the detail of the glass offers an interesting variant, and the two streams, one of crystal, one of red, show another original touch.

THE VISION OF THE THIRD ROBBER. From the *Fioretti* of Saint Francis, and from the *Actus* as well, we learn of the vision of the third robber, who did penance for his years of crime. One day after matins he was overcome with sleep:

"No sooner had he laid down his head than he was rapt and led in spirit to the top of a very high mountain ["in montem excelsum ualde"] over a steep place, and on this side and on that were broken and jagged rocks and monstrous crags that jutted forth from the rocks; wherefore this steep place was frightful to behold." Led by an angel, who flung him down the steep place, he suffered from the sensation that his bones had been broken by the rocks. The angel, however, bids him rise and heals him, and then shows him a "great plain, full of sharp and pointed stones and thorns and briars, and told him he must needs run across all this plain and pass over it with naked feet until he came to the end . . . ." Next he has to enter a furnace, and from this experience he is again healed.

[80] *La Vida de Santo Domingo de Silos,* ed. J. D. Fitz-Gerald, p. 41, lines 229ff.

He is then led to a "bridge, which could not be crossed without great peril, for it was very frail and narrow and slippery and without a rail at the sides; and beneath it flowed a terrible river, filled with serpents and dragons and scorpions, that it gave forth a great stench." He crosses to the middle and the angel flies to the other side up to the top of a high mountain leaving him helpless. He trembles for fear of the beasts, stoops and embraces the bridge with a prayer to God, whereupon he sprouts wings, and with these he attempts to fly up to the angel. But he falls back again and his wings drop off. Twice this happens. At last on the third attempt he attains to the door of the marvelous palace where the angel awaits him.[81]

Here the mountain and also the plain with stones and thorns and briars are traditional features, though more vividly presented than is usual. The bridge recalls the Purgatory of Saint Patrick and also Gregory's *Dialogues* with the addition of the motif of the wings.[82]

A vision of the same type has obviously influenced Saint Catherine of Siena in her *Libro della Divina Dottrina* where she speaks of the river and the bridge. The river is the tempestuous sea of this dark life. The bridge, of course, is the Incarnate Word, and though it is raised on high, it is not separated from this life. Walled about with stone, it has three steps: imperfect love, perfect love, filial love; and on crossing it, one reaches the gate of Eternal Life. In her letters, where she reflects the same idea, we learn also that some souls walk under the bridge — the sinners, the unjust; some seek refuge on the shore; some cling to the bridge and climb up by exercising virtue; and some sink into the bottom-

[81] *"The Little Flowers" and the Life of Saint Francis with the "Mirror of Perfection,"* trans. T. Okey, Miss E. Gurney Salter, and Robert Steele (Everyman's Library), ch. xxvi, pp. 47–52. The translation is based on the text of A. Cesari with help from the text of Passerini. See also *I Fioretti del Glorioso Messere Santo Francesco e de' suoi Frati,* ed. G. L. Passerini, cap. xxv, pp. 70–78; the *Actus Beati Francisci et Sociorum Eius,* ed. P. Sabatier, cap. 29, pp. 97ff.; Nino Tamassia, *S. Francesco d'Assisi e la sua leggenda,* pp. 193ff.; and H. W. L. Dana, *Medieval Visions of the Other World,* diss. unpubl., Harvard Univ., 1910, p. 151.

[82] For the bridge see *The Little Flowers,* Everyman's Library, p. 50, and *I Fioretti,* ed Passerini, p. 75. The text in the *Actus* runs as follows (p. 102, § 40): "ad quemdam pontem qui transuadari non poterat absque ingenti periculo, quia erat nimis angustus et excessiue politus. 41. Sub ponte uero fluuius terribilis defluebat serpentibus et draconibus, scorpionibus et bufonibus, et

less depths of the water.[83] Jorgensen thinks that Saint Catherine may have read the *Vision of Saint Galgano,* which has not been edited so far as I know but which, in the manuscript of which he has a report, runs as follows:

An angel appeared in a vision to Saint Galgano and said "Follow me!" Then Galgano with the greatest devotion followed him to a river, over which was a bridge. This bridge was very long and could not be crossed without the greatest labor. Beneath it was a mill which continually turned – signifying that all earthly things are in a continual state of flux. Passing beyond all this Galgano came to a delightful meadow.[84]

What follows in the manuscript we can guess with a fair degree of accuracy; for it is possible that this story was composed as early

horrendis fœtoribus plenus. . . ." Cf. also the use of the river, *The Little Flowers,* ch. xxxvi, p. 65 (*Actus,* 59, pp. 177ff.). The sources for the first part of the story of the three robbers are considered by Tamassia, *op. cit.,* pp. 193ff., and the analogues of this section go back to Gregory the Great; but the second part is not dealt with. The closest parallel I have noticed is the bridge over the river "spumans igne et corrupto sulfure" in a poem in a thirteenth-century MS printed by F. Böhmer in the *Zeits. f. d. Alt.,* V (1845), pp. 464ff. Note that here the righteous "induti uite pennis exuunt spurciciis" and cross with ease. This work is actually the *Visio de Gloria Paradisi* attributed to Joachim of Flora (cf. A. F. Ozanam, *Les Poëtes Franciscains en Italie au Treizième Siècle,* pp. 445ff.) and discussed by Francesco Mango in *Il Propugnatore,* XIX (1886) part ii, pp. 248f. Cf. also *Speculum* XXI (1946), pp. 343f. The vision includes a mountain with silver sides, ascent of which is made with a ladder. The plain of Paradise contains the usual elements. Oriental sources for the bridge motif in general are discussed, Mango, *op. cit.,* pp. 253ff.; the ladder is considered, *ibid.,* p. 255. In the poem itself cf. the negative formula for Paradise: "Abest anguis, abest rana, abest mala bestia" (Böhmer, *op. cit.,* p. 465, l. 53). The *Visio* is printed with other works of Joachim in *Expositio magni prophete Abbatis Joachim in Apocalipsim,* etc., Venice, 1527, p. 280. For the authorship see Henry Bett, *Joachim of Flora,* p. 23. Cf. the use of the ladder leading to the plain on "Montjoie de Paradis" in the *Voie de Paradis,* attributed by some to Raoul de Houdenc, in *Œuvres Complètes de Rutebeuf,* ed. A. Jubinal, III, pp. 213ff.

[83] *Santa Caterina da Siena, Libro della Divina Dottrina volgarmente detto Dialogo,* etc., ed. Matilde Fiorilli, pp. 43ff.: "E perchè Io ti dixi che del Verbo de l'unigenito mio Figliuolo avevo facto ponte . . . ." (p. 43); *Le Lettere di S. Caterina da Siena,* ed. Niccolò Tommaseo and Piero Misciatelli, IV, No. cclxxii, pp. 199ff.: ". . . dell' unigenito mio Figliuolo; del quale ho fatto ponte perchè tutti possiate giungere a gustare e ricevere il frutto delle vostre fadighe" (p. 203). Cf. Our Lady as bridge in the hymn, *Analecta Hymnica,* G. M. Dreves, I, p. 56, 14.

[84] Johannes Jorgensen, *Saint Catherine of Siena,* trans. Ingeborg Lund, p. 428, n. 5, and pp. 313f.

as the end of the twelfth century (Galgano died in 1181), and it seems to follow the manner of the others of this type. The mill, however, is an interesting feature and may recall the fiery wheel that accompanies the fiery river in the *Sibylline Oracles,* the *Apocalypse of Peter,* and the *Vision of Saint Paul* (where we also find the bridge). Reflections, on the other hand, of the general tradition are the "Pont qui tremble" in the *Grande Chanson des Pèlerins de Saint Jacques* [85] and the Brig o' Dread in the *Lyke-Wake Dirge,* both of a later period.

What seems to be generally indebted to material of this kind, although in this case the author himself claims an oriental source, and direct contact with Moslem literature is indicated,[86] is the first vision of Mirza in *Spectator* 159. Here, as Addison says he translates for us, Mirza ascended the "high hills of Bagdat" and sees a huge valley which is "the vale of misery," with a tide of water running through it which rises in thick mist at one end and again is lost in mist at the other. Across it is a bridge which "is human life" and which consists of threescore and ten arches with several broken ones bringing the total number up to something like a hundred. Once it had a thousand arches. At each end is a black cloud and over the bridge pass multitudes of people, of which several passengers fall through to the great tide beneath. It appears there are concealed trap doors that allow this. Vultures, harpies, ravens, cormorants, and "several little winged boys," which are the vices, hover near. Mirza is permitted to look beyond the mist at the end so that he sees that the valley opens into an immense ocean where are "innumerable islands" covered with fruits and flowers. These are the "mansions of good men after death." In this account the mountain, the valley, the river, and the bridge are all familiar elements in the Latin visions, but the

[85] *The Way of Saint James,* G. G. King, III, p. 541 and above p. 121, n. 73. The *Lyke-Wake Dirge* is printed in the *Oxford Book of English Verse,* No. 381, pp. 443–444.

[86] "When I was at Grand Cairo I picked up several Oriental Manuscripts, which I have still by me. Among others I met with one entituled, *The Visions of Mirza . . ." Selections from the Writings of Joseph Addison,* ed. Barrett Wendell and C. N. Greenough, p. 165. Cf. for another vision, in which there is a plain, a fountain, two rivulets, a column of diamond, and a black tower, *Spectator* 524.

ocean with its islands suggests the Celtic — or in this case more probably a classical antecedent.

But perhaps the most interesting reminiscence of all is the satiric use of the vision in Rabelais's *Pantagruel,* where Epistemon, who is at one point found "stark dead" with his head cut off, is restored to life and tells of his journey to Hell and the Elysian fields. He lists the people he has seen. For example, "All the knights of the Round Table were poor laboring slaves, employed to row over the rivers of Cocytus, Phlegeton, Styx, Acheron, and Lethe, when messieurs the devils had a mind to recreate themselves upon the water . . . ."[87] The classical element is obvious enough, but the whole pattern of the vision and its narration derives almost certainly from the medieval idea. Finally the journey to the land of the dead has been the subject of a modern study on the basis of Freudian psychology,[88] including an interpretation of the river, the bridge, the animals that in some accounts guard the bridge, and the fate of the damned and the saved, omitting only the framework of the vision or dream in which the soul, duly warned, returns for further life and activity.

Characteristic motifs that appear in many of these visions of the life after death include the following: the ascent; the river barrier or the fiery river, sometimes accompanied by the bridge; the mountain as barrier or as a feature in general; the dark valley; the wall as barrier. The ascent, which is found commonly in Hebrew lore and in Gnostic works, often adds the detail of a critical glance back at the earth. So it is in the *Apocalypse of Zephaniah* so-called, in the *Testament of Abraham,* the *Vision of Saint Paul,* and the *Vision of Saint Salvius.* Angels usually conduct the soul; but in the *Narrative of Zosimus* it is a storm, and in the *Vision of Alberic* a bird like a dove. In the *Vision of Fursa* when the soul looks down, what he sees is a dark valley that, in the light of other accounts, is probably Hell.

[87] *The Works of Rabelais Faithfully Translated from the French,* p. 207 (*Pantagruel,* II, ch. xxx); *Œuvres de François Rabelais,* ed. Abel Lefranc, IV, p. 311.

[88] Géza Róheim, *Animism, Magic, and the Divine King,* pp. 39ff., with a survey of the oriental instances and modern folklore accounts. For a considerably broader interpretation of the symbolism of the bridge see *Harvard Journal of Asiatic Studies,* VIII (1944), pp. 196ff.

The use of the river motif is general. As a barrier it is found in the *Apocalypse of Baruch,* the *Shepherd of Hermas,* the *Vision of Saint Paul* (where we are told that it is the ocean), the *Narrative of Zosimus* (with a wall of cloud), the *Dialogues* of Gregory (where it is black and smoky), in the *Vision of Godeschalc* (filled with steel knives), and in the many instances where it is burning. Fiery rivers appear in the Gnostic fragment, in the *Sibylline Oracles,* in the *Visio Esdrae,* in the *Apocalypse of Peter,* in the *Apocalypse of the Virgin,* as well as in the visions of Saint Paul, of Sunniulf, of the monk of Wenlock (a pitchy river), of Adamnán (fiery glen), of Alberic, and of the Knight Owen (*Saint Patrick's Purgatory*). In the *Visio Esdrae,* in Redaction IV of the *Vision of Saint Paul,* and in the other visions just listed, it is combined with the bridge, which is also found with a foul river containing dragons and serpents in the *Vision of the Third Robber,* and with a river (which is the tempestuous sea of this dark life) described by Saint Catherine of Siena and apparently taken from the *Vision of Saint Galgano.* In the *Vision of Tundale* there are two bridges, one over a deep valley, and one over a stormy lake. In the *Vision of Thurkel* the bridge spans a large, cold salt lake. In both instances the bridge over the lake is full of sharp nails. The Gjallar Bridge in the *Draumkvæde* is fitted with a row of hooks. Sinners are immersed to various levels in the fiery stream in the visions of Saint Paul, Sunniulf, the monk of Wenlock, and Alberic; and in the ice-cold waters in the account of Thurkel. The use of the contrast between cold and heat in the torture of sinners appears in the visions of Saint Paul (Redaction IV), Drythelm, Tundale, and the monk of Eynsham, where we have reference to regions part hot and part cold. Burning ice is in the Old Norse *Draumkvæde.*

The mountain, too, is a constant element in descriptions of this kind. The celestial realm in the *Apocalypse of Zephaniah* seems to be above the mountain Seïr, at least by implication. In the *Apocalypse of Baruch* there is a "very great mountain" with a serpent on it. The *Apocalypse of Peter* recalls the holy mountain of the Jews. From a breast-shaped mountain in Arcadia the Shepherd of Hermas sees twelve more mountains which in their variety almost recall the islands of the Celtic *imram.* In the

Vision of Wettin appear two mountains of great height and incredible loveliness, round which flows a fiery stream, making one think for an instant perhaps of the pillar in the *Sibylline Oracles* surrounded by the "river inexhaustible of fire." In the same vision is also the purgatorial mount reserved for the cleansing of the abbot on its top. The *Vision of Charles the Fat* tells of fiery mountains from which come burning rivers; according to the *Vision of Laisrén,* two mountains stand at the mouth of a cave, another at the very mouth of Hell. The last of these is black with a large glen in the upper part. In the *Vision of Tundale* there is a vast mountain, over which goes the narrow road bordered by fire on one side, and snow and ice on the other. In *Saint Patrick's Purgatory* a tempest sweeps naked souls from the top of a high mountain down to an icy river; and, according to the monk of Eynsham, the place of torment has one mountain followed by a deep, dark valley, and another giving forth fire on one side and cold with snowy storms on the other. The *Vision of Thurkel* shows the motif as the scene of the Earthly Paradise with meadow and garden and gate. The third robber, according to the *Little Flowers,* sees himself flung from a very high mountain down broken and jagged rocks, recalling a little the cliff down which sinners were hurled in the *Apocalypse of Peter.*

I have presented more details in the review of this theme because the tradition appears to be more varied than in the case of the river. Even so, it is clear, I think, that it can hardly derive from the Celtic *síd* or even from the hollow mountain of the Germanic. Like the fiery river, it seems definitely to be related to Jewish and oriental material; and the nature of the narrow (*angustus*) and slippery bridge points in the same direction. From the same source too may come the widespread reference to the dark (*tenebrosa*) valley, which seems deliberately to call up the image of "the valley of the shadow of death" of the twenty-third Psalm, and all the biblical associations of the region (e. g. Isaiah, ix:2). The idea is reflected also in the "deep and dark" places in the Book of Enoch.[89] In the *Sibylline Oracles,* it is true, we are told of Gehenna in "midnight gloom" "where darkness is

[89] See p. 14 above.

supreme," and of the "darkening shades" of Tartarus; the underworld is gloomy according to the *Odyssey*. But doubtless a psychological coincidence plays its part in all this material, as in other related fields; and Norse allusions to the realm of the Goddess Hel, which was certainly not too cheerful, may have had some added influence.

In the *Life of Saint Pachomius* we have an early reference to the deep, rocky valley, where sinners lay plunged in darkness, like the "deep and awful ravine" mentioned by Caesarius of Heisterbach. Fursa, according to Bede, saw a dark valley beneath him as three angels took him heavenward. A broad and deep valley with fire on one side and cold on the other is described in the *Vision of Drythelm*. The deep valley appears again in the *Vision of Bernoldus,* in that of Saint Anscar, in that of Charles the Fat (with the neighboring part delightful and most splendid), in that of Adamnán (plains, bare and parched), in that of Laisrén (the glen in the mountain), in that of Flodilda, in that of Tundale (*ad uallem ualde terribilem ac tenebrosam*), in *Saint Patrick's Purgatory* (the dark wilderness), and in that of the monk of Eynsham (a deep, dark valley). A thorny path leads to the place (and there is also a thorny valley) in the *Vision of Alberic,* recalling in a way the woods around Hell according to Heriger's prophet. A thorny moor is in the *Draumkvæde*; and a thorny plain is in the *Vision of Godeschalc,* and another appears to the third robber in the *Little Flowers*. Thorny brakes are in the land of pain in Adamnán's vision. In all this we may think of the "certain place precipitous" in the *Shepherd of Hermas,* where the sheep are caught in the thorns and thistles.[90] The approach to the region is actually underground according to the *Vision of Laisrén* and *Saint Patrick's Purgatory* as well as in Guibert Nogent's account of his mother's dream.[91]

As the approach to Hell is forbidding, so the path to Paradise or Heaven is delightful (*amoenissima*): for example, in the *Vision of Rotcharius* and in the *Vision of Saint Anscar*. The desired country may be surrounded by a wall, as in the fourth

[90] Cf. such biblical passages, however, as Isaiah vii:24.

[91] Cf. J. A. MacCulloch, *The Harrowing of Hell,* for a study of the descent.

Heaven (a river wall) of the Gnostic fragment (where Hell too has walls — of red-hot iron), the *Vision of Drythelm,* the *Vision of the Poor Woman* (two walls), the *Vision of Adamnán* (seven crystal walls), the *Vision of Tundale* (a silver wall and one of pure gold), and the *Vision of the Monk of Eynsham* (a crystal wall of vast size. In the *Vision of Adamnán* there is also a silver wall and one of fire in Hell too. Gates or doors into this region there are, of course: in the *Apocalypse of Zephaniah* (iron gates that scatter fire), the *Apocalypse of Baruch* (very great doors), the *Apocalypse of Ezra* (a narrow entrance), the *Testament of Abraham* (one narrow gate and one broad), the *Vision of Saint Paul* (twelve gates), the *Vision of Barontus* (four gates, the third of glass), the *Vision of Adamnán* (six guarded doors), and the *Vision of Thurkel* (a jeweled gate of the garden). A meadow is usually found within, and flowers and trees, with a perfume that has special properties in the *Vision of Salvius,* the *Vision of Drythelm,* and the *Legend of Saint Barlaam and Saint Josaphat.* Nearly always a fountain is here: in the *Sibylline Oracles* (three, of honey, wine, and milk), in the *Vision of Tundale* (the fountain of life), the *Vision of Adamnán* (a spring, § 16, that refreshes the righteous and annoys and scalds the wicked), and the *Vision of Thurkel* (the source of the four rivers). In Hell too the fountain sometimes appears, as in the case of the two fountains, one tepid, one hot, in the *Vision of Charles the Fat.* The four rivers of the garden of the Earthly Paradise (Phison, Euphrates, Geon, and Tigris, taken straight from Eden) are in the *Vision of Saint Paul;* and four others, like a counterpart but classical in origin,[92] appear in the region of pain in the *Vision of Saint Paul* and the *Vision of Adamnán.*

The trees are sometimes remarkable. In the *Sheperd of Hermas* one of the twelve mountains is covered with trees abundant with fruit. In the *Vision of Tundale* is a vast tree covered with flowers and fruit and birds. In the *Vision of Thurkel* a tree of great size stands over the fountain, vaguely reminding one of Yggdrasil, but bearing fruits and giving a spicy odor. The Tree of the Knowledge of Good and Evil is in the *Vision of Saint Paul.*

[92] Cf. Silverstein, *Visio Sancti Pauli,* pp. 65f., for the influence of Virgil.

Speaking or singing trees appear in the *Testament of Abraham* and the *Vision of Perpetua* (rose trees), while the trees in the legend of Barlaam and Josaphat seem to carry a reminiscence of music. Souls in the form of birds surround the fiery chair in the *Vision of Adamnán,* and three stately birds sing the canonical hours. In Hell bird-souls fly through the flames in the *Vision of the Monk of Wenlock.* One may also remember, in this connection, the wings that sprout, birdlike, on the robber who attempts to cross the bridge in the *Little Flowers.*

Such are the most conspicuous features of these visions, of which the most distinctive seem to be the river, often fiery, the bridge, the mountain as barrier, and the deep and dark valley. The wall of the celestial region, however, may also be mentioned and the varied gates or doors.

V

JOURNEYS TO PARADISE

BESIDES THE ACCOUNTS OF THE VISIONS of life after death, medieval literature gives us various descriptions of journeys to the Other World, some of which purport to be founded on fact. These frequently have to do with the Earthly Paradise or some island retreat, probably because these were the easiest to manage in a matter-of-fact narrative before the days of aviation. The Garden of Eden was universally believed to exist, and, although cut off from ordinary approach, was supposed still to be waiting for the saints before their ascent to Heaven. Medieval maps often showed its location. Travels of this type are sometimes legendary in nature, and the story of *Saint Patrick's Purgatory* might well be considered in this part of the study, although it shows an underground realm; but I have classified it instead with the visions to which its material is so obviously allied. Discussions of the general character of Paradise are common as a part of the use and transmission of the Book of Genesis by the Church Fathers, who also, it must be remembered, commented on the Book of Revelation and gave it currency. People of the time must have been led to think of Eden as scarcely "behind the beyond," but about as remote and just as accessible as certain other marvels – deserts, rich mountains, and strange seas, the nature of which is often quite analogous – of which travelers to the East told them. For the Garden was not of the "stuff of dreams" but was quite materially real to their minds, as Edoardo Coli has noted in a study which shows how widely the idea was spread.[1]

[1] Edoardo Coli, *Il Paradiso Terrestre Dantesco.* I am much indebted to this work for guidance in this chapter. Cf. p. 60: "È singolare questo affaticarsi a sostenere la materialità del Paradiso Terrestre anche a costo di sacrificare quello celeste, pure di non consentire a quei rari uomini di senno che sotto le parole Mosaiche videro o intravidero l'etnica e cosmica verità." Cf. also Baring-Gould, *Curious Myths of the Middle Ages,* pp. 242ff.

Something of a sense of the reality of the place for the popular imagination may be gained from a passage in Tertullian, where he argues that the poets derived their accounts of the Elysian Fields from this source: "And if we speak of Paradise," he observes,[2] "a place of divine beauty (*diuinae amoenitatis*) appointed to receive the spirits of the saints, severed from the knowledge of this world by that fiery zone as by a sort of enclosure, the Elysian plains have taken possession of their faith." So, too, Justin Martyr maintains that Homer took the words of Moses for the garden of Alcinous in the *Odyssey*.[3] But if the poets have borrowed from our religion, Tertullian goes on to say, then our accounts are truer "as being of earlier date" and "have higher claims upon belief." Theophilus of Antioch placed the scene in a middle region between heaven and earth,[4] Saint Irenaeus regarded it as the third heaven to which Paul the Apostle was rapt, and Hilary of Poitier had the same idea.[5] The proposal, however, was rejected by Athanasius,[6] who records another suggestion — that Paradise was in Jerusalem — as also mistaken: Scripture teaches it is in the East, and the fragrance of the trees in the Orient and near India suggests the neighborhood. But eventually the inference that the Garden shared something of earth and something of Heaven led to the further idea that it was on a high place, a mountain, a detail easily added in the Hebrew tradition.

An allegorical interpretation of the description of the Garden

[2] *Apology*, xlvii, in the *Ante-Nicene Fathers*, A. Roberts and J. Donaldson, III, p. 52. Gehenna, "a reservoir of secret fire," he relates to Pyriphlegethon, "a river among the dead." For the Latin see Migne, *Patr. Lat.*, I, col. 587; *Tertullian, Minucius Felix*, T. R. Glover, G. R. Rendall and W. C. A. Kerr, pp. 210–211 (Loeb Libr.); and *Tertulliani Apologeticum*, ed. H. Hoppe, *CSEL*, LXIX, p. 112 (xlvii, 13). I have modified the translation of the *Ante-Nicene Fathers* in part.

[3] *Justini Philosophi et Martyris opera quae exstant omnia*, etc. p. 28 (*Ad Graecos Cohortatio*).

[4] *Ibid.*, p. 366 (section 24, lib. ii), with an allegorical interpretation of the features of the Garden. Cf. also Coli, *op. cit.*, p. 69.

[5] *S. Irenaei contra omnes haereses libri quinque*, ed. A. Stieren, I, 728; and for Hilary, Migne, *Patr. Lat.*, X, cols. 172–173.

[6] *Quaestiones ad Antiochum*, q. xlvii (*Opera omnia*, II, p. 227). So too Epiphanius, *Adversus Haereses*, II, i, lxiv (Migne, *Patr. Gr.-Lat.*, XXIII, col. 577.).

was advised by Origen,[7] who, however, believed in the literal truth of Paradise as a place on earth for the reception and instruction of the saints after death.[8] The same view was held by Cyprian, who saw in the region the likeness of the Church, whose trees are watered with the four rivers of the Gospels.[9] The tendency further to read symbolical meaning into the Garden was followed by Saint Ambrose, Saint Jerome, Saint Augustine, Saint John Chrysostom, and others. All this writing spread more widely a knowledge of the details of the scene.

Most of the features which characterize Eden remain fairly constant. The trees are luxuriant, the fruits abundant; a river runs there, parted into four streams – the Gihon, the Phison, the Hiddekel, and the Euphrates; and there too are found the Tree of Life, and the Tree of the Knowledge of Good and Evil. Speaking of the trees, Philo (at the beginning of the first century A.D.) says that the Garden is full of all sorts, some everblooming, some coming into blossom every spring, some with fruit for man and some with fruit for the animals, and all these are endowed with a soul. But he adds, "This description is, I think, intended symbolically rather than literally; for never yet have trees of life or of understanding appeared on earth, nor is it likely that they will appear hereafter." [10] Flavius Josephus (also in the first century) briefly mentions the same details and refers to the same rivers: "Now this garden is watered by a single river whose stream encircles all the earth and is parted into four branches." [11] What these are and where they go occupies his attention for a moment. But the problem bothered other writers still more; for if the streams of Paradise represent, as they seemed to, the Ganges, the Euphrates, the Tigris, and the Nile, where do they meet? The suggestion was soon forthcoming that to accomplish their courses

[7] *De principiis,* IV, §16. See too his commentary on *Genesis* where he puts Eden "in the middle of the earth" like the pupil in the eye. However, he is not the first to interpret in this way: cf. Philo, *On The Creation,* and *On Genesis,* in *Philo,* F. H. Colson and G. H. Whitaker, I (Loeb Libr.).

[8] Origen, *ibid.,* II, ch. xi.

[9] *Ep.,* LXXII, 10 (R. E. Wallis, trans., *The Writings of Cyprian,* p. 266).

[10] *On the Creation,* 153 (*Philo,* I, p. 123). Cf. also, *Thesaurus patrum flores doctorum,* V, p. 188, *s.v. Paradisus.*

[11] *Josephus,* H. St. J. Thackeray, IV, p. 19 (*Antiq. Iud.,* I, 38, Loeb. Libr.).

they travel in part underground,[12] but it remained a suggestion and was not universally adopted. For the general description of the Garden, what are almost set formulae were established regarding its perfection; and many of these we find as early as the poetic account falsely attributed to Tertullian: "Est locus Eois Domino dilectus in oris"; the light is clear, the air wholesome; "Est secreta Deo regio"; the fields are fertile, the flowers rich, the air fragrant; [13] here gems have special lustre (the emerald [*prasinus*] and the carbuncle),[14] the trees are fair with fruit; "Nulla cadunt folia, et nullo flos tempore defit"; a lake is here, also a fountain whose stream divides in four parts; eternal spring reigns; no cold or night may be found, anger and treachery are absent; but Faith sits on the throne, and whoever fears God and is righteous has a place here and praises the Lord.[15] These lines apparently are indebted to the Latin poem (usually ascribed to Lactantius) *De aue phoenice,* which certainly in turn borrows the Earthly Paradise for the purposes of its own mythology.

Many of the details are the same: "Est locus in primo felix oriente remotus"; spring reigns here; nor death, nor illness, nor age, nor fear, nor any other evils may here be found; no storm or cold do injury; "Est fons in medio, quem uiuum nomine dicunt"; it floods the land each month; and here is a great tree laded with fruit. But one important difference is, we are told, that this smooth plain is on a very high plateau:

[12] Cf. Pomponius Mela, *De Situ Orbis,* I, ix (on the Nile); Bede, in Migne, *Patr. Lat.,* XCI, cols. 45–46 (*Hexaem.* i); Theodoretus, Bishop of Cyrrhus, *In Genesim, xxix* (Migne, *Patr. Gr.-Lat.,* XLI, cols. 755–756); and F. Cabrol and H. Leclercq, *Dict. d'Arch. Chrétienne,* XIII, cols. 1603–1604. The article last referred to contains references to the Garden as represented in art, cols. 1607ff.

[13] The fragrance of the trees of Paradise is a common theme, and one may see the idea in the Babylonian *Talmud, Seder Neziḳin* II, trans. I, Epstein, p. 652, where the leaves fill Rabbah b. Abbuha's robe with perfume.

[14] *Lapis prasinus* and *carbunculus* are an old rendering for what is translated (from Gen. ii, 12) as *bdellium* and *onyxus* in the Vulgate. Cf. Jerome, *Liber Hebr. Quaest. in Gen.* ii, 12 (Migne, *Patr. Lat.,* XXIII, col. 989). Choice stones in Caesar's diadem were carried by birds over "the fiery mountain" from Adam's Paradise according to the Irish translation of Lucan, *Irische Texte,* Stokes and Windisch, IV, 2, p. 389.

[15] Sixth century perhaps. Tertullian, Migne, *Patr. Lat.,* II, cols. 1151–1152 (*De iudicio domini, viii*). For the authorship and date of this poem see Martin von Schanz, *Geschichte der römischen Literatur,* IV, 2, § 1165, pp. 396f. (*Handbuch der Klassis. Altertumsw.,* VIII).

Sed nostros montes, quorum iuga celsa putantur,
Per bis sex ulnas imminet ille locus.[16]

The mountain barrier here is worth noting, and also, further along, the very considerable use of the negative formula, nec . . . nec: "Nec Mors crudelis nec Metus asper adest . . ." with much more.

Another poetic account which may also have influenced the pseudo-Tertullian is the passage in Cyprian's lines on Genesis. Here too are about the same features: the Tree of Life, a river divided into four streams (with their names, Phison, Gihon, Tigris, and Euphrates), gems (the emerald and the carbuncle), the fields and the fruit, but all more briefly.[17] Here, however, are dwellings by the river. A very brief description of the same pleasant (*amoena*) fields, leafy groves, and the four rivers, where perpetual spring reigns, is also found in the *Cathemerinon* of Prudentius.[18] Spring and summer are here too in the remarkable *Cento* of Falconia Proba, where we find the flowers and perfume, liquid fountains, the vine and the laurel, in a uniquely Virgilian background for the first couple.[19]

The *Cento*, however, stands by itself as an ingenious composite of verses taken straight from Virgil. How far the other poetic accounts are interrelated with one another or contribute to the

[16] E. Baehrens, *Poetae Latini minores,* III, pp. 253ff., for the whole description. The Old English version of this in some points seems closer to the lines in the pseudo-Tertullian: the Lord made this spot remote; no blossom falls from the trees; a holy fragrance spreads through the land. See *The Exeter Book,* ed. G. P. Krapp, E. V. K. Dobbie, pp. 94ff. Cf. also Cook, *The Old English Elene, Phoenix, and Physiologus,* pp. liiff. Baehrens (*op. cit.,* p. 250) notes that Gregory of Tours refers to Lactantius "de Phoenice," but with an account that differs in some respects from the Latin poem we know: here, too, however, is the fountain and the great fruit tree. Cf. also Sidonius Apollinaris, (Migne, *Patr. Lat.,* LVIII, col. 654): "Est locus oceani, longinquis proximus Indis"; "Axe sub Eoo . . ."; "Ver ubi continuum est . . ." Note especially, "Hic domus Aurorae rutilo crustante metallo." One may also compare something of the phraseology in the opening of Claudian's description of the land of the dead (*In Rufinum* i, 123); "Est locus extremum pandit qua Gallia litus," etc.

[17] R. Peiper, *Cypriani Galli poetae Heptateuchos, CSEL,* XXIII (1881), p. 3.

[18] *Cath.* III, 101ff. (Migne, *Patr. Lat.,* LIX, col. 803); and *Prudentii carmina,* ed. J. Bergman, *CSEL,* LXI (1926), p. 17. Cf. also *Cath.,* V, 113ff. (Migne, *op. cit.,* LIX, cols. 826–827), with reference to the fragrance of Paradise.

[19] *Poetae Christiani minores, CSEL,* XVI (1888), *Probae Cento,* ed. C. Schenkl, pp. 578–579 (ll. 157–172).

pseudo-Tertullian, it is very difficult to say. In all of them the typical ideas and mode of expression, or even the verbal formulae and the vocabulary itself, continue in a way that challenges the reader to discriminate between borrowing and coincidence. One might say that apart from the words in the Book of Genesis, an orthodox way of describing the Garden of Eden was pretty well established. The tradition goes on, and we may take for example the verses of the fifth-century African Dracontius: "Est locus in terra diffundens quatuor amnes;" it is filled with flowers and their perfume, and so on. According to an accurate and felicitous modern rendering:

A place there is diffusing rivers four,
With flowers ambrosial decked; where jewelled turf,
Where fragrant herbs abound that never fade,
The fairest garden in this world of God.
There fruit knows naught of season, but the year,
There ever blossoms earth's eternal spring.
Fair vesture clothes the trees, a goodly band;
With leaves and sturdy branches well entwined
A dense-grown wall arises; from each tree
Depends its store, or lies in meadows strewn.
In sun's hot rays it burneth not, by blasts
Is never shaken, nor doth whirlwind rage
With fierce-conspiring gales; no ice can quell,
No hailstorm strike, nor under hoary frost
Grow white the fields. But there are breezes calm,
Rising from softer gust by gleaming springs.
Each tree is lightly stirred; by this mild breath
From moving leaves the tranquil shadow strays . . .[20]

Further along, "Ver ibi perpetuum communes temperat auras." Hardly an idea is left out; hardly anything new introduced. The suggestion of a medicinal benefit to be derived from the leaves is like an echo of the promise of the Book of Revelation that they shall be "for the healing of the nations": "Pendet et optatae uiuax medicina salutis." [21] But the line is rather ambiguous.

[20] From *Latin Writers of the Fifth Century* by Eleanor S. Duckett, copyright 1930 by Henry Holt and Company, Inc., p. 85. For the Latin see Migne, *Patr. Lat.*, LX, cols. 704ff. (*Carmen de Deo*, I, 178ff.).

[21] Cf. Arturo Graf, *Miti, Leggende e Superstizioni del Medio Evo*, p. 22, with a parallel in the *Talmud*.

And the reference to a wall, which is rather interesting in view of the motif of the wall of heaven in the visions, is hardly more than figurative. The style, with some use of the negative formula (". . . no ice can quell," etc.), is familiar.

So, too, in the well-known passage written by Avitus *De mundi initio* appear the same features: "Est locus eoo mundi seruatus in axe"; "Secretis, natura, tuis . . ."; the air is always pure; no changes of season, but "uer floribus occupat annum"; no winds rage, no clouds appear; roses and lilies and other flowers are here, and fragrance and a light breeze; and a fountain flowing forth in the usual four streams with jewels.[22] Everything is about what we should expect, though rather sumptuously described, with more information about the rivers, and some discussion of the forbidden tree. One feature, however, is important: the grove of Paradise is on an inaccessible height ("lucus inaccessa cunctis mortalibus arce . . ."). The usual formulae appear also in the *Alethia* of Claudius Marius Victor: "Eoos aperit felix qua terra recessus"; "aeternum paribus uer temperat horis"; the trees are full of fruit; the flowers are fragrant; the jewels are here, the carbuncle and the emerald, and the four rivers with discussion of their courses (the Tigris for a time goes underground in caverns). But one feature is distinctive: the leaves of the trees are stirred —

sonat arbore cuncta
hymnum sylua deo, modulataque sibilat aura
carmina . . . .

Singing trees we have encountered in the visions,[23] and the idea here may represent one more bit of evidence of an oriental source; but I am willing to admit the possibility of mere coincidence.

Perhaps as a sort of offshoot from the poetry we have been considering, the poem *De ligno vitae* by an unidentified author uses at times similar material. It begins: "Est locus ex omni medius,

[22] Migne, *Patr. Lat.*, LIX, cols. 328ff.; also, *Auctores antiq., MGH,* VI (ed. R. Peiper), 208ff.

[23] See above pp. 90f. For the whole description see the edition of Victor by C. Schenkl, *CSEL,* XVI (1888), pp. 372–375 (*Alethias* i, 224ff.) and pp. 446–447 (Gen. i:224ff.).

quem cernimus, orbe." It speaks of the Tree of Life in the same way:

> Ecce sub ingenti ramorum tegminis umbra
> Fons erat: hic, nullo casu turbante, serenus,
> Perspicuis illimis aquis, et gramina circum
> Fundebant laetos uario de flore colores.

The fruit of the tree made strong the weak and healed the sick, and by its branches they found possible the ascent to Heaven:

> Hinc iter ad ramos, et dulcia poma salutis:
> Inde iter ad coelum per ramos arboris altae.[24]

Here we may be reminded of the *Vision of Saint Paul* in a passage summarized in the preceding chapter: "And I entered in further and saw a tree planted, out of whose roots flowed waters, and out of it was the beginning of the four rivers, and the spirit of God rested upon that tree, and when the spirit breathed the waters flowed forth." [25] It recalls still more, of course, the Tree of Life "on either side of the river" of life in the Book of Revelation (xxii:2), whose leaves are healing.

As Graf has observed, the descriptions of the Earthly Paradise are innumerable and continue even to our own day.[26] Doubtless in their early use of the mountain motif and their account of rivers, flowers, and fruit, they influenced some of the visions. It is unnecessary as well as impossible to list them all, and only the chief examples need occupy our attention. We have already noted how Athanasius remarked on the fragrance of Paradise, which affected the trees of even neighboring regions. He discusses, too, the question as to whether the fruit is incorruptible, and decides that compared with ordinary fruit it is, but that it is yet inferior to the glory of Heaven.[27] The discussion in *Oratio III* on Paradise [28] formerly attributed to Saint Basil gives material not unlike

[24] Migne, *Patr. Lat.*, II, cols. 1171–1174.

[25] M. R. James, *The Apocryphal New Testament*, p. 549.

[26] Graf, *Miti, Leggende e Superstizioni*, p. 31. For a reflection of Genesis and also Revelation see the lines in the *Altus Prosator* of Saint Columba, *The Irish Liber Hymnorum*, J. H. Bernard and R. Atkinson, I, p. 78, ll. 86–91.

[27] *Opera*, II, p. 228.

[28] *Sancti Basilii opera omnia*, I, Pars Altera, pp. 493ff.

that in the Latin poetry. As man is remarkable among created beings, so his home was made to be excellent, surrounded by limpid air with temperate climate. All unpleasant elements are excluded by a string of negatives — no winds, no storm, no ice, not the humidity of spring nor the heat of summer nor the dryness of the autumn; storms circle about the spot. The land flows with milk and honey and is abundant with edible fruits, and floral meads are here and birds and gentle animals. A river is here that in its course irrigates all Eden. Any comparison with our mortal life is injurious because it must range so far from the truth. *The Liber de Paradiso* of Saint Ambrose deals chiefly with the interpretation of the well-known features: the Tree of Life, the Tree of the Knowledge of Good and Evil, the fountain, the four rivers.[29] The Phison incidentally contains gold, the carbuncle, and the emerald. And the rivers, we may note, signify the four cardinal virtues.[30] The beasts of the field and birds of the air in Paradise represent the emotions and wandering thoughts. According to Ephraim Syrus, who thus develops an idea already suggested elsewhere, Paradise is located on a very high place and looks down on the highest of our mountains.[31] He himself has seen it with "the eye of the mind." Because of its eminence it was uninjured by the flood, but, high as it is, the righteous may ascend it without difficulty. It has all the traditional beauties and fragrance, the Tree of Life and the Tree of Knowledge. There the righteous have houses made of clouds. And it lies about the sea and the earth and contains them within itself.

In commenting on the phrase "in monte sancto Dei" and a reference, in Saint Paul's Epistle to the Hebrews, to Mount Zion and the city of the living God, the heavenly Jerusalem, Saint Jerome remarks, "Vel certe mons sanctus Dei, paradisus (ut diximus) intelligendus est." [32] Even if what he referred to was the spiritual Paradise, he shows how easily the two traditions were merged and the idea of Eden on a mountain top was maintained.

[29] C. Schenkl, *CSEL*, XXXII, 1 (1897), pp. 265ff.; and Migne, *Patr. Lat.*, XIV, cols. 291ff. Cf. also Migne, *op. cit.*, XVI, cols. 1191ff.

[30] The idea that the rivers represent the four cardinal virtues is found in Philo's *Allegorical Interpretation*, i, 63 (*Philo*, I, pp. 188–189).

[31] *Thesaurus patrum*, V, pp. 192ff.

[32] *Comm. in Ezech*, IX, xxviii (Migne, *Patr. Lat.*, XXV, col. 272).

In the same period, however, Saint John Chrysostom discusses the spiritual realm, but definitely places the earthly Paradise on earth.[33] In the same way, with some discussion of the Tree of Life and the rivers (according to which the main stream has an underground course after watering the garden, and thus conceals the approach), Severianus seems at times to have the heavenly kingdom in mind, but still asks why the Lord placed Eden in the east. It is because, he says, the course of heaven's luminaries is from the east to the west. The east is the beginning of life for men, and thus God signifies the future: the resurrection from the dead. In the west, therefore, where the stars set, is the place of death – an interesting inference in view of Celtic ideas.[34]

In this problem of the literal truth of Paradise, Saint Augustine observes that there are three general opinions: one by which its physical reality is understood and accepted; one by which it is taken in a spiritual and so figurative way; and a third by which at times it is understood as a material fact and at times interpreted spiritually. The third view is the one which he himself favors; so for him Paradise undoubtedly signifies the place in which man was first created, but it may also have a spiritual meaning, and he discusses the interpretation of the trees and the rivers.[35] But he recognizes also the spiritual paradise not only in derivative meaning but as an actual region – in fact, every place wherein it is well with the soul or where blessed souls are.[36] He continues the analysis of the symbolism elsewhere – the Tree of Life is wisdom, the four streams are the four cardinal virtues (an idea he may have taken from Saint Ambrose), the carbuncle is radiant truth and the emerald is eternal life.[37] In all these passages the

[33] *In Genesim sermo VII,* and *In Cap. I Genes. Homil. XIII.* Cf. Migne, *Patr. Gr.-Lat.,* XXIX, cols. 614 and 108.

[34] *De Mundi creatione oratio V,* §§ 5ff. (Migne, *Patr. Gr.-Lat.,* XXX, cols. 477ff.)

[35] *De Genesi ad litteram* viii, 1ff., (*Sancti Aureli Augustini de Genesi,* etc., ed. J. Zycha, *CSEL,* XXVIII, 1 [1894], pp. 229ff.). Note the reference to the subterranean course of the river, *ibid.,* 7 (p. 242).

[36] *Ibid.,* xii, 34 (pp. 430ff.).

[37] *De Genesi contra Manicheos* II, ix–x (Migne, *Patr. Lat.,* XXXIV, cols. 202–204). Cf. also *De civ. Dei* XIII, xxi (*CSEL,* XXXX, 1 [1899], ed. E. Hoffmann, pp. 645–646): the streams are also the four Gospels, the garden is the Church, the fruit trees the saints, and so on.

usual elements as found in Genesis remain constant with little change,[38] and the chief point appears in the consideration of what they properly signify.

After stressing the fact that Paradise is in the middle region of the east (κατὰ τὰς ἰσημερίας της ἠοῦς), Philostorgius discusses at some length the course of each of the four streams. Near the Phison grows the fruit or flower called *karyophyllum,* which, according to inhabitants of the district, comes from one of those trees that grew in Paradise; and anyone attacked by fever will be freed from disease if submerged in this river. Beyond is a district that is desert and barren. The Tigris and the Euphrates flow partly underground. As for the Nile or Gihon:

> This river then, if one may conjecture, takes its rise in Paradise, and before reaching any inhabited region, its waters are absorbed by the sand, whence it makes its way secretly into the Indian Sea, and there takes a sort of circular course, — for what man knows anything accurately concerning this matter, — and then passing under all the intervening continent, makes its hidden passage into the Red Sea, on the other side of which it eventually appears again beneath the mountain which is called after the Moon. There it is said to form two great fountains, situated at no great distance from each other, and throwing their waters up to a great height from below. The river then falls down a steep ridge of cliffs and passes through Æthiopia into Egypt."[39]

Here is an interesting jumble of many features ("for what man knows anything accurately concerning this matter"), but in a strange order at least we have the subterranean rivers, the mountain of the moon, the cliffs, the two fountains, and apparently for the garden itself, the desert barrier. Noteworthy too is the brief item regarding the healing power of the Phison for those who are bathed in its waters.

Under the word "Asia" in his *Etymologiae,* Isidore of Seville

[38] Note the echo of the negative formula: "Sicut in paradiso nullus aestus aut frigus, sic in eius habitatore nulla ex cupiditate uel timore accidebat bonae uoluntatis offensio," *De civ. Dei,* XIV, xxvi (*CSEL,* XXXX, 2 [1900], pp. 53, 21–23).

[39] From the epitome made by Photius of the *Ecclesiasticae historiae,* iii, 10, in *The Ecclesiastical Hist. of Sozomen, also the Eccles. Hist. of Philostorgius,* E. Walford, ed., pp. 449–450. For the Greek see *Eccles. hist. libri XII,* pp. 36ff. Cf. Migne, *Patr. Gr.-Lat.,* XXXV, cols. 249ff.

describes Paradise: it is located in the East; it is a garden of delights, and here is every kind of tree and fruit, including the Tree of Life; "non ibi frigus, non aestus; sed perpetua aeris temperies"; in the middle is a fountain that waters the whole grove and separates into four streams; it is surrounded by a wall of fire almost reaching to Heaven (with flames like swords).[40] Under the word "Insulis" he distinguishes this region from the Fortunate Isles, of which the tradition was still familiar.[41] In his *Differentiae* he distinguishes between two Paradises, the earthly and the heavenly; [42] and in his *Quaestiones in Vetus Testamentum* he interprets the allegory of the Earthly Paradise (the garden is the Church, the four rivers are the four Gospels, and so on).[43] In all this two features are of special interest in this study. First, in Isidore's awareness that the Earthly Paradise may be confused with the Fortunate Isles, the implicit suggestion is that the garden is situated on an island itself, an idea in harmony with hints found elsewhere, like that in Josephus regarding the way in which the river encircles the whole earth, and the evident way in which the description of Eden has influenced the far-off realm of the Phoenix. Secondly, the wall of fire is found in Tertullian and Lactantius, and here receives special emphasis.[44] Bede, with some echo of Augustine, speaks of the tradition that the Garden of Eden in the East is separated from the rest of the world by a very long space, either of ocean or of land, and was untouched by the flood; and he discusses at some length the jewels and the course of the four streams (including a subterranean journey).[45] While Paradise may represent the Church or a type of future

[40] *Isidori Hispalensis Episcopi etymologiarum siue originum Libri XX,* ed. W. M. Lindsay, II, XIV, iii, 2–3. For a poetic derivative from Isidore see Raby, *Secular Latin Poetry,* I, p. 158: note the line, "non est aestas neque frigus."

[41] Lindsay, *op. cit.,* XIV, vi, 8.

[42] Migne, *Patr. Lat.,* LXXXIII, col. 75; cf. also LXXXIV, cols. 926ff.

[43] Migne, *op. cit.,* LXXXIII, cols. 216f.

[44] Tertullian: *De anima,* lv, implies a wall; it is found in *Apol.* xlvii. For Lactantius see *Diuin. Inst.* II, *De origine erroris,* xiii (Migne, *Patr. Lat.,* VI, cols. 323–324).

[45] *Hexaem.,* i (Migne, *op. cit.,* XCI, cols. 43ff.). Much vaguer reflections of the tradition, at about this time, appear in the visions of Paulus Emeritanus (Migne, *op. cit.,* LXXX, cols. 119 and 121) and Saint Valerius (Migne, *op. cit.,* LXXXVII, cols. 431 and 433).

fatherland, we may not doubt, he says, that the place was and is on earth.

At this point it may be especially apropos to recall the fact that the Book of Genesis found its way, through paraphrase, into the vernacular languages and thus had a wider influence. Of this sort of literature I may mention simply the older Genesis in Old English, with its description of "Neorxnawang" filled, as the poet says, with gifts for man, with a fountain, and the four rivers: "Not at all did dark clouds carry rain over the spacious ground," but the earth was adorned with fruit.[46] In general, the material faithfully follows the reading of the Vulgate.

The comments and discussion go on with many writers. As man was created with both a visible and an invisible nature, observes John of Damascus, so Paradise has a physical and a spiritual reality. It was located in the East:

> In Oriente omni terra sublimior positus fuit, probeque temperatus, ac subtilissimo purissimoque aere undique collustratus, plantis nunquam non floridis uernans, suauissimo odore et lumine plenus, elegantiae omnis, quae quidem in sensum cadat, et pulchritudinis cogitatum superans, diuina plane regio. . . .[47]

Thus the old formulae reappear. We can well understand how the author of this passage may also have composed the corresponding vision in the Legend of Barlaam and Josaphat already considered. With regard to the four streams, however, he seems not quite ready, like certain others, to adopt the idea that they flow underground, but he does take the ocean as the river which Scripture says flowed forth from Paradise.[48] Here, too, are the well-known trees. Rabanus Maurus repeats, at times verbally, some of the material we have found in Augustine and Bede: Paradise has a real existence and is also a type of the future fatherland; it is separated from us by a long space of ocean or of land; it is so high it was untouched by the waters of the flood;

[46] *Die Ältere Genesis,* ed. F. Holthausen, p. 8, 206ff. For "Neorxnawang" see R. Jente, *Die mythologischen Ausdrücke im altenglischen Wortschatz* (*Angl. Forsch.* LVI), pp. 226ff. (iv, § 139).

[47] *De fide orthodoxa,* II, xi (Migne, *Patr. Gr.-Lat.,* XLVII, col. 464). Also cf. *S. Ioannis Damasceni, Opera omnia,* I, pp. 170ff.

[48] *De fide orthodoxa,* II, ix (Migne, *op. cit.,* XLVII, cols. 460–461).

some of the rivers go underground; Paradise is the Church, the rivers are the four cardinal virtues, and so on.[49] These are the established ideas, and it is not surprising to find some of them again much later in the *Sententiae* of Peter Lombard: [50] there are three ways of taking Paradise (as a physical realm, as a spiritual realm, sometimes as one and sometimes as the other); it is hidden from us, being separated by a long intervening space, of sea or of land – "et in alto situm, usque ad lunarem circulum pertingentem, unde nec aquae diluuii illuc peruenerunt." Rabanus also has the material, obviously derived from Isidore of Seville, regarding the wall of fire.[51]

In the tenth century Mosis Bar-Cepha made much of the problem as to whether there is a physical or a spiritual Paradise, dividing his treatise to devote a part to each. He discusses the whole matter thoroughly, deciding that there are not two Paradises but one, which is to be considered both mystically and as a physical fact. From the latter point of view, it is located on earth, in the east, and beyond an ocean; it is far higher than any part of the earth which we inhabit, as one can tell from the fact that its four streams flow down on the rest of the world; never were such trees and such fruits; the river which waters Paradise goes under the ocean and reappears (with God nothing is impossible); in the garden is the Tree of Life and the Tree of Knowledge of Good and Evil. In the second part of the work the mystical interpretation of these features is discussed: Paradise is the spiritual life; the four rivers are the four cardinal virtues or the four Evangelists, and so on.[52] In this treatise of Bar-Cepha, the great altitude of Paradise and the ocean barrier are both worthy of note.

The old formulae and the old vocabulary continue with various authors. Arnold of Bonneval has much to say: the beauty

[49] Migne, *Patr. Lat.*, CVII, cols. 476ff.

[50] *Sententiarum libri quatuor*, ii, dist. xvii (Migne, *op. cit.*, CXCII, cols. 686–687; also *Ad claras aquas*, 2nd ed., 1916, I, pp. 385–386).

[51] Migne, *op. cit.*, CXI, col. 334.

[52] *Mosis Bar-Cepha Syri, Maxima bibliotheca veterum patrum et antiquorum scriptorum*, etc., Leiden, 1677, XVII, pp. 457ff.; Migne, *Patr. Gr.-Lat.*, LVII, 2, cols. 247ff. Bar-Cepha quotes some material from a treatise by Philoxenus, Bishop of Mabbugh, including (col. 258) the statement that Paradise is in a middle region between heaven and earth.

of the place (*amoenitas*) was befitting to man who was made in the image of God; no hail or snow here, nothing sad and nothing corrupt; "non erat febris, et iam erat antidotum; nulla adhuc naturae defectio, et iam languorum remedia germinabant"; "neque horror hiemis, neque ulla intemperies ingreditur, sed continua ueris fixa est nouitas cum ex ipsius temporis harmonia quaecumque ibi sunt, in augmento sint . . ."

superne in ramis cedrorum uel aliarum arborum phoenix uiuax psallebat, et psittacus, et multiplici concinentium auium sono una erat consonantia: quorum hilaris uniuersitas laudabat secundum modum suum auctorem suum, in uice exsultationis iubilans Creatori . . . . Aliae singulae uolucres de statu praesentis uel futurae Ecclesiae praecinebant quasi quaedam oracula . . . .

In this instance I rather suspect that the song of the birds praising God is a figure of speech, rather than part of some mythological tradition; but, whatever be the case, it is elaborated at some length: "sed siue per arctas siue per amplas faucium fistulas circumflexiones iubilorum impellerentur, ascensiones et descensiones uocum conuenientibus in unum differentiis ad unius puncti reuertebant harmoniam."[53] Saint Bernard of Clairvaux develops the allegorical interpretation: here again the four streams are the four cardinal virtues, as they are also with Gottfried of Admont, Alexander Neckam, and others.[54]

By the twelfth century, then, the idea of the Earthly Paradise was fairly well established in many respects: it is located in the east, it is cut off from the rest of the world by its high location, or its ocean barrier, or perhaps by a fiery wall, its features are the familiar ones in Genesis described with almost a traditional form and vocabulary. Thus *De imagine mundi* (from about 1100),

[53] Migne, *Patr. Lat.*, CLXXXIX, cols. 1535ff. Helinandus also describes Paradise in the *Vision of Gunthelm, ibid.*, CCXII, col. 1062.

[54] Bernard of Clairvaux: *Genuina sancti doctoris opera,* II, col. 746; cf. *Opera genuina,* III, p. 145, *Sermo* CXVII (*fontes quatuor, id est, ueritas, caritas, uirtus, sapientia*); also Migne, *Patr. Lat.*, CLXXXIV, col. 1072, and CLXXXIII, cols. 741–742; Gottfried of Admont: Migne, *op. cit.*, CLXXIV, col. 147. Other interpretations are of course suggested for the streams, the trees, and other features. Cf. also Peter Damian, Migne, *op. cit.*, CXLV, col. 844; Hugh of St. Victor, Migne, *op. cit.*, CLXXV, cols. 638ff.; Alexander Neckam, *De naturis rerum,* II, ii (ed. Thomas Wright, p. 128, *Rolls Series,* XXXIV).

borrowing from Isidore of Seville, speaks of it as a region in the east, "locus uidelicet omni amoenitate conspicuus," with a fiery wall reaching to heaven, with the Tree of Life, the fountain that divides into four streams (which flow underground), and beyond it a desert waste with serpents and wild beasts.[55] Abelard quotes the material found in Bede, Isidore, and others, and in discussing the rivers observes that in Paradise there is but one, which once outside divides into four streams.[56] *De situ terrarum,* attributed doubtfully to Hugh of St. Victor, briefly describes the garden under the topic Asia "et partibus eius": it is in the east; has every kind of tree and fruit; "non ibi frigus est, non aestus, sed perpetua aeris temperies"; and it has a fountain that divides into four streams.[57] From the twelfth-century *Account of Elysaeus,* based partly on a letter of the legendary Prester John, comes also the information that the Earthly Paradise is at the top of four mountains in India (access to which is impossible because of a barrier of darkness), and there too is the fountain whose four streams (Tigris, Geon, Phison, and Euphrates) bring down precious stones and fragrant apples. If anyone even smells of these apples he has no desire to eat or drink, and they have a healing property.[58] The author of this document, whoever he was, contributed other material (from eastern sources or the letter or his own fertile imagination) which was useful for subsequent Otherworld accounts: for example, he sanctifies the idea of a mountain by saying that the Apostle Thomas was buried in a church at the top of one (in a stone tomb with four precious stones in it that can hold it up in the air); he tells of an elaborate palace, with many jeweled columns, some with carbuncles in the top which shed an amazing light, and describes its twelve rich

[55] Migne, *Patr. Lat.,* CLXXII, col. 123; borrowed by Gervase of Tilbury, *Otia imperialia* (ed. G. W. Leibnitz, *Scriptores rerum Brunsvicensium,* I), p. 911. The *Imago mundi* was translated into French, and from one of the French versions into Caxton's *Mirrour of the World* (ed. O. H. Prior, *EETS:ES,* CX). The French and the English add "giants rough and hairy" to the desert waste.

[56] Migne, *op. cit.,* CLXXVIII, cols. 775ff.

[57] Migne, *op. cit.,* CLXXVII, cols. 209–210.

[58] Ed. F. Zarncke, *Der Priester Johannes, zweite Abh., Abh. der . . . Königl.-sächsischen Ges. der Wissenschaften, Phil.-Hist. Cl.,* VIII, Leipzig, 1883, p. 123. For the rivers see also *ibid.,* 124 and 168, and *Abh.* VII (Leipzig, 1879), p. 839 and p. 912.

doors, its garden with a golden tree and golden birds of all kinds.[59]

Most of the accounts I have been considering are in prose, but the poetic descriptions also continue. Theodulph of Orleans (*fl. c.* 800) wrote some charming verses dwelling less on the strictly traditional motifs than on the flowers and fruits and trees:

> Primus amoena tenens factoris munere rura
> Helisii celsi tum bene factus homo,
> Floribus umbriferis uitam peragebat in aruis,
> Quo, paradise, tuus uernat amoenus ager.

Fruits and flowers never fail here. The scene is more redolent, I think, of Elysium than of the Book of Genesis, but at any rate the Tree of Life is included:

> Arbor in inmensum spaciatur nomine uitae
> Helisii medio e uertice surgit eri.
> Mille soporatas profert pulcherrimus herbas
> Campus inauditas, quas dat amoenus ager.[60]

Situated in the east, with temperate climate and a pleasant stream, the Paradise of Bernard Silvester also abounds with herbs and

[59] Vol. VIII, pp. 123 and 125f., §§ 15 and 35ff. For the location of Thomas's tomb see the letter of the Patriarch, *Abh.* VII, p. 840. In later accounts based on the letter of Prester John note the turning castle, VIII, p. 167, § 33: "Et ibi est speciale palacium presbiteri Iohannes et doctorum, ubi tenentur concilia. Et illud potest uolui ad motum rotae, et est testudinatum ad modum coeli . . ." For others, VIII, p. 168, § 37; cf. p. 167, § 34. See p. 160: "Die sich drehenden Palasträume . . . scheint er sogar aus französischen Romanen herübergenommen zu haben . . . ." Note also, p. 165, the rocky mountain and underground river; p. 168, the "terra feminarum," the island where women do not die; p. 170, the island of fruits and flowers and flying creatures singing sweetly (where the travelers spent three days and nights, although it seemed only three hours — "Et ibi non erat nox. Et uocatur illa insula 'radix paradisi' "); p. 170, the Earthly Paradise on a mount (high and steep, like a tower, so that none can gain access; the wall shines in the sun like a star). The land of Prester John extends from India to the Babylonian desert and the Tower of Babel, according to the original letter (*Abh.* VII, p. 910, §§ 12ff.): it flows with milk and honey; the river Ydonus is here, flowing from Paradise and bringing jewels of all kinds; at the foot of Mount Olympus is a grove, where the Fountain of Youth is located; the dry sea and stony river are near this land; an underground river carrying precious stones is here; also the palace of Prester John with jeweled columns and carbuncles for light. Zarncke traces the tradition of this material in other documents, including *Mandeville's Travels.*

[60] *Poetae Latini aevi Carolini,* ed. E. Dümmler, I, p. 573, *MGH.*

flowers and fragrance.[61] According to Alexander Neckam, the mountain peak on which the garden is situated is so high it almost touches the sphere of the moon; [62] no sterile tree is there, nor storm of winds with dense clouds; nor did it know the waters of the flood:

Hic mons, a prima nascentis origine mundi
Conditus, aurorae regna propinqua tenet.

And hither came Enoch and Elijah to enjoy tranquil peace,[63] and here are clear springs and precious fruits. Godfrey of Viterbo's description is somewhat more in the traditional manner: "Est locus excisus, nullo prius ordine uisus"; here grows the Tree of Life; the four rivers are mentioned and the jewels; here are apples whose fragrance alone is healing.[64] It is so high, it escaped the deluge, and it is far in the east.

Intellectual authority may speak for the Middle Ages in the writings of the Dominican Thomas Aquinas and the Franciscan Bonaventura, and also in those of the reputable encyclopedists. Saint Thomas Aquinas quotes the familiar dictum of Saint Augustine regarding the three general opinions that may be held and accepts the literal truth of Scripture. While he believes the garden is located somewhere in the east, he takes figuratively the idea that Paradise reaches to the sphere of the moon. He accepts the theory that the rivers flow underground, and that the region is shut off by mountains or seas or some "torrid region." In the same way he keeps the idea of the Tree of Life as a material fact, and he admits the possibility that Enoch and Elias still dwell in the garden.[65] Saint Bonaventura also quotes the observation of

[61] *De mundi universitate,* I, iii (ed. Barach and Wrobel, pp. 24–25). There is another scene of the kind with perpetual spring and all the rest in the region assigned as the home of Physis, II, ix (pp. 52f.)

[62] So Peter Lombard, above, p. 147. Cf. also Neckam, *De naturis rerum,* II, xlix (Neckam, *Rolls Series,* p. 159): it is higher than the lunar sphere; and Gervase of Tilbury, *Otia Imper.* (ed. G. W. Leibnitz, *Script. rer. Brunsvicens.,* I), p. 892.

[63] *De laudibus divinae sapientiae,* v, 35ff. (Neckam, *Rolls Series,* p. 441).

[64] *Pantheon,* ed. J. Pistorius (*Germanicorum scriptorum,* etc., 3d ed., B. J. Struve, II), pp. 29 and 58. For other poetic accounts see Graf, *Miti, Leggende,* pp. 152ff. Cf. also Peter Damian's *Hymnus,* Migne, *Patr. Lat.,* CXLV, cols. 861ff.

[65] *Summa theologica,* I, q. cii, *art.* i–ii. (*Opera omnia,* ed. Pope Leo XIII, V, pp. 448ff.). Translated by the Fathers of the English Dominican Province, IV, pp. 364ff.

Augustine and the material from Bede; he also rejects the theory that Paradise reaches the lunar sphere but believes it is on an elevated place where the air is pure. Perhaps his most important comment is on the question of the spiritual and the corporeal Paradise where he says there are both. One is in the Church militant and one in the Church triumphant: "Paradisus autem corporalis locus est deliciarum et amoenitatis. . . ." [66] The encyclopedists quote the old material to much the same effect. According to Vincent of Beauvais, borrowing from Isidore of Seville, Paradise is in the east; it is a garden of delights; it has all sorts of fruit trees including the Tree of Life; "Non ibi frigus: non estus"; it has a temperate climate; here is a spring dividing into four streams; and it is surrounded by a wall of fire.[67] So too with the *Polychronicon* of Ralph Higden, who gives specific reference to Saint Jerome, Isidore of Seville, and others: Paradise, we learn, is on a height from which its waters fall; the rivers are listed; the reality of the earthly region is accepted; the idea that it is as high as the moon is rejected because, among other reasons, it would cause an eclipse of the moon; it is temperate and its trees and flowers fade not; it is surrounded with a wall of fire.[68] So too with *De proprietatibus rerum* of Bartholomew Anglicus, where the same authors are quoted and the same ideas presented, including (from Isidore) the distinction from the Fortunate Isles; an interesting detail lies in the fact that when the waters fall from the hill of Paradise they make such a roar men are born deaf there.[69] Brunetto Latini tells us in the *Tesoro* [70] that Paradise is in India, not an unfamiliar suggestion: here is an abundance of fruit and trees, the Tree of Life, and the

[66] *Libr. sententiarum,* II, dist. xvii (*Opera omnia,* ed. A. C. Peltier, III, pp. 1ff.).

[67] *Speculum maius,* lib. xxxii, c. 11 (*Bibliotheca mundi seu Speculi maioris,* Douai, 1624, IV, p. 24).

[68] *Polychronicon Ranulphi Higden . . . with the English Translations of John Trevisa* etc., ed. C. Babington, I (*Rolls Series*), pp. 66ff.; also in *Life in the Middle Ages,* G. G. Coulton, II, pp. 28ff.

[69] *De propr. rerum,* Nuremberg, 1492, Hain-Copinger *2510, Proctor 2073, lib. xv, cap. xii; trans. John Trevisa, ed. Wynkyn de Worde, 1496, lib. xv, c. xi.

[70] In the Italian rendering of Giamboni, III, ii (ed. P. Chabaille, *Il Tesoro,* II, p. 28). For the French see *Li Livres dou Tresor par Brunetto Latini,* ed. P. Chabaille, p. 161.

rivers; "non v'ha nè freddo, nè caldo, se non perpetuale tranquillitade e temperanza"; the place is closed to all mankind. The ideas reappear in part in his *Tesoretto:* here is every delight without cold or heat or anger or grief; here are the rivers and the gems.[71]

From the testimony also of medieval maps we get some of the same material: Paradise is in the east, surrounded by wall or mountains, and sometimes cut off by an ocean.[72] The result in general in nearly all our evidence is the same. Whatever barriers made approach difficult, this earthly region was a place in actuality located somewhere on the globe, and it was a place therefore that might be visited by travelers even if they had to have recourse to supernatural means. The literature on the subject was immense.[73] With all due variations, the constant features of all this mass of writing of the early authors and the later ones, the encyclopedists, and makers of maps, are the following: Paradise is in the east (India or Asia, or perhaps so far as to be at the other side of the world); it is cut off from man because it is located on a high mountain[74] or by the ocean or by a fiery wall, or by more than one of these, making it an island;[75] it contains a garden with an abundance of trees and fruits and flowers which, in some accounts, are unfading, in some have a medicinal value; the fragrance of the fruit or the flowers is sometimes emphasized; the Tree of Life, the fountain, and the four streams with their names,

[71] *Il Tesoretto e il Favoletto di Ser Brunetto Latini*, G. Batista Zannoni, pp. 41–42 and pp. 79ff. (vi, 33ff. and xi, 15ff.). Also in the edition of B. Wiese, *Zeits. f. roman. Philologie*, VII (1883), ll. 458ff. and 943ff.

[72] So J. K. Wright, *The Geographical Lore of the Time of the Crusades*, pp. 71f. and 261ff., with much useful material. The idea that Paradise was in Asia was not universal: cf. *ibid.*, 262; it was in Africa in the earlier Leardo maps: cf. Wright, *The Leardo Map of the World*, p. 36. See also Coli, *Paradiso Terrestre*, pp. 93ff., with important reproductions.

[73] In addition to English, German, and French paraphrases of the Book of Genesis and other vernacular renderings, the commentaries of the Church Fathers and the like, cf. also Graf, *Miti, Leggende e Superstiz.*, pp. 111f., note 125.

[74] The constant features according to Coli (*Paradiso Terrestre*, pp. 60–61) are that it is in the east (according to the Bible), that it is on a mountain (from the Hebrew sacred mountain), and that it is a garden.

[75] Coli, *op. cit.*, pp. 111ff., gives maps showing the island motif. Cf. above, pp. 144–145, with regard to Isidore of Seville's distinguishing the region from the Fortunate Isles.

and the jewels, all as in Genesis, are mentioned almost everywhere; and sometimes there is reference to the birds and even the animals of the garden. In literary expression the negative formula (no winter, no summer, but only a temperate climate) is commonly adopted and sometimes much elaborated. As for the matter of climate, even where the garden is on the equinoctial circle the air is clear and agreeable and spring reigns. Of all these elements, perhaps none is so general or so likely to show influence when it appears elsewhere as the four rivers and their names. Finally we may note the tendency, from Philo on, to interpret these rivers allegorically as the four cardinal virtues.

The garden, the Tree of Life, and Adam and Eve, were represented, of course, over and over again in medieval art until indeed they appeared on the stage in the drama of the time.[76] It is interesting to see how often the rivers alone appear as an independent unit in new combinations with other figures. Christ depicted as standing on a mountain with the four rivers issuing therefrom is not unusual in painting.[77] From early times there are many examples also of the Agnus Dei on the mountain with the same streams, as on an early sarcophagus and in the sixth century mosaic of the Church of Saints Cosmas and Damian in Rome.[78] In one of the capitals in the abbey church at Cluny the rivers appear as the four cardinal virtues.[79] The Tree of Life and the rivers are found in the celebrated manuscript of the *Hortus deliciarum* of Herrad of Landsberg;[80] they represent the four Evangelists in a copper engraving of the thirteenth century;[81] and they are found again in the font of the cathedral at Hildesheim, roughly of the same period,[82] interpreted as both the

[76] See e.g. D. C. Stuart, *Stage Decoration in France in the Middle Ages,* pp. 103, 118, 197.

[77] Cf. Louisa Twining, *Symbols and Emblems,* p. 36, pl. xvii, fig. 4. Cf. also *ibid.,* pl. xxxvi, fig. 8 (the cross on the mountain).

[78] M. Didron, *Christian Iconography,* trans. E. J. Millington, I, p. 67, fig. 23, and J. R. Allen, *Early Christian Symbolism in Great Britain and Ireland,* p. 42 (cf. also pp. 35, 37, and 54).

[79] *Speculum,* VII (1932), plate iiid, opposite page 27.

[80] Ed. A. Straub and G. Keller, plate viii, f. 19*ro*. Note also the combination of the motif with Abraham, plate lxxvii.

[81] Twining, *op. cit.,* pl. xlviii.

[82] M. Viollet-le-Duc, *Dict. raisonné de l'Architecture Français,* V, 540.

cardinal virtues and the Evangelists. It is no wonder then, with these and many other examples, that they appear in the hymns,[83] and they are reflected ironically in the "Four Rivers which spring for Epicureans from the source of lust" in the *Policraticus* of John of Salisbury.[84] In Wolfram von Eschenbach's *Parzival*, the heathen enemy of King Amfortas came from the land where "Flow the streams of the River Tigris" from Paradise, and to the region they send for "Some plant from the wondrous garden" for healing.[85]

With the general certainty implied in all this material that Paradise is actually located somewhere on earth, even if exalted by a mountain to a higher level, it is not strange that travelers went in search of it, and it was inevitable that stories should be told of their occasional success. Foundation of sorts for this appears in the *Legend of Seth*, the story of the son of Adam who at his father's bidding went back to the garden to obtain the Oil of Mercy promised by our Lord. In an early form of this (the Latin version is of the third or fourth century A.D.) Eve as well as Seth makes the journey; they are stopped by the snake, and do not get the oil, but return instead with nard, crocus, calamus, and cinnamon. In one manuscript we read that the angel gives Seth a branch with three leaves from the Tree of Paradise but he drops it in the river Jordan.[86] The story was transmitted in various forms and is found incorporated in the legend of the Holy Cross with interesting elaborations. Here in its most popular version Seth follows a green path (*uiam uiridem*) marked by Adam's and Eve's footsteps back to Eden, which is eastward. The path begins at the head of a valley. When he arrives, he is stupified by the splendor of Paradise, thinking it a burning fire. Its

[83] F. J. Mone, *Lateinische Hymnen des Mittelalters,* I, pp. 159–160; P. G. Morel, *Lat. Hymnen des Mittelalters,* p. 26. Note also the reference to the one river of Paradise in the farced Epistle, Du Méril, *Poésies Populaires Latines du Moyen Age,* p. 60.

[84] *Policr.* viii, c. 16 (*The Frivolities of Courtiers,* etc., J. B. Pike, pp. 396ff.)

[85] *Parzival,* trans. J. L. Weston, pp. 275ff. (ix, 801–802 and 835–840). For the German see Wolfram's *Parzival und Titurel,* ed. E. Martin, I, pp. 169–170, ll. 479, 13ff., and 481, 19ff. Cf. Hagen, *Der Gral* in *Quellen und Forschungen* 85, p. 31, and L. E. Iselin, *Der morgenländische Ursprung der Grallegende,* pp. 35ff.

[86] W. Meyer, *Vita Adae et Evae, Abhandlungen der königl. Bayer. Akad. der Wissenschaften, Philos.-Philol. Cl.,* Bd. XIV, 3 Abt., Munich, 1878, pp. 185ff.

loveliness (*amenitas*) appears in various kinds of fruits and flowers with the harmony of birds and with delicious fragrance (*multum fulgebat inaestimabili odore adiuncto*). Here is the famous fountain (*fontem lucidissimum*) with the four streams; over it is the Tree of Life bare of leaves, but Seth eventually sees it elevated to the heavens with a babe in the top in swaddling clothes, and with its roots penetrating down to Hell where Abel is confined. Here again the placing of the Tree of Life distantly reminds one of Yggdrasil in the Norse. Still more perhaps, it recalls the great tree, in the verses *De Pascha* attributed to Cyprian, which extended its branches to the very sky, and stood over a fountain.[87]

From the tree come the three seeds which eventually produce the woods that later become united in the timber of the Cross. This timber is cast into the drain (*probaticam piscinam*) in Jerusalem, in one of its adventures, and then later is placed as a bridge across the brook of Siloam: "fecerunt ex ea ponticulum quodam trans torrentem Syloaticum ut memoria ligni illius sub pedibus conculcantium annichilaretur." The queen of the south, Sybilla, refused to walk on it; she withdrew her garments and did honor to it, wading in the water and uttering prophecies about it. Here the timber of the Cross seems almost reminiscent of the purgatorial bridge in its clear symbolism of Christ and His redeeming power. And that is in no way modified by the attitude of the queen as she does honor to it, interpreting it plainly as the holy symbol.[88] The fully developed legend, which had wide influence, is found in manuscripts at least as early as the thirteenth century, but the episode of the Queen Sybilla (who is the Queen of Sheba) [89] is found in a work of the twelfth.[90] The

[87] *S. Thasci Caecili Cypriani opera omnia*, ed. W. Hartel, *CSEL*, III, 3, pp. 305ff. Translation by Kuhnmuensch, *Early Christian Latin Poets*, pp. 232ff.

[88] For the Latin legend see W. Meyer, *Die Geschichte des Kreuzholzes, Abhandlungen der königl. Bayer. Akad. der Wissenschaften, Philos.-Philol. Cl.*, XVI, 2 Abt. (Munich, 1882), pp. 101ff. the legend itself, pp. 131ff.; A. S. Napier, *History of the Holy Rood-tree, EETS*, 103, pp. xxxiff.; cf. J. A. MacCulloch, *The Harrowing of Hell*, pp. 162 and 272ff. The many versions of the story in various languages are listed in these studies. On material in the legend from the Alexander cycle see *Medium Aevum*, V (1936), pp. 173ff.

[89] See *Zeits. f. d. Alt.*, XXVII (1883), pp. 19ff. Cf. e.g. R. Morris, *Legends of the Holy Rood*, etc., *EETS*, 46, pp. xviff.

[90] Meyer, *op. cit.*, pp. 115f.

Cross as bridge in this fashion is referred to in *Mandeville's Travels,* where the author says that "in the myddes of þat vale is a lytill ryuere þat men clepen *Torrens Cedron.* And abouen it ouerthwart lay a tre þat the cros was made offe þat men ȝeden ouer onne." [91]

According to a romantic account written in the twelfth century, and perhaps earlier, Alexander the Great made a journey to the Earthly Paradise and there learned something of the limits of his power. This is the well-known *Iter ad Paradisum,* which is independent of the Pseudo-Callisthenes for the most part. Yet in an episode already referred to,[92] the Greek story may have furnished a suggestion for the later narrative: there in certain versions of the Pseudo-Callisthenes (in the letter of Alexander to his mother and Aristotle) we learn that Alexander traveled through the land of darkness and came to a clear fountain in a region of fragrant and sweet air. This is the Well of Life, and in its water a dead fish, which Alexander's cook is washing, comes suddenly to life. Later the hero tries to enter the Land of the Blessed but may not do so.[93] This story became widely disseminated and lived on in oral tradition. With the *Iter ad Paradisum* there is a similar journey. Alexander chose five hundred of the bravest of the youth of his army and set forth with them in a ship to find Paradise. It seems that after the conquest in India he came to the Ganges and was told that its source was in the Garden of Eden. Inhabitants of the country round about had fished huge leaves out of the stream to cover the roofs of their houses, and these leaves, when dried, had a marvelous fragrance. With the youths and the ship he journeyed upstream

[91] *Mandeville's Travels,* ed. P. Hamelius, I, *EETS,* 153, p. 62, 32ff. Cf. also *The Ancient Cornish Drama,* E. Norris, I, 424–425. For the substitution of Cedron for Siloam see Meyer, *op. cit.,* p. 147, n. 8.

[92] Chapter I, page 25 above.

[93] For an Ethiopic text of this see E. A. Wallis Budge, *The Alexander Book in Ethiopia,* p. 161, which may be added to the Syriac version discussed by Krappe in *Philol. Quarterly,* XX (1941), p. 123 (cf. Budge, *The History of Alexander the Great,* pp. 171ff.) But for a list of places where the episode appears see *Romanic Review,* IX (1918), pp. 134ff., note 5. For other versions of the story see *Medium Aevum,* VI (1937), pp. 173ff. The connection with the *Iter ad Paradisum* is indicated by Crane, *Romanic Review,* IX, pp. 135–136 and Friedlaender, *Archiv für Religionswissenschaft,* XIII (1910), pp. 161ff.

for a month with great difficulty because of the force of the current and because the roar of the waters deafened them. At length they came to a city of wonderful height and extent with no towers or bulwarks and all overgrown with moss. Here from a narrow window an inhabitant gave them the Wonderstone, which outweighs all gold, unless the stone is covered with a little dust and then it weighs less than a single gold piece. They returned to Susa, and there Papas explained that the city they had seen is where the righteous await the day of judgment, and that the Wonderstone is intended to be a lesson against ambition.[94] Here the journey up the Ganges to get to its source in the Garden is especially interesting; and the fragrance of the leaves is a familiar theme.

Another episode in the Pseudo-Callisthenes should be mentioned in this connection, the story of the trees of the sun and moon. Here we are told how Alexander came to a garden: "locum arboribus consitum uel amoenissimis. Hunc illi paradisum uocitauere."[95] In this grove, with the sanctuary of the gods of the sun and moon, were two trees reaching almost to heaven, one male and the other female; the male tree is the tree of the sun and the other the tree of the moon. They tell Alexander that he will win the world but never return home again. The trees are carefully described: they are like cypresses but straighter and of the same species as the palm; their roots are covered with hides from animals (lions, panthers, and the like) – from male animals for the male tree, and from females for the female; the male tree speaks at sunrise, midday, and late afternoon, to those who consult it, and the female tree at night and during the hours of the moon. This garden is located in the east; iron, bronze,

[94] For the Latin text see the edition of Alphons Hilka in *La Prise de Defur and Le Voyage d'Alexandre au Paradis Terrestre,* ed. L. P. G. Peckham, P. G. Lawton, and M. S. La Du, pp. xliff. The earliest manuscript is of the twelfth century, and the legend goes back to the Babylonian *Talmud* and the fifth century A.D. See *ibid.,* pp. xxxiiiff. For the French and other versions see *ibid.,* pp. 73ff.; *Romania,* XI (1882), pp. 229ff.; and *Medium Aevum,* V (1936), pp. 31ff.; 79ff.; and 173ff. Note the shift to a river barrier in the Hebrew version, *Medium Aevum,* V, p. 39.

[95] *Iuli Valeri Alexandri Polemi* etc., ed. Bernard Kuebler, p. 132. The Julius Valerius represents the a-type of the Pseudo-Callisthenes. Cf. the Ethiopic in Budge's *The Alexander Book in Ethiopia,* pp. 95ff.

tin, and clay are unknown here as building materials, and one may never bring iron into Paradise.[96] Besides this story and the other two I have discussed, the many and tremendously varied documents of the cycle of Alexander contain a really vast amount of scattered material on desert barriers, mountains more or less sacred, jewels and marvels of various kinds, that possibly reflect Otherworld accounts or served to influence later descriptions.[97]

In the *Pantheon* of Godfrey of Viterbo we have an original account of a journey made by a group of monks from the shores of Britain. Paradise, we are told in the versified narrative, is at the end of the ocean:

> Finibus Oceani maris est locus ultimus orbis,
> Quo penitus nullis agitantur tempora morbis,
> Est ibi temperies, perpetuata quies. . . .

The monks leave in a boat to explore far and wide over the ocean, and in the midst of the seas find a bronze image in the shape of a female warrior on a rock pointing their way for them. Later they come across another image of the sort, and following this guidance they arrive at a great mountain of gold where the air is fragrant and they are attracted to beach their ship. Here they discover a city with powerful golden walls and buildings of gold, and a statue of the Virgin Mary with the Holy Child. At length they find two old men, Enoch and Elias, who tell them that the city is guarded by cherubim and seraphim; that angelic songs mark their festivals; that they are sustained by celestial food; and that one of their days is the equivalent of a hundred years on the rest of the earth. The monks are warned that when they get back home all will be changed. This proves most grievously to be the case:

[96] On the trees in later literature see *Medium Aevum*, V (1936), pp. 173ff. Note here too the reference to the "dry tree" and see also *Vassar Mediaeval Studies*, pp. 68ff. (R. J. Peebles, "The Dry Tree: Symbol of Death").

[97] Choosing at random, I notice, for example, the mountain crowned with a temple that shone like gold, with lovely garden and great fragrance, and two thousand five hundred steps, where Enoch reclines on a couch, in Budge's *Alexander Book in Ethiopia*, pp. 91ff.; the dark valley, the mountain with clear weather on the far side, and the land with fruit trees and nourishing crystal streams, in the *Prose Life of Alexander*, ed. J. S. Westlake, *EETS*, 143, pp. 90–91.

Non erat ecclesia, quam primitus hi tenuerunt,
Non abbas, non sunt monachi uelut ante fuerunt,
  Non urbs, non populus, moenia prima ferunt.
Antistes nouus est, noua plebs, nouus ecclesiae grex,
Est patriae noua lex, et principibus nouus est Rex,
  Mortua sunt uetera, singula nata noua.
Non loca, non homines, non cognouere loquelam,
Eruptis lachrymis, secum tenuere querelam,
  Nam sibi non patria; non homo notus erat.
Ipsi qui fuerant hodie forma iuueniles,
Mane senescentes sunt pelle piloque seniles;
  Decrepitos, uiles, se miserosque uident.[98]

In this account the emphasis on the passing of time is vivid. The motif of the voyage and the mountain and the perfume of the atmosphere are familiar features.

The Earthly Paradise is reflected in an amusing way in the *Travels of Marco Polo*. According to this famous work the Old Man of the Mountain "caused a certain valley between two mountains to be enclosed, and had turned it into a garden, the largest and most beautiful that ever was seen, filled with every variety of fruit. In it were erected pavilions and palaces, the most elegant that can be imagined, all covered with gilding and exquisite painting. And there were runnels too, flowing freely with wine and milk and honey and water; and numbers of ladies and the most beautiful damsels in the world, who could play on all manner of instruments, and sang most sweetly, and danced in a manner that it was charming to behold." [99] But as Marco Polo goes on to say, the Paradise the Old Man had in mind was that described by Mahommed. The garden was protected by a fortress, and the Old Man admitted his guests (limited to a very few) only after giving them a potion to cast them into a deep sleep. Polo also refers, a little earlier, to the Tree of the Sun, which he has confused with the Dry Tree.[100] In this case the mountain motif derives in all probability from the actual loca-

[98] *Pantheon,* ed. J. Pistorius (3d ed., B. G. Struve, II, pp. 58–60).

[99] *The Book of Ser Marco Polo,* etc., trans. Sir Henry Yule, I, pp. 139–140. On the Old Man of the Mountain cf. *Speculum,* XXII (1947), pp. 497ff.

[100] *The Book of Ser Marco Polo,* I, pp. 127–128. Cf. the note, I, pp. 128ff. (note 2).

tion of the protective retreat where the great leader of assassins, the Old Man, hid himself, and may have suggested in turn the use of other and genuine reminiscences of the Moslem Earthly Paradise when the garden itself was to be described.

Joinville in his *History of Saint Louis* refers to the river "that cometh through Egypt and from the earthly Paradise. . ." No brooks flow into it. Before it gets into Egypt men cast their nets loose in the stream in the evening

> and when morning is come, they find in their nets such goods as are sold by weight as they bring from that country — that is, ginger, rhubarb, *lignum aloes,* and cinnamon. And men say that these things come from the earthly Paradise; for the wind bloweth down the trees that are in Paradise, as the wind bloweth down dry wood in the forests of our land . . .

The water from the stream when put in water pots and hung up will grow cool even in the heat of the day. The Sultan of Cairo often tried to find whence the stream came and sent men to discover. "And they brought tidings to him that they had searched the stream and had come to a great cliff of sheer rock, where no man could climb." [101] Out of this flowed the river, and at the top of this eminence there seemed to be an abundance of trees.

The river appears again in the garden of the Admiral (Emir) of Babylon, according to the thirteenth-century *Huon de Bordeaux*: "Li ruisiaus vient del flun de paradis";[102] about this spring grows every imaginable kind of fruit tree, and a serpent guards it. Any damsel who drank of its waters became such as she was on the day she was born. Huon washed his hands in it. In the sixteenth-century English version of the story (based on fifteenth-century French prose) by Lord Berners we read the following account:

> & in the myddes of this garden there was a fayre founteyne commynge out of þe ryuer Nile that commyth from paradyce, the whiche founteyne

[101] Jean Sire de Joinville, *The History of Saint Louis,* trans. Joan Evans, pp. 55–56; *Histoire de Saint Louis,* ed. Natalis de Wailly, pp. 66f. (xl). With this account cf. the description of Mount Amara in Milton's *Paradise Lost,* iv, ll. 280–285.

[102] *Huon de Bordeaux* in *Les Anciens Poètes de la France,* V, ed. F. Guessard and C. Grandmaison, pp. 165ff. (5540ff.).

as than was of such vertue that yf any sycke man dyd drynke therof, or wasshyd his handes & face, incontynent shulde be hole & also yf a man had bene of grete age he shulde retourne agayne to the age of .xxx. yere and a woman to become as freshe & lusty as a mayde of .xv. yere. this founteyne had that vertue ye spase of .lx. yere but .x. yere after that Huon had ben there that was dystroyed and broken by ye Egypsyence, who made warre to the admyrall that was as than in Babylon.[103]

There is much Otherworld material in this *chanson de geste:* for example, the castle of Dunostre, built close to the sea and guarded by two copper men with iron flails, which has three hundred windows and twenty-five rooms. It was built by Julius Caesar, the father of Oberon, and here dwells the giant called l'Orgueilleux. A basin of gold hangs on a pillar near by, and this Huon strikes three times with his sword. The sound reaches the ears of a damsel inside, Sebile, and she comes to open the wicket gate, an act that quiets the action of the copper warriors so that Huon is enabled to enter.[104] Much later in the English version there is also the episode of the crystal rock to which a griffon carries Huon. Here he discovers a beautiful forest and a fountain of great virtue; after combat with the bird he also comes upon another great fountain in rich masonry "all of whight Iasper wroughte rychely with flowers of fyne gold and Asure." [105] At the bottom the gravel is of precious stones: it was called the "fountayne of youth" and cured sickness. Near at hand was an apple tree with marvelous fruit that restores youth, and beyond was an orchard. "This gardayne was so fayre that it semyd rather a paradise then a thyng terrestryall." [106] Huon gathers three apples, follows a path by a stream full of precious stones, and comes to a richly garnished ship. The boat takes him

[103] *The Boke of Duke Huon of Burdeux,* etc., ed. S. L. Lee, *EETS:ES,* 40, (*The English Charlemagne Romances,* Part VII), pp. 116–117.

[104] *Huon de Bordeaux,* ed. Guessard and Grandmaison, 4550ff., pp. 136ff.

[105] *The Boke of Duke Huon,* ed. Lee, *EETS: ES,* 41 (*Charl. Rom.* VIII), pp. 433–434. For another journey in the air see *ibid.,* pp. 595–596. Huon and Esclarmonde reach a deserted castle where they have food. The castle vanishes; they climb a mountain, cross a river, and reach Oberon's palace.

[106] *Ibid.,* p. 435. On the apples see pp. 464–465 and 568. This whole episode derives from the *Chanson d'Esclaramonde.* See p. xxxix; cf. Graf, *Miti, Leggende,* p. 90, and note 118 (p. 136); M. Schweingel, *Esclarmonde* (*Ausg. u. Abh.* LXXXIII), ll. 1172ff. (but cf. the closer version in P, p. 47); L. Jordan, *Archiv für das Studium der neueren Sprachen,* CXII (1904), pp. 338ff.

down a river and eventually through an underground passage where voices are heard cursing fortune and there is the thunderous sound of falling waters. Bars of red hot iron threaten but do not touch the ship; it runs aground and Huon discovers all the gravel in the water is of precious stones. He manages to push off again, however, and at last arrives at daylight and the Persian Sea.

The whole episode is clearly oriental in origin, and the flight with the griffon recalls the story of Alexander's experimental journey in the air and also that of Sindbad's adventure with the Rukh.[107] The underground voyage at the end as an escape from the Paradise is just the reverse of Alexander's journey through the Land of Darkness to the country of the Well of Life.[108] Of the same type too and probably of similar origin is the whole account of the Lodestone Rock, which rises as an island in the midst of the sea, and has woods and a white house on it. Huon's ship is drawn toward it and nearly wrecked at its shore. Sir Arnold climbs the three hundred and eighty steps up its side, and instead of a white house finds a castle at the top guarded by a serpent. When Huon ascends he sees that the castle is marvelously fair with walls and towers of alabaster and fine gold: he fights the serpent and slays it, and on visiting the chambers within he discovers that the furniture is of ivory and jewels; outside is a garden garnished with sweet-smelling flowers and fair fruit trees.[109]

[107] See Chapter I, p. 24 above and Jordan, *Archiv*, CXII (1904), pp. 338ff. In Lord Berner's account the crystal rock is said to be the place to which Alexander came after passing through the deserts of India and speaking with the trees of the sun and moon, and was actually called "the rock of Alexander": *The Boke of Duke Huon*, p. 427. So too in version P of the Old French: see Schweingel, *op. cit.*, p. 47. According to the C version, however, Christ had once visited the place and blessed it: see *ibid.*, p. 46 and ll. 1253. The traces of Paradise are here clearly indicated:

Sains est li lix *et* la montaigne bele
Ains ni vit nuls orage ne tempeste
La repoza Jesucris nos salueres
Si le saigna de sa main digne *et* bele
De tous les fruis con a vëu sor terre
I a plenté gisant sont desor lerbe.

[108] Pp. 157f. above; and *Philol. Quarterly*, XX (1941), p. 123.

[109] *The Boke of Duke Huon*, ed. Lee, *EETS:ES*, 41, pp. 368ff.; Jordan, *Archiv*, CXII (1904), p. 340. For the Old French cf. the P version, Schweingel, *op. cit.*, pp. 42–43.

As everybody knows, *Mandeville's Travels* is really a compilation from various sources and in itself represents perhaps no travels at all. Here is a kind of hodgepodge of almost everything we have so far considered in this chapter. The story of Seth appears and the Dry Tree;[110] the royal estate of Prester John is described at some length and the Lodestone Rock and the river that comes from Paradise. Here we are told that the whole country of India is divided into islands because of the rivers that come from Paradise, and it is some of these islands that Prester John has under his rule. In his empire too is the "grauely see": "And a .iij. journeys long fro þat see ben grete mountaynes out of the whiche goth out a gret flood þat cometh out of Paradys and it is full of precious stones withouten ony drope of water and it renneth þorgh the desert on þat o syde, so þat it maketh the see grauely And it bereth into þat see and þere it endeth." [111] It flows three days a week. Near by grow small fruit trees: "But noman dar taken of þat frute for it is a thing of Fayrye." [112] Prester John's palace is full of jewels and its steps are of precious stones; the pillars of his chamber are of fine gold, and with carbuncles give light even in the nighttime. In his realm too is the isle belonging to the Old Man of the Mountain, whose garden of delights is described in the familiar way and is called Paradise. Near the river Phison is the Vale Perilous, about four miles long, supposed to be full of devils because of its storms and mysterious noises, with a devil's head under a rock at its midst. Beyond the land of Prester John is a desert and the "derke regyoun," which extends to the real Earthly Paradise located quite clearly on the other side of the earth. The real Paradise is so high that it nearly touches the circle of the moon; Noah's flood could not reach it. It is enclosed with a wall covered with moss and having one gate, which is sealed with burning fire. Here are the rivers with their precious stones, *lignum aloes*, and gold gravel. The

[110] *Mandeville's Travels*, ed. P. Hamelius, *EETS*, 153, pp. 7f. and 44f.

[111] *Ibid.*, p. 181. In an Irish version of Lucan's *Pharsalia*, as noted earlier, Caesar's diadem had stones brought in the claws of birds and winged things "over the fiery mountain out of Adam's Paradise to the land of India," *Irische Texte*, ed. Stokes and Windisch, IV, 2, p. 389.

[112] *Mandeville's Travels*, p. 182.

author has never been here, nor any other mortal, although many have tried to enter by the swift rivers.[113]

An Italian story familiar in the fourteenth century tells how three monks visited Paradise, which the extant version places "in the eastern region of this earthly world, upon a mountain lifted high above all other mountains and this earth of ours . . ." [114] Here spring the four rivers with the usual names. "Now, beside one of these rivers which is named Gihon, there stood a convent of monks who were great friends of God and lived a truly angelic life." Three of these monks were one day bathing their feet and hands here and saw drifting down the stream a "bough of a tree, enamelled with every colour that is fairest to see; for one of its leaves was golden, another silvery, a third azure, a fourth green, and so forth of all motley hues. . . ." On it were apples and fruits. The monks decided to search for the sacred place whence that bough had come. Up the river banks they went, finding herbs "all full of manna" and trees "laden with the sweetest fruit." For a year they traveled and came to the mountain of Paradise, from whose top comes the song of angels. Here they ascended the sides, which were covered with fruit trees and flowers "of marvellous hues and of divers and marvellous scents; and that mountain was an hundred miles high." The gate of Paradise was closed, guarded by an angel of the Cherubim with sword in hand. After five days and five nights they were admitted, and the monks heard the music of the "wheel of heaven" "so sweet, so soft, so delightful, that they knew not where they were. . . ." They met Enoch and Elias; they saw the "living spring, whereof whoso drinketh can never grow old, and whosoever is already old, he turneth to the age of thirty

[113] *Ibid.*, pp. 201ff. Note also in India the Fountain of Youth (*ibid.*, p. 113), which, men say, comes out of Paradise. The author drank of it three or four times, "and yit me thinketh I fare the better." Cf. E. W. Hopkins, *Journal Amer. Oriental Soc.*, XXVI (1905), pp. 32ff. and G. F. Warner, *The Buke of Maundevil*, Roxburghe Club, 1889, p. 84. For the apples of Paradise and the apple tree of Adam see *Mandeville's Travels*, ed. Hamelius, p. 31.

[114] G. G. Coulton, *Life in the Middle Ages*, IV, pp. 272ff. The Italian may be found in the *Manuale della Letteratura Italiana*, A. D'Ancona and O. Bacci, I, pp. 437ff. (citing C. Bosio, Venice, 1846) and *Leggende del Secolo XIV*, ed. I. Del Lungo, I, pp. 489ff.

years"; they also saw the Tree of Good and Evil and the Tree of Salvation, from which came the wood of the Cross. "Then they saw another tree, whereof whosoever eateth shall never die. After that they saw four fountains, whence issued the four rivers that encompass the world." Here too was a fountain five miles in length and breadth in which were fishes that "chanted day and night in answer to the song of Paradise." "Then they saw the tree of glory, which was so great that it spread its branches for the space of a mile around." Its leaves were gold, its fruit "as it were of sugared confections," and it was full of small birds with red wings which sang as though they had been angels of the celestial Paradise. The monks asked to be allowed to stay fifteen days and were told they had already been there seven hundred years. When they asked how that could be, they were told that the fruit of the Tree of Life and the water of the Fountain of Youth had made them partake somewhat of the glory of eternal life. Their own brethren and companions in their convent had long been dead and others must receive them. They were instructed that the missal on their high altar had their names and would identify them for admission on their return. After forty days they would themselves become dust and go to the holy quiet of eternal life. And so it came to pass when they went back.

This narrative bears an obvious similarity to, or even relationship with, the story of the monks in the *Pantheon* of Godfrey of Viterbo. Older than that,[115] perhaps going as far back as the seventh or eighth century, and perhaps indirectly connected, is the tale of Theophilus, Sergius, and Hyginus, three monks in the legend of Saint Macarius of Rome as found in the *Vitae Patrum*. These three came to a monastery in Syria between the Tigris and the Euphrates. One day when sitting on the banks of the Euphrates, Theophilus suggested to the other two that they seek the spot where the heavens join the earth. Thereupon they traveled to Jerusalem and Bethlehem, ascended the Mount of

[115] A Greek text is listed in an eleventh century MS., *Analecta Bollandiana*, XXI (1902), p. 19; and a Latin text appeared at least as early as the fourteenth century, *ibid.*, XXVIII (1909), p. 458. For further discussion of this and the preceding legend see Coli, *Par. Terrestre*, pp. 133ff.

Olives, and going on, crossed the Tigris, entered Persia, went to India, and at length reached the lands of the dogheaded men and pygmies. Then they ascended some very high and terrible mountains: "ubi sol non intrat, nec arbor nec herba crescunt; ibi ergo serpentes innumerabiles, et dracones, et aspides, sed et basiliscos, et uiperas, et unicornes, et bubalos uidimus multos . . . . ." [116] Led by the Lord they came to a place filled with rocky heights, and after that to an open plain where there were elephants. In one place they found fruit: "Iam ergo tenebrae densissimae cuncta illa repleuerant loca: nec aliquid lucebat, sed nebulae obscurissimae erant. Tunc nos nimium turbati et afflicti . . . ." They called on God for help and were encouraged on their way by a dove. They came to an arch (*absida*) made by Alexander the Great when he was pursuing Darius.[117] After further adventures, in which they passed between two very high mountains where a giant was enchained, they came to a place with many large trees in which were many winged creatures like birds crying out with human voice to God asking Him to spare them. Four men with jeweled crowns and golden palms guarded their road with fire and sword. They saw a church of crystal, from whose altar flowed a liquid like milk.[118] The land was parti-

[116] *Acta Sanctorum* (Bolland.), Oct. x, die 23, pp. 566ff.; also Migne, *Patr. Lat.*, LXXIII, cols. 415ff. Cf. A. D'Ancona, *Scritti Danteschi, I Precursori di Dante*, etc., 33; Graf, *Miti, Leggende*, pp. 63f.; and Asín Palacios, *La Escatalogia Musulmana*, pp. 180ff.

[117] Apparently this is not the famous gate. Cf A. R. Anderson, *Alexander's Gate, Gog and Magog, and the Inclosed Nations.* But the terrain is sometimes similar: compare the detail of the two mountains in the Syrian *Christian Legend Concerning Alexander, ibid.*, p. 23, and E. A. Wallis Budge, *The History of Alexander the Great*, pp. 152–153; in the *Pseudo-Callisthenes*, Anderson, *op. cit.*, p. 35; and elsewhere. The legend is undoubtedly influenced by some form of the story of Alexander: cf. the valley of darkness, the reference to the dog men, the region of serpents, in both. Certain points in the *Iter ad Paradisum* show similarity: the huge leaves from the Garden of Eden and the journey in a ship up the Ganges. The arch referred to in the present passage is vaguely like the pillars with table of gold and inscription in *The Prose Life of Alexander*, ed. Westlake, pp. 95–96. Cf. also, Wright, *Geographical Lore*, pp. 263f. and p. 464, n. 51.

[118] The description of the church suggests the Otherworld elements: "Ipsa uero ecclesia a parte Meridiana similitudinem habebat lapidis prasini pretiosi, a parte Australi colorem sanguinis mundissimi praetendebat, a parte autem Occidentali tota erat alba, instar lactis et niuis candidissimae: stellae super ipsam ecclesiam plus quam huius mundi sidera lucebant, sol ibi sep-

colored: "id est una facies alba erat ut nix, et alia rubicundissimis coloribus erat. . . ." Going across a river they come to a pleasant spot where they find "herbas candidas et albas, sicut lac, dulces uelut mel . . ." Finally they reach the cave (*speluncam*) of Saint Macarius, who informs them that Paradise is twenty miles further along, guarded by one of the Cherubim, and that no one still in the flesh may visit the place. He narrates to them his own story, and at length the brothers return to their monastery by the various lands through which they have traveled.

According to the fourteenth-century satiric *Romans de Bauduin de Sebourc,* Baldwin III, King of Jerusalem sailed far across the sea and reached the *Paradis Terrestre:*

> Qu'l ont véut .j. lieu moult noble et souffisant,
> Muret trestout autour de cristal reluisant;
> Et li crestal estoient con fin or reluisant
> Et quant Bauduvins vint à che lieu avenant,
> Ne vit tour, né chastel, né dongon, en estant;
> Fors arbres qu'en tous tamps sont vert et fruit portant.[119]

The crystal is a unique feature of the scene. At the gate Bauduin and his companion Polibant found two "preudhommes" sitting – Enoch and Elias. Here the birds sing in a manner to make anyone rejoice, and perpetual summer reigns:

> De trestoutes mannières d'oysiaus du firmament
> I ost-on le son chanter si douchement,
> Que de la mélodie n'a, el mont si dolent
> Qui n'en fust resjoïs à che démainnement.
> Adès i fait estés, n'i keurt pluie né vent;
> Li arbre i sont tout vert, en tous tamps, oraiëment.
> Li fruit y sont pendant, sans chéoir nullement,
> Né jà ne kerra fruis, s'escripture ne ment,
> Dès-si jusques au jour de très grant jugement
> Que Diex fera le monde finer parfaitemans.[120]

---

templiciter lucebat et calebat, quam in huius terrae regione; alpes et arbores omnes plus altae, et folia ac fructus plures et dulciores, quam istius mundi arbores habebant; sed et aues coeli aliter resonabant quam aues terrae istius . . ."

[119] *Li Romans de Bauduin de Sebourc,* II, p. 46 (*chant* xv), ll. 29ff.

[120] *Ibid.,* p. 49, ll. 131ff.

Here is the fruit that brings youth and also that which bestows old age. Elias and Polibant try the apple of youth. When Polibant tasted it:

> Leus qu'l en ot mengiet, li est le vis mués:
> Il devint gratieus et biaus et coulourés,
> En l'age de .xxx. ans fu esrant figurés.[121]

Bauduin ate the apple of old age:

> Il a pris une pomme, vistement le menga.
> Quant avalée l'ot; li piaus li hirrecha,
> Vielles fu et barbus, sa véue troubla:
> Il ne vit sé poi non, à terre se geta
> Et ne poot aler s'au baston n'apoïa.
> Qui le vit par devant et adont l'esgarda,
> Il ne créest jammais che fust Baudewin là,
> Car en povre point fu et si vielles sambla
> Que de .m. ans et plus . . . .[122]

Enoch gives him the apple of youth to restore him. In such details one is vaguely reminded of the Fountain of Youth in *Huon de Bordeaux*. Later the travelers also see the Dry Tree, and they come to an island where they find the entrance to Hell and meet Judas, who has been released for his day of rest.

Other significant material in this poem appears in the account of the visit to the Old Man of the Mountain.[123] His palace, just as tradition had it, and indeed pretty much as Marco Polo describes it, is on a mountain (*en le rouge montaigne*), with a garden "from which a hundred silver steps" lead up to "un Paradis." Here is a palace, and all is of gold and azure. Three streams flow here: one of claret, one of honey, and the third of some other wine. Here a hundred damsels sing melodiously and we see the usual features that go to make up the Moslem and oriental scene of luxury.

Perhaps the most famous instance, however, of a description of Eden in medieval literature is that in Dante's *Purgatorio*, where we find the general location on a mountain on an island,

[121] *Ibid.*, p. 51, ll. 212ff.
[122] *Ibid.*, p. 52, ll. 239ff.
[123] Vol. I, p. 359 (*chant* xiii), 80ff.

and the river barrier is also used. Here, it happens, the four rivers are not referred to, but instead we have a classical reminiscence in Lethe and Eunoe springing from a single fountain. Because of influence from Dante, without doubt, Federico Frezzi introduces a visit to the garden in the *Quadriregio* in his account of the realm of Virtue. Both examples must receive further consideration later when we come to the allegorical tradition of the Other World. In the *Faustbuch* Dr. Faustus is "on the hill of Caucasus" where he "sawe the whole lande of India and Scythia" and towards the east "he sawe a mightie cleare strike of fire comming from heauen vpon the earth, euen as it had been one of the beames of the Sunne." This, he learns, is the fiery wall of Paradise and in a valley there he sees the four rivers issuing out of a "well." The names of these are the Ganges or Phison, the Nile or Gihon, the Tigris, and the Euphrates. No one is allowed to come any nearer to this region.[124] Faustus also has the experience of riding up into the heavens in a wagon carried by two dragons. He looks down and sees the earth enclosed "in comparison within the firmament, as the yolke of an egge within the white" and "the whole length of the earth was not a span long."[125] Lorenzo de' Medici also refers to a place "alto e silvestre" as an Earthly Paradise:

> e quivi il primo secol si rinnuova:
> se trista e lassa, in quelle parti alpestre
> avvien ch'ogni dolcezza e grazia muova. . .[126]

It was inevitable that in time the Earthly Paradise should be used for satiric purposes. The most famous example of such a treatment perhaps is the thirteenth-century *Land of Cockaigne,*

[124] *The English Faust-Book of 1592,* ed. H. Logeman, pp. 72–73. For the German see *Das Volksbuch vom Doktor Faust,* J. Fritz, pp. 63–64; also Robert Petsch, (*Neudrucke deutscher Litteraturwerke des XVI und XVII Jahrh.*) pp. 70–71. In the German concerning the wall we read of a "Fewrstrom" that goes from the earth to heaven.

[125] *The English Faust-Book,* pp. 47ff.; Fritz, *Das Volksbuch,* pp. 49ff.

[126] *Selve d'Amore,* "Selva Secunda," st. 122, Lorenzo de' Medici, *Opere,* I, ed. Attilio Simioni, p. 283. There are many other examples of this kind of influence. Cf. the use of the Earthly Paradise as a means of comparison in John Gower, *Complete Works,* ed. G. C. Macaulay, I, p. 344; IV, p. 24.

where a corresponding but superior region is described as the background for an attack on the corruptions of monasticism. This country is "Fur in see bi west Spayngne" fairer than Paradise itself,[127] where, the poet says:

Þer nis met bote frute;
Þer nis halle, bure no benche,
Bot watir man is þursto quenche.
Beþ þer no men bot two,
Hely and Enok also . . .

In Cockaigne is everything, food and drink, joy of a very earthly character and bliss. The negative formula is extensively used:

Al is dai, nis þer no niȝte.
Þer nis baret noþer strif,
Nis þer no deþ, ac euer lif,
Þer nis lac of met no cloþ
Þer nis man no womman wroþ . . .

and so on. The rivers are here but unnamed, and they flow with oil, milk, honey, and wine. A great abbey of white and gray monks is here: the shingles are of cakes, the walls of pasties; in the cloister the pillars are of crystal with jasper and coral base and capital. Within are four wells of treacle and syrup and spiced wine, apparently a repetition of the rivers, with jewels including the carbuncle and "prassiune." Many birds are here singing day and night; and roasted geese fly to the abbey crying, "Geese, all hot, all hot." Near at hand is a nunnery by a river of sweet milk. In this case obviously the satire is not directed at the idea of a Paradise on earth, although the island motif, the negative formula, the rivers, and the garden are used as a part of the conventional picture.

Much less closely related to the tradition is Rutebeuf's *La*

[127] *Die Kildare-Gedichte*, ed. W. Heuser (*Bonner Beiträge zur Anglistik*, XIV), pp. 141ff. On different forms of the story in different languages see Paul u. Braune's *Beiträge*, V (1878), pp. 389ff., especially pp. 404ff.; and Elfriede Ackermann, *Das Schlaraffenland in German Literature and Folksong* (note the emphasis on the mountain as barrier, pp. 14ff.).

Voie de Paradis,[128] where we are told how the poet dreamed of his journey on a road "estroite," which was so unpleasant that many people left it to take another road to the left and this of course, flowery and delightful, led to the realm of grief and distress. Rutebeuf follows his more difficult route to the city of Penitence and has many subsequent adventures that do not concern us here, except perhaps to notice the valley of Envy:

> El fons d'une obscure valée
> Dont la clarsez s'en est alée . . .

a scene that recalls the dark regions in some of the vision literature. Clearly this work springs more from the allegorical influence of the *Roman de la Rose* and works of that kind than from ideas of Eden.[129]

In accounts of the journey in general, however, we still see the familiar features. These are clearest perhaps in Mandeville, although they also come into the story in various ways in Godfrey of Viterbo, Joinville, and others. The mountain and the four rivers are fairly constant. The fiery wall referred to by Tertullian, Lactantius, and Isidore of Seville, reappears in the *Faustbuch.* A land of darkness on the way is in the story of Alexander and in the "derke regyoun" of Mandeville and Rutebeuf's *Voie de Paradis.* Crystal is found in the church in the legend of Saint Macarius and the walls referred to by Bauduin de Sebourc. Swift passage of time in Paradise is indicated by Godfrey of Viterbo and in the story of the three monks; and the Well of Life in the Alexander cycle makes one think of the waters

[128] *Œuvres Completes de Rutebeuf,* ed. Achille Jubinal, II, pp. 169ff. Also, as a matter of general influence, may be noted the vision of the garden on the Mount of Olives in Berceo's *Vida de Sancta Oria, Virgen,* stanzas 139ff. (*Biblioteca de Autores Españoles,* 57, *Poetas Castellanos ant. al Siglo XV,* ed. F. Janer, p. 142). Cf. also the tree in the celestial vision, *ibid.,* stanzas 43ff. In the same author's *Milagros de Nuestra Sennora* (*ibid.,* pp. 103ff.) the garden at the beginning uses the material, with the four clear springs interpreted as the four Gospels, and the birds as saints who sing the Virgin's praises (stanzas 21ff.)

[129] For the counterpart of such works cf. the journeys to hell summarized in Legrand d'Aussy's *Fabliaux ou Contes du xiie et du xiiie Siècle,* II, pp. 17ff. and 36ff. For texts see A. Jubinal, *Mystères Inédits,* II, pp. 384ff.; and *Jongleurs et Trouvères,* pp. 43ff.

of youth in *Huon de Bordeaux* and the apple of youth in the romance of Bauduin.

Finally we may recall the fact at this point that later journeys were taken to the Earthly Paradise. When Christopher Columbus discovered the New World, he thought he was close to the Garden of Eden; Ponce de Leon went in search of the Fountain of Youth and was followed by various other navigators.[130] In Spenser's *Faerie Queene* the Bowre of Blisse shows indebtedness to several sources but one of them is probably the medieval idea of the Garden of Eden.[131] Here on an island is a "large and spacious plaine" mantled with green grass and flowers where the heavens "Ne suffred storme nor frost on them to fall" and there are "trembling groves, the Christall running by" and a beautiful fountain. As Spenser says:

> There the most daintie paradise on ground
> It selfe doth offer to his sober eye . . .[132]

Even more clearly Milton borrows from this tradition in his account of the garden in Book IV of *Paradise Lost*,[133] where we find the mountain and the subterranean river:

> Southward through Eden went a River large,
> Nor chang'd his course, but through the shaggie hill
> Pass'd underneath ingulft . . .[134]

[130] For the whole matter cf. S. E. Morison, *Admiral of the Ocean Sea, A Life of Christopher Columbus,* II, pp. 282ff. and Olschki in the *Hispanic American Historical Review,* XXI (1941), pp. 361ff.

[131] *Faerie Queene,* II, xii, stanzas xliiff. For a suggestion of influence from the Celtic see Lois Whitney, "The Literature of Travel in the 'Faerie Queene,'" *Mod. Philol.,* XIX (1921–1922), especially pp. 159ff. The poet himself refers to Eden and to Paradise. Another similar description in the poem is that of Mount Acidale with the plain and garden at its top, but this recalls Claudian's *De Nuptiis* and scenes in the allegory of Courtly Love. Cf. also *Faerie Queene,* III, v, st. xl and the Garden of Adonis, III, vi, stanzas xxixff.

[132] *Faerie Queene,* II, xii, st. lviii.

[133] This influence has been noted by Grant McColley in his *Paradise Lost, An Account of its Growth and Major Origins,* pp. 142ff., where he also draws attention to Spenser's description of the mount in the Garden of Adonis, *Faerie Queene,* III, vi, st. xliii. Here we find continual spring and harvest, trees in flower and bearing fruit, and it too is a "joyous paradize."

[134] *Par. Lost,* IV, 223–225. On Milton's use of the bridge motif cf. above p. 61, n. 7.

Also in later years various scholarly attempts were made to discover the actual location of Eden, although of course the idea that it still retained its old delights had vanished forever.[135]

[135] Cf. for example Marmaduke Carver's *A Discourse of the Terrestrial Paradise* (London, 1666), combatting the ideas on the subject held by Junius. He notes, p. 46, that according to Pliny the Tigris runs underground "for the space of 25 miles . . ." A serious attempt to locate the region seems made in *Exercitium Academicum de Situ Paradisi Terrestris,* Eric Klint, Upsala, 1714, and a more satiric work related to the question is *The Situation of Paradise Found Out,* by Henry Hare (London, 1683).

VI

ALLEGORY

THE TRANSITION FROM MYTH to poetry is usually accomplished by means of allegory. The literature of vision may transmit a vast amount of material, and stories of travels in search of mythical realms may perpetuate many of the old ideas; but presumably in both cases a degree of faith in the actuality of what is dealt with persists and will persist as long as the narrative is more or less offered on those terms. When the gods and goddesses, the scenes and structures of an old religion, however, are used merely as symbols to imply some meaning on another level of thought, we are in the presence of the metaphorical, and the numinous gives way to the poetic. The process is delicately gradual, of course, and one may never be quite sure how far some writer like Aeschylus, say, keeps to the old mythology or how skeptical was Euripides. How much even Virgil believed in the literal truth of the underground realm in the *Aeneid* may be a matter of conjecture, and no one can tell exactly when the three Fates ceased to be deities and became a figure of speech. But by the time when nearly all the writings we are now considering were set down, little if any faith in the mythology remained and the allegory stamps them with the seal of another purpose.

There are plenty of suggestions for allegory in the classical period. When Ovid describes the Palace of the Sun and the House of Fame in the *Metamorphoses* it is safe to say that he did not believe in their real existence. They are different too in that respect from the idea of the underworld in other Greek and Latin sources because they had never been regarded as real, but were symbolic contrivances pretty much of Ovid's own invention. They fall into the tradition of the Other World, however, since they derive in some respects from the mythological and offer material for later use of that kind. The Palace of the Sun, as we see from the end of Book I of the *Metamorphoses,* is located in the east beyond Ethiopia and India. Book II tells us that it "stood high on lofty columns, bright with glittering gold and bronze." [1] On its doors Mulciber had carved in relief "the waters that enfold the central earth, the circle of the lands and the sky that overhangs the lands." A "steep path" leads thither. The House of Fame (or in this case more properly Rumor) is at a place "in the middle of the world, 'twixt land and sea and sky, the meeting point of the threefold universe." [2] It is specifically "upon a high mountaintop" and it has "countless entrances, a thousand apertures, but with no doors to close them." It is all built of "echoing brass," and is full of people engaged in spreading "falsehoods mingled with the truth." In this instance the mountain may have been introduced to harmonize with the central location between earth and sky, but probably it derives from the many examples of the holy mountain of the Latins and Greeks.

The same feature appears in the *Epithalamium* of Claudian, who speaks of "a craggy mountain . . . unapproachable by human foot" on the island of Cyprus.[3] This region is the home of Venus:

The hoar frost dares not clothe its sides, nor the rude winds buffet it nor clouds obscure. . . . The year's less clement seasons are strangers to it, whereover ever brood the blessings of eternal spring. The mountain's height slopes down into a plain; that a golden hedge encircles, guarding its meadows with yellow metal. . . . Fair is the enclosed country, ever bright with flowers though touched with no laboring hand, for

[1] *Ovid, Metamorphoses, with an English Translation,* F. J. Miller (Loeb Library), I, p. 61 (ii, 1ff.).

[2] *Ibid.,* II, pp. 183f. (xii, 39ff.). The hollow mountain abode of Morpheus should also be mentioned, *ibid.,* II, pp. 162f. (xi, 592ff.)

[3] *Claudian, with an English Translation,* Maurice Platnauer (Loeb Library), I, pp. 247ff. (ll. 49ff.). With the palace here one may compare the temple of love visited by Psyche in Apuleius (*Metam.* V, 1, in *Apuleius, The Golden Ass,* W. Adlington, rev. S. Gaselee [Loeb. Libr.], pp. 198ff.). Psyche is on the top of a high rock and is carried by the "softly breathing Zephyrus from the hill" to a deep valley where she spies a "pleasant wood" and a crystal spring. Near the spring is the edifice, with pillars of gold, silver walls, pavement of precious stone. Beasts are depicted on the walls, and the pavement is also carved with scenes. Another temple in the story is that of Juno, (*ibid.,* VI, 3, pp. 254f.).

Zephyr is husbandman enough therefor. Into its shady groves no bird may enter save such as has first won the goddess' approval for its song. . . . The very leaves live for love and in his season every happy tree experiences love's power: palm bends down to mate with palm, poplar sighs its passion for poplar . . . .

Here spring two fountains, the one of sweet water, the other of bitter, honey is mingled with the first, poison with the second, and in these streams 'tis said that Cupid dips his arrows. . . .

Afar shines and glitters the goddess' many-colored palace, green gleaming by reason of the encircling grove. Vulcan built this too of precious stones and gold . . . Columns cut from rock of hyacinth support emerald beams; the walls are of beryl, the high-builded thresholds of polished jasper, the floor of agate . . .

The turf is perfumed, and here grow spikenard, cassia, and cinnamon; and "balsam creeps forth slowly in an exuding stream." In this case we notice the island, the mountain, the garden, the fountains, and the jeweled palace. Especially interesting is the use also of the negative formula: "The hoar frost dares not clothe its sides" and so on. Perhaps both island and mountain are derived from Cyprus itself, and the rest is symbolism; even so, the Otherworld tradition is undoubtedly represented here in the total picture.

A mountain seems also to be the foundation for a temple of Venus according to the *Epithalamium* of Sidonius.[4] The precious stones used for the temple's construction, including topaz, sardonyx, amethyst, beryl, and the like, came from five different regions. Outside were towering walls of rock "roughened by the constant lashing of the waters" of the sea, but within Mulciber had imitated the crags in gold and portrayed other scenes of nature. The whole account, however, is brief and does not contribute much. Such temples as this, nevertheless, and fabulous palaces of one kind or another doubtless made a contribution to the details available for Otherworld scenes. The possibility has been made clear that solar palaces of the type already considered in Ovid, as well as other magnificent edifices in actuality

[4] *Sidonius, Poems and Letters, with an English Translation*, W. B. Anderson (Loeb Library), I, pp. 201ff. The text at the beginning is a corrupt jumble.

and in Greek and oriental romance, had some influence on European story telling of a much later date.[5]

i

With such a background of classical material, in which the mountain is fairly constant, it is not surprising to come upon the allegorical description in Godfrey of Saint Victor's *Fons Philosophie*, written in the twelfth century to display the intellectual conflict of the period and the intellectual life.[6] The author in this fragmentary piece tells of a dream in which he seems to awaken out of sleep and takes a long journey to a delightful place:

Loca quedam de longe uisa sunt amena
Mire celsitudinis facie serena
Et quasi delitiis Paradysi plena . . .

Here one wonders whether Godfrey was led by his master, Bernard Silvester, to think rather of the Earthly Paradise and so to be influenced by that.[7] The murmur of a thousand streams comes to his ears, however, and at length he arrives at the foot of a mountain. Below are the seven poisonous rivers of the mechanical arts, but at the top is a spring from which flow the beautiful rivers, some shining like gold, some like silver, of the Seven Liberal Arts. Here different representatives of the Arts drink from the streams and engage in dispute. Theology receives due emphasis in the scene where Jerusalem is located on both sides of the river of that name, over which passes a connecting bridge presumably to unite the Old Law with the New.[8] Here sit Gregory, Ambrose, Jerome, and Augustine.

Another of Bernard's disciples and a more famous one is Alanus de Insulis, whose *Anticlaudianus* shows obvious indebtedness to the material already considered and had great influence

[5] See Miss Schlauch's treatment in *Scandinavian Studies*, X (1928–1929), pp. 189ff.; *Speculum*, VII (1932), pp. 500ff.

[6] Edited by M. A. Charma, in *Memoires de la Société des Antiquaires de Normandie*, XXVII, pp. 11ff.

[7] See above pp. 150f. Cf. the river in the garden of Physis, *De mundi universitate*, II, ix, ll. 39ff. (ed. Barach and Wrobel, p. 53.).

[8] Stanza 167. For another bridge, again not in any way the Bridge of Judgment, see stanzas 70–73 including a sumptuous description with reference to the name of Adam du Petit-Pont.

on numerous works to follow. In this poem there is, first, the elaborate description of the realm of Nature:

It is a place secret and in a region far from our clime, that makes mock of the foments of our abodes. . . . What the munificent hand of Nature can accomplish, and in what she may pour forth more graciously her gifts, she lavishes in this place: where, felted with the soft down of flowers, stellated by their stars, flaming with the dye of roses, earth strives to paint a new heaven (*terra nouum contendit pingere coelum*). Not there does the beauty of the budding flower fade, dying in its bloom; nor does the morning girl-rose droop into the evening old-wife; but ever rejoicing in the same aspect, she grows ever young by the gift of eternal spring. Winter pinches not this flower with its cold, nor does summer consume it in heat. Not here does the wrath of wanton Boreas rage, nor the South Wind threaten . . .[9]

And so the negative formula is used again and again. Every kind of tree and fruit and bird is here, and a stream that nourishes the soil. In the center of the grove "an elevated plain rises upon the airy summit of a mountain and gives kisses to the clouds." Here the palace of Nature is erected:

Suspended on tall columns it pierces the air, gleams with the starriness of gems, burns in gold, nor is less than appropriate honor given to silver. . . . Here the grace of painting describes the customs of men and inscriptions attach with fidelity to the work so that the thing depicted deviates little from the truth. . . .

In these pictures we find various classical scenes taken from such stories as those of Priam, Midas, and Paris. In the whole description of this region the first part is clearly indebted to ideas of the Earthly Paradise as even the opening line suggests ("Est locus a nostro secretus climate tractu") and the mention of eternal spring. The mountain plateau may also come from this tradition or from that of Claudian and classical writers, from which also the account of the palace would seem to derive.

Another section of the poem also indebted to Claudian, I

[9] From the translation of W. H. Cornog, *The Anticlaudian of Alain de Lille*, pp. 53f. For the Latin see Thomas Wright, *The Anglo-Latin Satirical Poets and Epigrammatists of the Twelfth Century*, (Rolls Series), II, pp. 275ff. (i, caps. iii–iv), and Migne, *Patr. Lat.*, CCX, cols. 488ff.

feel sure, is the description of the realm of Fortune, which I shall examine again in another connection. But here we may note the interesting fact that in general the same elements are used: the mountain, the garden, the house, and something like the same formulae; but the appropriately contrasting features are introduced to symbolize the evil effect of Fortune when she is adverse. Thus:

the rock rejoices in much grassland, while Zephyr blows upon it with gentle breath. But soon fell Boreas deprives it of flowers . . . Here a changing grove and an inconsistent tree spring forth. That remains sterile, this gives forth fruit. . . . One flourishes, the many wither. . . Here two rivers run along . . .[10]

one is sweet and one is foul. The house of Fortune is partly on the mountain, partly in the valley; part is magnificent with jewels, and part is falling to pieces. The whole account is like that of Nature's realm of which half has now been devastated.

A feature of special interest in this allegory, however, is the flight which Prudence takes in the chariot led by the horses of the five senses to travel through the universe.[11] In this vehicle she visits several regions and at last Heaven itself, which, on the whole, may seem less inviting than the Earthly Paradise. Such journeys were taken when the griffon carried Huon up to the crystal rock, Sindbad had his adventure with the Rukh, Alexander rode in the chariot of the griffons, and Faustus went up to the heavens in the wagon conveyed by two dragons; but perhaps closer than any of these is the journey to heaven of Philology in Martianus Capella's *De nuptiis* and the suggestion implied in Elijah's experience, with possibly something of the *Somnium Scipionis* added thereto.[12] Alanus has given a vivid account of

[10] Cornog, *op. cit.*, p. 139ff.; Wright, *op. cit.*, pp. 396ff. (vii, caps. viii–ix). Alanus likes to paint contrasts: cf. his abode of Saturn (*Anticl.* iv, cap. viii).

[11] *Anticl.* iv, caps. ivff. The idea of such a mission is derived, of course, from *De mundi universitate* of Bernard Silvester, II, v, (ed. Barach and Wrobel, 40ff.).

[12] The influence of the *Somnium Scipionis* would come at least by way of Bernard's allegory. We may also note that Nature descends from the celestial region in a chariot drawn by the birds of Juno in *De planctu naturae,* prose ii (Wright, *op. cit.*, p. 445): "curru uitreo ferebatur; ipsae uero Iunonis alitibus."

the flight through the air and the ether, and his story prompted Chaucer much later to describe a comparable trip in his *House of Fame*.

The mountain is used again in the *Architrenius* of Jean de Hauteville (or Hanville [13]) as the site of the golden palace of Venus,[14] suggesting knowledge of Claudian, and in another passage as a symbol of Ambition, recalling a little some accounts of the Earthly Paradise.[15] The Mount of Ambition, according to this poem, rises higher than the moon into the neighborhood of the stars. Here Zephyr blows and every kind of tree flourishes, including each kind of pear. A river flows down shining with silver and gold and jewels. At the top is an abode, richly built with marble and precious stones, and decorated with tapestries showing various scenes of classical stories and with cups whose pictures make the modern reader think of a Greek amphora.

In the early part of the thirteenth century one of the most influential allegories was Robert Grosseteste's *Chasteau d'Amour*.[16] Here the castle to symbolize the body of the Virgin Mary suggests borrowings from the Otherword tradition.[17] Painted green, blue, and rose, it is founded on a high rock (*roche dure e bise E bien poli de ci k'aval*) with deep ditches (*fossez*) around it. It has seven barbicans, four small towers, three baileys, and a strong wall. Within what appears to be the dungeon or high tower is a spring with four streams that murmur over the gravel and fill the ditches outside. Within is an ivory throne surrounded by a rainbow. The foundation (with what is really a moat) and the four streams clearly suggest a reminiscence of the Earthly Paradise, but it is of course not certain that in this case we have more than the operation of sheer coincidence. The

[13] Cf. F. J. E. Raby, *A History of Christian-Latin Poetry*, p. 337, note 3.

[14] Wright, *Anglo-Latin Satirical Poets*, I, p. 252.

[15] *Ibid.*, pp. 292ff.

[16] Edited by J. Murray, *Le Château d'Amour de Robert Grosseteste.* See for bibliography *The Writings of Robert Grosseteste*, S. H. Thomson, pp. 152ff.; for the English translations, R. F. Weymouth, *Castel off Loue*; Carl Hortsmann, *The Minor Poems of the Vernon MS*, (*EETS*, 98, pp. 355ff.); and *Anglia*, XIV (1892), pp. 415ff.

[17] Murray, *op. cit.*, pp. 105ff. (ll. 571ff.). The castle, says the author, is the ladder (*l'eschiele*) by which God descended from heaven (*ibid.*, p. 112, ll. 825–826).

castle itself derives from a tradition of symbolism that is independent.[18] The rock, of course, (which is the heart of the Virgin) may be explained simply by the use in the parable of the house founded upon a rock; and the four rivers possibly offering nothing more than a detail from Genesis or what may be accounted for by the author's sense of symmetry. On the whole, however, considering the frequent reference to the rivers in literature and their appearance in art with the mountain,[19] it seems quite unlikely that Robert Grosseteste did not receive some hints for his allegory from the tradition we have followed in the previous chapter. The four towers here are interpreted as the Four Cardinal Virtues and the rivers or streams are simply Divine Grace. A similar pattern is found again and again in later allegorical usage, even as late as the pageants and masques.[20] In this case, in all probability, certain Otherworld scenes have been enriched by details from a strictly allegorical source. It is clear, however, one must be on one's guard against complete confidence that even the rock, the four towers, and the four rivers, always come down from the mythological tradition wherever they occur.[21]

[18] Miss Cornelius is responsible for demonstrating this. For the sources in general see R. D. Cornelius, *The Figurative Castle,* and cf. Owst, *Literature and Pulpit in Medieval England,* pp. 77ff. A comparison of the English and the French is found in F. K. Haase's *Die Altenglischen Bearbeitungen von Grosseteste's Chasteau d'Amour verglichen mit der Quelle,* pp. 28ff. The symbolism of the ladder introduced here (ll. 825ff.) is, however, overlooked in both studies. Doubtless it has scriptural origin.

[19] See p. 154 above.

[20] It was taken over in the *Cursor mundi,* ll. 9877–10094 (ed. R. Morris, *EETS,* 59, pp. 568ff.). The castle with the four virtues symbolized in the towers appears, I believe, in the *Somme le Roi* by Frère Lorens. I have not seen the manuscript. It is found also in the translations of the *Ayenbite of Inwyt,* ed. R. Morris, *EETS,* 23, p. 124; the fourteenth-century *Book of Vices and Virtues,* ed. W. Nelson Francis, *EETS,* 217, p. 122; and elsewhere. The four virtues are timbers in the house of the Virgin according to Honorius of Autun (Migne, *Patr. Lat.,* CLXXII, col. 502; cf. Bernard of Clairvaux, Migne, *op cit.,* CLXXXIII, cols. 675–676). For a Castle of Love in a thirteenth-century ivory casket, showing the four figures which may just possibly stand for the virtues, see A. Schultz, *Das Höfische Leben zur Zeit der Minnesinger,* I, p. 577, fig. 171.

[21] So with the bridge of the castle in Mirk's *Festial* as examined by Miss Cornelius, *op. cit.,* p. 47. So too with the *Songe du Castel, PMLA,* XLVI (1931), pp. 321ff., which comes from the late thirteenth century, it seems, and suggests some elements that appear in allegories of the vision of Courtly

Another allegory of the early thirteenth century, the *Besant de Dieu* by William the Clerk of Normandy, gives us the symbolism of the two roads, one broad and easy to the city and one narrow ("estraite e aspre e dure") to the Castle of Virtues. On the highest tower of the Castle are Patience, Humility, and Obedience the Queen. There is a corresponding castle of vices.[22]

In Brunetto Latini's allegorical framework of his *Tesoretto* the author loses his way and finds himself in a wood where he sees a mountain with a throng of animal life about – men, women, beasts, creatures of all kinds.[23] It is here he finds Nature, who later directs him to a plain where he will meet various important people. He goes through a narrow path (*sentiero stretto*) and finds himself in a desert place where there is no road:

De, che paese fero
Trouai in quella parte! [24]

Here all living creatures are absent, all streams and forms of life:

Et io, pensando forte,
Dottai ben dela morte.

It is three hundred miles wide at least. Through a dark valley he goes (*una ualle schura*) and on the third day comes out upon a vast and pleasant plain (*Lo più ghaio del mondo*) where he sees

---

Love. In this case the castle is constructed upon two slender pillars, presumably derived from nothing more than human legs; the main part symbolizes the head. But the dream, the field, and the assembly of people at the start, are found in the documents of the love visions. A clear combination of Otherworld material with elements from the tradition of Courtly Love and the symbolism of the Castle is found in Nevill's *Castell of Pleasure,* edited by Miss Cornelius, (*EETS,* 179,) who, however, fails to take full account of the Otherworld background (cf. *ibid.*, pp. 18–19 and below pp. 221f.). On the symbolism of the body see Archer Taylor, "A Metaphor of the Human Body in Literature and Tradition," *Corona,* 1941, and Powell in [*N. Car.*]*Studies in Philol.,* XVI (1919), pp. 197ff.

[22] *Besant de Dieu,* ed. Ernst Martin, pp. 52ff., ll. 1813ff. (for the roads); 1865ff. (for the Castle of Virtues). Note the roads in *Yder,* ll. 3557ff. (ed. Gelzer, p. 102. Cf. p. lxv).

[23] See the edition of Wiese, *Zeits. für romanische Philol.,* VII (1883), pp. 337ff. (ii, 188ff.).

[24] *Ibid.*, pp. 355ff. (xiii, 1183ff.).

sights he dare not tell. Here are emperors and kings and various personified abstractions, including Virtue and her daughters, the Four Cardinal Virtues. Further on in the poem the author visits the realm of Love. He passes by valleys and mountains, woods, and bridges, and comes to a fair plain covered with flowers, which, however, has, like love itself, a changeful aspect:

Ma or parea ritondo,
Ora auea quadratura,
Ora auea l'aria schura,
Ora è chiara e lucente,
Or uegio molta gente,
Or non uegio persone,
Or uegio padiglione,
Or uegio chase e torre.
L'un giace e l'altro chorre,
L'un fugie e l'altro chaccia . . .[25]

and so on, a sort of embodiment of the paradoxical ideas often expressed in the oxymora of love poetry. Something of the contrasts of the realm of Fortune in the *Anticlaudianus* of Alanus de Insulis may have been in Brunetto's mind here, but there is no proof of that; a similar use of the paradox is found later in the twofold inscription of the gate of Love's garden in Chaucer's *Parlement of Foules*.

From Brunetto's dark valley and desert region Dante may have got the "selva oscura," where he too found himself lost at the beginning of the *Inferno*.[26] But as we have seen, such a region was possibly familiar to him from many sources; and after it he comes to a hill at the end of the valley and Virgil asks him why he does not ascend the delectable mountain, the beginning and end of all joy.[27] Dante's Otherworld excursion is a complete view of most

[25] The whole description begins *ibid.*, p. 374 (xix, 2197ff.).

[26] Brunetto's desert is "saluagio" (*ibid.*, p. 355, xiii, 1197). Grandgent (*La Divina Commedia*, p. 12) compares only *Tesoretto* ii, 75–78 and iii, 1. But see his *Power of Dante*, pp. 160ff.

[27] *Inferno*, i, 77 (*dilettoso monte*). A useful summary of various accounts of the Other World, especially in the visions and legendary material, is found in *Forerunners of Dante* by Marcus Dods, citing the older studies by Ozanam and Labitte. Cf. too August Rüegg, *Die Jenseits Vorstellungen vor Dante*. For the island motif in the *Purgatorio* see the material cited by Silverstein, *Harvard Theological Review*, XXXI (1938), pp. 53ff.

of the forms of such a journey available to him in medieval literature. He goes underground, like Virgil in the sixth book of the *Aeneid* and various figures in the Latin visions; he ascends the mountain of the Earthly Paradise in the *Purgatorio*; and in the *Paradiso*, like Scipio in the *Somnium Scipionis* and various others elsewhere, he goes up through the spheres to the empyrean and beyond.

For our purposes, the second of these is most significant. With Dante the Otherworld scene of the Earthly Paradise combines nearly all the elements available in literature of this type. It is located on an island (directly opposite Jerusalem on the globe and thus both east and west according to the point of view); it is on a mountain top; [28] and it seems to use the wall of fire (in the circle of Lust) and the river barrier as well (in the poet's approach to Lethe). Within the garden is the characteristic fragrance; the song of birds here is accompanied musically by the leaves of the forest; the Tree of the Knowledge of Good and Evil is here despoiled of foliage. Flowers, of course, are everywhere, which the garden bears without seed. The mountain is so high it is clear of all storms; and here is the usual fountain, dividing in the present case, however, into two rivers, Lethe and Eunoe, instead of four [29] – an astonishing change for Dante to make from the traditional picture of Eden, a point in his originality and in the classical influence to which he was subject. He began with taking over Lethe and then invented Eunoe for obvious reasons. Another somewhat paradisial scene in the *Purgatorio* that should be mentioned is the charming valley on the side of the mountain.[30] The path leading there was something between steep and level; the grass and flowers were of surpassing colors; and there too was the fragrance of a thousand scents.[31]

[28] The ladder figure is used here too, *Purg.* xxvii, 124. See also the steps of three colors, white, perse, and red, *ibid.*, ix, 76ff.; and Jacob's ladder itself in the *Paradiso* xxi, 29ff., all of gold and extending out of sight. In this sphere is Saint Romuald, who according to legend had a vision of Jacob's ladder, which became his symbol in artistic representations.

[29] See Grandgent, *op. cit.*, pp. 580 and 583. Dante refers to the names Euphrates and Tigris (*Purg.* xxxiii, 112).

[30] *Purg.* vii, 70ff.

[31] Full documentation for the material regarding Dante's sources need hardly be given here. The parallel to Virgil's description of the Elysian fields

Like the scene of the Paradise in the *Purgatorio* the garden in Imperial's *Decir de las Siete Virtudes* has the river barrier.[32] In this work of the fifteenth century, Imperial is so considerably influenced by Dante and Brunetto Latini [33] that it may well be discussed here. Though not asleep, the poet has a vision at dawn in a green meadow by a spring where a rosebush is in flower. He sees a garden encircled by a crystal rivulet which flows from a spring, and walled about by a very high wall of jasmine, where the water makes sweet music:

> Era çercado todo aquel jardin
> De aquel arroyo á guissa de cava,
> E por muro muy alto jazmin
> Que todo á la redonda lo çercava:
> El son del agua en dulçor passava
> Harpa, duçayna, vyhuela de arco,
> E non me digan que mucho abarco
> Que non ssé sy dormia ó velava.[34]

At first he can find no entrance, bridge, or gate, but then in the jasmine sees a door of ruby brighter than flame. He has great desire to go in:

> Muy á vagar passé allen la puente,
> Oliendo del jardin los dulçes olores,
> Por que de entrar ove mayor talante
> E fise entrada entre flores é flores.[35]

And so he goes over the bridge he apparently discovers, and meets various personified Virtues, some of whom are singing, and sees the Deadly Sins as snakes.

(*Aeneid* vi, 637ff.) has been pointed out with reference to this scene and also that of the realm of Limbo in the *Inferno*. Further influence in the latter scene from the *Visio Sancti Pauli* is indicated by T. Silverstein in [*Harvard*] *Studies and Notes in Philology and Literature*, XIX (1937), pp. 231ff. On the question of Dante's indebtedness to Moslem ideas here or elsewhere see for a recent discussion August Rüegg, *Die Jenseits Vorstellungen vor Dante*, I, pp. 435ff.

[32] *El Cancionero de Juan Alfonso de Baena*, ed. P. J. Pidal, no. 250, pp. 243ff.

[33] Among other studies of the sources see especially *Mediaeval Spanish Allegory*, C. R. Post, pp. 171ff.

[34] Pidal, *op. cit.*, p. 245.

[35] *Ibid.*, p. 246.

In the fourteenth century Federico Frezzi, also an imitator of Dante, has still more Otherworld material in his *Quadriregio,* in the difficult road of the valley in his approach to Fortune's realm ("Per l'aspero cammin di quella valle") [36] and in his full account of the Earthly Paradise in the traditional manner.[37] He includes also a descent to the lower world, obviously much indebted to the *Inferno,* and for symbolic purposes makes considerable use of the valley and the mountain.[38] Related material in his section devoted to the Realm of Love will be considered when we come to the allegory of Courtly Love. The Earthly Paradise seems to be in the east:

It is a garden full of flowers of greater fragrance than any we know, and provided with every fruit. This is the region the Lord placed where the sun has most virtue; here the air is serene and is full of sweet songs. At its gate stands the angel with the flaming sword. While the poet is listening to the music of the birds he sees two venerable figures approaching: Enoch and Elias – to their direction his guide Minerva now relinquishes him. He sees the Tree of Knowledge of Good and Evil all stripped of foliage and dry; around it coils a serpent, and on it no bird sings. The Tree of Life is here with its roots in the heavens and its branches on the earth. Here too are the rivers springing from a stream of great size but they are indicated chiefly by their derivatives. Here is the grove in which Adam concealed himself to taste the apple. And the great height of the whole plateau leads the poet to ask for an explanation of the temperate climate.

For all its special touches of originality here and there, chiefly prompted by Dante, this description reflects largely the Garden of Eden as we know it in the story of Seth. Notable, however, is the height of the region so that the ninth heaven and the Primum Mobile affect the quality of its atmosphere.[39] In the chapters that

[36] *Il Quadriregio,* ed. Enrico Filippini (*Scrittori d'Italia,* 65), p. 158 (ii, cap. xiii). Cf. also Filippini's, *La Materia del Quadriregio.*

[37] *Il Quadriregio,* pp. 275ff. (iv, cap. i).

[38] Classical influence appears in the mountain scene of Vulcan's home, pp. 70ff. (i, cap. xiv) and that of the cave of Eolus, p. 78 (i, cap. xv) and doubtless in the temples on high mountains (iv, cap. vi; iv, cap. xv). The Mountain of Vices, however, seems imitative of Dante's *Purgatorio,* pp. 202ff. (iii, cap. ii). The two paths, the broad to pleasure and the narrow one to duty, leading respectively to Hell and to Heaven, are described, p. 109 (ii, cap. iii).

[39] Cf. *Purg.* xxviii, 97ff.

follow the poet visits the castles of the Four Cardinal Virtues. They have high walls: that of Justice is of crystal; that of Prudence, of sapphire; and so on. From the realm of Caritá the poet also ascends to Heaven.[40]

Apparently quite independent of the tradition from Dante, and technically far closer to the *Roman de la Rose*,[41] Guillaume de Guileville's three pilgrimages show a comparable pilgrim's progress and include much Otherworld material of importance. These fourteenth-century allegories have an encyclopedic inclusiveness that make them potential contributors of the greatest importance in the field of symbolism. Guillaume uses the dream motif, and his general pattern at once suggests the sort of experience familiar in the Latin visions. In the *Pélerinage de Vie Humaine* [42] he at first sees in his dream the heavenly Jerusalem as in a mirror. On his journey thither he has to be plunged in the River of Baptism. An interesting detail is introduced when Reason tells him to use his staff as a bridge over the river of this world when necessary, wherefore he is to be called "pontifex." [43] The broad road to pleasure and the narrow way to duty are described with the thorny hedge of Penitence between them.[44] At length he swims in the Sea of the World, where he comes upon various islands: the tree and wheel of Fortune; a hill of sand which is the island of Astronomy and Astrology; an island with a revolving tower; and so on.[45] The Ship of Religion finally rescues him.

De Guileville's *Pélerinage de l'Ame* has been very thoroughly

[40] The description of the journey through the spheres is not extensive. The earth, as he looks down, appears like a grain of millet, p. 384 (iv, cap. xxii).

[41] The most significant study of his sources for our purposes now is that of S. L. Galpin regarding the *Pélerinage de l'Ame, PMLA,* XXV (1910), pp. 275ff.

[42] Ed. J. J. Stürzinger, *Le Pélerinage de Vie Humaine* (Roxburghe Club).

[43] *Ibid.*, p. 23, 696ff.

[44] *Ibid.*, p. 203, 6503ff. The broad way and the thorny narrow way are described in Baudoin de Condé's *Voie de Paradis* (*Dits et Contes de Baudoin de Condé,* etc., ed. August Scheler, I, pp. 205ff.). Also see Rutebeuf's *Voie de Paradis* (*Œuvres Complètes de Rutebeuf,* ed. A. Jubinal, II, pp. 171ff.) deriving probably from the *Roman de la Rose,* and cf. the *Besant de Dieu.*

[45] These appear in De Guileville's later version of his poem, and in the rendering by John Lydgate. See *The Pilgrimage of the Life of Man, Englisht by John Lydgate,* etc., ed. K. B. Locock, (*EETS: ES,* 92, p. xix). For the French of the later version see *Le Rommant des Trois Pélerinaiges,* c. 1500, fols. lxvj *vo.*

analyzed,[46] showing the unquestionable indebtedness to the visions in its main outlines and many details. Here we find the Soul in a dream with a good and a bad angel, journeying above the earth, which appears as a small town. The Soul visits Purgatory, Hell, and Heaven. Above the earth it sees the Dry Tree. Heaven, when it gets there, is shown to be surrounded by a body of water. Toward the end of the poem the Soul also beholds the Tree of Life with a long dry branch on which is a cross. Details of the influence from the visions have been indicated and include the angel as guide, the description of fire enclosing the earth, the punishment by alternating heat and cold, the stench of Hell, the fragrance of Paradise, and the precious stones in the divisions of Paradise. On two details in the aforementioned study, however, special comment is necessary. The precious stones in Paradise are compared with those in Revelation (xxi: 19–20) and the *Vision of Tundale*, and for the carbuncle "Old French poetry is responsible." [47] Here we may notice that the emerald and the carbuncle are fairly constant among the jewels in the descriptions of the Earthly Paradise we have examined.[48] Elsewhere in the same study the reference to birds singing praises is proved to be from the Latin visions of Irish origin and the *Vita Sancti Brendani*.[49] We may also notice the same idea in Arnold of Bonneval's description of Paradise.[50]

A classical echo with medieval modification appears, on the other hand, in the *Trionfi* of Petrarch when the captives of love visit the Isle of Venus in the Aegean: "Un' isoletta dilicata e molle," [51] where there is an "ombroso e chiuso colle." Here are sweet odors, fountains, streams, birds, and all the attributes of

[46] By Mr. Galpin, *op. cit.*, see especially pp. 279ff.

[47] See Mr. Galpin's study, *op. cit.*, p. 303; *Pélerinage de l'Ame*, ed. J. J. Stürzinger (Roxburghe Club), pp. 9456ff.

[48] See pp. 137ff. above.

[49] Galpin, *op. cit.*, pp. 305f.; *Pél. de l'Ame*, 9685ff. A more important passage, however, is that describing the larks which sing "Jesus, Jesus" — 8777ff. In the *Pélerinage Jhesucrist* birds take Guillaume in a dream to the top of a mountain from which he sees the whole world. See the edition of J. J. Stürzinger (Roxburghe Club), p. 5, ll. 89ff.

[50] See pp. 147–148 above.

[51] *Trionfi*, iii, 101 (*Die Triumphe Francesco Petrarcas*, ed. Carl Appel, p. 217. Cf. p. xxii.). Cf. also *I Trionfi di F. Petrarca, Testo Critico*, ed. Carl Appel. See Neilson, *Origins and Sources of the Court of Love*, p. 115, for the

Paradise in a valley somewhat like that described by Claudian; but the effect seems to be debilitating, and here is the entrance to Love's Hell, a place of fire and ice and eternal darkness.[52] In the Middle English poem *Wynnere and Wastoure* the poet lies down alone to sleep by the bank of a stream near a fine hawthorne; and though for a while kept awake by the noise of the waters, he sleeps at last and dreams of a "loueliche lande (clearing)" that "laye loken by a lawe (hill) the lengthe of a myle." [53] The apparatus of the dream and the similarities to other allegorical works of this type suggest that here too is an Otherworld reminiscence, even if the influence is vague. A clearer example that has long been recognized,[54] however, is that of the *Pearl,* where in a dream the poet goes toward a forest in which are hills and towering crystal cliffs. Here are the fragrance of fruit, the singing birds, and a stream passing over precious stones with banks of beryl on the other side of which he thinks is Paradise. At the foot of a crystal cliff he sees the maiden he is seeking. Later he also beholds the Celestial City as he tells us in lines indebted to Revelation. The river barrier suggests something of the Latin visions, and the jewels in the stream and the fragrant fruit remind one of the Garden of Eden, but the whole account is highly original.

The *Testament of Love,* which, incidentally, also deals with a lady called Pearl, introduces a different motif. The author tells of remembering how once toward winter he set forth to see the

---

similarity to descriptions like that in Claudian. On the medieval element, cf. Post, *Mediaeval Spanish Allegory*, pp. 82–83.

[52] Such is the reading of one group of manuscripts. See Appel, *Die Triumphe Francesco Petrarcas,* p. 220, ll. 157–158.

[53] *The Parlement of the Thre Ages,* ed. Israel Gollancz (Roxburghe Club), p. 91 (*Wynnere and Wastoure,* ll. 48–49). A somewhat similar beginning appears in the *Vision of Piers Plowman,* which has also its tower, deep dale, and fair field.

[54] See the analysis of C. G. Osgood, *The Pearl, A Middle English Poem,* pp. xxxvii–xxxviii. For the journey to the hill near the river's source, in going to the Celestial City, cf. above p. 161. Another religious poem with a beginning like that of many poems of Courtly Love is the alliterative *Quatrefoil of Love,* ed. Israel Gollancz and M. M. Weale, *EETS,* 95. Note the "welle" and the "mery orcherde" and the birds. Cf. also the opening of Berceo's *Milagros de Nuestra Sennora* (in the *Biblioteca de Autores Españoles,* LVII, pp. 103ff.) with reminiscences of the Earthly Paradise.

world and found himself wandering alone in the woods. Great beasts frightened him there and he took to sea in a ship called Travail. After a voyage over a stormy sea he was driven to an island where he was met by Love and where he discovered his "Margaryte-perle" in a blue shell. All this is presented without much description,[55] but the woods and their significance seem to offer a parallel to the scene in Dante's *Inferno.* A comparable forest with very different symbolic meaning is that in the *Desert of Religion,* in early fifteenth-century manuscripts, written on the text *Ductus est Jesus in desertum a spiritu, ut temptaretur.* Here religion itself is the desert, a thorny place ("thorne-garth"), which is sharp with the "scharpenes of strayt lyfynge," a protection really against "wykked bestes." [56] The good trees are various virtues and include the Tree of Life that "standes in-myddes paradyse" and the Tree of Joys in Heaven, but there are also trees of sin and damnation. The desert is penitence of heart.

The Earthly Paradise itself was represented in a pageant for Henry the Sixth's triumphal entry into London in 1432. John Lydgate describes the scene for us.[57] At Cheapside at the conduit the water, running "like welles off Paradys," was turned into wine drawn by three virgins, Mercy, Grace, and Pity. Trees with fresh leaves offered fruit: oranges, almonds, pomegranates, and others. Here too were Enoch and Elias, who addressed the king. One cannot be sure in this arrangement that the four rivers were represented at the conduit, but the episode as a whole shows its origin. The pageants for other occasions show a use of Otherworld material from time to time, and they transmitted much of this to the masques and Lord Mayor's shows of a later period. For example in the pageant of 1377 for Richard II, a castle was erected at Cheapside which had four towers recalling the arrangement in

[55] *Testament of Love,* i, ch. iii (*Complete Works of Geoffrey Chaucer,* ed. W. W. Skeat, VII, supplt. vol., pp. 15–16).

[56] The poem is edited in *Archiv für das Studium der neueren Sprachen,* CXXVI (1911), pp. 58ff.

[57] And perhaps he was responsible for the verses used on that occasion. For his description see *The Minor Poems of John Lydgate,* ed. H. N. MacCracken and Merriam Sherwood, Part II, (*EETS,* 192,) pp. 641ff. For the authorship see the discussion in Robert Withington's *English Pageantry, An Historical Outline,* I, pp. 141f., n. 2, and *Archiv für das Studium der neueren Sprachen,* CXXVI, pp. 76ff.

Grosseteste's poem. In each of them stood a beautiful virgin in garments of white who blew leaves of gold at the King and threw counterfeit golden coins before him. On the top stood a golden angel, and on the two sides of the castle wine flowed forth.[58]

Damsels representing the four Cardinal Virtues stand in the four corners of the House of Reason (which, however, is not a castle) in Alfonso de la Torre's *Visión Delectable*. This Spanish prose work of the first half of the fifteenth century describes the child Understanding with the damsel Instinct at the foot of a great mountain and tells how he visits the abodes of the Arts. At the top of the mountain he finds the wonderful road that leads to the Quadrivium, and there too he at last meets Truth, queen of the whole region, and her sisters, Wisdom, Nature, and Reason. They live in an enclosure which has no night but always clear day, one in which the sun shines with unobstructed splendor and the air is always delightfully warm – here is no excessive heat or cold, a garden in which grow odoriferous trees and trees that bear delicious fruit. The birds sing here with angelic melody; and here is the Tree of Life and of the Knowledge of Good and Evil, at the foot of which runs a stream on a bed of jewels. In this place is no sickness, no decay, no death, no sadness – and the negative formula listing the evils missing or banished runs on for many lines, with some mention too of the good things that are included by way of contrast. In this picture the mountain with the Earthly Paradise at its summit falls in with a long tradition familiar in the

[58] Thomas Walsingham, *Historia Anglicana*, ed. H. T. Riley, (*Rolls Series*), I, pp. 331–332. Cf. Withington, *English Pageantry*, I, p. 128. Perhaps the same structure is what appeared in 1415: see Withington, *op. cit.*, I, p. 134 (at Cheapside); and cf. again the scene at Cheapside in 1522, *ibid.*, pp. 177–178; and *Hall's Chronicle*, London, 1809 (*The Union of the Two Noble and Illustre Famelies of Lancastre and Yorke*), p. 639: ". . . in maner quadrant with fower towers. . . . In the fower towers were fower fayre ladyes for the cardinall vertues. . . ."; also that for Anne Boleyn in 1533, A. F. Pollard, *Tudor Tracts* (Arber's English Garner), pp. 17–18, a "fair tower with four turrets with vanes" with music and singing children, and *Antiquarian Repertory*, III, p. 209: "in every turrett stood one of the cardinal vertues." This type of castle seems to have become conventional, but here again coincidence is easy. Cf. Withington, *op. cit.*, I, 94, for a French instance as early as 1330; and *ibid.*, I, 113, for one in a "disguising" of 1501. Mountains of various sorts also appear in entertainments of this kind: cf. the Mount of Love, *ibid.*, I, 114.

present study,[59] but its symbolic application is in some points new and original.

A most lavish description of the garden, of a type not dissimilar, appears in the late fifteenth-century *Court of Sapience.* The author tells of a vision such as one often encounters in the literature of Courtly Love: he finds himself in a desert place in which he has lost his way:

> In moche derknesse, in caues, in couert,
> Wyth wylde bestes in deuouryng expert . . .[60]

At length he discovers a path "thorny and strayte" and comes to a meadow surrounded by a river. We are told that the desert place is Worldly Occupation and the river is Quiet. He comes to a bridge of marble on arched pillars with pinnacles and towers, and as he crosses it he sees that the banks of the stream are filled with all kinds of precious stones, which he proceeds to list and describe in the manner of a Lapidary. There is no good property which the river does not have:

> In Paradyse he hath hys soueraynte
> Bothe owte and in to ren wyth liberte . . .[61]

In it are, of course, all kinds of fish, as in the neighboring garden are all sorts of flowers and trees. The birds here, listed in detail, sing so sweetly that their song pierces through to heaven and they bid the cherubim to "lerne wyth what tewne thow shalt syng *Sanctus.*" [62] After telling of the animals in the garden, the poet beholds a comely castle with seven towers. Its moat is filled from the river Quiet; it is set on a rock; and from the towers come seven

[59] For the whole treatise see *Biblioteca de Autores Españoles,* XXXVI, pp. 341ff. The Paradise is on p. 352; the reference to the Cardinal Virtues in the corners of Reason's house is on p. 388 (cf. p. 377). See also Post, *Mediaeval Spanish Allegory,* pp. 256ff., and the present author's *Tradition of Boethius,* p. 91.

[60] *The Court of Sapience,* ed. Robert Spindler, pp. 128ff., ll. 130ff. The garden motif by itself is of course found again and again: for example in the *Pietosa Fonte* of Zenone da Pistoia (ed. Francesco Zambrini, *Scelta di Curiosità,* 137) of the fourteenth century. The garden is entered by a path; there are the usual trees, meadows, fountains, and flowers (white in this case), and birds singing so sweetly they make the poet long to sleep.

[61] Spindler, *op. cit.,* p. 170, ll. 1152–1153.

[62] *Ibid.,* p. 179, l. 1393.

Virtues: the three Theological and four Cardinal. From the chief tower (the "dongeon"), which rose to heaven, came Philosophy and here among others are also the seven Liberal Arts. In this elaborate allegory many features point to influence from Robert Grosseteste, whose ideas, however, when they are introduced, are considerably developed. Interesting features which are independent, however, are the dark wilderness, the river, the bridge, and the song of the birds; and these seem derived from the tradition of the symbolism used in the poetry of Courtly Love. Behind the influence of Grosseteste and also that of Courtly Love, I may add, are the suggestions which come from the Earthly Paradise.

The mountain is used in the fifteenth-century *Defunnsion de Don Enrique de Villena* written by the Marquis de Santillana. Here at a desolate season when the wind has stripped the trees of their leaves, the poet found himself at the foot of a wooded mountain:

> Me ví todo solo al pié de un collado
> Selvático, espesso, lexano á poblado,
> Agreste, desierto, é tan espantable . . .[63]

Without any guide he proceeds on the solitary path and meets wild beasts and also strange monsters which fill the air with the clamor of their grief. At the top of the mountain he finds the nine Muses lamenting the death of Villena. A notable fact is that the atmosphere of the mountainside is foggy and the place dark, on the whole like the Inferno described in Santillana's *Bías contra Fortuna,*[64] where we have, however, the addition of the Elysian Fields. In the *Defunnsion* we find the influence of Dante's *Inferno* and Virgil's Hades, but in the *Bías contra Fortuna* chiefly that of Virgil. The Elysian Fields, it is true, seem to be located on a mountain;[65] the waters of the river harmonize with the songs of the birds; the negative formula (there is no excessive heat or cold) is used. And one might argue that in the first two of these

[63] *Obras de Don Iñigo Lopez de Mendoza, Marqués de Santillana,* ed. Don José Amador de los Rios, pp. 241ff. For a discussion with some consideration of similar descriptions, see Post, *Mediaeval Spanish Allegory,* pp. 49f.; 220ff.

[64] *Obras,* p. 205. Cf. Post, *op. cit.,* pp. 230–231.

[65] *Obras,* pp. 212–213. Does the "montaña" refer merely to the wooded region?

features there is a faint reminiscence of the *Purgatorio,* and certainly in all three there is evidence of something derived from the Otherworld tradition in general.

Much of the poetry in Middle Scottish with an allegorical framework belongs to the literature of Courtly Love, which will be considered later. But *King Hart* by Gavin Douglas, of a more strictly didactic nature, may receive attention now, although its few details of special interest to us here probably derive from the conventions of that genre. In this poem the King's castle is sursounded by a stream "Blak, stinkand, sowr, and salt as is the sey" —

> That on the wallis wiskit, gre by gre,
> Boldning to ryis the castell to confound,[66]

and the "pretty place" of Dame Plesance near by with its bulwarks has a bridge

> that hegeit was, and strang;
> And all that couth attene the castell neir,
> It made thame for to mer amiss, and mang.[67]

With all their startling resemblance, however, to the foul river and the difficult bridge of the Latin visions, we cannot be sure that in this case we have more than a coincidence provided by a moat in the one instance, and a drawbridge in the other, and the poet's imagination at work on them. One may compare, nevertheless, the corresponding items in the Old French romance *La Mule sanz Frain.*

ii

A large number of medieval allegories are devoted to the use of certain forms of presentation which become so conventional that the productions may be classed together, within reasonable limits, as forming a tradition of their own. In one such group may be considered the poems and treatises of Courtly Love and in another those that have to do with the Goddess Fortuna. In both cases, however, the documents have already been submitted to so

[66] *The Poetical Works of Gavin Douglas,* ed. John Small, I, p. 88.
[67] *Ibid.,* p. 89.

much scrutiny in other monographs [68] that it hardly seems necessary to examine the greater part of them in much detail here. Yet it may be illuminating to take up outstanding examples, and for the rest refer to significant details as discussed in the various studies.

The typical framework in the literature of Courtly Love is the dream or vision, and one may be tempted to see in this some influence from the sort of visions we have already discussed. Something of the sort is, of course, probable, but I see no great evidence for it. The chief elements in these works,[69] seem ultimately indebted to classical allegory as far as palace or dwelling and perhaps even the mountain are concerned. Christian works offered material rather for the personifications.[70] Still the problem of sources is far from simple, and each document is likely to raise special questions of its own. In *De arte honesti amandi* of Andreas Capellanus (completed by 1186) we find the Palace of Love "in the middle of the world" (*in medio mundi*) "with four very splendid façades" in each of which is a gate.[71] Three of these entrances are "assigned to three definite classes of ladies" suggesting a kind of maidenland as we find it in Irish, but the indications of Celtic borrowing are too vague to be reliable. Near at hand is a garden with beautiful meadows, "every kind of fruitful and fragrant trees," and in the center a "marvellously tall tree, bearing abun-

[68] For example, *The Origins and Sources of the Court of Love*, by W. A. Neilson, ([*Harvard*] *Studies and Notes in Philology and Literature, VI*); Patch, *The Goddess Fortuna in Mediaeval Literature*; Post, *Mediaeval Spanish Allegory*, especially chapter vii (pp. 75ff.), "The Erotic Hell"; and A. Doren, "Fortuna im Mittelalter und in der Renaissance," *Vorträge der Bibliothek Warburg*, II, i (Leipzig, Berlin, 1924), pp. 71ff.

[69] As Mr. Neilson suggests, *op. cit.*, pp. 8–17 and 23. Note that here we find the Otherworld features. For the dream setting see *ibid.*, p. 213, and cf. Langlois, *Origines et Sources du Roman de la Rose*, pp. 55ff.

[70] Cf., however, above pp. 181–183 and especially note 21.

[71] *The Art of Courtly Love by Andreas Capellanus*, ed. J. J. Parry, (*Records of Civilization, Sources and Studies*, XXXIII), p. 73. For the Latin see the edition *Andreae Capellani De amore libri tres*, E. Trojel, pp. 89ff. Cf. the comment with Celtic parallels by A. C. L. Brown, *The Origin of the Grail Legend*, pp. 344ff. and (on the square palace) pp. 358ff.; and note instances in the Latin visions, Genesis, and Revelation, of the square Paradise, *ibid.*, pp. 368–369. See this book, pp. 15, 89, 117, 213, and 301 n. 216. On the bridge episode see *Mod. Lang. Rev.*, XXVI (1931), p. 73, n.1.

dantly all sorts of fruits." [72] At the roots of this "gushed forth a wonderful spring of the clearest water, which to those who drank of it tasted of the sweetest nectar, and in this spring one saw all sorts of little fishes." From this source "many brooks and rivulets flowed out in all directions." The garden itself is divided into three parts: the inmost (in which is the tree) called Delightfulness, the next Humidity, and the third Aridity. This third section has baked earth and intense heat, and bundles of thorns each on a pole and thus held by two strong men. It is difficult to identify any special tradition in all this material; but the third section recalls the familiar motif of the desert tract, and the tree with the spring at its roots may seem like that in *De Pascha* attributed to Cyprian, or even the Norse Yggdrasil.[73]

Later in the treatise of Andreas a knight comes to "a certain river of marvellous breadth and depth, with great waves in it, and because of the great height of its banks it was impossible for anyone to reach it." [74] He finds, however, a bridge of gold with one end at each bank and the middle, which rested in the water, often covered by great waves. It is guarded by a knight "of ferocious aspect" who tells the traveler that if he wishes to cross the bridge he must be "seeking death." After their combat another bridge keeper "of tremendous size" appears across the river who, as the traveler sets his horse to pass over, shakes the bridge so that "much of the time it was hidden by the waves." The hero drowns his opponent, however, and on the other side finds a region of beautiful meadows and flowers. Here is a circular palace with no door that he can discover. After a while, nevertheless, one appears and opens with a shock like that of thunder, and a man "of gigantic size" comes with a copper club to challenge him. Still later he finds another palace of gold with many rooms where King Arthur sits in state. In these details the explicit reference to the Arthurian story would lead one in all fairness, I believe, to suspect Celtic origins. The bridge crossing to the scene of the meadows and flowers is like that in Latin visions, but I

[72] Parry, *op. cit.*, pp. 78f.; Trojel, *De amore*, p. 100.
[73] Cf. above, p. 156.
[74] Parry, *op. cit.*, pp. 178ff.; Trojel, *De Amore*, pp. 298ff.

think there is a touch of Celtic fantasy in the way it is managed.[75]

Such gardens and palaces or castles become a constant feature in the literature of Courtly Love. Specific influence is seldom apparent, nor need such indebtedness be presupposed. The Provençal Guiraut de Calanso describes a palace with five portals "two of which having been passed, the other three are easy of entrance" but "the exit is hard." [76] In the *Chastel d'Amours* a noble castle is to be built with hard-hearted ladies for the high towers, gates of speech for portals, and keys of prayer.[77] A garden with fountain and singing birds appears in the verses of Jaufre Rudel and Peire Guillem.[78] In the famous altercation of Phyllis and Flora in the *Carmina Burana,* which appears also in English and French versions and had a wide popularity, there is a visit to the "Paradise of Love." [79] At the entrance of the grove murmurs a stream; the wind is filled with perfume. Here instruments make sweet music, and there is the song of birds. Immortality is the share of anyone who stays in this delightful spot, and here are the usual fruit trees; the paths are fragrant with myrrh, cinnamon, and balsam. In the French version of this, known as *De Florence et de Blancheflor,* we have a palace with sides of roses and other flowers and a surrounding wall of Cupid's bows. A bird parliament is held in the garden inside.[80] In *Li Fablel dou Dieu D'Amours* there is a garden plainly influenced by the Earthly

[75] Certain points of similarity in Chrétien's *Lancelot* are obvious. Cf. Brown, *op. cit.*, p. 348.

[76] Neilson, *Origins and Sources,* p. 24. Cf. *ibid.*, p. 26. For the text see Karl Bartsch, *Chrestomathie Provençale,* (rev. E. Koschwitz,) cols. 183–184.

[77] Neilson, *op. cit.*, p. 28. For text see Bartsch, *op. cit.*, col. 299. Such a castle besieged with fruit and flowers is described in an entertainment held at Treviso in 1214. See L. A. Muratori, *Rerum Italicarum scriptores,* Milan, 1726, cols. 180–181, (translated in G. G. Coulton's *Life in the Middle Ages,* III, pp. 47ff.) Also cf. the ivory carving of a Castle of Love under siege, Schultz, *Höfische Leben,* I, p. 577, fig. 171; and for further examples in art, *American Journal of Archaeology,* second series, XXIII (1919), pp. 255ff.

[78] Neilson, *op. cit.*, pp. 26–27. Bartsch, *op. cit.*, cols. 59 and 296.

[79] *Carmina Burana,* ed. J. A. Schmeller, pp. 162ff., stanzas 59ff. For Courtly Love see Neilson, *op. cit.*, pp. 34ff.

[80] Neilson, *op. cit.*, pp. 36–37. For the text, E. Barbazan and D. M. Méon, *Fabliaux et Contes,* IV, pp. 360ff. Neilson describes another fantastic palace (pp. 37f.) with a wall "no snow or rain or fire can pass." This is *Hueline et Aiglantine* in Méon's *Nouveau Recueil de Fabliaux et Contes,* I, pp. 353ff., where again there is a palace of flowers and of course singing birds.

Paradise.[81] In fact from Paradise flows a stream that waters its meadow, and if an old man bathes himself therein he becomes at once youthful, and an old woman becomes a girl. Its sands, of course, are of precious stones. Trees, flowers, and singing birds are here; no winter causes harm. About the garden is a ditch with water running through it from the river. Before the gate is a bridge all of fine gold and marble, but if any churl walks on it the bridge is raised and the portal shut. For a courtly visitor this does not happen, and this power of discrimination is startling; but a reminiscence of the Bridge of Judgment in this case is, I would suspect, remote [82] and even then as a logical derivative from the same feature in Andreas Capellanus's description.

What seems to be derived from the typical river barrier appears again in the *Roman de la Rose*. The scene here is too familiar to need close analysis, but it may be noted that the river is "grant e roide," the water clear and cold, and its bed paved with gravel.[83] The poet bathes his face and, without having to cross the stream, follows along its bank. Soon he comes to the garden wall, which is crenelated and on which a number of personified abstractions are represented. Within are trees and birds singing in sweet accord. A wicket gate "petitet e estroit" admits the poet who sees a "parevis terrestre" and again hears the celestial song of the birds:

[81] For the text see *Li Fablel dou Dieu D'Amours*, ed. Achille Jubinal, pp. 13ff. On the sources of the poems of this group see E. Langlois, *Origines et Sources du Roman de la Rose* (*Bibl. des Écoles Françaises d'Athènes et de Rome*, LVIII), pp. 12ff. Material in the *Fablel* has been sometimes found similar to that in *De Venus la Deesse d'Amor*, ed. Wendelin Foerster. In the latter see the Otherworld castle with tower, wall, foss (where the water springs from tears), and a hall of crystal paved with amber and coral: stanzas 221, 239, and 241.

[82] The poet says "Moi fu avis que fuisse en paradis" (p. 17, *Li Fablel*, ed. Jubinal). Note also: a bird parliament is held; in the second dream the poet is led to a palace surrounded by a ditch or moat in which was water and over which was a bridge; the ditches are interpreted as sighs, the water as lovers' tears, and the bridge was made of songs (*ibid.*, pp. 24–25); a phoenix was doorkeeper; the pillars of the palace represented the months; and outside the palace was a meadow in the midst of which stood a tree filled with singing birds (*ibid.*, p. 31). For other palaces see Neilson, *op. cit.*, pp. 39 and 43 (the door of coral, the building of crystal).

[83] *Le Roman de la Rose*, ed. E. Langlois, (*SATF*, CVIII), II, pp. 6f., ll. 103ff.

Trop par faisoient bel servise
Cil oisel que je vos devise.
Il chantoient un chant itel
Con fussent ange esperitel.[84]

Every kind of tree and every sort of fruit may here be found; fountains and brooks too, with the Fountain of Narcissus of which the bed is a sand brighter than fine silver. At the bottom are two stones of crystal that mirror the garden, and the waters run through two channels. In one of the stones the dreamer sees the rosebush reflected which symbolizes what he is searching for, and which by considerable forcing of correspondences may be taken as the substitute in this Paradise for the Tree of Life. It is surrounded by a hedge of thorns and briars. Jealousy builds a castle to protect the rose: it is square with towers at the four corners and another in the center; it is founded on a solid rock and has a moat; a gate opens on each of the four sides toward the four points of the compass (ll. 3800ff.). The resemblance here to the palace in Andreas Capellanus's description is obvious enough and, it seems clear, shows indebtedness; [85] but how it is related to the similar structure in Grosseteste's *Chasteau d'Amour*, it would be difficult to say. They both may derive from Andreas; or — considering the details of the foundation and the towers — De Lorris may be the rather flippant borrower from Grosseteste;[86] or we may have another startling example of the play of coincidence.

In Jean de Meun's part of the *Roman* the symbolism of paths through the garden is introduced. The poet leaves the righthand path and takes the left, which is guarded by Richesse. Later the usual broad and narrow ways are referred to (ll. 20213ff.); and a long account of the true Paradise (ll. 20267ff.) gives us again

[84] *Ibid.*, pp. 34–35, ll. 661–664.

[85] On the sources of the poem see Neilson, *op. cit.*, especially pp. 52ff.; and Langlois, *Origines et Sources du Roman de la Rose*, especially pp. 10ff., 24, and 33–34. F. M. Warren proposed a Byzantine source written in the twelfth century. See *Publ. Mod. Lang. Assoc.*, XXXI (1916), pp. 232ff. The Byzantine story has a park enclosed by a wall decorated with allegorical figures, a carved stone fountain, and a pillar of "many-colored stone."

[86] For the transference of apparatus from the veneration of the Virgin Mary to the cult of Venus, see Neilson, *op. cit.*, p. 221, and the *Carmina Burana*, ed. Schmeller, pp. 141ff., No. 50.

the flowery meads, the fountain of life which flows forth on a bed of crystal sand and then under the roots of the (olive) Tree of Salvation (reminiscent perhaps of the *Legend of Seth*), and a three-faceted carbuncle within the fountain which radiates light and fragrance. Indeed one could say:

> Qu'onques en si bel paradis
> Ne fu fourmez Adans jadis.[87]

The fountain banishes sickness and old age; the carbuncle does away with night. The Book of Revelation could be in the author's mind here, but almost the reverse of that seems to be what has happened. The Earthly Paradise gave suggestions for the account of the Garden of Love and just possibly (in the square castle) a hint or two came from Revelation; the whole picture was taken over by Jean de Meun from the composition of Guillaume de Lorris in this heavenly counterpart with corresponding meadows, flowers, and fountain, and the olive in place of the rose.[88] The olive also appears, incidentally, in a Spanish piece of the same century, the so-called *Romance de Lope de Moros,* where the poet is under the tree in an orchard in April. He sees a vessel of wine and another of cold water. He lies down in a meadow filled with flowers and cooled by a spring, when a beautiful lady approaches singing of love.[89] Here the setting is parallel.

In *La Messe des Oisiaus* of Jean de Condé, the poet dreams one night in May that he is in the midst of a forest in a most beautiful glade. He is sitting on a mound by a pine tree, and all about him the birds are singing. A parrot announces the approach of Venus and a throne is set up for her. Here in the temperate weather are the flowery meadow and varied trees with sweet and clear fountains pouring down on fine sand, already so familiar and as usual suggesting the Earthly Paradise. Led by the nightingales, the birds sing the Mass in the presence of

[87] *Roman,* ed. Langlois, V, p. 49, ll. 20595–20596. For Jean de Meun's knowledge of the literature of visions see *Romanic Review,* II (1911), pp. 54ff., dealing, however, with details regarding references to Hell.

[88] Jean has also brought in earlier the House of Fortune taken from Alanus de Insulis, ll. 5947ff.

[89] *Romania* XVI (1887), pp. 368ff. Cf. Post, *Mediaeval Spanish Allegory,* pp. 130ff. on the nature of the work.

Venus.[90] The idea of the birds singing the liturgy introduces a feature that recalls other examples of their songs being offered in worship, especially in Celtic Otherworld material.[91] In *La Panthère d'Amours* the poet in a dream is carried off by birds to a forest full of many and varied animals making a tempestuous noise. At the entrance of a valley blocked with rocks and thorns appears the beautiful Panther. The poet meets the God of Love, and then on horseback goes in search of the Panther until he comes to a "fosse" protected by a thorny hedge where the Panther hides. Much later he pays a visit to the House of Fortune which is described with detail borrowed from Alanus de Insulis, but is here constructed on a rock of ice.[92] The thorns and rocks of the poem are interpreted allegorically; with the forest they seem related to a type of waste country or desert of love found elsewhere,[93] and more broadly to the forest and dark valley of vision literature perhaps and Dante's "selva oscura."

In *Li Mireoirs as Dames* Watriquet de Couvin tells of riding along through a great forest when he meets Aventure, who leads him to the fountain or source of beauty "Au chastel c'on claime Thopasse." To reach this he has to climb thirteen steps, each of which is guarded by one of the Virtues.[94] In *Li Tournois des*

[90] *Dits et Contes de Baudouin de Condé et de son Fils Jean de Condé*, ed. Aug. Scheler, III, pp. 1ff.

[91] See above pp. 54f. The motif is found also in the *Vision of the Monk of Wenlock*, the *Vision of Adamnán*, and in the writings of Arnold of Bonneval, and cf. in this chapter, p. 189, n. 49, and p. 193 above. For many uses of the bird motif in allegorical literature see Neilson, *op. cit.*, pp. 216ff. Cf. also *Archiv für das Studium der neueren Sprachen*, CXXX (1913), pp. 310f.

[92] Edited by H. A. Todd, (*SATF*, LXXVII). For the House of Fortune see below pp. 222ff.

[93] For other examples see *Mod. Lang. Notes*, XXXIV (1919), pp. 321ff. and Post, *Mediaeval Spanish Allegory*, pp. 75ff. Cf. Charles d'Orléans and his "forest damoureuse tristesse," translated into Middle English (see E. P. Hammond, *Eng. Verse between Chaucer and Surrey*, p. 229). A forest which is wholly agreeable in a scene like that of Paradise is in *La Prise Amoureuse* of Jehan Acart de Hesdin (see the edition by Hoepffner in *Gesellschaft für Romanische Literatur*, 22, p. 6, ll. 153ff., describing the four symbolic roads). The desolate scene with rocks and thorns is also pictured (*ibid.*, p. 8, ll. 225ff.). So, too, in the *Jardin de Plaisance* there is the pleasant forest (*SATF*, LI, folio e ii vo) and the dark region of fumes and rocks and thorns (folios f iii and h ii vo).

[94] *Dits de Watriquet de Couvin*, ed. Aug. Scheler, pp. 1ff.

Dames Watriquet gives us a striking account of a "Pont perilleus" over a flowing river:

Si parfonde, noire et hideuse
Que c'estoit une orribletez.[95]

The bridge, however, is beautiful, rich with stone and of fine workmanship, on what appears to be a hopelessly weak foundation of wood. Men tread fearlessly on it only to fall into the stream. The whole picture is presented as a parable of the false hopes of man building his towers and castles on such a structure:

Li un tours, maisons et chastiaus,
Sales de pierre et à crestiaus
Y avoient amoncelé,
Li autre de lonc et de lé
Touz les biens qu'il porent avoir.
Onques pont si garni d'avoir
N'oi mais veü en tout mon tans,
Mais il estoit cent mille tans
Plus perilleus que je ne di . . .

because the foundation is so insecure. Here the river shows the general source of the idea; but in this case the Bridge of Judgment is certainly put to quite novel uses with a twist of what is a kind of mixed metaphor. In a walk to the Fountain of Love in another poem Watriquet goes through a garden full of trees where the birds are singing and flowers are in bloom. The fountain itself is of gold and silver and precious stones.[96] Such gardens with their fountains again recall the Earthly Paradise.[97] This is specifically the case with the scene in Guillaume de Machaut's poem *La Fonteinne Amoureuse,* in which the poet is led to the garden where the fountain flows into a vessel of marble on a column of ivory. The ivory is carved with the story of Narcissus, and the basin with that of Venus, Paris, and Helen. The

[95] *Ibid.,* p. 246, lines 474ff.

[96] *Ibid.,* pp. 101ff. For such fountains see Neilson, *op. cit.,* pp. 73–74.

[97] Which was, of course, known to Watriquet. Cf. the *Mireoir as Dames,* ll. 942–943, *ibid.,* p. 30. Such a reference is, of course, conventional; see John Gower's *Balades,* xxxvi, ll. 1–2, and more strikingly, vii, st. 4 (*Complete Works,* ed. G. C. Macaulay, I, pp. 366 and 344 respectively).

meadow surrounding is planted with trees to moderate the sunshine, and the woods and fields are filled with the songs of the birds. All fruits and flowers are there, so that in the whole world there is no fairer Earthly Paradise.[98] The carvings here recall the pictures that so often adorn the palaces or the walls of the Other World in the literature of Courtly Love, and derive from the similar imagery in the *Roman de la Rose*.

In the *Dit dou Vergier* Machaut again is walking in a garden full of blossoming trees and the songs of birds where he follows a path to a flowery meadow. This too he can only describe with reference to the Earthly Paradise. Under a bush covered with flowers of marvelous fragrance in the midst of the meadow sits the God of Love.[99] The *Jugement dou Roy de Behaingne* finds the poet in a similar situation among trees and flowers and the songs of birds, this time near a stream by a fair tower.[100] He sees approaching along a narrow path a lady who has lost her lover by death. In the *Dit dou Lyon* Machaut is wakened by the song of birds, which render "Au printemps loange et servise." He is at a place near a river which surrounds a beautiful garden with all fruits and all plants and flowers including healing herbs. Here too are fountains of surpassing worth. He finds no bridge nor plank nor passageway over the stream, and is troubled thereat because the water is broad and deep; but at length he discovers a beautiful and sumptuous boat in which there is no other creature, but which conveys him. He is met by a lion who leads him over a pathless tract

> Parmi ronces, parmi orties
> Et par espines plus agües . . . .

He sees many cruel beasts but finally goes along a stream until he comes to the customary meadow and fountain where there is a fair pavilion and a noble lady who is the queen of this country.[101]

This work of Machaut's reflects considerably more of the material with which we are familiar, including the river motif,

[98] *Œuvres de Guillaume de Machaut,* ed. Ernest Hoepffner, III, pp. 189ff. (*Font. Amour.*, ll. 1299ff.).

[99] *Œuvres,* I, pp. 13ff.

[100] *Ibid.*, pp. 57ff.

[101] *Œuvres,* II, pp. 159ff.

some implication of the bridge, the thorny waste tract, the rudderless boat (a little recalling that in the lay of *Guigemar* of Marie de France), the fountain and the garden with birds that sing songs of praise, and the guiding animal. This poem has been compared with the Middle English *Chaucer's Dream*.[102] There the poet begins dreaming beside a well in a forest, and he sees an isle with wall and gates of glass where there is a host of fair ladies. The gates have a thousand fanes of gold, towers shaped like flowers, and turrets. Singing birds of course are here, and all is more wondrous than a joyous Paradise.[103] Out on a rock in a "strange se" is a holy hermitage to which the voyage is perilous. A tree with three apples grows there: the first apple keeps youth and beauty, the second nourishes one in pleasure, and he who eats the third may not fail in his delight. The ship that voyages thither has sails ornamented with flowers, "castles" with huge towers, and birds that fly down and sing ballades and lays. The island motif is thus doubly represented in this poem, once with a resemblance to the Celtic maidenland; the tree with the apples and the garden recall the Earthly Paradise. The glass wall with its gates is found elsewhere, for example, in the Book of Enoch; but it may be a reflection of the wall in Revelation made of jasper, which, we are told (xxi:11), was as "clear as crystal," or it may simply show the fondness for glass and crystal in Otherworld scenes in general.

The garden and the fountain, whether derived from scenes in the kind of poetry we have been considering or from actual experience, appear in Boccaccio's *Ameto*, where with the fauns and dryads in the neighboring woods, and satyrs and naiads too, the "bellissimo prato d'erbe copiose e di fiori" and the "chiara fontana" suggest a classical background suitable to the temples it describes.[104] In the *Amorosa Visione* the poet is led through a gate into a garden "Fiorito e bello com' di primavera," where we discover a fountain with carved marble figures and a throng of noble ladies dancing, suggesting again, though doubtless by

[102] Neilson, *op. cit.*, p. 62. See *The Works of Geoffrey Chaucer*, ed. John Urry, pp. 572ff.

[103] Lines 127–128.

[104] *Opere Volgari di Giovanni Boccaccio*, XV, *Ameto*, pp. 29–30.

coincidence, the scene of maidenland.[105] The noble castle with its elaborate paintings, which the poet enters earlier, is a characteristic feature of the literature of Courtly Love.[106] In the *Teseida* the prayer of Palemon rises "sopra'l monte Citerone" to the temple of Venus where there is a kind of garden full of plants and flowers with clear springs and singing birds.[107] The whole scene is familiar in Chaucer's rendering in the *Parlement of Foules*, with the birds, the animals, the fountain (in which Cupid tempers his arrows), the ladies dancing about the temple, and the allegorical figures; but the English poet adds a reminiscence of the Book of Revelation which he doubtless took from the *Roman de la Rose:*

> No man may there waxe sek ne old;
> Yit was there joye more a thousandfold
> Than man can telle; ne nevere wolde it nyghte,
> But ay cler day to any manes syghte.[108]

The fact that Chaucer introduced this negative formula and also lines which seem to come from Dante's description of the Earthly Paradise [109] is significant here. Further details regarding a journey to the Other World, and appearing in the *Teseida* in the account of the flight of Arcite's soul, have been discussed elsewhere in this study [110] with special reference to the influence of the *Somnium Scipionis*; this work too, it will be recalled, was utilized by Chaucer.

Elaborate material of another kind appears in Boccaccio's prose *Corbaccio*. Here the writer, grieving over the treatment he receives from his cruel love, falls asleep and in his dream sees before him a delightful and fair path. Presently he seems even to be furnished with wings and flies along with great speed until his way becomes rocky and full of weeds. A thick mist closes down

[105] *Opere Volgari,* XIV, pp. 151ff. (caps. xxxviiff.). Cf. also the meadow in the painting, p. 63, (cap. xv), which again suggests springtime.

[106] *Ibid.*, pp. 10ff. (caps. iiff.)

[107] *Giovanni Boccaccio, Teseida,* ed. Salvatore Battaglia, pp. 197ff. (vii, stanzas 50ff.)

[108] *Complete Works of Geoffrey Chaucer,* ed. F. N. Robinson, p. 365. (*Parl.* 207–210). For the sources of the whole description, see *ibid.*, p. 903.

[109] Cf. *Parl.* 201–203 with *Purg.* xxviii, 9–15.

[110] Pp. 23–24 above.

on him which holds him from progress, but when it clears he finds himself at night "in una solitudine diserta aspra e fiera, piena di salvatiche piante, di pruni e di bronchi," without path and surrounded by mountains which seemed to touch the sky. Here was the bellowing of wild animals but there appeared to be no escape from the valley, which we learn later is called the "Laberinto d'Amore," the "Valle incantata," the "Porcile di Venere," and the "Valle de' sospiri e della miseria," as it is variously regarded.[111] In all this we have a clear instance of the desert of love as we have seen it also in the *Panthère d'Amours*. With Boccaccio there seems to be just the briefest echo of Dante's "selva oscura," and with the startling element of the mist it quite possibly goes back to the "Val des faux amants" in Arthurian romance,[112] and beyond that to the dark valleys familiar in the Latin visions.

An anonymous work in Italian in the fourteenth century called *L'Intelligenza* shows a framework borrowed largely from the literature of Courtly Love. The scene is laid in the springtime, and the poet is standing by a stream in a garden in the shadow of a pine tree. Near by is a fountain and the usual flowers, and birds are singing. The poet's lady Intelligence appears and is elaborately described. In "una ricca e nobile fortezza" she dwells, a palace of great beauty, surrounded by a "ricca fiumana." The palace is all of marble with doors of ebony, and its entrance is toward the rising sun. Its rooms are richly ornamented, and famous characters are depicted in sculpture and painting within them.[113] The river barrier here is interesting, but the poem is on the whole conventional and overweighted. In the allegorical interpretation we are told that the palace is the soul and body, recalling the general motif of the castle of the body as in the *Songe du Castel*.[114]

[111] *Opere Volgari*, V, pp. 161ff. For possible influence on Chaucer see *Mod. Lang. Notes*, XXXIV (1919), pp. 321ff., with reference to the *House of Fame* and the motif of the desert of love.

[112] Cf. L. A. Paton, *Studies in the Fairy Mythology of Arthurian Romance*, (*Radcliffe College Monographs*, 13,) pp. 81ff., and in the present study pp. 288ff. below. Cf. also the material on pp. 210ff. and 253.

[113] A. F. Ozanam, *Documents Inédits pour Servir a l'Histoire Litt.*, pp. 321ff.

[114] See above in this chapter pp. 182f., n. 21.

A castle symbolically representing a pure woman is in the fourteenth-century German poem *Der Minneburg.* Here the poet comes to a wild mountain surrounded by a stream. Using a raft, he crosses and enters a fair and flower-bedecked meadow, where he sees a strongly defended castle, whose drawbridges are guarded by giants, lions, and dogs. Within he finds a round pillar decorated with gold and precious stones and furnished with five mirrored windows ("fünf spiegelfenstern"). Inside this is a glass image of a man and a steel figure of a woman. Later in the poem another castle is introduced, also guarded like the first.[115] The mountain and its stream offer well-known motifs and with the drawbridges of the castle and their protection, suggest a borrowing from the field of romance. Beyond that they may go back to German folklore or even the Eastern tradition.[116]

In his *Paradys d'Amours* Jean Froissart gives us the sort of description we have seen already in the works of Guillaume de Machaut. The dream opens in a beautiful grove with trees and flowers and the songs of birds. The poet sits near a stream by some blossoming bushes and utters his complaint. Plaisance and Esperance lead him to a clearing in the wood to the pavilion of the God of Love. Later he comes to a meadow all full of flowers and singing birds.[117] A similar scene is offered with flowers and birds and streams in the *Cour de May*[118] where Love holds his

[115] For this summary I have been able to use only the outline given by Ehrismann in Paul u. Braune's *Beiträge,* XXII, (1897), pp. 303ff., and that in Ehrismann's *Geschichte der deutschen Literatur bis zum Ausgang des Mittelalters,* zweiter Teil, Munich, 1935, pp. 501ff. Here note the motif of the storming of the castle (p. 502), derived from the *Carmina Burana.* Cf. also Neilson, *op. cit.,* pp. 123ff. Cf. the columns in the *Voyage of Maeldúin* (§ xxvi); *Voyage of the Húi Corra* (51); the Irish life of Saint Brendan (xxxviii); and especially the "high pillar, all of diamond," *Spectator* 524.

[116] For such mountains in German see pp. 73f. and 78f. above and P. S. Barto, *Tannhäuser and the Mountain of Venus;* and cf. his article in the *Journal of Eng. and Germ. Philol.,* XV (1916), pp. 377ff. Arthur F. J. Remy argues for Celtic origins in some points of the Tannhäuser legend in the *Journal,* XII (1913), pp. 32ff. and is answered by Barto, pp. 295ff. in the same volume. Cf. also, A. H. Krappe, *The Science of Folk-Lore,* pp. 106f. Examples of other motifs familiar in German literature of Courtly Love, including the forest, the garden, the castle, are indicated by Neilson, *op. cit.,* pp. 126, 128, 129, 130, 132.

[117] *Œuvres de Froissart,* ed. Aug. Scheler, I, pp. 1ff.

[118] *Œuvres,* III, pp. 6ff., (*Cour,* ll. 150ff.; 370ff.).

court and the poet finds the lady Leesse guarding a fountain. He then goes to a spot so beautiful that in his opinion the Earthly Paradise could not surpass it.[119] Here is the dwelling of Love in a sumptuously described tent with cords of gold and with jewels of all kinds. The finest ornament of all was a carbuncle on high with eight rubies. The place was enclosed with a hedge of flowers, and a stream ran there which made anyone who washed in it joyous and was a medicine of good fortune and sweetness for the lover. The portal of the dwelling had a tablet engraved with a warning for all false men, liars, and the proud, to flee from the place. A garden, two tents, and a palace, appear also in the *Trésor Amoureux,* if that may be listed as Froissart's work, but they show little special interest here.[120] In the *Temple d'Onnour* the poet in a vision finds himself in a pleasant forest, and is led on horseback along "une voie herbue" until he sees a fair temple in a lovely spot between two rivers. The door of the temple is open and without any guard, and within is a throng of people. Here is the throne of Onnour, to which seven steps lead up with a knight representing a virtue standing on each of them.[121] The pleasant forest and the two rivers are worthy of note. The steps with the virtues imitate the motif in Watriquet de Couvin's *Mireoirs as Dames.*[122]

Les Eschez Amoureux, an anonymous French poem of the last third of the fourteenth century, which gathers up most of the ideas in the literature we have been studying, begins with the poet in bed kept awake by the loud singing of birds. Nature appears to him and bids him behold the beautiful world. There are two paths, one of which starts in the east, goes west, and then returns to the east again; the other does just the reverse of this, starting in the west. These represent the two sides of man's nature at variance, and Reason prefers the first road, while the senses like the second. The poet goes forth on a pleasant green

[119] *Ibid.,* p. 20 (*Cour,* ll. 641–642).

[120] *Ibid.,* pp. 52ff.

[121] *Œuvres,* II, pp. 164ff.

[122] Cf. Neilson, *op. cit.,* pp. 79–80 and above in this chapter p. 202. Four steps appear in the palace of Guiraut de Calanso (Neilson, p. 24). We may also recall the three steps at the gate of Dante's Purgatory (*Purg.* ix, 94ff.), variously interpreted, and the *scala* motif in general.

path. After various experiences he comes to a forest of evergreen trees whose fruit never decays; from Diana he learns of the orchard of Deduis where there are fountains full of poison, "pleasant to see and taste," trees that are usually barren or bear fruit that is worthless or vile, and poisonous herbs among the flowers. He goes on to the garden and there sees a beautiful river flowing over clean gravel and a wall on which various images are depicted. Having entered the gate he finds a spot so beautiful "it seems rather a heavenly than an earthly place," with trees of every kind, flowers and fragrance, wild animals and singing birds. Here is where Jalousie built a castle to imprison Bel Acueil, and here is the fountain of love of Narcissus with gravel all of precious stones and crystal.[123] The indebtedness to the *Roman de la Rose* and other works of the kind in all this will be immediately apparent. Features of special interest, however, are: the two roads, which have not been commonly borrowed and have what is literally their own special twist in this case; and the garden described as having barren trees or trees with worthless fruit, and poisonous fountains and herbs.

In the *Lay du Desert d'Amours,* the title of which is significant, Eustache Deschamps refers to the fountain of Narcissus and speaks of the happy days of yore in the garden of love, a "mondain paradis," where the grass was green, the trees covered with flowers, and the nightingales sang. Now he is in the desert itself:

> Ne venez pas en ce desert
> Ou il n'a fueille, ne boys vert,
> Herbe, fleur, fruit n'autre verdure;
> Tout chant d'oisel y ert desert;
> Fors que bruiere n'y appert,
> Noif, gresil et toute froidure;
> Esté fault la, l'yvers y dure
> En tous temps . . . .[124]

[123] For this analysis I have followed, sometimes even verbally, the synopsis made by Stanley L. Galpin, (*Romanic Review,* XI [1920], pp. 283ff.) The French poem was rendered in English by John Lydgate, whose version, called *Reson and Sensuallyte,* is edited in the *EETS:ES,* 84 and 89, by Ernst Sieper. The sources are indicated in the second of these (pp. 59ff.) and in Sieper's *Les Échecs Amoureux,* (*Litterarhistorische Forschungen,* IX), pp. 127ff.

[124] *Œuvres Complètes de Eustache Deschamps,* ed. Le Marquis de Queux de

Morgan Library MS. 245. *Courtesy of the Pierpont Morgan Library*

THE GARDEN OF THE *ROMAN DE LA ROSE*

THE FOUNTAIN OF NARCISSUS

Here is the perfect counterpart of the Earthly Paradise. The same unhappy idea appears in his *Balade* DXXXV where we read that in the "desert d'amours":

> Verdeur n'y a, esbatement ne joye,
> Fors espines, ronses, tristesce, esmay,
> Langour, freour, dur penser qui m'anoye;
> Le chahuant ses chans de mort m'envoye . . .[125]

and so on. Here is nothing but hail and snow and cold, a kind of negative formula in reverse, with the owl representing the usual singing birds. Both scenes remind us somewhat of the *Corbaccio*.[126] The *Lay Amoureux* presents in contrast a background of lovely weather, trees, bird songs, flowers, fountains, fragrance, all that is delightful, in which the poet has his dream one night. He seems to be walking in a wood and comes to a meadow where there are a fountain, a clear stream, and a tall pine tree. In this place, under a thorn tree, he observes a meeting of Love and many famous lovers.[127] This gives us one more instance of the garden, of course, with the usual properties, but nothing unique except, perhaps, the shining figure of Love descending in a fiery chariot among the group.

Something like the forest of love appears in John Gower's *Confessio amantis*, where in the month of May lamenting his ill success in such matters, the poet goes to the woods to make his complaint.[128] A real desert, however, perhaps symbolizing ideas like those in Deschamps,[129] is found in Chaucer's *House of Fame* (480ff.), where the Otherworld material is elaborately used. Its temple of glass with jeweled pinnacles and ornamentation in pictures and sculpture suggests the Court of Love palace. The flight with the eagle calls up thoughts of the journeys of Elijah, Ganymede, Alexander the Great, and Scipio, to all of whom

---

Saint-Hilaire, (*SATF*, XXIV–XXXIV), II, p. 190, ll. 236ff. See for the fountain, ll. 11ff.; the Paradise, ll. 87ff.

[125] *Œuvres*, III, p. 374, ll. 22ff.

[126] See above in this chapter pp. 202, 204 and 206–207.

[127] *Œuvres*, II, pp. 193ff.

[128] *Complete Works*, ed. Macaulay, II, p. 38. (*Conf.* i, 109ff.) Considerable influence of the Earthly Paradise appears in the description at the beginning of the *Vox clamantis*, i. 60ff. (*Complete Works*, IV, pp. 24ff.)

[129] Cf. *Mod. Lang. Notes*, XXXIV (1919), pp. 321ff.

reference is explicitly made. Fame's abode in the middle space between earth and sea and sky on a rock of ice, beside borrowing from Ovid and Nicole de Margival and showing added indebtedness to Alanus de Insulis, gives us the motif of the mountain, while the rumor machine shows the influence of various turning castles in the tradition from Celtic. All this is well known and the sources have been carefully studied.[130] So, too, is the description of the dream in the *Book of the Duchess*,[131] where the birds with their songs derive from the French poems of dreams; and that of the garden in the *Parlement of Foules* together with the paraphrase of the *Somnium Scipionis*, both of which we have already considered.[132] Also the flowery meadow with the birds and their song in the two prologues of the *Legend of Good Women* shows the conventional picture familiar in love poetry for many years after the publication of the *Roman de la Rose*. The enclosed garden in the *Merchant's Tale*, Chaucer tells us, was so fair that it would have defied the efforts of the author of the *Roman* to describe it.[133]

The *House of Fame* made a contribution in turn to John Lydgate's Temple of Glass, in which the temple on a craggy rock like frozen ice shone in the sunlight as if it were crystal.[134] This, we are told, was "ful fer in wildirnes." Like other structures in the poetry of Courtly Love this temple has pictures of famous lovers on the walls. The typical garden, with stream and fountain, flowers, trees, and birds, somewhat indebted to the *Book of the*

[130] Notably by W. O. Sypherd, *Studies in Chaucer's House of Fame*, (Chaucer Soc., 1907). But for details see Robinson, *Complete Works of Geoffrey Chaucer*, pp. 886ff. For the further tradition of the rock of ice, see Patch, *Goddess Fortuna*, pp. 134, n. 1, and 145, n. 2; *Handwörterbuch des deutschen Märchens*, ed. L. Mackensen, II, pp. 621–627; for glass mountains and a glass bridge, see Garrett, [*Harvard*] *Studies and Notes*, V (1896), 151ff.

[131] Perhaps an adaptation of the forest motif appears in ll. 416ff. The "derke valeye" between two rocks, which is the abode of Morpheus (ll. 155ff.), should also be noted. It derives from Machaut, and ultimately Ovid's hollow mountain. For later examples see *Mod. Lang. Notes*, V (1890), 9–21.

[132] See in this chapter p. 206 above, and pp. 23–24 earlier, where the flight of the soul of Troilus is also mentioned.

[133] E 2031–2033.

[134] *Lydgate's Temple of Glass*, ed. J. Schick, (*EETS:ES*, 60), pp. 1–2, ll. 16ff. For the sources and motifs see pp. cxvff.

Duchess perhaps, is found in Lydgate's *Complaint of the Black Knight.*[135] The forest and the birds appear in his *Flour of Curtesye,*[136] and walls painted with instructive stories surround the foursquare "herber" in his *Assembly of Gods.*[137] It will be remembered also that Lydgate made his own rendering of De Guileville's *Pélerinage de la Vie Humaine* which we have discussed earlier. A dream of a scene including a grove of oaks with bird songs, path, "herber," a field, and a blossoming medlar tree, is found in the anonymous *Flower and the Leaf,* which seems to owe some details to Chaucer.[138] Another dream in the *Assembly of Ladies* offers a "strait passage," a "herber" with masonry and paved floor and stairs down "with turning wheel."[139] A marvelous castle with towers and high pinnacles, glittering with gold and jewels, the windows and walls of which are decorated with pictures of famous lovers, is described in *The Court of Love,* but here the dream motif is not used.[140] In this work appears the birds' parody of the offices of matins and lauds,[141] a motif related to that already considered in the *Messe des Oisiaus* of Jean de Condé.[142]

Motifs already familiar in French and Italian and English appear in various fifteenth-century works, sometimes developed further, and sometimes showing fantastic changes for their new setting. The mountain, the forest, the birds, come into the somewhat despairing love poem of Alfonso Álvarez de Villasandino:

> En muy esquivas montañas
> Apres de una alta floresta . . .[143]

Again in the *Sueño* of the Marquis of Santillana we have the dream with a garden, nightingales, fragrant flowers, and all the

[135] *Chaucerian and Other Pieces,* ed. W. W. Skeat, (*Complete Works of Geoffrey Chaucer,* VII), pp. 246ff., (ll. 36ff.).

[136] *Ibid.,* pp. 266ff.

[137] *The Assembly of Gods,* ed. O. L. Triggs, (*EETS:ES,* 69), pp. 44f. (lines 1478ff.).

[138] *Chaucerian and Other Pieces,* ed. Skeat, pp. 362ff.

[139] *Ibid.,* pp. 381–382.

[140] Skeat, *op. cit.,* pp. 411ff. (ll. 71ff.); Neilson, *op. cit.,* pp. 1ff.

[141] Skeat, *op. cit.,* pp. 445ff. (ll. 1352ff.).

[142] See above in this chapter pp. 201f.

[143] *El Cancionero de Juan Alfonso de Baena,* ed. P. J. Pidal, p. 48 (No. 42).

rest of it; but interestingly enough, the trees become gnarled and fierce trunks to symbolize the same idea as that of love's desert,[144] and the birds change into sluggish asps. Forest and fountain are in the *Triunphete de Amor*; [145] and in the *Infierno de los Enamorados* [146] Fortune transports the poet to a forest on a mountain from which eventually he travels through a dark valley:

> Por un valle como bruno,
> Espesso mucho é fragoso . . .

until he reaches a fearful castle surrounded by fire as by a moat. With his guide Hippolytus he crosses this by a bridge,[147] and in the castle he finds the Inferno of Love. The apparatus of most of this [148] is connected with the motif of the desert familiar to us in Deschamps's poem and elsewhere, quite as much perhaps as with Dante's *Inferno*. Beyond that kind of influence the tradition seems to go further back to the dark valley of the Latin visions.[149] On the other hand, the Comendador Juan Escriva, stricken by love, describes a journey in a cloud accompanied with melodious songs to "un campo florido" where the fragrance revives him. The place is surrounded with high mountains, and in the midst of its "florida floresta" he sees a "pequeño monte" (hill or grove?) of blossoming orange trees filled with music so sweet that the birds pause in the air to listen. Round this is a clear stream; and he crosses it in a bark, of which the boatman is Care, to the abode of Love.[150] Here the river barrier is interestingly used after the flight in the cloud.

[144] Post sees influence here of the *Corbaccio*. Cf. *Mediaeval Spanish Allegory*, pp. 208–209. Note also the "selva steril" in the description of the temple of Mars, *Teseida* vii, st. 31 (ed. Battaglia, p. 192). For the text see Santillana, *Obras*, pp. 345ff.

[145] Santillana, *Obras*, p. 366.

[146] *Ibid.*, pp. 373ff.

[147] So it seems in stanza xlv.

[148] As Mr. Post has suggested, *op. cit.*, pp. 77ff. with discussion and several examples of the "erotic hell." See the wooded vale, the river, and a bridge, p. 84.

[149] The motif of a prison of love, as in Baudouin de Condé, appears with a later journey to a mountain and grove in the *Sátira de Felice e Infelice Vida* of the Constable, Dom Pedro of Portugal, written in a work of prose and verse, 1449–1455, printed in *Opúsculos Literarios*, ed. A. Paz y Mélia, (*Soc. de Bibl. Españoles*, XXIX) pp. 47ff. The seven virtues appear in the grove.

[150] *Cancionero General de Hernando del Castillo*, II (*Soc. de Bibl. Españoles*, XXI 2), p. 434.

An astonishing development of the motif of the mountain appears in Baudet Herenc's *Parlement d'Amour,* once thought to be by Alain Chartier. In a dream the poet saw a surpassingly beautiful garden on top of a shining rock of topaz where Love held his bow in hand. The place was planted with cypresses and rose trees. The gate was bordered with lilies and also lilies of the valley. Birds sang here, and in the four corners were fountains that gave forth an abundance of water. In the midst was an "auditoire" of green marjoram, where in flowers were told the stories of Paris and Helen and the Chatelaine de Vergy.[151] Love's throne too is ornamented with flowers of various kinds. In this poem the four fountains may possibly be a reminiscence of the four rivers of the Earthly Paradise. One might suspect that they were suggested more by a desire for symmetry in the picture; but it should be conceded that the "roche viue" of topaz, with the garden at its top, does correspond to the well-known foundation for the Garden of Eden.

In *L'Hospital d'Amours* once attributed to Chartier, the poet, Achille Caulier, speaks of being in the "assemblee de plaisir" where was the "montioye" of honor, but after being rejected there, he withdrew and later had a dream at night in which he was wandering along a great thorny road at the bottom of a valley. It was a desert great and long where the earth was mingled with weeping and tears. This was the "Montioye de doulours," and here there was no tree which was not full of people who had hanged themselves for despair. Under the trees were streams, wells, and ditches, with drowned lovers. The fountain of Narcissus was here too, and swords of suicides and fires in which desperate lovers had been burned. In this region the wind was full of sighs and the thunder made of loud cries. The poet was now taken by Esperance and Sapience, who like spirits entered him invisibly, to the Hospital d'Amours built on a rock of ruby and all enclosed with a wall of crystal and marble. It was also surrounded with a thick hedge of flowers.[152] Within he found a hall

[151] *Les Œuvres de Maistre Alain Chartier*, ed. André du Chesne, p. 696. Cf. Neilson, *Origins and Sources,* p. 86. On the authorship see Gustav Gröber, *Grundriss der romanischen Philologie,* 4, *Geschichte der Mittelfranzösischen Lit.*, II, pp. 53 and 245 n., and *Romania,* XXX (1901), pp. 317ff.

[152] Chartier, *Œuvres,* pp. 722ff.; Neilson, *op. cit.*, pp. 87ff. On the author-

with the pavement strewn with flowers, and a chapel with an altar of Venus and Cupid. He visited the garden, where he saw "Dames sans nombre," and returning to the Hospital found a "riche portal" leading to the cemetery where lovers are buried. Through a postern gate he came to a sad valley which was "vng abisme de mal" because here were the bodies of those whom Love had excommunicated. In this complicated work the mountain motif may be found in the ruby foundation for the Hospital, and the deserted valley perhaps inspired the corresponding scenes in Santillana's *Infierno de los Enamorados,* and elsewhere.[153]

The *Hospital d'Amours* was imitated in the *Livre du Cuer d'Amours Epris* by King René of Anjou. In this composition of prose and verse the author dreams that Love takes his heart out of his breast and turns it over to Desire to be equipped with armor. The heart then goes on various adventures including a ride through the "forest de Longue-Actente" where there is a thicket with tormenting branches and thorns, and a storm-making spring like that in Chrétien's *Yvain.* Heart has a dream of a bridge "long et estroit, lequel estoit viel et pourry, fraesle, feible, rompu et persé, froissé et cassé souvent et menu," on which one could go only on foot. Under it runs a river "forment parfonde et roydement bruyant dont l'eaue estoit laide, noire et trouble." Heart gets almost to the middle of the bridge when a great monster with flaming eyes and bellowing roar attacks him and hurls him into the river. Though he is weighted down by his armor, a siren

---

ship see Gröber, *Grundriss,* 4, *Gesch. Der Mittelfranzös. Lit.* II, pp. 53 and 245 n.; *Romania,* XXXI (1902), pp. 315ff., and XXXIV (1905), pp. 559ff.

[153] Cf. Post, *op. cit.,* pp. 79ff. and 223–224. Cf. the "grant val" in *La dame Leale en Amours, Romania* XXX, p. 325., with the motif of the flight (p. 329) to a series of different heavens:

> Après ces mos fusmes ravis
> Et en hault en l'air eslevés,
> Et noz corps materiez vis
> Angeliquement ordonnés . . .

Also after being in a fair forest, the poet of Caulier's *Cruel Femme en Amour* finds himself in a dark valley (*Romania,* XXXI, p. 323), by a river "d'eauue salee," where are no flowers or verdure of any kind. In a vision he sees a palace, and is presently transported up in the air to a beautiful city with walls of crystal. Here too are palace and garden. Cf. also the *Jugement du Povre Triste Amant Banny* with the dreamer transported, he did not know how, to the celestial city and the jeweled palace, *Romania,* XXXIV, pp. 379ff.

stretches out helping hands and saves him. In his waking adventures he comes to a great and marvelous valley in a dark and deserted land, where there is a river "parfonde, hideuse, trouble et espouventable durement." This is "Le val de très Parfont-Penser," and the river is the "Fleuve de Larmes" that comes from the Fountain of Fortune (the storm-making spring). Over the river is a very high wooden bridge "foible, fraesle, d'ancienne façon et estroit à merveilles" so that a horse could hardly cross it, called "Le Pas-Perilleux." On the other side is a knight in black armor on a black charger, who guards the bridge and with whom Heart now fights to his own discomfiture, being hurled into the stream and rescued. Later he comes to the sea, and in a boat, guided by two damsels, is carried by a fresh breeze to the isle of the God of Love, after weathering a storm with high waves, and stopping for a while at the "rochier" of Compaignie and Amictié. On Love's island is a fair castle, and further exploration reveals a most beautiful church, which seemed like a "chose celestial." It was built on a rock of diamond, and had walls of marble and jasper and a roof of silver enameled with azure stars. All this is part of the Ospital d'Amours, behind which is a cemetery whose portal is emblazoned with the arms of famous men. The fair castle is on a rock of emerald with crystal walls "et y avoit a chacun pan au bout d'une grosse tour faicte de chailloux de rubiz fins et reluisans . . ." On every tower is a great carbuncle, and jewels and precious stones ornament the place in many ways. In the courtyard is a crystal fountain with a basin of gold ornamented with precious stones, and near this Heart meets Dame Oyseuse.[154]

This extraordinary mélange of motifs covers nearly everything we have considered thus far. The dream in which the heart removed from the breast has various adventures in another world, the double use of the river and bridge, the dark valley, the rock of diamond and the rock of emerald suggesting fantastic transformations of the mountain, call to mind the typical pattern of some of the Latin visions. The storm-making spring and the river and bridge also make one think of the romances, as perhaps the journey in the boat to Love's island does as well. The Ospital

[154] *Œuvres Complètes du Roi René*, ed. le Comte de Quatrebarbes, III, pp. 1ff.

and the cemetery show undoubted influence from Caulier's *Hospital d'Amours.*[155]

In the poetry of Charles d'Orléans many motifs are introduced, but without extensive description. The Manor of Love is well located and pleasant to the view in *La Retenue d'Amours.*[156] Reference is made to the "paradis des amoureux" and the "purgatoire de Tristesse." [157] The manor of Nonchaloir comes into the *Songe en Complainte*; [158] and Charles too had reason to know what it was like to ride in the "forest de Longue Actente," [159] and he speaks of the "desert of desperaunce" where he will dwell in torment and penance till he dies.[160] Michault Le Caron, called Taillevent, describes the allegorical construction of the "ostel dolloureux d'Amours" as follows:

> Le fondement est de merancolie,
> Et les murs sont faiz de desconfiture . . .

and so on.[161] And many other poets include reference to the desert or forest or hospital or castle of Love in one way or another.

The so-called Scottish Chaucerians use some of the familiar features. The *Kingis Quair,* attributed to James I of Scots, tells how the poet in a dream seemed to go through a door and then, lifted by his two arms, was raised up into the air and, surrounded by a crystal cloud, was conveyed from sphere to sphere to the "glade empire" of Venus – apparently among the constellations, since he has arrived at the "circle clere" of the Zodiac. Her "place" was all wrought with crystal stones. The flight itself makes one think perhaps of some of the derivatives of the *Somnium Scipionis* and Caulier's *Cruel Femme en Amour.*[162] Later, on descending

[155] For another view of the sources see Neilson, *op. cit.*, p. 93; and Gröber's *Grundriss,* IV, 2, p. 173, suggesting the influence of Charles d'Orléans.

[156] *Charles d'Orléans, Poésies,* ed. Pierre Champion, I, p. 4, lines 103–104.

[157] *Ibid.*, I, p. 42, xxiv, ll. 2 and 8.

[158] *Ibid.*, p. 115, ll. 444–446.

[159] See for example *ibid.*, p. 165.

[160] *The English Poems of Charles of Orléans,* ed. Robert Steele, (*EETS,* 215), p. 143, lines 4286ff. Cf. also above, p. 202, n. 93.

[161] *L'Ediffice de l'ostel dollouréux d'Amours, Romania,* XVIII (1889), pp. 449–450, gives excerpts.

[162] Cf. the material referred to in p. 216, n. 153 above. See *The Kingis Quair,* ed. W. W. Skeat, (*Scottish Text Soc.*), p. 20, stanzas 74ff.

to earth again, the poet finds himself in a "lusty plane" by a river, where the crystal waters run over gravel "bryght as ony gold" and are full of fishes (somewhat reminiscent of Chaucer's in the *Parlement of Foules*). Fruit trees are here and all sorts of animals, and here too are Fortune and her wheel.[163] Gavin Douglas in the *Palice of Honour* is wandering in a garden that is like a "paradice amiabill" when he has a vision or dream of being in a desert place "Amyd a forest by a hyddeous flude" which contains "grysly fische." Here he meets the cavalcade on its way to the Palace of Honour.[164] Later after a long journey over most of the world (passing, among others, the rivers Tigris and Phison, and pausing at the fountain of the Muses), he comes to a pleasant plain at the foot of a fair green mountain, where with temperate clime and herbs, flowers, and fruit, the songs of birds, the "beriall stremis," we have the usual meadow of Courtly Love and an apparent reminiscence of the Earthly Paradise.[165] The pavilion of the Muses stands here. With further travel the poet comes to the Palace of Honour itself, which is on a rock of "slid hard marbell stone" that shines like glass and at the foot is protected by a narrow stream of burning brimstone, pitch, and boiling lead. Over all this to the top of the "hill" the poet is lifted by the hair "As Abacuk was brocht in Babylone." Now he looks down and sees how small the earth is and in an assaulting tempest how dangerous the climb.[166] The troubles of the world are symbolized by the spectacle of a ship tossed in the waves with its crew perishing. On the rock's summit is a "plane of peirles pulchritude" with the trees, flowers, and birds and crystalline water essential to a Paradise, and finally the Palace of Honour, which is "all of cristall cleir" ("Wrocht as me thocht of poleist beriall stone").

In this remarkable work the palace is decorated in the manner of Courtly Love; but the burning river and the high rock with its garden strikingly recall corresponding elements in some of the descriptions of the Earthly Paradise and may in that respect show more than mere coincidence. At the end of the poem the poet,

[163] *The Kingis Quair,* pp. 37ff., stanzas 151ff.

[164] *The Poetical Works of Gavin Douglas,* ed. John Small, I, pp. 3ff.

[165] *Ibid.*, pp. 44f.

[166] *Ibid.*, pp. 50ff.

in emerging from the garden, has to cross a surrounding stream of water by going over a "tree." His guide proceeds safely but he himself falls in and thus is wakened from his swoon. Here we possibly have a parallel to the familiar bridge motif in an episode such as may be found in the Latin visions. These are the clearest examples of our motifs used in the poems of this group. Dunbar has, to be sure, the flowery meadow in which the poet falls asleep, in the *Goldyn Targe* and elsewhere,[167] but it is doubtful whether we may include every garden and every stream in such a survey. Most interesting of all perhaps is the episode of the ascent through the spheres in the *Kingis Quair* and the journey up the rock, pulled by the hair, in Douglas's poem; and it is important to remember that features like the crystalline "place" of Venus in the first and the rock that shone like glass in the second, along with other details, show some connection with Chaucer's *House of Fame,* where the eagle takes the poet up through the skies to the castle (all made of beryl) on the rock of ice. Also in Lydgate's *Temple of Glass,* influenced by Chaucer's poem, the poet in a dream is "Rauysshid in spirit" into the temple, which is founded, as we have seen, on a craggy rock like frozen ice.[168]

Following the tradition from Chaucer and Lydgate we have in Stephen Hawes's *Pastime of Pleasure* a late use in English of much of the familiar material. The two paths are here, one "sharpe" and one "more playne," of contemplation and worldly dignity, known to us in different guise in the *Pélerinage de Vie Humaine* and Jean de Meun's part of the *Roman de la Rose.*[169] The garden appears with flowers and dulcet spring "To paradyse ryght

[167] *The Poems of William Dunbar,* ed. John Small, II, pp. 1ff. (*The Goldyn Targe*). Cf. p. 174 and 183ff., and even perhaps p. 30. The river and the bridge come into Henryson's *Traitie of Orpheus.* After Orpheus has passed the Hound of Hell he arrives at a "rywir wonder depe" over which is a "brig," and this is guarded by the three Fates who superintend Ixion's wheel. Orpheus crosses the bridge without apparent difficulty and comes to "a wonder grisely flude" where Tantalus has his torture. See *Pieces from the Makculloch and the Gray MSS,* etc., ed. George Stevenson (*Scottish Text Society*), pp. 225–226, lines 144ff., and *The Poems of Robert Henryson,* ed. G. G. Smith (*Scottish Text Society*), III, pp. 44–45.

[168] Cf. p. 212 above.

[169] See above pp. 188 and 200. On the sources of the *Pastime* cf. *The Pastime of Pleasure by Stephen Hawes,* ed. W. E. Mead, (*EETS,* 173), p. xliii; Neilson, *Origins and Sources,* pp. 167f. For the paths see the *Pastime,* lines 76ff.

well comparable." [170] The tower of gold of La Bel Pucell is beyond a "grate see" in a goodly land full of fruit and joy and bliss.[171] The Tower of Doctrine made of fine copper is far in the west on a craggy rock,[172] and in its court is a noble spring pouring forth water through the mouths of dragons in four streams sweeter than "Nysus (Nilus?) or Ganges . . . Tygrys or Eufrates." The hall in this place is made of jasper with crystal windows and jeweled ornamentation. The Tower of Music has a crystal temple.[173] The Tower of Geometry is on a craggy rock and that of Chivalry on one of "merueylous altytude." Thus the adventures proceed with a monotony of towers on craggy rocks and jeweled halls and the like. A wilderness with wild beasts and "dyssolate derkenes" has to be traversed on the way to the palace of La Bel Pucell, and it thus seems to have a traditional meaning.[174] The palace again is on a craggy rock and has a fountain in its court. Its lower tower has four images that blow clarions, and the golden fanes above make sweet harmony with the wind. The hall is ornamented with the story of Troy and is, of course, jeweled. Such is the collection of details that Hawes has made use of, with little originality or invention on his part.[175]

In Nevill's *Castell of Pleasure,* just a little later and undoubtedly taking certain ideas from Hawes,[176] the situation is about the same, although the poem is much shorter. In a dream the poet led by Morpheus comes to the Mountain of Courage and ascends it. Forth he walks on that "goodly hyll" until he sees a castle

[170] Lines 2008ff. Here Graunde Amoure meets La Bel Pucell by the fountain. Cf. also 2668ff.

[171] Lines 266ff.

[172] Lines 344ff.

[173] Lines 1464ff.

[174] Lines 4921ff.

[175] Similar borrowings with adaptation are found in Hawes's earlier *Example of Virtue.* For this I have had access only to the modern rendering in *The Dunbar Anthology,* ed. Edward Arber, pp. 217ff. Note the voyage and the island, pp. 222ff.; the castle to which approach is made only over the little bridge "Not half so broad as a house-ridge," pp. 262ff. (cf. stanza 179, only the pure may cross to the "Kingdom of Great Grace" — others fall into the water); the dungeon of darkness, p. 287; the valley of sorrow and pain and burning fire, p. 288; the gardens, pp. 277–278; the wilderness of darkness and thorns, pp. 258–259.

[176] See *The Castell of Pleasure by William Nevill,* ed. Roberta D. Cornelius, (*EETS,* 179), pp. 15ff.

by a river and pauses there to wait for low tide. The river, it seems, destroys people oppressed with pride and runs over stones of steadfastness. The castle is protected on every side with hounds and other beasts; the walls are of adamant, the windows of crystal. The poet gets safely over the river to the castle, and after visiting it comes to the Garden of Affection all surrounded with gems so that "Me thought it a new paradyse delycate and delycyous." This is "set full" of trees and goodly flowers, especially the primrose. Perhaps the most interesting feature of the whole description, however, is the writing in two "scryptures," one of gold and one of blue, on the gates of the castle, the first telling of the way of worldly joys (dancing and singing and worldly wealth) and the second offering the love of beauty, as a choice of roads to be followed — recalling for us the paths in the allegory of Hawes.

iii

The allegorical tradition of the Goddess Fortuna includes various accounts of her dwelling place, and this I have considered in detail in another study elsewhere.[177] But it will be illuminating at least to summarize some of the pertinent material here, inasmuch as we again find in the literature of that tradition the motifs of the island, the mountain, the garden, the fountains and springs, the palace, and the trees and flowers. At the outset we have the elaborate account of the scene in the *Anticlaudianus* of Alanus de Insulis, as we have already noticed. Here the dwelling is on a high cliff in the midst of the sea, suggesting both the island motif and the mountain. At times the cliff is submerged in the water and again lifted high above it, symbolizing, like nearly all the rest of the detail, the shift from bad to good fortune or the opposite. The garden is at one time flowering with the breeze of spring and again devastated by the north wind, in contrast to the perennially temperate weather of the Earthly Paradise. Some trees are barren and some bear fruit. Thorns and yews pierce the hands. Two streams are here, one sweet and one bitter: the sweet seduces many to plunge into it, and the other, dark and sulphurous, drowns many. The house on the cliff and sloping to the valley

[177] *The Goddess Fortuna in Medieval Literature,* pp. 123ff.

is partly bright with silver and gems and partly in ruins and squalid.[178]

This description was taken over by Jean de Meun for the *Roman de la Rose* beginning "Une roche est en mer seianz." [179] Here is the craggy rock again. The translation is close, and all the details are here, including the bird songs (the nightingale, Alanus told us, sang seldom, but the owl prophesied dire events). In the laments and weeping by the dark river we see the reason perhaps for René d'Anjou's calling the stream from his Fountain of Fortune a river of tears. At any rate the general idea of the picture is taken over in the *Régime de Fortune* by Michault Le Caron (called Taillevent), where the house is "Sur lac de dueil, sur riuiere ennuieuse" and once more

> D'vne part clere, & d'autre tenebreuse
> Est la maison aux douloureux meschans,
> D'vne part riche & d'autre souffreteuse:
> C'est du costé où les champs sont prochains,
> Et d'autre part a assez fruictz & grains.[180]

From the *Roman* too the idea went into the *Disguising at London* by John Lydgate.[181] At least the mountain as foundation for Fortune's home went into the scene of Nicole de Margival's *Panthère,* where, as we have observed, we have the rock of ice, and then into Chaucer's *House of Fame* for the dwelling of Fame.[182] In Watriquet de Couvin's *Dis de l'Escharbote* a city of which Fortune is porter is located on the mountain, and the unlucky citizens are those who fall to the valley below. To get to this city the poet in his dream goes along the valley until he sees the incredibly beautiful place shining with marble, and it seems like an Earthly Paradise. Here is a fair castle and the place below is described as

> . . . cel orible val parfont
> Où toute joie faut et font.[183]

[178] *Anticl.* VII, viii–ix. Cf. above pp. 179–180.
[179] *Le Roman de la Rose,* ed. Ernest Langlois, II, ll. 5921ff.
[180] Chartier, *Œuvres,* p. 713, bal. iv.
[181] Brotanek, *Die Englischen Maskenspiele,* pp. 309ff.
[182] Pp. 202 and 212 above.
[183] *Dits de Watriquet de Couvin,* ed. Scheler, pp. 399ff.

In the *Chevalier Errant* of Thomas, Marquis of Saluzzo, the house of Fortune is on a high rock at the top of which are two fearful precipices, and from this height the wretches are hurled.[184] According to Fregoso's *Dialogo di Fortuna,* an approach over a hard and thorny road leads to the goddess's palace on a mountain,[185] and Ariosto is right in seeing the idea of this barrier as the equivalent of the wheel.[186]

The garden in Fortune's realm, according to Aeneas Sylvius, is surrounded by a stream and also by a wall, in which, with an obvious borrowing from Virgil, there are two gates, one of horn and one of ivory. The approach must be made over a bridge in either case, which may be raised to prevent access. Here are flowery meadows, cold fountains, groves, fruits, jewels, lovely maidens and splendid youths — all, we are told, like the Paradise of Mahomet.[187] Fregoso's *Dialogo* has a great apple tree from which Fortuna dispenses the fruit. A variant on this theme is found in De Guileville's idea of a tree in mid-ocean where the nests contain people at different levels, according to the favors Fortune bestows on them.[188] It may be, however, that the genealogical trees in manuscripts and the extraordinarily familiar motif of the Tree of Jesse in art had something to do with this. The palace in Fregoso has four large portals with a triumphal arch and tower toward the four points of the compass, and at the top is a colossus of gold.[189] The square palace recalls a little the abode of Love in the description of Andreas Capellanus already considered.[190]

In all these allegorical treatments of the material it is difficult to decide in some cases how far the familiar motifs appear

[184] E. Gorra, *Studi di Critica Letteraria,* 45ff.

[185] Antonio Phileremo Fregoso, *Dialogo di Fortuna,* caps. xiiiff.

[186] Lodovico Ariosto, *Rime e Satire* (*Opere* VIII), p. 207 (sat. iii). Quite similar is the mountain of treasure, with fragrant grove, of the Fata named Plutina in Trissino's *Italia Liberata,* II, 78f. (lib. xi) : G. G. Trissino, *L'Italia Liberata da' Goti,* ed. A. Antonini, 3 parts. Also cf. the mountain where Palestine guards her treasure in *Melusine,* lines 4621ff. (*The Romans of Partenay,* ed. W. W. Skeat, *EETS,* 22.).

[187] Aeneas Sylvius, *Pontif. Epist.* I, cviii (*Opera omnia,* pp. 611f.).

[188] Cf. Patch, *The Goddess Fortuna,* pp. 138f.

[189] *Dialogo,* caps. xiii–xv.

[190] Cf. above p. 196, especially note 71.

simply as an invention of the particular author in question, and how far they are taken over from the general tradition we have been studying. Where there is verbal evidence of literary borrowing we know, of course, that tradition has played its part thus far, but we can hardly be sure how much further it has gone. To illustrate what I mean I may cite a document which presents something perhaps midway between a vision and an allegory by a thirteenth-century Welsh mystic. Considering the developments in the literature of Courtly Love in this period, his symbolism is striking.[191]

As his narrative goes: "In a fair castle crowning a lofty mountain dwelt my Love. Fairer than all other castles in the world was this one, and beautiful the gardens and pleasaunces within its walls. . . . I lay down one day to rest from the heat of the sun, and straightway came to my mind the vision of the castle of my first Love." "Right cunningly were derived its approaches and strong towers," he says, "so that none might hope to win it by stealth. . . ." A path leads at first gently upward, and then downward "towards a gloomy chasm where lay a bottomless lake whose black waters were never lightened by the sun, and whose shores were inhabited by many fierce dragons, while venomous serpents and other vermin lurked in its depths. . . ." Love points out a "winding, narrow rugged path which was soon lost in the woods, instead of the straight and spacious road leading to the castle." The broad road proves easier at first, but at length it comes to a spot where the author sees it has been washed away to a deep ravine. The narrow path is of course the one that brings him to his goal.[192]

Here we find the mountain and the castle along with the two paths. On the one hand it reminds us instantly of the Latin visions, and on the other one might think it belonged among the numerous allegories of Courtly Love. Except perhaps for the suggestion in Scripture of the strait and narrow way and the broad road, however, there is nothing in the whole account that

[191] For an interesting essay on the interplay between vision and allegory, although the survey is not extensive and is a little out of date, see Eugenia dal Bò, *La Visione nell' Arte Medievale*.

[192] *Dublin Review* 175 (1924), 21ff. (translated by Mons. P. E. Hook).

would require much strain on the imagination of its author for pure invention. The mountain with a castle could often be seen in the medieval landscape and presents in any case a natural obstacle. Only the great number of documents of this general type in the twelfth and thirteenth centuries, offering the same elements over and over again, together with the medieval habit of borrowing ideas, would argue in favor of the theory that the author was indebted to the tradition. Even then the material was so widely spread that he may have been unaware of the debt, and it may conceivably have involved a process taking place largely in his "unconscious self." A different example of the same problem is found in Nicole Bozon's comment "De periculoso transitu huius mundi": "La nature del asne si est qe il doute mout passer ponte od veit desouz l'ewe profonde. Et nous qe sums en ceste vie passantz par un ponte mout estreit e perilous. . . ."[193] In the discussion that follows we see that falling from the bridge is tantamount to falling into Hell, and it is obvious that one succeeds in passing over by righteousness. In this case I feel sure that Nicole knew of the Bridge of Judgment, especially since he has occasion to add "com dit seint Gregor: 'Il est prest de perir qe ne pens poynt coment deit eschaper.' "

Two modern instances of use of the material, in what seems to have symbolic qualities, if not the literalistic variety of allegory, may be found in Hilton's *Lost Horizon* and Barrie's play, *Mary Rose*. In the first of these the region known as Shangri-La is found in the mountains of Tibet. It is reached by a journey in a plane, and its foundation seems to be the cone-shaped mountain so covered by a glacier that it resembles for us, after the present survey, the well-known mountain of ice. Up there on the heights, which incidentally are scaled by passing through a mist, is a valley which is

> nothing less than an enclosed paradise of amazing fertility, in which the vertical difference of a few thousand feet spanned the whole gulf between temperate and tropical. Crops of unusual diversity grew in profusion and contiguity, with not an inch of ground untended. The whole cultivated area stretched for perhaps a dozen miles, varying in width

[193] *Les Contes Moralisés de Nicole Bozon,* ed. L. T. Smith and Paul Meyer, (*SATF,* XV), p. 45 (29).

from one to five, and, though narrow, it had the luck to take sunlight at the hottest part of the day. The atmosphere, indeed, was pleasantly warm even out of the sun, though the little rivulets that watered the soil were ice-cold from the snows.[194]

It may not be inapropos to recall the fact that the planes which in the war went to bomb Tokio were said to have taken off from Shangri-La, and that an airplane carrier has been named for this pleasant spot. But even while the mountain, the delightful valley, and certain details, suggest a conscious reminiscence of the Earthly Paradise, I venture to say that what we have here is nothing more than psychological coincidence. It is tempting to the scholar to find "influence" everywhere, and one might see another familiar motif out of the medieval past in Wilder's *Bridge of San Luis Rey,* where, I am sure, the connection is no closer.

On the other hand, the island in Barrie's *Mary Rose,* to which, guided by the little old woman, the girl pays a visit and disappears for periods in which she grows no older, that, I am equally confident, has been taken out of folklore modern or ancient. Other examples in the literature of our day might be cited in which we have similar elements with overtones of symbolic meaning, like the voyage in *Outward Bound.* But the problem of exactly where a contact with our tradition may be properly recognized or where, on the contrary, there is only chance similarity, we must leave to others. In medieval documents it is probably almost as nice a question, and the best we can do is to present the material for consideration.

Certainly through Claudian and Sidonius the mountain found its way into allegory and thus into the works of Alanus de Insulis, Jean de Hauteville, and others. Instances of its use appear almost everywhere in varying forms. It is not too much to say that the rocky foundation in Grosseteste's *Chasteau d'Amour* and the similar feature in the *Court of Sapience* and many other works, belong in this category. Fantastic developments are found in the rock of ice in the *Panthère d'Amours,* the rock of topaz in Herenc's *Parlement d'Amour,* the rock of ruby in Caulier's *Hospital d'Amours,* and the rock of diamond described by King René. But

[194] James Hilton, *Lost Horizon,* p. 129.

the classics were not the only source in some of these cases, where it is obvious that the tradition of the Earthly Paradise has played its part, and also vision literature has contributed something. Traces of the first appear in Godfrey of Saint Victor's *Fons Philosophiae* and in Alanus's realm of Nature, and the idea comes clearly into Frezzi's *Quadriregio,* the *Visión Delectable,* Dante's *Purgatorio,* and elsewhere, notably of course from time to time in the literature of Courtly Love. Latin visions too had great influence, as we know from Jean de Meun's and De Guileville's acquaintance with them; ultimately from such documents derive some examples of the mountain, the river, the bridge, the dark valley, probably even the desolate tract and the gloomy woods.

The river we know in the *Pearl,* the *Court of Sapience,* Imperial's *Decir de las Siete Virtudes,* and elsewhere. It is black and stinking in Douglas's *King Hart,* "grant e roide" in the *Roman de la Rose,* destructive of pride in Nevill's *Castell of Pleasure,* and thus occasionally suggests in one way or another the foul stream of the visions and of oriental mythology. This is the more evident when it is combined with the bridge motif, as in the hideous example in Watriquet de Couvin's *Tournois des Dames,* and in that described as "parfonde, hideuse, trouble et espouventable durement" in René's *Livre du Cuer d'Amours Epris.* The dark valley and desolate tract are widely used motifs. We find them in different forms in the *Tesoretto* of Latini, the *Corbaccio* of Giovanni Boccaccio, the *Defunnsion* of Santillana, and in many other examples; and they constitute, together or singly, what has been appropriately called the Inferno of Love, as in the *Infierno de los Enamorados* of Santillana, and rather vividly displayed in Caulier's *Hospital d'Amours.* The thorny path is also another feature that may come from the same tradition, as it appears in such works as Fregoso's *Dialogo di Fortuna* and Caulier's *Hospital* and also the *Court of Sapience.*

An interesting development from Biblical sources is that of two paths, the strait and narrow and the broad and pleasant one. These are introduced into the *Besant de Dieu,* the *Roman de la Rose,* the *Pélerinage de Vie Humaine* (with a strange doubling on themselves), *Les Eschez Amoureuse,* and elsewhere. Four roads appear in Hesdin's *Prise Amoureuse.* From Celtic mythology perhaps, although there are instances in vision literature, comes the idea of the birds that sing sacred music, as in the *Pélerinage de l'Ame,* the *Court of Sapience,* and notably Jean de Condé's *Messe des Oisiaus.* From Celtic or the classics is derived too the motif of the island, rather less common than that of the mountain or that of the river barrier. It appears in Claudian, the *Anticlaudianus* of Alanus de Insulis, the *Pélerinage de Vie Humaine,* Petrarch's *Trionfi, Chaucer's Dream,* and a few other works. On the other hand, the idea of a flight of some sort to the Other World, perhaps less familiar in the mythologies, is used several times: in the *Pélerinage Jhesucrist,* the *Panthère d'Amours,* the *House of Fame,* the *Teseida,* the allegory of the Comendador Juan Escriva, Caulier's *Cruel Femme en Amour,* the *Kingis Quair,* and other works. If we attempt a brief summary of the whole situation, then, it may be said that on the face of it classical influence seems to dominate in the allegories in general; but actually the ultimate indebtedness to vision literature, to the tradition of the Earthly Paradise especially in the garden, and perhaps even to Celtic, is extensive too.

VII

THE ROMANCES

AS SCHOLARS HAVE LONG BEEN AWARE, a great mass of material drawn from the tradition of the Other World appears in medieval romance. Here particularly it is impossible to be exhaustive, but important instances at least may be noted with some indication of the general sources from which originally they may have been derived. Folklore of this kind was widely available in the period; and here and there, in literature other than the strictly romantic, what look like reminiscences or fragments of Otherworld scenes are found which seem to represent much more that was being passed about in popular rumor. Thus in Nennius's *History of the Britons* we have the account of how the three sons of a Spanish soldier came to Ireland, and later "saw a glassy tower in the midst of the sea," in which were persons who made no reply when spoken to. After a year the three sons went by boat with all their company of men and women to attack the tower, but one of the ships was wrecked. The others sailed on for the attack, but when the voyagers landed on the shore round the tower, the sea "overwhelmed them and they were drowned." The island motif and the tower of glass, and perhaps the proximity to Ireland as well, suggest Otherworld origins.[1] One cannot be so sure of the vase symbolizing an island in the Arabian embroidery on the eleventh- or twelfth-century robe prepared for the body of Saint Cuthbert.[2] In this case the familiar motif may have been used simply as a reference to Holy Island and its fruits. On the other

[1] *Nennius's History of the Britons*, trans. A. W. Wade-Evans, (*SPCK*), pp. 40–41; *Historia Britonum*, ed. T. Mommsen, *Monumenta Germaniae historica, Auct. antiq.*, XIII, part 1, p. 155. Cf. d'Arbois de Jubainville, *Le Cycle Mythologique Irlandais*, pp. 117ff.; *Romania* XXIV (1895), p. 328; Cross in *Am. Journal of Theology*, XXIII (1919), p. 374; Loomis, *Celtic Myth*, p. 201.

[2] G. F. Browne, *The Venerable Bede, His Life and Writings*, (*SPCK*), plate xi (cf. p. 167).

hand, the Triads of the Red Book refer to the burial of Arthur in the island of Avalon (Avallach) – "the other world *par excellence* in the 'matter of Britain' " [3] – but here we perhaps have a literary influence from Geoffrey of Monmouth and others.[4]

Ultimately some form of literary influence or more likely straight folklore should account for the story told by William of Malmesbury which he says he picked up as a boy from a monk of Guienne. On a journey to Italy the monk saw a "montem perforatum" where he heard there were the treasures of Octavian. With the help of a string to guide their return, he entered a cave with a group of men, saw a road covered with bare bones and corpses, and a fearful river near by, and finally came to a placid pool stirred with ripples that played on its shores. Over the pool was a brass bridge and on the other side golden horses with golden riders. When one of the group set foot upon the bridge to cross, "quod mirum auditu sit," the near side sank and the other side was raised "producens rusticum aereum cum aereo malleo, quo ille undas uerberans, ita obnubilauit aera, ut diem caelumque subtexeret. Retracto pede, pax fuit. . . ." This happened again, and the attempt was abandoned. Next day they found the exit of the cave guarded by demons. It is worth noticing, however, that on the first journey they did get a silver cup, which they shared among themselves; and at another time a Jewish necromancer entered and obtained some dust by which anything became changed to gold.[5] If, as seems probable, William's memory did not betray him and he did get the story from the traveler to Italy, the bridge in this case leaps with Celtic agility but really comes from the south and almost certainly from vision literature

[3] L. A. Paton, *Studies in the Fairy Mythology of Arthurian Romance*, (*Radcliffe College Monographs*, 13), p. 40, n. 2.

[4] D'Arbois de Jubainville and J. Loth, *Les Mabinogion*, II (*Cours de Litt. celtique* IV), p. 215 (cf. pp. 202–203). Cf. pp. 284ff. below.

[5] William of Malmesbury, *De gestis regum Anglorum*, ed. William Stubbs, I, (*Rolls Series*, XC), pp. 198–200 (ii, § 170). Cf. Ogle in *Mod. Lang. Notes*, XXXV (1920), pp. 129ff., giving other examples of the motif of the wonderful cave, especially in Italy, and observing (p. 132) that "many of the details which adorn the tales are of extraneous origin, chiefly oriental." Two notable instances, which, he suggests, may be related, are those of the underground palace, lighted by a carbuncle, with treasures guarded by automata (William of Malmesbury, *op. cit.*, I, pp. 196–197, [ii, § 169], and the *Gesta Romanorum*, ed. Oesterley, cap. 107, pp. 438–439).

and from the Far East. Moreover, the cave itself is like some we shall examine presently in the writings of Walter Map and others, often associated with Welsh folklore, but in some points calling up the Italian scene.

Remote literary influence of a different kind just possibly appears in Walter Map's story of the knight in Little Britain who found his dead wife at night in a throng of women "in the depths of a most lonely valley" (*in conualle solitudinis amplissime*).[6] This may actually be a reworking of the story of Orpheus with Celtic modifications, or it may be a form of story among the Celts that later took on details of the Orpheus plot in the well-known lay. Here the elements of the night and the lonely valley suggest in any case a connection with stories of the underworld. The underworld, too, appears in Walter's famous story of King Herla, who, to carry out his contract with the pygmies, goes to their home and enters "a cavern in a lofty cliff" where "after a space of darkness they passed into light." This came not from the sun or moon but from lamps, and the mansion was "like the palace of the sun in Ovid's description." On Herla's return he is warned to let none of his company dismount until the dog with which they have been presented shall leap from the arms of the man who carries him. Some of the retinue disobey the order and are changed to dust. King Herla learns that although he supposed his stay to have been but three days, he has in reality been there for well over two hundred years.[7] To this ending (which has a parallel in the *Voyage of Bran* [8] and elsewhere, and notably, for the passage of time, in the *Pantheon of Godfrey of Viterbo*) a curious addition appears in the fact that Herla spent the rest of his days wandering as leader of the "wild hunt." [9] We may also note that

[6] *Master Walter Map's Book De nugis curialium* (*Courtiers' Trifles*), trans. Frederick Tupper and M. B. Ogle, p. 218. For the Latin see *Walter Map, De nugis curialium*, ed. M. R. James, (*Anecdota Oxoniensia*, Med. and Modern Series, XIV), dist. iv, cap. viii (pp. 173–174). For the tale as a Breton parallel to *Sir Orfeo* see *Mod. Lang. Notes,* LI (1936), pp. 28ff. and p. 492, and *Mod. Lang. Rev.*, XXXI (1936), pp. 354ff.

[7] Trans. Tupper and Ogle, pp. 15–18. *Walter Map,* ed. James, dist. i, cap. xi (pp. 13–16).

[8] As Loomis points out, *Mod. Lang. Notes,* LI, p. 29.

[9] The home of the pygmies resembles the later realm of the dwarfs in the *Wartburgkrieg,* ed. Simrock, 168 (pp. 218–219). Note the reference to such realms in Germany and in Wales (line 6).

in Map's tale of Henno cum Dentibus, Henno's supernatural bride, who carries the traits of the snake-lady Melusine, arrives with her father by ship.[10] In this detail it may not be too much to see the remnant of the ocean barrier and the voyage from the Other World. And in Map's story of Sadius and Galo, Galo's journey through a "deep grove" (*uiam altissimi nemoris*) to the scene of lofty palaces within high walls (with ivory homes and other marks of beauty, where no inhabitants appear, but the giant's lady awaits under a cherry tree in the garden), may offer a reminiscence of the motif of the forest.[11]

The lower world again is introduced into the story of the priest Eliodorus according to the *Itinerary Through Wales* of Giraldus Cambrensis.[12] As a boy the priest had on a certain occasion gone to hide "under the hollow bank of a river" (*in concaua fluuii cuiusdam ripa*), and there two pygmies joined him and invited him to come along with them to their country. He followed them on a path "at first subterraneous and dark, into a most beautiful country, adorned with rivers and meadows, woods and plains, but obscure, and not illuminated with the full light of the sun. All the days were cloudy, and the nights extremely dark, on account of the absence of the moon and stars." The path "per uiam primo subterraneam et tenebrosam" is clearly that of the continuously underground journey to the familiar realm no longer lit by the sun and stars; but the river and the cave in its bank suggest tantalizing vestiges of another idea, the river barrier perhaps and the Other World in a hill. The rest of the adventure does not concern us, except the end where the boy is punished by losing all traces of the subterraneous road "though he searched for it on the banks of the river for nearly the space of a year" (*intra concauas aquae praedictae ripas uiam inutilis explorator inquireret*). Such a place appears in the account by Gervase of Tilbury of the swineherd who, searching for one of his swine,

[10] *Walter Map*, ed. James, dist. iv, cap. ix (pp. 174ff.)

[11] *Ibid.*, dist. iii, cap. ii (pp. 114–115). See *Speculum*, XVI (1941), pp. 34ff. Cf. Caldwell, *Eger and Grime*, pp. 144ff. The river appears in another version of the story: *Perceval le Gallois*, ed. Potvin, III, p. 101 (l. 11983).

[12] *Itin. Kambriae*, I, viii, ed. J. F. Dimock, *Giraldi Cambrensis opera*, VI, (*Rolls Series*, XXI), pp. 75–76. Trans. R. C. Hoare, *The Itinerary through Wales*, ed. W. L. Williams, (*Everyman's Library*), pp. 68–69. Cf. Hartland, *The Science of Fairy Tales*, pp. 135ff.

entered a notoriously windy cave when its winds were quiet, and following a path, came from darkness into light *(ab opacis in lucidum locum)* on a spacious plain where men were gathering a ripe harvest. On his return with the pig he found winter still in progress outside. Here the entrance to the cavern is in a mountain *(in monte cauerna foraminis)*.[13] So is the entrance to the lower world in Gervase's story of the demonic palace, which is underground near a lake at the top of a mountain in Catalonia.[14] At the foot of this inaccessible eminence runs a stream with golden sands, and its peak suffers continual snow and ice.

The approach through a mountain may perhaps be found again in Gervase's account of Mount Etna — as he says, "vulgarly" called Mongibel. A servant, he tells us, went in search of his bishop's lost horse, and after wandering about the place he discovered a very narrow path *(arctissima semita sed plana)*, which led him out to a delightful and spacious plain full of all delights. There he saw a marvelous palace, and within, recumbent on a couch, King Arthur himself, who had the horse in his possession.[15] In this case we have no definite indication of the cavern or lower world, but the chief elements of the tale are found elsewhere. Étienne de Bourbon says that a certain man in or on a mountain near Etna *(in quodam monte iuxta Vulcanum)*, where is said to be the place of Purgatory *(ubi dicitur locus purgatorii)*, was seeking his master's horse. He came to a city with a little iron gate and inquired of the porter concerning the horse. The porter directs him to the hall of his lord, who will restore the horse. In the city the fellow sees as many people as there are in the world, and in a certain hall the prince himself, who offers him food.

[13] *Otia Imperialia, In Einer Auswahl,* etc., ed. Felix Liebrecht, III, xlv (p. 24). For a windy cave see also the *Marvels of Britain* in *Auct. Antiq.* XIII, ed. Mommsen, *MGH,* p. 215. Cf. MacCulloch, *Medieval Faith and Fable,* pp. 30ff. The folklore of the hollow mountain was widespread. Cf. the stories of Pilate, Theodoric, Frederick II, Frederick Barbarossa, and others. See A. Graf, *Miti, Leggende,* pp. 341ff., and *Roma nella memoria e nelle Immaginazioni del medio Evo,* 644ff. and note 60; *Anzeiger für Kunde des deutschen Mittelalters,* IV (1835), cols. 421ff.; *Studi Medievale,* IV (1912–1913), pp. 213ff.; Krappe, *The Science of Folk-Lore,* p. 90.

[14] *Otia Imperialia,* III, lxvi (pp. 32–34): "Asserebat, iuxta lacum in subterraneo specu palatium esse latum, in cuius aditu ianua est, et intra ianuam interior quaedam obscuritas . . . ."

[15] *Otia Imperialia,* II, xii (p. 12).

The servant, however, who has been warned by the porter to touch no food, refuses all dishes. Here there are four couches, one of them prepared for his own master, who will someday come. He accepts a gold cup and his horse is returned to him. On his return home, the cup, when opened, pours forth flames and, thrown into the sea, sets that too on fire.[16] We may recall the fact that in the story of the monk of Guienne told by William of Malmesbury a cup was obtained in the Under World. Caesarius of Heisterbach also has the same story as Gervase, but according to his version when the servant of a dean goes in search of the horse, he finds again that it is in or on Mount Gyber, where Arthur has it (*In monte Gyber*). The mountain vomits flames.[17]

The narrative of Étienne de Bourbon seems more primitive than the other two, as if it represented the form of the story as it was originally known in Sicily. Otherwise it is hard to see how Étienne would have failed to keep the great name of Arthur. Moreover, the fiery cup suggests that the prince's realm was understood to be within the mountain. With due consideration of the extensive folklore regarding the Purgatory or Hell inside Mount Etna, and the fact that Caesarius accompanies his story with three others regarding such a place of torture, it is fairly certain that in all these accounts the authors thought of the realm as inside. Anyhow, Caesarius himself took it that way, as he shows by the question "Cum animae in eos mittantur, estne ibi purgatorium siue infernus?" [18] In the light of Gervase's use of "anti-

[16] Étienne de Bourbon, *Anecdotes Historiques*, ed. A. Lecoy de la Marche, p. 32 (§ 25). Note too the vision described by Étienne, p. 123 above. On the motif of the cup cf. "The Magic Horn and Cup in Celtic and Grail Tradition," R. S. Loomis and J. S. Lindsay, *Romanische Forschungen*, 45 (1931), pp. 66ff.

[17] Caesarius of Heisterbach, *Dialogus miraculorum*, ed. Joseph Strange, II, pp. 324–325 (dist. XII, cap. xii).

[18] *Ibid.*, II, p. 326. A legend of Dagobert I has it that a hermit sees Dagobert's soul on a bark driven by demons over the waves to the realm of Vulcan, but rescued in time by Saint Denis, Saint Maurice, and Saint Martin (*Gesta Dagoberti I*, ed. Bruno Krusch, *Scriptores rerum Meroving.* II, *MGH*, p. 421, § 44. The editor compares Gregory's *Dialogues*, iv, 31). See too Collin de Plancy, *Légendes de L'Autre Monde*, pp. 68–69. Cf. the *Wartburgkrieg*, ed. K. Simrock, 83–84 (pp. 110–113) and see *Publ. Mod. Lang. Assoc.*, XXXVIII (1923), pp. 404ff. On the whole matter see the comprehensive discussion by Loomis, *Mod. Philol.*, XXXVIII (1941), pp. 289ff., especially p. 298, where he urges the interpretation of Gervase's "circa montis opaca" as a reference to

podibus" in his title for his story of the swineherd, we may also suspect that the idea of Arthur as lord of the Antipodes was somehow related to this conception of his stay in the lower world. Thus some men may have understood the "hemispherium inferius" in which (in 1169 or thereabouts) the *Draco Normannicus* says that Arthur holds sway.[19] The cup in Étienne's story may incidentally recall another anecdote by Gervase: that of a small hill, the height of a man, where if one ascended it alone and said "I thirst" a stranger appeared offering a horn of delicious liquid. This horn was one day kept by a knight and went into the possession of Henry I, as indeed did an Otherworld chalice described by William of Newburgh when it too began its wanderings.[20]

The mountain or volcano as an entrance to the lower world comes several times into the *Dialogus* of Caesarius. In addition to the story about Arthur in Mount Gyber or Etna, he tells one of Bertolph, Duke of Zähringen, for whom some men walking near the place hear orders given to kindle the fires.[21] At this point the Novice asks whether Purgatory or Hell is there, and the monk tells him it is said to be Hell. In the same way three stories are told about Stromboli; in one we hear of the kindling of the fires,

---

the underground passage. Cf. also Wright, *Geographical Lore*, p. 311; Graf. *Miti, Leggende*, pp. 461ff.; Krappe, *The Science of Folk-Lore*, pp. 108f.; Loomis, *Celtic Myth and Arthurian Romance*, p. 194; Tatlock, *Mod. Philol.*, XXXI (1933), pp. 1ff. and 113ff.; MacCulloch, *Medieval Faith and Fable*, pp. 98ff.; Hartland, *The Science of Fairy Tales*, pp. 207ff. Cf. Gardner, *Arthurian Leg. in Italian Lit.*, pp. 12ff. ("The local traditions of Etna are classical . . ." but the story is Norman).

[19] Howlett, *Chronicles of the Reigns of Stephen*, II (*Rolls Series*, LXXXII), pp. 703ff., *Draco Normannicus*, ll. 1162ff. Cf. Loomis, *Mod. Philol.* XXXVIII, p. 296. Cf. the idea among the Greeks according to Franz Cumont, *After Life in Roman Paganism*, pp. 80–81, and see Wright, *Geographical Lore*, pp. 158 and 160–161, and Loomis, *Celtic Myth*, pp. 197–198.

[20] For the small hill see *Otia Imperialia*, III, lx (p. 28). Other folklore pertinent to Otherworld considerations is found in Gervase's story of the rope and anchor coming down from a cloud (*ibid.*, I, xiii, p. 2). Cf. Thomas Wright, *Saint Patrick's Purgatory*, pp. 27ff.; MacCulloch, *op. cit.*, p. 20. Note also the palaces of the sun and moon (*Otia Imp.*, III, lxxviii, p. 36): here the land of the sun is "ad modum insulae" two hundred stades in length and breadth, and is surrounded by a wall. Here are two similar square temples of gold and cinnamon, a couch of the sun in gold and ivory and precious stones, and a golden vine. Cf. Loomis, *Celtic Myth*, pp. 194ff. Gervase also makes reference to the "insula Fortunatorum" (*Otia Imp.*, II, xi, pp. 10–11).

[21] *Dialogus miraculorum*, II, pp. 325–326 (dist. XII, cap. xiii).

and in another the victim enters howling.[22] Clearly with Caesarius the region is different from the examples we have encountered in the narratives of Gervase of Tilbury and Giraldus Cambrensis. With him there is something purgatorial or diabolic even in the short account of Arthur in Mount Gyber which sends forth flames (*flammas euomit*), and we may recall the fact that he knew at least some of the Latin visions and refers specifically to Gregory's story of the bridge and to Saint Patrick's Purgatory.[23] In his case, however, the Other World in a mountain seems to have been combined with an underground place of torture, probably through folklore interpretations of what goes on inside a volcano, which after all suggests its own mysterious preoccupations. He seems to be recording folk tales rather than developing his own idea from the visions.

On the other hand the realm of happiness is depicted in the story told by Ralph of Coggeshall regarding the boy and girl who emerge from a place near a small pit in Suffolk. They are dressed all in green and will touch no food except beans. The boy dies but the girl lives on and tells of the country from which they have come. No sun shines there, but they have about as much light as glows after sunset. The mouth of the cavern from which they wandered has disappeared.[24] The same tale appears as well in the *Historia rerum Anglicarum* of William of Newburgh, who says that the episode occurred not far from the monastery of Bury Saint Edmunds. He adds that the underworld region is called Saint Martin's Land and that the people there are Christians. Not far away across a river (*amne largissimo utramque dirimente*) is a brighter country.[25] In this case the river motif suggests a reminiscence of the visions. William also writes of a hill in which was heard the sound of music and festival. A rustic sees a door in the side and there in a spacious and bright dwelling he beholds

[22] *Ibid.*, II, pp. 322–324 (dist. XII, caps. vii–ix).

[23] *Ibid.*, II, p. 331 (dist. XII, cap. xxi); pp. 347–348 (dist. XII, caps. xxxviii–xxxix).

[24] Ralph of Coggeshall, *Chronicon Anglicanum*, ed. Joseph Stevenson, (*Rolls Series*, LXVI), pp. 118ff.

[25] *Historia rerum Anglicarum of William of Newburgh*, ed. Richard Howlett, (*Chronicles of the Reigns of Stephen, Henry II, and Richard I*, vol. I, *Rolls Series*, LXXXII), pp. 82ff. (I, xxvii).

men and women feasting. From an attendant he takes a cup which was given to Henry I and later became the property of Henry II.[26] Here we seem to have the Celtic *síd* in a form clearer than that of the hill in the story told by Gervase,[27] but we cannot be so sure of the story of the boy and the girl from the cave. Quite possibly in that account and also in the examples of the lower world cited from Walter Map, Giraldus, and Gervase, we have a combination of ultimate indebtedness. By the twelfth century Germanic, Celtic, classical, and Eastern ideas all contributed to the general notion that the Other World was somewhere underground — wherever else it might also be found.[28] What in the early form of some story may have been a hollow hill could also be modified later as a mountain under the influence of Welsh scenery, the Germanic tradition, the Latin visions, Italian stories, or the general folklore associated with the volcano. Such a conclusion is suggested by the Welsh origin of some of the material, but with the widely scattered examples we cannot be sure.

The mountain as a symbol comes into a story in the *Gesta Romanorum* where we read that Gauterus[29] in his wandering search for abundance, joy, and light comes to the "montem altum" to be ascended on a ladder which has six steps. At the top is a most beautiful palace, and here, he is told, he will find what he seeks. The ladder, we learn, with the seven steps it requires for ascent, represents the life of holiness with the seven works of mercy by which one comes to everlasting life. The whole picture recalls something of the arrangement in the *Visio de gloria Paradisi* attributed to Joachim of Flora.[30] On the other hand, the

[26] *Ibid.*, p. 86 (I, xxviii).

[27] Cf. above pp. 234–235; and see MacCulloch, *Medieval Faith and Fable*, pp. 32–33.

[28] Ralph of Coggeshall's story of the hairy man from the sea (*op. cit.*, pp. 117–118) implies an under-water realm. In telling such marvelous or miraculous anecdotes, no author seems troubled by the problem of consistency in his localization of the Other World. Thus one author's several narratives may be based on as many or more traditions.

[29] Oesterley has "Ganterus." I suspect that the Middle English reading "Gauterus" is correct. See for the story Hermann Oesterley, *Gesta Romanorum*, cap. 101, pp. 426–428. Cf. S. J. H. Herrtage, *The Early English Versions of the Gesta Romanorum*, (*EETS:ES*, 33), pp. 365–367, lacking the mountain, and having a ladder with three steps.

[30] See above p. 126, n. 82.

bridge used for monitory purposes appears in the story of the "certain man" who had to cross from one realm to another and found himself at a "certain bridge" by which the passage had to be made. Before him was a very ferocious lion; on his right was a dragon; and on his left the sea. Fearing to go further he began to return home when an angel with a drawn sword stood before him and urged him on. With the sword the man killed the lion and the dragon, and received a crown from the angel.[31] In this case, as so often, the bridge obviously leads to the Other World. So too it does in the *Disciplina Clericalis* of Petrus Alfonsus in the exemplum of the travelers who seek advice of an old man regarding the road to a city they desire to reach. There is a long way and also a short path; but, according to the old man, one travels more quickly by the long way. The travelers nevertheless take the short cut and get lost. So too the travelers on the long road come to a river where there is a ford and also a bridge: the old man says that the route by the ford is shorter by two miles but one arrives sooner by the bridge. They ridicule the old man, but those who go by the ford lose horses and baggage, and those who cross by the bridge arrive without harm. "Tale est prouerbium quod audiui: Magis ualet longa uia ad paradisum quam breuis ad infernum." [32] Thus the bridge, here without any test, is combined with the two paths, one of which is the longest way round but the shortest way home. With the *Disciplina Clericalis,* moreover, we presumably have renewed contact with the Moslem tradition and the East.

On the other hand, the hollow hill comes into the fourteenth-century *Disputisoun bytwene a cristenemon and a Jew.* In the vision described, the Christian and the Jew cross a field to a place where they see the hill. Then as they looked

Þe eorþe cleuet as a scheld
On þe grounde grene.

[31] Oesterley, *op. cit.,* cap. 191, p. 597. The story does not appear in the Middle English versions.

[32] *Die Disciplina Clericalis des Petrus Alfonsi,* ed. Alfons Hilka and Werner Söderhjelm, (*Sammlung mittellat. Texte* 1), pp. 28–29, xviii. Cf. Victor Chauvin, *Bibliographie des Ouvrages Arabes ou Relatifs aux Arabes publiés dans l'Europe chrétienne de 1810 à 1885,* vol. IX, pp. 15–40, tale 16. Cf. too the MS illustration of the man walking on a plank over the Slough of Hell noticed

Sone fond þei a stih:
Þei went þer-on radly

. . . .

After þat stiȝ lay a stret
Clene Ipauet wiþ grete.

There they found a manor with sculpture and with high walls.

To a place weore þei brouht
As paradys þe clene.

Here was the song of birds; the place was adorned with rich hangings and decorated with wonderfully wrought windows; herbs, spices, and flowers grew here; and most remarkable of all, here was the Round Table of Arthur. Near by was a nunnery where were tables with rich meats and with wine, but the Christian would not partake of anything. At length when he shows the Sacrament, the whole spectacle vanishes away, and

Heo þo stoden ope hulle
Þer þey furst were.[33]

In a similar astonishing way the earth opens in the story of *The Adulterous Falmouth Squire* of the fifteenth century. A child is grieving for his dead father when an angel leads him to "A comly hille" where "The Erthe opened, and in thay yode . . ." Here he finds his father in torment for his sins. The angel next leads the boy "Oute of that wrechidly wone" to a great forest "long in brede" where there is a "fayre Erbere" with gates of "clene Cristall" and walls of gold. The birds are of course singing:

The pellycan and the papynjaye,
The tymor and the turtille trewe,
An hondered thousande in her laye,
The nyghtyngale with notis newe.
On a grene hille he saw a tre,
The savoure of hit was stronge & store,
Pale it was and wanne of ble,
Lost it had bothe frute and floure.

---

by G. R. Owst, *Literature and Pulpit in Medieval England*, p. 105, where one is reminded of the first bridge in the *Vision of Tundale* (above p. 112).

[33] Horstmann, *Sammlung Altenglischer Legenden*, first series, pp. 204ff.

And it is bleeding, for it is the tree from which Adam picked the apple. Next the lad is conducted to a "pynacle" (tent) of cloth of gold, where he finds his uncle waiting for him.[34] Of these two poems the *Disputisoun* is the one which more clearly preserves the idea of the Celtic *síd*. In the case of the *Adulterous Falmouth Squire* there is obviously some influence from the visions and the tradition of the Earthly Paradise.

No collection of material, of course, offers more in the way of folklore than the ballads. While few of those we know are actually medieval in their present forms, many of them go back to the Middle Ages and preserve for us at times old examples of the familiar motifs. The field has been carefully studied [35] and need not be reviewed by us in detail here. Suffice it to say that once more we find the Other World in the grave or barrow; we have the boat burial; the river as barrier; the bridge; the sea as barrier; the island; the mountain of Paradise and mountains too of Heaven and Hell; the forest and the enchanted wood; the realm under the sea; the garden of the Other World with flowers, fruit trees, streams, and birds; the mist barrier; the hollow hill; bird souls; and Otherworld music. The *Bitter Withy* gives an especially interesting example of the bridge, one which in this case is built by the Lord out of sunbeams to show His power, and which in the loss of the three "jerdins" seems to include the element of testing.[36] The river barrier in *Thomas Rymer* is of "red blude to the knee." [37] In the *Wee Wee Man* the Otherworld castle was of gold and crystal: "The flure was o the crystal a'." [38] Finally, though the period of stay in the ballad Other World is sometimes as long as seven years, there seems to be no indication of a supernatural lapse of time.[39]

[34] *The Adulterous Falmouth Squire*, in *Political, Religious, and Love Poems*, ed. F. J. Furnivall, (*EETS*, 15), pp. 93ff. Cf. *Engl. Studien* XVI (1892), pp. 89ff. The poem is outlined by Wright in his *Saint Patrick's Purgatory*, pp. 85ff.

[35] By Mr. Lowry Charles Wimberly. See his *Folklore in the English and Scottish Ballads*, pp. 108ff. and 401ff. for Otherworld material in general.

[36] For some discussion see *ibid.*, pp. 114–115, with the suggestion of an oriental origin. For the original see *Notes and Queries*, 10, IV (1905), 84f.

[37] Wimberly, *op. cit.*, pp. 109–110; F. J. Child, *English and Scottish Popular Ballads*, I, p. 324 (37, A7).

[38] Wimberly, *op. cit.*, p. 146; Child, *op. cit.*, I, p. 330 (38, A7).

[39] Wimberly, *op. cit.*, pp. 328–330.

i

In the coming of Scyld in a pilotless boat according to the *Beowulf,* and in the burial ship with which he departs (of which it is said that no one knows who received that freight), we have undoubted reference to the Otherworld journey across the sea. It is quite possible, however, that in the haunted mere we have a scene that is ultimately indebted to ideas of the strange realm under the sea or Under-Wave-Land. Indications of this may be found in an analogue which has been suggested in the Norse saga of *Samson the Fair* and other literary connections.[40] The cave with various treasures found under water and inhabited by supernatural creatures may derive from the underwater realm as well as from general notions of underground regions supplied with riches of one sort or another. Our attention has also been drawn to the most popular of all ballads, *Lady Isabel and the Elf Knight,* for a parallel to the story of a supernatural creature who lures a person to destruction; as it has been said, "there are indications that [the lady] is to be taken to an other-world country." [41] In some versions of the ballad the Elf Knight puts the lady on his steed and takes her to a region by the sea (and in B3 according to Child,[42] "to that water That they ca Wearie's Well"). We may add that the episode thus far is astonishingly like that in the Old French lay, *Tydorel,* where a beautiful queen of Bretagne is one day visited in her garden by the handsome knight who puts her on his horse and takes her off with him to a lake. From this point on the stories differ, but scholars seem agreed that the knight in this case too represents an underwater creature.[43]

[40] See Mr. W. W. Lawrence in *Klaeber* [*Anniversary Volume*], "Studies in English Philology," pp. 172ff

[41] Mr. Lawrence, following Child, *ibid.*, p. 181. Cf. Child, *op. cit.*, I, p. 50: "The nearest approach to the Elf-Knight, Halewyn, etc., is perhaps Quintalin, in the saga of Samson the Fair." Child speaks later of the "subaqueous cave of Quintalin's mother, who is a complete counterpart to Grendel's, and was probably borrowed from Beowulf."

[42] Child, *op. cit.*, I, p. 55, ballad 4.

[43] *Romania* VIII (1879), pp. 66ff.; *Le Lai de Guingamor, Le Lai de Tydorel,* ed. Erhard Lommatzsch, (*Romanische Texte*, VI), pp. 23ff. Cf. Paton, *Studies in the Fairy Mythology of Arthurian Romance*, p. 168; Leach, *Angevin Britain and Scandinavia*, p. 217; *Mod. Lang. Review,* XXIV (1920) pp. 200ff.; *Publ. Mod. Lang. Assoc.,* XX (1905), pp. 152ff.

Tydorel is definitely Celtic in some of its details. Among the lays *Sir Orfeo* has long been regarded as a story presenting an instance of the Celtic Other World which replaces the classical Hades.[44] Heurodis fell asleep in an orchard under an "ympetre" (grafted tree) and had her dream of the fairy king coming with a hundred knights and more and a hundred damsels to take her on his palfrey to his palace, where he showed her castles, towers, rivers, forests, and flowers. Later, when Orfeo discovers his lady with the others of the fairy king's train, he follows them and sees them go "In at a roche." He goes after "Wele þre mile oþer mo" and comes to a fair country as bright as the sun on a summer's day, smooth and flat and all green. Here is a castle with the outermost wall as bright as crystal and with a hundred towers. Within are gold and precious stones which shine as bright as the sun at noon.

> Bi al þing him þink, þat it is
> Þe proude court of paradis.

Here the ladies alight and enter.[45] Orfeo knocks at the gate and the porter admits him. He sees many supposedly dead people about him, and among them his wife sleeping under an "ympetre." In the king's hall he finds the king and queen enthroned, to whom he then makes entreaty with his harping.

Among the lays of Marie de France *Guigemar* offers a well-known example of the "rudderless" or unpiloted boat. The hero, who has been out in a forest hunting a white doe, follows a green path to a plain:

> En la plaigne
> vit la faleise e la muntaigne
> d'une ewe ki desuz cureit.[46]

[44] *Amer. Journal of Philology,* VII (1886), pp. 176ff. Here it is interesting to note the parallel suggested to *Tydorel,* pp. 190–191. Cf. also Loomis, *Mod. Lang. Notes,* LI (1936), pp. 28ff. and above page 232 n. 6.

[45] *Sir Orfeo,* ed. Oscar Zielke, Breslau, 1880. The ballad *King Orfeo* (Child, *op. cit.,* I, pp. 215–217, 19) adds nothing except an apparent reference to the "roche" as "grey stane" and to the lady as "Isabel." The latter detail has interest here because the use of music in *Lady Isabel and the Elfin Knight* suggests some influence or connection between the ballads.

[46] *Die Lais der Marie de France,* ed. Karl Warnke, (*Bibliotheca Normannica,* III), p. 11, ll. 147–149.

This is an arm of the sea, and here he sees a solitary ship with a pavilion on it, with sails of silk and timbers of ebony. Inside the pavilion is a sumptuous bed, on which Guigemar rests because of his wound. The boat takes him to "une antive cité," where there is a castle owned by an old lord and his fair wife. The castle has a garden below its great tower, round which is a wall of green marble with only one gate. On the other side is the sea, so that none can leave or enter without a boat. Within the wall the lord has had a room constructed: "suz ciel n'aveit plus bele." At the entrance is a chapel, and inside are the most beautiful paintings. Here Guigemar and the young wife are united in love, and his wound is healed. They dwell for a year and a half until their affair is discovered and he returns to his own land in the vessel. Later the wife, who has been shut in a tower of grey marble, makes her escape and finding the ship in the harbor rides in it to the realm of Meriaduc, where eventually she joins her lover again. The plot has long been recognized as in part an example of the story of a healing fée; and, in that respect at least and the motif of the boat, it derives from the Celtic.[47]

A comparable set of details, as readers know, may be found in the lay of Guingamor, sometimes attributed to Marie, where the hero goes forth to hunt the wild boar in the "aventure de la forest" where:

> La lande i est aventureuse
> Et la riviére perilleuse.[48]

Guingamor rides through the clearing and apparently across the river right through the green and blossoming meadowland, until he sees a great palace enclosed with green marble all about. At the entrance is a tower of silver and the gates are of ivory inlaid with gold. He enters but finds no one. The rooms are set with stones of Paradise. After looking around he goes back and rides

[47] Cf. Köhler's comments, *ibid.*, pp. ciff.; and A. Ewert, ed., *Marie de France, Lais,* p. 165. Both editors compare the ship in *Partonopeus of Blois* which is sent by Melior. Cf. pp. 251ff. and 256f. (*Floriant et Florete*) below. Note the ship bearing the dead body of Raguidel and conveying Gawain in *La Vengeance Raguidel,* ed. Friedwagner, p. 6, ll. 105ff.; p. 140, ll. 4197ff.

[48] *Romania* VIII (1879), p. 53, ll. 177–178; *Le Lai de Guingamor, Le Lai de Tydorel,* ed. Erhard Lommatzsch, p. 6, and for the motifs cf. pp. vf.

along the bank of the river. At length in a clearing he discovers a fountain under an olive tree wide-spreading and green and in blossom. Its waters flow over gold and silver gravel. Here he finds bathing the lady whom he thenceforth loves, and with whom he has his affair. They meet again at the palace, now filled with a fair company of knights and ladies, and decked richly in his honor. At length he returns to his own country by riding back to the river, which this time, it is clear, he crosses in a boat (S'est el batel outre passé"). He is warned not to partake of food or drink again until his return to this strange region or he will be in trouble. From a charcoal burner he learns that the king and people he knew in his own country have been dead for more than three hundred years and the castles are in ruins. Being famished, he eats a wild apple; whereupon he grows physically old and feeble and is rescued by two damsels who, reproaching him, get him across the river again in the boat.

In the motif of the hunt and in the journey over water to the region of the fairy mistress one may find a general similarity to the story of *Guigemar*. It is striking, however, that the water barrier is here much reduced, although the boat is still necessary. If there is any relation between the two lays, we may suspect that the amount of water is less in this case because of some outside influence, perhaps ultimately from the Germanic or from the tradition of the Latin visions. Such a conclusion is suggested by the emphasis on the forest and on the peculiar nature of the river. It seems doubtful that the motif of the ocean would be cut down merely for the sake of convenience.[49] In the Celtic voyages there is no stress on the danger of crossing the sea, whether in coracle or pinnace; but here, although the boat may come from such a story, the perilous river itself seems to belong to another tradition, that of the turbulent and ugly streams of which there are so many instances.

A vivid possibility of oriental influence is suggested by the

[49] Cf. the opposing view of Philipot, *Romania*, XXV (1896), p. 267, with special reference to the influence of the *imrama* in Arthurian romance; and also that of Loomis, *Romania* LIX (1933), pp. 557ff., regarding the *Contes del Graal*. Further material regarding the "peculiar nature of the river" is offered in my comments on the subject, *Publ. Mod. Lang. Assoc.*, XXXIII (1918), pp. 630ff.

use of the motif of the hunting of the deer, which leads to the discovery of the fée, as it is recounted in an early fifteenth-century manuscript of the *Historia septem sapientum*,[50] based on a Hebrew version of a much earlier period. The rest of the plot need not concern us here. The episode reappears in the *Dolopathos* of Johannes de Alta Silva, where it is connected with the Swan Knight story and where the hero finds the damsel bathing in a fountain.[51] It is preserved in the thirteenth-century *Naissance du Chevalier au Cygne*, where the king's attempt to return from the hunt is impeded by a mountain, and near an oak tree he looses his horse to feed and by the beautiful fountain takes his own rest.[52] Here we are told that the water from the fountain flowed over gravel more precious than that found in the Tigris: it was all of diamonds, topazes, and other precious stones. Moreover, the fée comes from the mountain, within which is her dwelling along

[50] *Historia septem sapientum*, ed. Alfons Hilka, Heidelberg, 1912 (*Sammlung mittellateinischer Texte*, 4, 1) pp. 11ff. (6). A magic fountain, which changes the hero's sex, appears later. Hilka calls the whole work the first Latin translation of an oriental redaction (p. xiii). On the story of the hunt and the fée cf. *ibid.*, pp. xivff. Note that the Hebrew text uniquely combines the story of the hunt and that of the fountain. Cf. Domenico Comparetti, *Researches Respecting the Book of Sindibâd*, London, 1882, (Folk-Lore Society) p. 46. For the Syriac, the oldest text left of the oriental versions, see the translation of Hermann Gollancz, *Folk-Lore*, VIII (1897), pp. 109f. (the hunt of the wild ass) and 112f. (the spring). For the Spanish, which is based on the lost eighth-century Arabic, see the text and translation in Comparetti, *op. cit.*, pp. 86ff. (trans. pp. 131ff., the hunt) and pp. 89f. (trans. pp. 134f., the fountain). On the other hand, cf. *Die Sage von der verfolgten Hinde*, Carl Pschmadt, especially pp. 65ff., showing how widely spread the motif of the hunt is, but not strengthening a case for Celtic origins. For a parallel in German folklore cf. Siuts, *Jenseitsmotive im deutschen Volksmärchen*, p. 145 (§ 360).

[51] The development of the episode has been traced by M. B. Ogle in the *Amer. Journal of Philology*, XXXVII (1916), pp. 387ff., who calls the story "demonstrably oriental" (p. 415). With special reference to *Guingamor*, *Lanval*, and *Desiré*, cf. Schofield, "The Lay of Guingamor," [*Harvard*] *Studies and Notes in Philol. and Lit.*, V, pp. 221ff. See, however, the Celtic instances of the motif of the fée by a spring or ford indicated by Cross, [*Kittredge*] *Anniversary Papers*, pp. 377ff., and for the deer in Irish see *Mod. Philol.*, XVI (1918–1919), p. 656. In the Old French *Dolopathos* the forest is "espesse et drue" (*Li Romans de Dolopathos*, ed. Charles Brunet and Anatole de Montaiglon, p. 318, l. 9215), and the fountain's stream runs "Blanche et nete sor la gravelle" (p. 319, l. 9232).

[52] *La Naissance du Chevalier au Cygne*, ed. H. A. Todd in *Publ. Mod. Lang. Assoc.*, IV (1889), Nos. 3–4, pp. 4ff.

with other damsels.[53] Except possibly for this last detail the argument for ultimate derivation from the East is substantial, but in none of these versions do we have the motif of the river itself as a barrier.[54]

In the lay of *Graelent*, where the hero follows a white hart, he too rides through a great forest, but as with the lay *Guingamor* there is a river which he must later cross. The damsel he eventually loves he finds with two other maidens by a fountain. After the episode of the test like that in the *Lanval* story, when he follows his lady back to her realm through the forest she warns him that the river (which is described as "clere et bele") is dangerous for him. As he enters it the waters do close over his head, and she has to pull him back by his bridle. On the second attempt he is carried off his saddle by the stream, and the lady gets him across by pulling him out of the water on the far side.[55] In this case the danger of the river is made even more emphatic. At this point we may notice that in *Graelent*, where the river thus assumes a special peculiarity, the parallel to the story of the hunt as we have it in *Dolopathos* is closest. But we have observed that the oriental account of that episode, as it comes down in the tradition of the Seven Sages, does not include the river barrier so far as we know. It is quite possible that it derives instead from a wholly different document, such indeed as that which has been assumed as a source of the hunting of the white stag and the sparrow-hawk episode in Chrétien's *Erec*.[56] On that score we may turn

[53] *Ibid.*, p. 5, ll. 161ff.

[54] Curiously enough, the river does turn up in the prose English version, where the deer escapes by leaping into it: "Helyas, Knight of the Swan," ed. W. J. Thoms in *Early English Prose Romances*, III (London, 1858), p. 25.

[55] *The Lays of Desiré, Graelent and Melion*, ed. E. Margaret Grimes, (Institute of French Studies), pp. 76ff. Cf. Pschmadt, *Die Sage von der verfolgten Hinde*, pp. 73ff. In this connection Schofield's idea of the influence of the Wayland story, and thus of Germanic elements in the plot, is interesting: see *Publ. Mod. Lang. Assoc.* XV (1900), pp. 121ff. But cf. Cross in *Mod. Philol.* XII (1914–1915), pp. 585ff. (including some discussion of *Guingamor*) and [*Kittredge*] *Anniversary Papers*, pp. 377ff. Note that in *Desiré* the hero is riding in a forest, that of La Blanche Lande, when he comes upon his lady by the fountain: Grimes, *op. cit.*, p. 52, ll. 118ff.

[56] Cf. *Mod. Philol.*, XI (1914), pp. 450–451. See also Gardner, *Arthurian Legend in Ital. Lit.*, pp. 121ff. and 321ff.; and Nutt, *Voyage of Bran*, I, p. 284, n. 1, on the white deer.

again to the treatise of Andreas Capellanus where he deals with some of that material. Here one of the knights of Britain on his way to see Arthur goes alone through the royal forest and finds a girl of marvelous beauty sitting on a horse. She invites him to undergo the test for the hawk. He walks on alone through the wood, and "At length, as he was passing through a wild and lonely place, he came to a river of marvellous breadth and depth, with great waves in it, and because of the great height of its banks it was impossible for anyone to reach it." [57] He then has the adventure of the bridge of gold and the fight with the bridge keeper. Something like this, then, may have been familiar to Marie when she composed her *Lanval,* and also known to the author or authors of *Guingamor* and *Graelent,* where it could be fitted in neatly with the Eastern story of the hunting of the deer.

In Marie's lay of *Lanval,* although we do not have the episode of the hunt, the stream ("une ewe") is again fearful. In this case the horse is so disturbed ("mes sis chevals tremble forment") that Lanval sets him free to graze in the meadow and lies down to rest. We are not told how the damsels who come for Lanval get across the water barrier or manage to transport him. He simply sees them approaching as he looks along the river: "guarda a val lez la riviere." But at the end of the poem the whole idea shifts to the other conception, and we are told that the hero has gone to Avalun "en un isle qui mult est beals." [58] We learn, however, that the first scene of the lady's pavilion of silk and gold, which is presumably across the river, is not the same as her own land from which she says she has come ("fors de ma terre"). In the Middle English versions of the story the only possible reminiscence of the detail of the horse's fear is that the animal "slod and fel yn þe fen" according to Chestre,[59] who, however, omits the river and has a "fayr forest" lacking in Marie's poem but for us recalling the same feature in *Graelent* and *Guingamor* and

[57] *The Art of Courtly Love,* ed. Parry, p. 178. Cf. the discussion above in the study of allegory, pp. 196ff.

[58] Warnke, *op. cit.,* p. 88, ll. 45ff., and p. 112, ll. 659ff., and Ewert, *op. cit.,* pp. 59ff. and p. 74.

[59] W. H. French and C. B. Hale, *Middle English Metrical Romances,* p. 352, line 214.

even perhaps that in *Desiré*. *Landavall*, on the other hand, refers to the hero's ride as taken "Be-twene a water and a forest," although there is no allusion beyond that to the river; and the water and fair forest occur again in *Sir Lambewell* and *Sir Lamwell*.[60]

In *Tyolet* we have something like the Perceval story of the young hero brought up in ignorance of knighthood by his widowed mother. One day at her bidding he goes into the forest to slay a stag, and at last he finds one, which, however, wanders off out of the woods until it comes to a stream:

> L'eve estoit grant et ravineuse
> Et lée et longue et perilleuse.[61]

This the creature goes over in safety and on the other side changes into a fully armed knight. Apparently the youth is unable to follow, but later sees many knights, indeed two hundred, in the meadow on the far side of the river. In another episode Lodoer, who seeks the stag's foot to win the princess, comes to what seems like the same place, and again the stream is described:

> Qui molt estoit et grant et lée,
> Et noire et hisdeuse et enflée:
> Quatre cent toises ot de lé
> Et bien cent de parfondée.[62]

The brachet that led him thither plunges into the water, but Lodoer refuses to follow since he has no desire of death:

> Il dit que il n'i enterra,
> Car de morir nul talent n'a.[63]

[60] For *Sir Landavall* see the *Amer. Journal of Philology*, X (1889), p. 22, line 34; *Sir Lambewell*, see *Bishop Percy's Folio Manuscript*, J. W. Hales and F. J. Furnivall, I, London, 1867, p. 146, line 54; *Sir Lamwell*, see *ibid.*, I, p. 523, line 40. Kittredge attempts to minimize the significance of the forest: *Amer. Journal of Philology*, X, pp. 17–18; but, considering its place in the three lays, such a recourse seems of doubtful validity. It is interesting to find both forest and river in the modern Italian analogue *L'Isola della felicità* (*Novelline Popolari Italiane*, Domenico Comparetti, I, pp. 212ff.), where the hero waits "dietro al bosco che c'è sulla riva del ruscello."

[61] *Romania*, VIII, pp. 42–43, ll. 95–96.

[62] *Ibid.*, p. 46, ll. 379–382.

[63] *Ibid.*, p. 46, ll. 387–388.

But Tyolet on his corresponding adventure does take this risk, where again we are told of the

grant eve ravineuse,
Qui molt ert parfonde et hisdeuse.[64]

In the meadow he finds the stag he is looking for, with seven lions that guard it and love it with a great love. The rest of the story does not tell us exactly how the hero or any other characters came back across the stream, but in what we already have there can be little doubt that the lay presents an adaptation of the river barrier of the Other World of the type familiar in *Guingamor* and *Lanval.*

Marie's lay *Yonec* shows a combination of motifs. The description of the realm of the knight begins with the lady following a path until she enters a hill which has one entrance and no light. From this she issues forth and comes to a fair meadow where soon she beholds a city enclosed with a wall and having no house, nor hall, nor tower, but apparently all made of silver. Near by is a forest and from the other side runs a river all about, in which ships are arriving. Within the town the lady finds no man or woman, but in two rooms of the palace she sees a sleeping knight. In a third she finds her own knight lying on a bed, and this chamber is richly described with the detail that here the candles and chandeliers are lighted day and night. When she leaves this scene at last, the lady goes back through the hill and thus returns to her own country.[65] In the whole episode we obviously have the motif of the Celtic type of realm within the hill, but it seems to be somewhat awkwardly combined with the material regarding the meadow and the city. In this part of the description the forest and the river suggest details from another source.[66]

[64] *Ibid.*, p. 47, ll. 435–436.

[65] For the whole account see Warnke, *Die Lais der Marie de France*, pp. 137ff., ll. 349ff.

[66] Inconsistencies in the story are noted by Cross in *Rev. celtique*, XXXI (1910), pp. 460ff., and Ewert, *Marie de France, Lais*, p. 179. It has been suggested that the Inclusa episode at the beginning (of the wife shut up for protection) comes from oriental sources: see Johnston, *Publ. Mod. Lang. Assoc.*, XX (1905), pp. 326ff. and 338; Ogle, *Romanic Review*, X (1919), pp. 136ff.; and Cross, [*North Carolina*] *Studies in Philology*, XI (1913), p. 48.

The motif of the hunt and the journey over water reappears in the romance *Partonopeus de Blois,* which seems beyond question to be indebted to some story that also furnished material to the lays *Guigemar* and *Guingamor.* In *Partonopeus* the hero is hunting the wild boar in a forest, becomes lost, gets off his horse to let him feed, sits down under an oak tree, spends the night in distress, and on the next day finds a broad path which he follows:

Il entre en un moult let sentier,
Batu le voit moult et plenier,
Traces i voit de tels manières,
Onques n'avoit véu tant fières,
De serpens et de wivres grans,
Et de venimos vers volans.[67]

At last he and his horse come to a place from which they see the ocean. He goes down to the shore and finds the fair ship, which has a bridge let down to the land whereby he can get on board. There he sees no living creature; but he lies down and falls asleep, and when he wakens the ship is of course far out to sea. Going very fast, the ship sails all night and all the next day, and on the next evening comes to a town with a castle "Qui moult est buens et moult est beaus." With his steed Partonopeus leaves the ship. Before him shine the city walls, which are all of marble, red and white. Its splendor makes him think it is fairyland. The palaces too are richly described and their ornamentation:

Li enfès a tot esgardé,
En paradis cuide estre entré.[68]

On the other hand, Mr. Cross's articles here cited present a wealth of Celtic analogues for many details in the Otherworld material.

[67] *Partonopeus de Blois,* ed. A. C. M. Robert, I, p. 24, ll. 671ff. On the whole problem of the tradition of the plot in this romance see the fine study by Helaine Newstead, in *Publ. Mod. Lang. Assoc.,* LXI (1946), pp. 916ff.

[68] *Partonopeus,* I, p. 31, ll. 873–874. The same story is followed in the English version: cf. *The Middle English Versions of Partonope of Blois,* ed. A. T. Bödtker, (*EETS:ES,* 101, pp. 15ff. In the British Museum MS the hero when lost in the forest spends the night in a hollow tree; the path is omitted, but on horseback "Mony a perlows water he paste" — in fact he crossed twenty, we are told, according to the "ffrenshe boke"; the meadow by the seaside is full of wild beasts. On the Norwegian version cf. Leach, *Angevin Britain and Scandinavia,* pp. 262–263, noting Icelandic romances in which an aerial vehicle is substituted for the boat.

Up to this point, it should be noted, the hero's distress for food and drink and especially for fear has been mentioned by the poet from time to time. On the sea especially he felt great grief:

> Péors de terre est mioldre assés
> Que n'est de mer, bien le savés:
> A terre a mainte garison,
> Mais en la mer n'a se mort non.[69]

He wished he were back in the forest. This almost unique example of the hero's feeling of terror at the sea he crosses suggests a reminiscence of the dangerous and fearful river in *Guingamor*, *Graelent*, and lays of that type, from which the romance has certainly derived many details.

The palace into which the hero at length goes is of course magnificent, none being so fair in all the world. It has great ditches or moats about it, and high walls with two towers. Within the walls is also a tower all of bright marble, and spacious gardens and fair arbors. Inside he finds no living creature, but now his hunger is appeased by wonderful food served to him although no servant or vassal appears. After this feast he is led by lighted tapers to a room where he sees a marvelous bed, and on this he falls asleep. When the lady Melior wakens him and they achieve amicable conversation at last, she tells him that it is she who arranged all his previous experiences that brought him to her. She says Besance (Byzantium) is her realm, a detail that for the twelfth century may connote the Other World,[70] or perhaps only indicates some connection with Greek romance, such as we find evidence for in the Cupid and Psyche motif later utilized. Partonopeus has a wide view of the surrounding country from the tower; but, aside from the fact that everything including gardens, a castle, and a forest are here, the description has nothing especially noteworthy. He learns from Melior that the castle he is in is called Chef-d'Oire, and after some further experiences he goes back to his own country by the reverse process of boarding the ship, falling asleep, and finding himself again at Blois.

[69] *Partonopeus*, I, p. 26, ll. 745–748.

[70] For the significance of Constantinople cf. *Mod. Philol.*, XXV (1928), p. 334, and *Engl. Studien*, XXXVI (1906), pp. 356f.

The ship, which is clearly an example of the motif of the rudderless or pilotless boat, appears again in the story; and perhaps a further instance of Otherworld material may be found in the forest tract into which Partonopeus wanders in his time of grief, and certainly another in the island of Salence to which Urrake takes him for healing. Of the forest, which functions here somewhat as the Desert of Love does in medieval allegory much later, we read that the hero reached a spot infested with dangerous creatures:

Partonopex passe les mers
Où li serpent ont lor convers:
Tant est alez, que nuit que jors,
Qu'il est venuz el halt des hors
Et des lions et des liéparz;
D'iluec n'eschape nus coarz.
Passez s'en est par moult serpenz,
C'onques un n'i a gita les denz.[71]

It is a marvel, as the poet says, that he was not devoured; and here in this forest he is found by Urrake and Maruc, who take him by boat to the Isle of Salence "buens et beaus et purs et nés." [72] It was a gift to Urrake from her sister Melior, and in spices, fruits, fountains, flowers, it has everything including a fair castle, where Urrake assumes the rôle of healing fée. In general in this important romance there is little in the Otherworld material to suggest Eastern or even characteristically Greek sources, in spite of its initial and rather nominal connection with the classical cycle. On the contrary the main outlines show nothing that cannot be explained in terms of the Celtic (at least as modified in the twelfth-century *lais*), especially in the instance of the voyage for healing. Perhaps the forest, however, and the terror of the sea, and the "desert" tracts with reptiles and wild animals, are derivatives from another tradition.

In *Florimont*, written by Aimon de Varennes and dated 1188,

[71] *Partonopeus*, II, p. 25, ll. 5737ff. Cf. the similar episode, with the less forbidding forest, in Chrétien's *Yvain*, ed. Foerster, (*Romanische Bibliothek*, vol. V), pp. 72ff., ll. 2774ff.

[72] *Partonopeus*, II, p. 39, ll. 6168ff. For reference to Otherworld material one may note also the story of the Phoenix, *ibid.*, II, pp. 181f., ll. 11333ff.

we have the story of the fée again, who this time comes on a steed with magic sword and ring to offer the hero her love.[73] The romance is loosely connected in plot with the Alexander cycle, and directly or indirectly derives some material from the Orient. The damsel says she has crossed the sea in a ship for him from "l'Ile Selee" where she will make him king,[74] but this part of the story may well be associated with episodes already familiar in European literature in this period. Something like the forest is suggested in this scene too, in the "boscaige" along the sea where the ship waits.[75] But some question may be raised regarding the bridge, which appears in the account of the castle Clavegris much later. This powerful castle is on a mighty rock in the midst of the sea [76] on an island named Magalon, and its entrance is reached by a castle on another rock connected with the first by a bridge:

> Desoz le pont est grans li onde
> Et la meirs hate et perfonde.[77]

To cross here men must go one by one, and it is lowered only from Clavegris. Beyond are two lions to destroy invaders. If more than one traveler tries to get over, the bridge rises and the rest are smashed against the rock and thrown into the sea.[78] Here apparently we have an adaptation of the Bridge of Judgment with some reminiscence of the turbulent river in the description of the sea. In the subsequent rich description of the interior of the castle, where the Lady of Carthage and her damsels live, and in the whole episode there is the atmosphere of the Other World with what is perhaps the oriental form of Maidenland. One suspects, therefore, that the detail of the bridge itself came ultimately from some Eastern document.

In *Floire et Blanceflor* of the third quarter of the twelfth century we have what seems to be undoubted oriental material. The castle of maidens in Babylon, where Blanceflor is kept in

[73] *Aimon von Varennes: Florimont*, ed. Alfons Hilka (Göttingen, 1932), (*Gesellschaft für Romanische Literatur*, 48) pp. 93ff., ll. 2421ff.

[74] On the question of parallels to *Partonopeus, Lanval*, and *Graelent*, and on the invisible island motif, see *ibid.*, pp. cxif.

[75] *Ibid.*, p. 98, ll. 2543ff.

[76] *Ibid.*, pp. 455ff., ll. 11563ff.

[77] Lines 11599–11600.

[78] Lines 12577ff.

hiding, is clearly a type of harem. Features of the Earthly Paradise appear in the Emir's garden, where

> De l'autre part, cou m'est a vis,
> Court uns fleuves de paradis,
> Qui Eufrates est apelés.[79]

The place is fair and spacious, no better exists in the whole world; and it is all enclosed with a wall of gold and azure. It has all sorts of birds with their joyous songs; the stream that surrounds it so that no one may pass over except by flying flows on a bed of many precious stones; all sorts of fruit trees are here, spices, and flowers; in the middle is a fountain pouring forth in a channel of silver and crystal over gold gravel, and also the beautiful red tree of love always in flower. A peculiarity here is that when a girl who is a virgin crosses the rivulet from the fountain its waters are clear, but they become muddy for the wife of the Emir, who is then cast into the fire. However, he has his maidens walk under the tree, and the one on whom a blossom falls becomes his lady for the succeeding year.[80] But perhaps the most interesting detail of all is that in the approach to this splendid place there is in Babylon a broad and deep river over which Floire has to cross by a bridge.[81] It is from the keeper of this bridge that he gets all the present description, and learns how the maidens live in the ancient round tower, which has a carbuncle to illumine it

[79] *Floire et Blanceflor,* ed. Édélestand Du Méril, p. 72. So too in Fleck's *Flore und Blanscheflur,* l. 4444 (ed. W. Golther, p. 372). On the whole garden, identifying it as an Otherworld scene, cf. O. M. Johnston in *Zeits. f. roman. Phil.,* XXXII (1908), pp. 705ff. In the Middle English thirteenth-century version too the "stremes come fram paradis": *Floris and Blauncheflur,* ed. Emil Hausknecht, (*Sammlung Englischer Denkmäler,* V) p. 188, l. 696. For other versions see *ibid.,* pp. 4ff.; *Floire und Blantscheflur,* Lorenz Ernst, in *Quellen und Forschungen* 118 (1912); Hibbard, *Mediaeval Romance in England,* pp. 184ff.

[80] In the Middle English this test remains the same; but in the case of the rivulet, if the unchaste damsel comes to wash her hands, the water boils up as if it were maddened, and changes to blood: *Floris and Blauncheflur,* ed. Hausknecht, p. 189, ll. 719–720. Cf. Fleck's *Flore und Blanscheflur,* ll. 4472ff. (ed. Golther, p. 372) where, when the unchaste damsel goes by, the water turns red.

[81] *Floire et Blanceflor,* ed. Du Méril, pp. 54–55 ("Un flun moult le et moult parfont.") Cf. the *Floire et Blanceflor* (*ibid.,* p. 193) where the river is "ravinose," and Fleck's version ll. 3625ff. (ed. Golther, p. 349).

day and night and also a clear fountain to furnish water. The pavement and the pillars are of marble, and the ceiling of gold and azure. The whole setting is in part derived from the Otherworld tradition, and one cannot help suspecting that the bridge and its keeper represent the familiar motif rather directly taken from Moslem sources.

Another thirteenth-century romance that in certain details suggests the use of oriental material is *Floriant et Florete*, loosely connected with the Arthurian cycle. According to its story three fairies, including Morgain, who have been in the sea, come to take the newborn Floriant to Mongibel "lor mestre chastel," and there the hero stays until he is fifteen.[82] At that age he has to depart and sails in a well-made boat of ebony to seek out King Arthur. The ship is elaborately adorned with pictures of the firmament, Adam and Eve, the story of Troy, Amor, and Tristan and Yseult la Blonde. At dawn Floriant awakens and sees near at hand a castle surrounded by vineyards and fields, woods and meadows, where Moradas is lord, who has subdued and confined fifteen of Arthur's barons. Floriant liberates the prisoners by doing battle for them, and then he sails away. He next comes to a fair city with walls of marble of many colors, in which are many streets, chapels, churches, and dwellings, and here he finds a great number of damsels. He goes to a beautiful palace with massive silver pillars and adorned with gold and precious stones, where he is met by four damsels and finds a thousand more within. He kills a monster here that has daily devoured one after another of the maidens. With twenty of the damsels he sets forth again in his ship and arrives at Cardigan, where Arthur holds court. In the same way he goes in his ship from one adventure to another, coming once to a little castle, old and dilapidated and without man or woman, and another time to an island of savage beasts. On one adventure, at the time of the fight between Arthur and the Greek emperor, he meets Florete, with whom he falls in love and whom he calls "la Plaisant de l'Isle." His voyages are numerous; but finally at Palermo, when he is out hunting, a stag leads him to

[82] *Floriant et Florete*, ed. Francisque Michel, (*Roxburghe Club*), p. 21, ll. 569–570; ed. H. F. Williams (*Univ. of Michigan Publ., Lang. and Lit.* XXIII), p. 55, ll. 568ff.

a castle where he is to get immortality. The animal has been sent by Morgain to draw him back to her as she also will bring Arthur. Three fays are sent to fetch Florete so that they may be together at Mongibel. In all this the frequent voyages and the numerous ports instantly suggest a comparison with the Celtic *imram*, and indeed one need go little further than Irish tradition to explain most of the material in this plot. The city of many damsels looks like a clear instance of Maidenland, and the ebony ship and the hunting of the deer recall the lay of *Guigemar*.

The association of Arthur with Mongibello reflects the idea already noticed in the stories of Gervase of Tilbury and Caesarius of Heisterbach, but here emphasis is laid on the point that Morgain's castle is beyond the sea and she herself has been in the sea.[83] The whole narrative is filled with episodes concerned with what is clearly the magic boat she gives the hero, and not with a realm inside or on the mountain. In fact, this would seem to offer a prime instance of the wanderings of what is really the rudderless boat, used of course by Morgain when she took Arthur to Avalon, but widely familiar elsewhere. An outstanding example is that which conveys the Swan Knight in his wanderings in the Lohengrin story and in the thirteenth-century *Chevalier au Cygne*. Incidentally it may be worth noting that while *Floriant et Florete* has both the motif of the hunt and that of the ship, the *Naissance du Chevalier au Cygne* has the hunt, familiar in *Guigemar* and other lays, and the *Chevalier au Cygne* has the ship. In this last romance the swan brings it to Elyas and guides it on its journey, which includes some adventures: [84]

A tant es vous venant
Le chisne qui amaine le batel traïnant,
A une grant caaine qui'st de fin or luisant,
Que Dex i envoya par son disne commant.[85]

[83] Cf. Paton, *Studies in the Fairy Mythology of Arthurian Romance*, pp. 250–251. On the boat see also E. G. Gardner, *The Italian Legend in Arthurian Literature*, p. 104, and *Mod. Lang. Review*, XX (1925), p. 332; and *Floriant*, ed. Michel, p. xliv, n. 17, for the parallel to *Guigemar*. On this latter point and some connection with other romances here discussed see Miss Newstead's article, *Publ. Mod. Lang. Assoc.*, LXI (1946), pp. 916ff., especially 931ff.

[84] *La Chanson du Chevalier au Cygne et de Godefroid de Bouillon*, ed. Hippeau, I, pp. 90ff. (xxff.).

[85] *Ibid.*, I, p. 92.

In this case and in some instances elsewhere God is ultimately in charge of the wanderings of the boat; but in other stories another supernatural agent, perhaps Morgain or the fairy mistress herself, is responsible for sending the vessel. It would take us too far afield to attempt to catalogue all the examples.[86] The motif of the so-called rudderless boat derives in part from an occasional practice of putting a malefactor adrift according to the custom in some parts of the medieval world, but it comes too from fairy-mistress stories and even from boat burials, where it clearly implies the journey to the Other World. How much ultimately taken from these traditions may be found in the various documents of the Constance Saga it would be hard to say, but there we do seem to have something of both ideas, that of punishment and that of the journey. This is not the place to attempt to follow all the intricacies of that complicated cycle of story telling, but we may note that the motif of punishment appears in the account of the second Offa, whose wife-to-be arrives in a boat in the *Vitae duorum Offarum*, and it is clear also in *La Manekine* and other romances. In *La Manekine* the heroine prays to God and her prayer is heard; obviously then, although the boat is "Sans aviron, sans gouvernal," [87] to take only one instance, God directs her ship and thus as with some other romances the background of the story is Christian. But we may perhaps see in the fact that, when she lands, Constance does not readily reveal her name [88] – a detail that recurs in this and some other versions of the story – a hint of taboo and something of fairy origin, and thus a suggestion that the Otherworld journey of the fairy-mistress type has here made its contribution.[89] Finally, it is interesting to recall the fact that in some forms of the story, notably

[86] For one extensive list see Paton, *Fairy Mythology*, pp. 16–17, n. 1. Cf. too the *Journal of Eng. and Germanic Philol.*, XIX (1920), pp. 190ff., with special reference to the boat of Sceaf; and above pp. 52 and 61. For the punishment of putting a malefactor adrift on the sea and the boat as instrument of torture see *Publ. Mod. Lang. Assoc.*, LVI (1941), pp. 33ff.

[87] *Œuvres Poétiques de Philippe de Remi, Sire de Beaumanoir*, ed. Hermann Suchier, I, (*SATF*, 72), p. 36, l. 1081; cf. p. 148, l. 4785. For Divine control see p. 39, ll. 1161ff. For another instance see p. 147, ll. 4749ff.

[88] *Ibid.*, p. 40, ll. 1206ff.; p. 151, ll. 4865ff. So too, for example, in *Emare* and in Chaucer's and Gower's versions.

[89] For the introduction of the idea of the fée see Miss Rickert's discussion

in the history of Offa I, the heroine is exposed in a forest and there the king finds her when he is out hunting. This feature seems to have no special significance for us here since it has to do merely with banishment; but one may be tempted to read more into the episode in the light of such a story as the lay of *Graelent* or that of *Dolopathos,* in which the hero happens to meet his fairy mistress when he is hunting in the forest.

In the fourteenth-century *Sir Degare,* the hero, and his servant ride west into what is called "þeld (the old) fforest," and here after going many a mile and many a day, during which he saw many wild beasts, he came to a "water cler" – a river amidst which there was a fair castle. The drawbridge was down, and on entering the castle he found fodder for his horse and in the hall a fire kindled. But nobody seemed to be there, until at last four damsels appeared, a dwarf, and the lady of the castle with ten maidens.[90] In this episode we have an instance of Maidenland; but the forest and river seem related to corresponding features in such a romance as *Yder,* where we find also the "empty castle," the fodder for the horse, the fire, and a dwarf.[91] In *Yder* the episode in question includes a damsel riding a mule and may show some reminiscence of *La Mule sanz Frain,* where we have the forest, here full of wild animals, and a black and turbulent river crossed only by an iron bar, the deserted castle, and also a dwarf.[92] *Sir Degare,* however, may also derive something from a source or analogue of Renaut de Beaujeu's *Le Bel Inconnu,* where the

---

in *Mod. Philol.,* II (1904), pp. 362f. The story of Offa II and the motif of the boat do not come into Mr. Krappe's study in *Anglia,* LXI (1937), pp. 361ff.

[90] W. H. French and C. B. Hale, *Middle English Metrical Romances,* pp. 309ff., ll. 726ff.

[91] *Der Altfranzösische Yderroman,* ed. Heinrich Gelzer (*Gesellschaft für Romanische Literatur,* 31), pp. 108ff., ll. 3750ff. The forest is thick and dark, see p. 102, ll. 3563ff. For the parallel in *Yder* cf. Faust, *Sir Degare* (*Princeton Studies in English,* XI), pp. 76ff.

[92] Païen de Maisières, *La Damoisele a la Mule,* ed. Boleslas Orłowski, pp. 159ff. *Yder* may of course be based instead on an analogue or source of this poem: see Kittredge, *Gawain and the Green Knight,* 1916, pp. 64–65. The forest, the river (which has no ford [gué] unlike *Yder,* l. 3763), and a bridge, are found in Chrétien's *Perceval* near the castle of the Fisher King: *Der Percevalroman* (*Li Contes del Graal*), ed. Alfons Hilka, Halle, 1932, pp. 133ff. (cf. ll. 2988, 3015, 3034, 3066). For empty castles see G. P. Faust, *Sir Degare,* pp. 74ff.

hero on his way to the *cité gaste* passes through a forest, and there are other parallel details.[93] The city itself is located between two rivers "molt bruians," and it is desolate.[94] When the hero is about to enter his lady's chamber, he has a kind of vision of a turbulent river and a bridge that causes him much trouble. In this episode the author was obviously using the motif familiar in Latin visions; and all these instances would indicate that the river barrier to the empty city in *Sir Degare* had a similar derivation, although by the time it reached the present poem its origin was forgotten.

Reminiscences of familiar motifs turn up in the fourteenth-century *Brun de la Montaigne,* loosely connected with the Arthurian cycle and surviving in a fragment of a little less than four thousand lines. According to this poem, Butor de la Montaigne exposes his infant son near a fountain in the enchanted forest Bersillant, and there three fées bestow their gifts on him. The knights who convey the child go through the thick forest by a path until they come to the spring:

> Que dedens Bersillant qui est grande et fueillue
> La riviere ont oye de bien courre esmeüe.
> Or ont tant alé sus la gravele menue,
> Que la fontaine fu d'aus .iiij. perceüe.[95]

In this case the stream seems to be that which issues from the fountain, and the knights ride along its sands until they come to a fine chestnut tree, where they dismount and sit down. When the child is left, we are told how beautiful the "fontenelle" is with waters more shining than silver. Later in the poem, when

[93] Cf. Hibbard, *Mediaeval Romance in England,* pp. 304–305. Faust's note (*op. cit.,* p. 78, n. 37) hardly disposes of the question.

[94] Renaut de Beaujeu, *Le Bel Inconnu,* ed. G. Perrie Williams (Paris, 1929), in *Les Classiques Français du Moyen Age,* p. 85, ll. 2779–2780 (the rivers); p. 87, l. 2854 (the bridge before the city gate); p. 88, ll. 2871–2872 (no one is there); pp. 139f., ll. 4553ff. (the river and the bridge). Schofield urged that the line describing the river (4555) echoed the *Erec* (ll. 5374–5375): see [*Harvard*] *Studies and Notes in Philol. and Lit.,* IV, p. 132; Wendelin Foerster, *Kristian von Troyes, Erec und Enide* (Halle, 1909), in *Romanische Bibliothek,* 13, p. 149.

[95] *Brun de la Montaigne,* ed. Paul Meyer (Paris, 1875), *SATF,* XVI, p. 28, ll. 814–817. Cf. the corresponding scene on the later visit, *ibid.,* pp. 106–107, ll. 3092ff.

the hero, now a young man, has his adventures, he visits the castle of Morgan the Fay which is called "la Tor Ferrée" or "le Muable Manoir." [96] It is situated in the midst of a meadow in a valley, and here are damsels, virgin and married:

> si trés grant planté
> C'onques mais tant n'en vit en tretout son aé.[97]

The inevitable suggestion here of Maidenland, the evidence of some connection with the story of Ogier,[98] and the fact that the castle is Morgan's, leave us in no doubt about the nature of the scene. But the detail is too limited to permit us more than a conjecture that it comes from the tradition of Celtic lore.

The visit of Ogier the Dane to the Other World is described in a fourteenth-century French romance that has several times been summarized but, so far as I know, has not yet been fully edited. For the plot we may consider the outline given by Child in his notes on the ballad *Thomas Rymer*:[99]

Six fairies made gifts to Ogier at his birth. By the favor of five he was to be the strongest, the bravest, the most successful, the handsomest, the most susceptible, of knights: Morgan's gift was that, after a long and fatiguing career of glory, he should live with her at her castle of Avalon, in the enjoyment of a still longer youth and never wearying pleasures. When Ogier had passed his one hundredth year, Morgan took measures to carry out her promise. She had him wrecked, while he was on a voyage to France, on a lodestone rock conveniently near to Avalon, which Avalon is a little way this side of the Terrestrial Paradise. In due course he comes to an orchard, and there he eats an apple which affects him so peculiarly that he looks for nothing but death. He turns to the east, and sees a beautiful lady, magnificently attired. He takes her for the Virgin; she corrects his error, and announces herself as Morgan the Fay. She puts a ring on his finger which restores his youth, and then places a crown on his head which makes him forget all the past. For two hundred years Ogier lived in such delights as no worldly being can imagine, and the two hundred years seemed to him but twenty;

[96] *Ibid.*, pp. 113ff., ll. 3268ff.
[97] *Ibid.*, p. 124, ll. 3587–3588.
[98] Cf. *ibid.*, p. 117, ll. 3398–3399, where we are told that at this castle Morgan kept her lover Ogier for a month, and see the Introduction, p. xi.
[99] *English and Scottish Popular Ballads*, I, p. 319.

Christendom was then in danger, and even Morgan thought his presence was required in this world. The crown being taken from his head, the memory of the past revived and with it the desire to return to France. He was sent back by the fairy, properly provided, vanquished the foes of Christianity in a short space, and after a time was brought back by Morgan the Fay to Avalon.

Morgan transports him to Avalon in a chariot (*char*) which at least in appearance is fiery (*tout de feu sembloit*)[100] – a biblical reminiscence, no doubt, rather than a derivative from some such episode as Alexander's flight with the griffons. That some form of the whole story existed earlier and was known to the authors of *Floriant et Florete* and *Brun della Montagne* is obvious enough.[101] The general plot resembles a little the Partonopeus account of the fée; and the lodestone rock and the allusion to the Earthly Paradise make one think perhaps of the adventures of Huon of Bordeaux. The use of the motif of the change in time, including a magic object (often fruit, but in this case the ring) to restore Ogier's youth,[102] are not unusual features in Otherworld journeys, as we have seen. In at least some of the versions of this story Ogier is taken in a cloud back to this world, and in the prose romance he is similarly carried to Avalon at the end,[103] a type of journey that can be paralleled elsewhere, but in this case looks like original invention for the purpose.

The general similarity of this plot to that of the fourteenth-century *Thomas of Erceldoune* has long been recognized. According to the latter, the hero Thomas lay under a "semely tree" by Huntley Banks listening to the songs of birds when a fair lady rode up on a palfrey. He followed her over a "mountayne hye" and at "Eldonetree" addressed her as Queen of Heaven. She replied that she was not Queen of Heaven but of quite an-

[100] Renier, *Mem. della R. A. delle Sc. di Torino, Morali, Storiche e Filologiche*, second series, XLI, pp. 431–432.

[101] See Paton, *Studies in the Fairy Mythology of Arthurian Romance*, especially pp. 74ff. and p. 136, for a study of the material in these and other romances; also Newstead in *Publ. Mod. Lang. Assoc.*, LXI (1946), pp. 916ff.

[102] See Renier, *op. cit.*, pp. 431–432.

[103] Paton, *op. cit.*, pp. 77–78; and Renier, *op. cit.*, pp. 445–446; and *Kong Olger Danskis Kronicke* in *Christiern Pedersens Danske Skrifter*, V (Copenhagen, 1856), pp. 298 and 309. Cf. for such a flight p. 218 above.

other country. After they had lain together seven times, all her lustrous beauty vanished away. But she told him to take leave of sun and moon and the leaves of the trees, for this twelvemonth he was to go with her and see "medillerthe" no more:

> Scho ledde hym in at Eldonehill
> Undirnethe a derne lee,
> Whare it was dirke als mydnyght myrke
> And ever water till his knee.
>
> The montenans of dayes three
> He herd bot swoghynge of þe flode . . .[104]

She led him to a fair "herbere" where grew plenty of fruit, and birds were flying about and singing, but she warned him not to touch the fruit or his soul would go to Hell. Then she showed him the way to Heaven over a high mountain, the road under "rysse" (brushwood) to Paradise, the third way (which was by a green plain) to Purgatory, and the fourth over a "felle" to the burning fire of Hell. On a high hill before them she pointed out a fair castle which belonged to her, and there they went together and found knights and ladies and revelry. There dwelt Thomas until she announced to him he must leave. Against his protest that he had been there only three days she told him he had spent all of three years (seven according to the Cambridge MS) and more in that country. Thus she brought him again to Eildon Tree and bade him farewell. In this remarkable story, the motif of Eildon Hill suggests Celtic connections, but the flood up to the knee and the use of the mountain would indicate some contamination from vision literature.[105]

The mountain realm of the fée appears again in the strange story of *Guerino detto il Meschino,* written by Andrea da Bar-

[104] *Thomas of Erceldoune,* ed. Alois Brandl, (*Sammlung Engl. Denkmäler,* II), pp. 83–84, ll. 169–174. For an identification of Eildon Tree and Huntley Banks see *The Romance and Prophecies of Thomas of Erceldoune,* ed. J. A. H. Murray, (*EEST,* 61), pp. 1ff.

[105] On this romance see *Publ. Mod. Lang. Assoc.,* XXIII (1908), pp. 375ff., suggesting various analogues. Parallel details in the ballad of *Thomas Rymer* (Child, no. 37) are considered by Wimberly, *Folklore in the English and Scottish Ballads,* especially pp. 117ff., 127ff. and 153ff. (the fruit). Note that in the ballad the river is of blood, and crossing it takes forty days and forty nights (A7). In the C text (9) they come to a desert.

berino in 1391 and associated by some scholars with the origins of the Tannhäuser legend. Here we read of the hero going in search of the enchantress Alcina. He is told that her abode is in the Apennines, and traveling thither he comes to a savage place with "aspre selve" and at length, after passing a hermitage, to a very high mountain with four dark entrances.[106] Another adventurer there was stopped by a terrific blast of air. He enters with drawn sword and lighted candle and comes into a great dark cavern in which a stream of water is falling. Crossing this ("la qual era tanta, che averia macinato 2. molini") he finds a serpent which turns out to be a lost soul, and he learns that once changed to this form it could not pass over the stream. He next arrives at a metal door (inscribed "chi entra in questa porta, e passa l'anno, che non esce, non morirà fin al dì del Giudizio"), opened for him by three damsels. On the other side is a garden with fifty damsels and more, among which the most beautiful is the Signora Fata herself. She takes him to a room of her great palace and shows him the treasures, jewels, gold, and silver, she possesses, though of course all is false. They feast together; and, after he resists the temptations she offers (she is revealed as the Sibyl who guided Aeneas through the lower world), they go to a garden which seems like a veritable Paradise. Next morning she comes to see him "con molte damigelli" and they ride together through a fair plain. There are various other experiences. He learns how the inhabitants are here changed to serpents, dragons, scorpions,

[106] Andrea da Barberino, *Guerino detto il Meschino*, pp. 213ff. He first arrives at a mountain with two peaks: ". . . quella montagna dove li conveniva andare era fatta come un pesce marino, detto Aschi cioè come la schiena, il qual nasce nel mare. Questo poggio avea un barbacane di muro, di circa un braccio, poco più, e la cima di questa schiena del poggio donde si aduna la terra, questi dirupi, che non si potrebbe dire la sua oscurità, e quando parea fondo, e quel fondo è circondato d'alpi, di modo, che la luce del Sole non opra nel fondo alcuna cosa, e tutte queste alpi sono nude d'ogni sorte d'alberi ma vi è sassi, e alcune poche erbe" (pp. 220–221). One could only go there three months of the year. For the blast of air, see p. 215; for the identification with the Sibyl, pp. 234–235; for the visit to the Pope, p. 248. There is much folklore in this romantic document: note the river and the mountain of the giants with its mysterious cavern, pp. 47ff.; Alexander's gate, p. 77; the journey to the Tree of the Sun, pp. 78ff.; the journey to the land of Prester John, pp. 139ff. For the hermitage cf. Siuts, *Jenseitsmotive im deutschen Volksmärchen*, pp. 25 and 45.

and worms, from Saturday to Monday for deadly sins. But the hero himself is allowed to depart; he goes, as he came, by the cavern, and he seeks the Pope for absolution. The scene in this story has no resemblance to the Celtic hollow hill, despite the motif of Maidenland. Instead, it is like the realm depicted by Étienne de Bourbon, Gervase of Tilbury, and Caesarius of Heisterbach, discussed earlier,[107] which shows some indication of Italian origin and reminds one at times of scenes in the Latin visions. Also perhaps we should note that the idea of the transformation of sinners into reptiles seems hardly reminiscent of Dante's punishment of thieves in the *Inferno*.

A theory of Italian origin for the adventure of Guerino receives some support from the story, set down about 1440, by Antoine de la Sale in his *Salade,* of what purports to be an actual visit to the "Mont de la royne Sibille." [108] According to Antoine's account, the Mountain of the Sibyl is also in the Apennines between Norcia and Ascoli, and not far from the "Lake of Pilate" (or "of the Sibyl"), from which it is separated by a small stream.[109] This lake is on a high mountain, on which there is snow at all seasons of the year. In the lake (said to be bottomless) is an island of rock which seems to have supernatural protection; for when an enemy comes there, a great storm arises that devastates the whole country, recalling astonishingly the mountain lake (*aquam continens subnigram et in fundo imperscrutabilem*) described by Gervase of Tilbury, where there is continual snow and where, if anyone throws a rock into the water, the demons

[107] See the whole discussion of the underworld motif, above pp. 231ff. On the motif of the snakes, cf. Siuts, *Jenseitsmotive im deutschen Volksmärchen*, p. 115 and pp. 138ff.

[108] For a discussion of this episode see, among other works, the essays by Gaston Paris in *Revue de Paris* (December 15, 1897) pp. 763ff., and (March 15, 1898) pp. 307ff., both reprinted in his *Légendes du Moyen Age*, pp. 67ff.; Werner Söderhjelm in *Mémoires de la Société Néo-Philologique a Helsingfors*, II, (1897), pp. 101ff.; Joseph Nève, *Antoine de la Sale, Sa Vie et ses Ouvrages*; C.-A. Knudson Jr. in *Romania*, LIV (1928), pp. 99ff.; Fernand Desonay, *Antoine de la Sale, Le Paradis de la Reine Sibylle*, and MacCulloch, *Medieval Faith and Fable*, pp. 48–49. On the identification of Guerino's Alcina with the Cumaean Sibyl and for the use of the Sibyl in this connection see Desonay, *op. cit.*, pp. xcvi–xcvii.

[109] Desonay, *op. cit.*, pp. 7ff.

raise a tempest.[110] At the foot of the mountain, in Gervase's account, there is also a river; and near the lake itself is a subterranean palace of the demons. All this, according to Gervase, is in Catalonia; and the parallel details, which suggest at least a common source in folklore, may of course represent only coincidence.[111] In the scene described by Antoine, the Mountain of the Sibyl is next to the lake and its mountain. There are two roads that go to the top, one on the right hand and the other on the left. The left-hand one (by which are two good fountains) is the shorter but more difficult to climb because of its condition and because of the rocks; the one on the right, which Antoine himself took, is much easier because of its many turns on the slope and allows riding on horseback, although Antoine went on foot and led his horse after him. On the side of the mountain was the "chastel" (fortified town) of Montemonaco (recalling for us perhaps as "le mont du moyne" the mountain where Guerino sees a hermitage) and meadows with interesting flowers. Antoine's climb, however, took him by a dangerous and fearful route to the "crown," where there were two passages (the better of which would strike fear in any heart that could feel fear) leading to the cave.

The entrance to the cave was like a shield in form, sharp at the top and broad at the bottom. It could be entered only by stooping and crawling on all fours. Within was a small room, lighted by an opening only as big as a man's head. From this point on, details in the description were derived by Antoine from the stories he heard of various adventurers there. From these he learned of the metal doors that crashed night and day; [112] of the

[110] *Otia Imperialia*, III, lxvi (p. 32). For the location see the note *ibid.*, pp. 139–140. Cf., however, the account of the lake given by Bersuire according to Söderhjelm, *op. cit.*, pp. 137–138.

[111] But it is hard at times to separate the folklore from other elements in the *Salade*. Note the material on the Earthly Paradise, the Purgatory of Saint Patrick (Nève, *op. cit.*, p. 46), and the journey to the Lipari Islands with the visit to the volcano (*ibid.*, pp. 159ff.; Knudson in *Romania*, LIV, pp. 99ff.).

[112] Desonay, *op. cit.*, p. 16, ll. 26–27 ("portes de metal qui jour et nuyt batent . . . "); p. 17, ll. 17–18 ("portes de metal, qui jour et nuyt sans cesser batent, clouant et ouvrant."). On slamming doors as a barrier cf. Kittredge, *Gawain and the Green Knight*, p. 245; A. C. L. Brown, *Iwain*, in [*Harvard*] *Studies and Notes in Philol. and Lit.*, VIII, pp. 80ff., n. 1; Krappe, *Balor*, pp. 108ff.

narrow corridor that led at length to the larger chamber; of the "vaine de terre" from which came a terrible blast of air preventing all advance (though for those who did go on, it proved to be really violent only at first); and of the bridge over the abyss and the great river which made a hideous noise. The bridge seemed very long, but not a foot wide. When, however, one set both feet on it, the width was sufficient; as one progressed it became wider and the noise of the stream was less. In this account the blast of air may recall a similar detail described by Gervase of Tilbury in his story of the swineherd and his journey underground in "Britannia." [113] The bridge and the river are clearly reminiscent of vision literature.[114] Beyond the bridge the road widened, but at the end of this cave were two artificial dragons with shining eyes.[115] From this spot a narrow passage led to a "petite placete toute carree," and here were the clashing metal doors which might have crushed anyone who attempted to pass through. According to popular rumor, a German knight and his squire who ventured beyond these found a great door further along shining as if it were made of crystal, and on being admitted came through still another door to various rich halls and chambers and a great company of people with whom he was led to the presence of the queen.

[113] *Otia Imperialia,* III, xlv (p. 24: "et in monte cauerna foraminis, quae uelut fistula uentum pro tempore ualidissime eructuat." The swineherd enters when the wind is quiet).

[114] Curiously enough, the priest who narrates this part of the story has a dream or a kind of vision in an episode a little earlier (Desonay, *op. cit.*, p. 18). Details regarding the bridge and the river include the following: "Dessoubs ce pont a tresgrant et hydeux abisme de parfondeur, et au fons oyt on une tresgrosse riviere, qui fait un tel bruit qu'il semble proprement, de point en point, que tout cela fonde, tant en est la hideur merveilleuse. Mais aussi tost qu'on a les deux piez sur ce pont, il est assez large et, tant vait on plus avant, tant est plus large et moins creux, et le bruit de l'eaue se oyt moins" (*ibid.*, p. 19, ll. 60–67). Cf. the pit, the river, and the bridge which grows wider, in the *Purgatory of Saint Patrick* (see above p. 115), a story known to Antoine (cf. Nève, *op. cit.*, p. 46). We may also note he was a tutor of the son of René d'Anjou (*ibid.*, p. 9), whose allegory introduces the bridge (see above pp. 216f.).

[115] For animal automata cf. Stith Thompson's *Motif-Index* under magic dragon, magic serpent, flying horse, artificial animal, etc. For human automata in romance see *Publ. Mod. Lang. Assoc.*, XXXVIII (1923), pp. 436f., n. 41; *Mod. Lang. Notes*, XXXV (1920), pp. 129ff.; and *Mod. Philol.*, X (1912–1913), pp. 511ff.

Time passed swiftly in this place ("un jour ne lui estoit pas une heure")[116] and leaving was difficult. If the knight did not leave on the ninth day, he had to stay till the thirtieth and then until the three hundred and thirtieth; if he did not leave on the three hundred and thirtieth, he would never depart. He and his squire each had to select a lady as companion. On Fridays after midnight the ladies left them and joined the throng with the queen in rooms especially appointed, and there they were "en estat de couleuvres et de serpens."[117] After midnight on Saturday each returned to her companion more beautiful than ever. They never grew old; they never knew grief; garments, food, riches, and pleasures, were all they could wish. Here was no cold nor excessive heat. No heart could think, no tongue could tell, of the earthly delights of this place, and the knight's conscience was touched so that an hour of all this seemed ten days. The story goes on that on the three hundred and thirtieth day the knight and the squire departed with candles to light their way in the underground passages, and they journeyed to Rome to seek absolution of the Pope. When this seemed to be denied, they returned to the grotto forever. The plot as a whole was apparently based on an actual visit to a grotto together with someone's embellishment of the adventures of Guerino or a narrative related to that, to which have been added certain details from vision literature, such as the bridge and the Paradise, and others from folklore, such as the stormy lake and the wind barrier in the cave. The localization seems to reinforce the argument for Italian origin, and there is of course an ultimate debt to Virgil. But one must note that the travelers in this case were German,[118] and in some ways the *Salade* may well represent an adaptation from an earlier form of the story than Andrea da Barbarino's. The barrier of the wind, the rushing torrent, and the metal door in *Guerino* suggest a simplified memory of details presented in their proper form by de la Sale; and the entertainment actually

[116] Desonay, *op. cit.*, p. 27, ll. 95–96. Cf. a somewhat similar example noted by Barto, *Publ. Mod. Lang. Assoc.*, XXXVIII (1923), pp. 408f.

[117] Desonay, *op. cit.*, p. 28, l. 8.

[118] Cf. too the German name inscribed at the entrance, *ibid.*, pp. 39–40. Among other details of interest in *La Salade* is the material on the Purgatory of Saint Patrick and the Earthly Paradise, Nève, *op. cit.*, p. 46.

provided by the lower-world fées in his version is surely closer to that in the usual account of the fairy mistress.[119]

Some light may perhaps be thrown on the whole problem by the Melusine story, where the fairy mistress takes a mortal lover and becomes his wife, where too the motif of the lower world appears, where the idea of the snakes is an essential, and finally where the male hero seeks absolution of the Pope. The plot opens with a double use of the motif of the hunt in the forest and the discovery of the fairy mistress near a fountain, the episode that appears in *Guingamor* and the other lays we have discussed a little earlier.[120] In this fashion both Elinas and Raymondin found their wives. When Elinas breaks the taboo against visiting his wife at the time of her accouchement, she leaves him and departs for Avalon or the Lost Isle (so-called because though a man had been there several times, he could not find his way there again without great danger).[121] One of his daughters, Melusine, to punish him, shuts him inside a mountain. But at this the mother is angry, and condemns Melusine to be changed to a serpent from the navel down every Saturday. The plot proceeds of course with the episode in which Melusine's husband, Raymondin, breaks her taboo against looking upon her on Saturday. This, as scholars have pointed out, is found in Gervase of Tilbury's collection of folklore, in Walter Map's *Courtly Trifles,* and elsewhere; [122] and its use may explain the corresponding transformation of the ladies into snakes in *La Salade* and possibly for that reason the detail of the punishment of sinners in *Guerino.* Jean d'Arras, who wrote his version of the story in Latin or perhaps French prose, beginning its composi-

[119] But cf. Söderhjelm, *op. cit.*, pp. 142ff., and Gaston Paris, *Légendes du Moyen Age*, pp. 133ff.

[120] See above pp. 244ff. Both fountains here are in wonderful spots, cf. *La Légende de Mélusine* by Jean Marchand, pp. 7 and 34; *Melusine par Jehan d'Arras,* ed. Charles Brunet, (*Bibliothèque Elzevirienne*), pp. 18 and 35. In the second episode there are three fées at the fountain as in *Graelent* and apparently *Lanval.*

[121] *Melusine . . . Englisht about 1500*, ed. A. K. Donald, Part I, (*EETS:ES*, 68), p. 12; *La Légende de Mélusine*, by Marchand, p. 13; *Melusine*, ed. Brunet, p. 21. Cf. the "Ile Selee" in *Florimont*, discussed above pp. 253–254.

[122] *Otia Imperialia,* I, xv (pp. 4–5); for Map, cf. p. 233 above. See MacCulloch, *Medieval Faith and Fable*, pp. 50ff.; Hartland, *The Science of Fairy Tales*, pp. 272–273.

tion in 1387, and shaping the plot as we know it in English prose and verse of about 1500, cites Gervase of Tilbury on the idea of the serpent-woman in his prologue, thus indicating quite directly the lines of indebtedness and development. Finally we may note that Melusine's sister, Palatine, is imprisoned by her mother in a mountain "de Guigo" with her father's treasure until freed by a knight.[123]

In all these romances there is abundant evidence for a combination, or what may be called a contamination, of material from various sources.[124] The same may be said for the two versions of the fifteenth-century *Eger and Grime,* where the barrier to the Other World is the ocean for the Percy Folio narrative (the "forbidden country" is "a fresh Iland by the sea")[125] and also a forest and a river,[126] while that for the Huntington version is only the forest and river.[127] The Huntington version has indeed a reminiscence of the sea in its reference to the salt water and salt sand, and as further details it offers also another river, a wilderness and "all wasted land," as well as the forest, before the hero may come to the fair castle with halls and bowers, orchards and arbors. Perhaps too it has the mountain, but not as a barrier.[128] One may guess that the version with the island is

[123] *Melusine,* ed. Brunet, p. 24; *La Légende*, by Marchand, p. 17; *Melusine,* ed. Donald, p. 16. Cf. the verse form, derived from the French of La Coudrette, *The Romans of Partenay,* ed. W. W. Skeat (London, 1866), *EETS,* 22, pp. 160 and 196f. ("Where many A cruell serpent enhabit," 5727; many a knight hath gone there but none returned if he stayed there long "But that he were ded or foule destroed," 5733). Knights attempt to win the treasure but are killed by serpents or monsters. One adventure leads a knight to an iron door guarded by a monster who eventually devours him. The English prose seems to locate the prison "on" the mountain, but the scene is clear in the English verse and the French prose. The episode of the adventurers introduced by La Coudrette may suggest a remote reminiscence of the material in *Il Guerino* or its analogues.

[124] On the lower world, for example, see above pp. 237–238.

[125] *Eger and Grime,* ed. J. R. Caldwell, (*Harvard Studies in Comparative Lit.,* IX), p. 186 and cf. p. 103. Note the editor's careful analysis of the materials of the story and their analogues, pp. 51ff., and the discussion of the relation of the versions, pp. 20ff. Cf. p. 169, n. 109, and p. 212, l. 411.

[126] *Ibid.,* p. 188, l. 105; cf. p. 192, l. 187 ("a running strand"); and p. 212, ll. 414–415.

[127] *Ibid.,* p. 187, ll. 122–123; cf. p. 193, l. 215 ("a river strand"); and p. 237, ll. 881ff. (where there is also "wasted land").

[128] The hero goes "beside a mount upon a moor," *ibid.,* p. 187, l. 118. Cf.

the more primitive and is closer to the Celtic, and that the other details come later from other sources. If so, this is another instance of the ocean barrier's being replaced by the river, which is accompanied by other details which show contamination from the literature of vision or ultimately from the Orient.[129] As for the Otherworld scene in this romance there are no special points of interest in the description. There is a castle, a town, an arbor, and the "fairest bower that euer saw I." Birds sing in the green arbor.[130]

ii

Among the cyclical romances, those of the English or Germanic group show rather less striking instances of folklore motifs than the others. In late versions there is likely to be more of this material, however, probably from the influence of the other cycles. Thus in the development of the story of Guy of Warwick, the part that deals with the adventures of the hero's son tells how Reinbrun and the steward sailed from Africa ("Schyp þey fownde þere redy dyght"),[131] and after a long voyage came to a lonely country, where they found a castle wasted with war and fighting. They are told by the porter that the lord of the castle has disappeared. But the lady gives them food, and they learn her husband is Amys de la Mountaine, who has been exiled. Her abode is in an elvish land ("Thys cuntre ys full of eluys," 11315). Next morning they depart and come to a hill with gates fair and wide. Reinbrun enters and the gates close behind him.[132] Inside, it is at first dark, and then a light appears. Further along is a water "depe and brode" and beyond that a greensward with

---

p. 105, where the editor suggests a parallel to *Maxen Wledig's Dream*, but that too is a combination of different motifs, and we can hardly say on such a basis that Eger's path "is leading us to the fairyland of Celtic story." Cf. above p. 50 and n. 51 and p. 53, n. 58.

129 See pp. 245ff. and note 49 above. For the forest cf. the use of this motif in the analogues (Caldwell, *op. cit.*, pp. 82, 91, and 145, and cf. p. 233 above).

130 For the references see Caldwell, *op. cit.*, pp. 194–195; p. 204 (P 297) and p. 203 (HL 357ff.).

131 *The Romance of Guy of Warwick*, ed. Julius Zupitza, (*EETS:ES*, 25–26), p. 323, l. 11241.

132 Cf. the closing entrance of the mountain in the Persian story outlined in *Romanic Review*, IX (1918), p. 149.

all manner of flowers. There too is a splendid palace with posts of fine coral, beams of cedar, ornamented with precious stones and with carvings of flowers on the battlements. At the gates is a tree on which birds are singing a merry lay by day and night.[133] Reinbrun tests the river with his spear, crosses himself, and with his horse plunges in. The water rises high, but he gets across. The palace at first seems empty but there he finds Amys kept prisoner.[134] This is a simple and clear instance of a journey to the Other World over an ocean barrier, which is followed by another journey in which the hollow hill motif is used and then the river barrier.

One cannot be always quite so sure, however, as to what was used in the early formation of the plots of some of these romances. In *King Horn,* for example, we have the episode of Horn's being put to sea in a ship and of his landing in the country where he meets Rimenhild. Like the heroine of the fée type, she sends a messenger (Athelbrus) to bring him to her bower and she makes most of the amorous advances.[135] Again Horn is forced to depart on a vessel and once more he reaches a country where a lady is ready to his hand and heart, a manifest duplication, as has been often recognized, of the first part of the plot. In both cases one is bound to see examples at least of the rudderless boat, so-called, in which hero or heroine may be put to sea as a penalty or for banishment.[136] Yet it is also possible that here as in the Constance

[133] Note the Celtic use of the bird motif, pp. 54–55 above. Cf. the silver trees with singing birds in the letter of Prester John, interp. D: Zarncke, Leipzig *Abhandlungen, Phil.-Hist. Cl.*, VII (1879), p. 923.

[134] Cf. the version in the Auchinleck MS: Part III, (*EETS:ES*, 59), pp. 657–658. The water of the river was stern and grim; the walls of the castle are of crystal. Cf. too *Guy of Warwick, Nach Coplands Druck*, ed. Gustav Schleich, (*Palaestra*, 139), pp. 229 ff.: Raynburne and Heraude ride "homeward to their countrye" and see the castle on a mountain; Raynburne enters a "roche of stone" by a strong gate, comes to a "water brode" and sees the green place beyond where is a palace with crystal walls.

[135] Cf. Hodges in *Mod. Lang. Notes*, XXXII (1917), pp. 280 ff.; also *Amer. Journal of Philol.*, XXXVII (1916), p. 405.

[136] In the first case Horn's Saracen enemies thus treat him lest he take revenge on them for the death of his father: cf. "þare fore þou shalt to streme go," L, l. 105, *King Horn*, ed. Joseph Hall, p. 6; notes p. 102. Day and night the men in the boat rowed until they could see land, and at last they heard the birds sing and saw the grasses spring. Horn blesses the ship. The episode is missing in *Horn Child*; but it is even clearer in the French, where the

story and certainly in *Partonopeus* we also have the Otherworld journey vaguely reflected, as indeed it is in an episode of the romance of Tristram. It may be significant that the Anglo-Norman Thomas's *Tristram* certainly included the story of Tristram's first voyage to Ireland, where he travels in a rudderless boat before landing. In this case too [137] the hero arrives in the country where he finds the healing fée who becomes his *amie*.

On the other hand, a curious light is thrown on the problem by some details in the development of the story of Bevis of Hampton, where what at first appears to be Otherworld material may be the product of sheer coincidence. In the Middle English version of this romance, Bevis's mother plots against him and he is sold to heathen merchants who take him by boat to Armenia. There eventually he meets Josian, who becomes his love. She seems to make more advances than he does, and she gives him healing baths. Something like the motif of the forest may be read into the episode where Bevis goes hunting for the wild boar, and his lady, witnessing his might, is lost in admiration for him. Later the king is informed that Bevis has deflowered his daughter and Bevis then is forced to leave (much as Horn departs under the same charge regarding Rimenhild). Somewhat later again, Bevis enters Damascus, which is surrounded by a ditch over which is a remarkable bridge. Below it are sixty bells that ring when one crosses, and on it is a tower painted with gold and azure and ornamented with a golden eagle which has precious stones for

---

miraculous protection they enjoyed is emphasized almost as in the story of Chaucer's Constance: *Horn at Rimenhild, Recueil de ce Qui reste des Poëmes relatifs a leurs Aventures,* ed. Francisque Michel, (Bannatyne Club), p. 4, ll. 71ff. Here the boat is an old one, smashed once in a tempest. On the possibility that this represents an earlier version cf. Hibbard, *Mediaeval Romance in England*, pp. 86f. The use of the boat for punishment or exile is discussed in *Publ. Mod. Lang. Assoc.*, LVI (1941), pp. 43–44.

[137] The episode is discussed by F. Piquet, *L'Originalité de Gottfried de Strasbourg dans son Poème de Tristan et Isolde (Travaux et Mémoires de L'Université de Lille* I, 5), pp. 165ff., and *Mod. Lang. Review*, XIV (1919), pp. 39ff. Cf. Gertrude Schoepperle, *Tristan and Isolt, (Ottend. Mem. Germ. Monogr.* 6–7,) I, pp. 194ff.; II, pp. 370ff. On the question of the old idea of the common authorship of the Anglo-Norman Horn story and that of Tristram, cf. Michel, *op. cit.*, pp. xlix–l; *Romania*, XV (1886), pp. 575ff. For the influence of the *Tristram* cf. Hibbard, *op. cit.*, p. 83.

eyes. Damascus itself has all the appearance of an Otherworld realm:

> All the wyndowes and all the wallis
> With cristall was peynted, chamber and hallis,
> Pelouris and durris were all of brasse,
> With laten sett and with glasse;
> Hit was so riche in many wyse,
> That it was like to paradise . . .[138]

The Irish version is of course even more elaborate with "seven strong, impregnable fortifications around" the city and "deep, dark, impassable ditches." And "between the walls there was a swift, tidal stream, and a mad, tempestuous sea coursing around it in those broad, great ditches." There was a drawbridge going into the city supported by a pillar of brass, and ten bells that clattered and jingled, five on each side. At the end was a "splendid, great tower" with the figure of a "dark, ugly-colored dragon" cut on it with stones as eyes. In the windows of the city were "stones of crystal and carbuncle and full splendid precious gems." When Bevis is imprisoned at last, the water in the cell comes up to his chin when he sits and up to his buttocks when he stands.[139] On his escape from the city, as in other versions of the story, he has to cross a rushing torrent; and he and his horse leap into it and swim across (a day and a night in the Middle English, and twenty-four hours in the Celtic). From there he goes over dale and over down until he comes to the giant's castle, where he finds another important lady.[140]

In all this we may see the Josian story as another example of the healing fée to whom the hero travels by boat, with the scene at Damascus as definitely an Otherworld adventure, which includes the wild stream and the bridge and perhaps from the Latin visions the water of torment that comes up to the chin or

[138] *The Romance of Sir Beues of Hamtoun*, ed. Eugen Kölbing, Part I (*EETS:ES*, 46), M. ll. 1131ff. (pp. 66ff.).

[139] *Zeits. f. celt. Philol.*, VI (1907), pp. 308f.

[140] In a Picard version, after crossing the stream, Bevis goes into some woods by a path that leads him eventually to a wonderful castle surrounded by ditches and arrows (*Gesellschaft für romanische Literatur*, 25 [1910], p. 93, ll. 3062ff.).

the buttocks. But certain points in the available evidence give us pause. In the Anglo-Norman version of the story, which certainly represents an early form in some ways, much less is made of the description of Damascus: it is the richest city that ever was, and it is covered with silver and gold everywhere, but that is about all.[141] Still less appears of anything that would correspond in the Continental versions and the Italian. Even the bridge in the Middle English is astonishingly like that in the Middle English *Ferumbras,* which protects a city but so far as I can see does not take us to an Other World of any sort: in *Ferumbras* we find a bridge all of marble with sixty piers, a tower on each, ten chains across the forty-foot breadth, and a tower on which is a golden eagle. A giant is keeper here and takes a toll from the passerby of a hundred maidens and a hundred falcons and a carbuncle for each hoof of each steed.[142] In the Anglo-Norman Bevis we have only a suggestion that might later have been developed into all this with a borrowing from the Ferumbras story or some other: although we have no bridge we have the master tower decorated with a golden eagle.[143] Finally the stream into which the hero and his horse take their mighty leap escaping from Damascus, even that tidal river of which the Celtic says "it was not possible for any creature in the world to swim it," is not so far as one may tell derived from the ocean or river barrier at all. The whole episode of the perilous leap is independent of such matters and appears in the *Sermones Vulgares* of Jacques

[141] *Der Anglonormannische Boeve de Haumtone,* ed. Albert Stimming (*Bibl. Normannica,* H. Suchier, VII), p. 31, ll. 867ff. The Welsh is similar: cf. *Selections from the Hengwrt, MSS,* ed. Robert Williams, trans. G. H. Jones, II, p. 527.

[142] *The English Charlemagne Romances,* Part I, *Sir Ferumbras,* ed. S. J. Herrtage, (*EETS:ES,* 34), pp. 58–59, ll. 1680ff. Kölbing in his edition of *Sir Beues* (Part III, *EETS:ES,* 65, p. 283) pointed to the resemblance. The French version is simpler: see A. Kroeber and G. Servois, *Fierabras, Chanson de Geste* (*Anciens Poètes de la France,* IV), pp. 140f. The tower is here and the chain.

[143] Stimming, *Der Anglonormannische Boeve,* p. 31, ll. 870ff:

desur le mestre tour tot saunz mensounger
out li roi Bradmunt fet un egle de or founder,
que entre se pates tint un charboncle cler,
ke doune si grant clarté, ne vus quer celer,
ke ja ne serra si oscur ke l'em ne pus aler,
com si deus feit le solail luser cler.

The Welsh version is similar: Williams, *The Hengwrt MSS,* II, p. 527.

de Vitry (among other places),[144] and there perhaps the French poet found it.

We are left then with practically no real proof of any influence from Otherworld stories. Some details, it is true, like the nature of the terrible stream, the crystalline beauty of Damascus, the idea of the dragon on the Celtic bridge or that of the giant keeper in *Ferumbras,* may have come from the flotsam and jetsam of such material which was always available in the period. The journey of Bevis to his *amie* who healed him suggests a current narrative pattern of fairy lore, but one can be hardly sure. At any rate, early in the formation of this romance there was apparently almost nothing of this kind, and only as time went on were such suggestions added or developed. It is the reverse of what appeared in the case of *King Horn,* where one may suspect an original journey by boat to the fairy realm, and yet where the situation is so similar that all such conjectures are obviously quite precarious. The only positive comment to make is perhaps that Otherworld material was so widely scattered in the twelfth and thirteenth centuries that it was hard for an author to escape it.

A question not unlike this arises too with reference to an episode in the lost Middle English romance of Olive, loosely attached to the Charlemagne cycle as we find the story retold in Old Norse and elsewhere. In this case, according to the Old Norse translation, Olive's son Landres goes into the woods to escape from his stepbrother, and there he meets some dwarfs from whom he wants to obtain food; later he makes his way to the dungeon where his mother is imprisoned. In the adventure in the forest he climbs a hill and he crosses a stream ("var hann kominn heldr fram í einn stríðan straum ok djúpan"),[145] and he has negotiations with his foster-mother in this part of the story which have

[144] As Mrs. Loomis has made clear in *Mod. Lang. Notes,* XXXIV (1919), pp. 408ff. See the *Exempla of Jacques de Vitry,* ed. T. F. Crane, (*Publ. Folk-Lore Soc.* XXXVI), p. 41 (*Serm. Vulg.* XC).

[145] *Karlamagnus Saga ok Kappa Hans,* ed. C. R. Unger, p. 72. The whole story is told on pp. 50–75, and the episode here discussed is on pp. 66–73 (sections 13–15). Cf. Leach, *Angevin Britain and Scandinavia,* pp. 241ff. Note the translation from the Norse by H. M. Smyser in *Connecticut College Monographs I, Survivals in Old Norwegian,* H. M. Smyser and F. P. Magoun, Jr., pp. 3–27.

made some believe that here we are dealing with a journey to the Other World of the type that leads through the grim forest.[146] Nothing of all this is found in the later French and Spanish versions, however; but the interesting fact is that there we have instead the trip to Constantinople, which, as scholars have long been aware, often appears as the fairy realm in disguise or converted.[147] Thither Landri goes by boat and there falls in love with the Emperor's daughter, who makes rather violent advances to the hero. One may well ask whether here it was taste or misunderstanding or both that led to the substitution of one type of adventure for the other, and whether the author who made the change was conscious of the supernatural quality of the scene in each case. That is, if we may fairly assume that the journey to Constantinople implied as much as all that.

That it did cannot be safely inferred from the *Pèlerinage de Charlemagne,* another romance of the French cycle, because in this case the Byzantine episode is touched with a quality of burlesque that would render any such meaning doubtful as a part of the author's intention — even if there were other signs of it. But the question of the origin of the material here is quite another matter. Did the story begin as an Otherworld adventure or was it first a pilgrimage to which details from such stories were later added? Although the plot is well known, a brief outline may serve to make discussion clearer:

One day Charlemagne, girding on his sword and putting on his crown, said to his wife, "Lady, did you ever see a king under heaven whose sword and crown became him so well?" His wife replied that she knew someone who appeared even better in these circumstances, and after some difficulty she was prevailed on to tell that she meant Hugo the Mighty, Emperor of Greece and of Constantinople. Charles then planned to take the twelve peers and seek out this remarkable man. After visit-

[146] See Mr. Smyser in *Publ. Mod. Lang. Assoc.*, LVI (1941), p. 83. The foster-mother "has four traits of the Otherworld benefactor:" she lives in the land to which the hero goes; she gives him gifts which vanish; she gives him a "wise" horse; she is rich.

[147] On Constantinople as the Other World, cf. above p. 252. Landri goes by boat and meets the Emperor's daughter Salmadrine: *Doon de la Roche*, ed. Paul Meyer and Gédéon Huet, (*SATF*, 46), pp. 53ff., ll. 1380ff. Cf. the Spanish *Historia de Enrrique Fi de Oliua*, (*Sociedad de Bibliófilas Españolas*), pp. 44ff. On the episode cf. *Doon de la Roche*, p. lxxii.

ing the Holy Land he finally arrived at Constantinople. His journey, one may note, was by land and he crossed "La grant eve del flun" at Laodicea (106) before coming to Jerusalem. In the realm of Hugo, after having passed through a region of mountains, hills and plains, the travelers saw Constantinople, a mighty city all shining with splendor, beautiful gardens, twenty thousand knights in satin and ermine playing chess and backgammon, and three thousand damsels also richly clad. Charles was riding on a mule and at length found Hugo with his golden plow in the fields. They went to Hugo's palace and it is sumptuously described: the tables and chairs and benches were of gold; it was decorated with pictures of beasts, serpents, and flying birds; it was vaulted, had a hundred columns of marble; images of two children in copper and other metal held ivory horns to their lips; if the northwest or north wind blew it struck the palace and turned it like a cart wheel; the horns sounded and made a noise together like drums or thunder. At the impact of the wind Charles saw the palace turn like a mill wheel; the horns sounded and the images smiled at each other as if they were living. Whoever heard the horns thought he was in Paradise ("Qu'il seit en parais," 376). The storms of snow and hail were great there and the wind powerful; but the windows were of fine crystal cut and set with jewels, and within all was soft and calm as when the sun shines in May. The French were upset by the spectacle and dared not look at the turning palace. But they went within, and Charles's bedroom with the twelve beds around it and one in the middle was also a magnificent scene, vaulted, decorated with crystal, and lighted by a carbuncle set in a pillar. It is here they make their boasts which lead to present embarrassment.[148]

More than once scholars have noted that the palace in this account bears striking evidence of Otherworld origin; we may infer that it has something very much like the river barrier in the "grant eve qui si bruit a cel guet" (l. 555) to which Bernart refers in his *gab,* the stream that by divine aid he later forces out of its channel. There are Celtic parallels for the turning castle and for the arrangement of the beds, and a convincing argument

[148] *Karls des Grossen Reise nach Jerusalem and Constantinopel,* ed. Eduard Koschwitz (*Altfranzösische Bibliothek,* II), pp. 1ff. For the palace see pp. 21ff. In the Old Norse and Welsh versions instead of just the two images with horns, there is one for each of the hundred pillars; see the *Karlamagnus Saga,* ed. Unger, p. 471, and *The Hengwrt MSS,* ed. Williams and Jones, II, pp. 442–443. Cf. *Philologica: Malone Anniv. Studies* (Baltimore, 1949), p. 122.

has been offered that in this story an Otherworld journey is embodied and perhaps not entirely concealed.[149] Somewhat later material has been published, based on a suggestion made by Gaston Paris, to indicate a more or less direct influence from Byzantium itself. For there, as the author shows us, was a similar palace with a pair of statues over the gate, and such scenes appear again in Greek romance, leading us to think perhaps that the *Pèlerinage* is after all just a comic pilgrimage with material really derived from the East.[150] We are thus left with a situation like that in the case of Bevis of Hampton. What appears to be an Otherworld adventure on such terms was originally nothing of the kind but took on details of that sort later.

But such, I believe, is not quite the proper conclusion to reach in this instance. Many years ago, following suggestions offered by Gaston Paris and Child, one scholar examined the parallel between the ballad *King Arthur and King Cornwall* and the *Pèlerinage,* and drew attention to the story in *Diu Crône* by Heinrich von dem Türlin, where we have the initial episode of the Queen's taunting speech and an Otherworld excursion of sorts. In all three cases there is the reproving wife, the incipient jealousy, and the journey to find the rival. Moreover, in the ballad and *Diu Crône* what must have been the original plot is clearer; for there we see that the rival was once the Queen's Otherworld husband. For this and other reasons we infer that the *Pèlerinage* shows a later and disguised version, since Hugo has no wish to recover Charles's lady, nor is there any suggestion of

[149] Mrs. Loomis has drawn attention to this in *Mod. Philol.*, XXV (1927–1928), pp. 331ff. Note also Cross's contribution on the question of Celtic origin for the gabs.

[150] Miss Schlauch in *Speculum*, VII (1932), pp. 500ff. Miss Schlauch does not object to a theory of Celtic origin: "To me it seems very likely that the palace of Bricriu and the palace of Hugon are both modified Regiae Solis, or Abodes of the Sun, and they may be Celtic for all I know, but I do not think they are therefore primitive" (p. 513). For Gaston Paris see *Romania*, IX (1880), 1ff. and *Hist. Litt. de la France*, XXX, pp. 110f., and cf. Briggs, *Journal* [*Eng. and*] *Germ. Philol.*, III (1901), pp. 342ff. Miss Schlauch had earlier published other material on the solar castle, including a consideration of the *Rémundar Saga* "framed on the same type of plot" as *Arthur of Little Britain: Scandinavian Studies and Notes*, X (1928–1929), pp. 189ff. For an ultimate source of the plot in Eastern literature see Krappe's study in *Engl. Stud.*, LXVIII (1933–1934), pp. 351ff.

his having any interest in her or indeed of his having even known her.[151] Let us look at the story in *Diu Crône*:

One day after a hunt King Arthur, stricken with the cold, came in to warm himself by the fire. The Queen Gînôver began to poke fun at him: he suffers from the cold like a woman, she says, he has to wear heavy clothing. He is not so hot as a knight she knows, who rides summer and winter in nothing more than a white shirt and sings love songs. His horse is ermine white, his shield white, and his banner white too. He haunts the ford before Noirespine. The King consults three knights, Kei and two others, and they go to the ford. Kei falls asleep there, and he is wakened by a strange knight but learns nothing and is defeated in combat. The other two companions suffer in the same way, and eventually it is Arthur who finds out the stranger's name and learns that he has held Gînôver for seven years. He was her real husband.[152]

From all this it seems evident that the story holds together, and that we must include the episode of the taunt with that of the excursion to the realm of the rival. In the *Pèlerinage,* therefore, the original idea of the poet was undoubtedly a pilgrimage, but immediately it was fused with that of the reproving wife (to start the journey going) and that in turn by implication brought in the Otherworld excursion and scenery.[153] We cannot see the story as merely a reflection of Western ideas of Constantinople, whether from travelers' accounts or Greek romances, inserted in the narrative of a trip to the East. The turning castle is enough to show the presence of Otherworld material,[154] and this evidence is supported by the taunting scene at the beginning.

[151] Mr. Webster in *Englische Studien,* XXXVI (1906), pp. 337ff. Cf. too the episode in *Amadas et Ydoine,* ed. J. R. Reinhard, ll. 5735ff., and see Reinhard, *The Old French Romance of Amadas et Ydoine,* pp. 88–89.

[152] *Diu Crône von Heinrîch von dem Türlîn,* ed. G. H. F. Scholl, (*Bibl. des Litt. Vereins in Stuttgart,* XXVII), pp. 42ff. (ll. 3356ff.). On the battle at the ford see *Mod. Philol.,* XLIII (1945–1946), pp. 63ff., and below, p. 293, n. 195.

[153] Webster and apparently Kittredge would not have agreed with this last point: cf. *Engl. Studien* XXXVI, pp. 352–353 and p. 368 ("the reproving wife and the visit at Constantinople are unrelated episodes combined by the narrator"). I think Webster successfully disposed of Paris's attempt to establish the scene of the taunt as an independent motif, *ibid.,* pp. 353f.

[154] See above pp. 56 and 150, n. 59. In the story of *Arthur of Little Britain* there are the turning castle and four golden images blowing horns (see p. 316 below), and Loomis holds that it derived from the same source as that

But there is another curious fact that seems to have been overlooked in this connection. In all the discussion of the parallel between the *Pèlerinage* and *Diu Crône* it has been apparently forgotten that in Heinrich's romance, along with the scene of the reproving wife and the excursion to the ford and the settling of Arthur's difficulties with his rival, we have (immediately afterward) the story of what we elsewhere know as *La Mule sanz Frain,* but in an earlier form than that in Old French.[155] In this occurs the episode of the turning castle:

Sgoidamur comes to Arthur's court and asks for help in getting back her throne. Kei attempts the expedition and on muleback he rides through a throng of lions and leopards and a dark valley filled with frogs, snakes, and dragons. He comes to a deep and broad river ("swarz, tief unde breit," 12839) but dares not cross by the steel bridge there ("smaler denne ein hant," 12848). Gawain later takes up the adventure, and of course succeeds, crossing the river by the narrow bridge (12926ff.). He follows a narrow path from the stream to a house with walls like glass, a deep ditch round it full of water that turns the walls and makes them revolve. The house also has stakes on which are mounted human heads.[156]

When we read of the hero's journey on the mule we may be reminded of Charles "sor un fort mul amblant" (*Pèl.* 298), and recall that he too came up the path to the Other World, "un antif sentier" (300). The deep black river and the narrow bridge in *Diu Crône* are, with the dark valley and other details, clearly derived from the tradition familiar to us in the visions; and if the *Pèlerinage* was indebted to some source, immediate or remote,

---

of the *Pèlerinage: Celtic Myth and Arthurian Romance,* p. 224. Brown, *Iwain,* p. 80, n. 1, saw a resemblance in the *Mule sanz Frain* to the use of the castle in the *Fled Bricrend;* Loomis argues that the *Mule* and *Diu Crône* drew on the same source, *op. cit.* pp. 110ff. I am not taken with Miss Schlauch's implied suggestion regarding the dome of the circular church in Constantinople: "Apparently if one gazed long enough. . . the whole thing seemed to move. This is attested by several witnesses" (*Speculum,* VII, p. 503). There is too much material nearer home.

[155] As Mr. Loomis thinks, in *Celtic Myth and Arthurian Romance,* pp. 110ff. Cf. Kittredge, *Gawain and the Green Knight,* pp. 251ff. and L. L. Boll, *The Relation of Diu Krône of Heinrich von dem Türlin to La Mule sanz Frain,* (*Cath. Univ. of America, Studies in German,* II).

[156] *Diu Crône,* ed. Scholl, 12613ff.

of Heinrich's poem, then it too would apparently show the same influence (in the "grant eve del flun" perhaps or the "grant eve qui si bruit") in addition to whatever, like the turning castle, came to it ultimately from the Celtic.[157]

In the cycle of Alexander, on the other hand, another process appears in the development of the narrative of the journey to Paradise.[158] The adventure as a whole is broken up, and the fountain of life comes to be treated by itself in a story regarding Enoch and his leading an expedition for its search. He bathes in the water and is dealt with accordingly. After that is over, according to the *Roman d'Alexandre* (of the latter part of the twelfth century), the travelers come to a place beside a river where trees are growing and where there is an orchard that bears fruit in summer and in winter. Here is a fountain rushing forth in clear streams over white gravel. Under each tree is a damsel, and, though the travelers are taken with the beauty of these lovely creatures, approach is difficult. Over the stream which borders the place is a drawbridge with pillars of marble, sides of gold, and planks of ivory, but standing there are the golden images of two youths (*enfans*) with scrolls bearing warnings that they will defend the place. As the travelers draw near, each image seizes a hammer; but at length one of the figures is thrown in the water by enchantment (as the poet maintains, to be food for the fishes), and the other is carried away by a demon.[159] The

[157] The Celtic examples of the turning castle seem to be the oldest. Huet's discrimination between the types hardly seems to have real point here: "Il y a entre les deux conceptions cette différence essentielle que le palais du roi Huon est mis en mouvement d'une façon naturelle, par le vent, tandis que le château tournant des récits français aussi bien qu'irlandais appartient manifestement au monde magique et surnaturel," *Romania,* XL (1911), p. 241. But cf. the house in *Diu Crône* turned by water (see above p. 281), and note the iron wheel with knives turned by water in the *Wigalois,* ed. J. M. N. Kapteyn, p. 285, ll. 6773ff. If the *Pèlerinage* shows a degree of rationalization, many scholars will feel, I believe, that enough supernaturalism remains for purposes of indicating the origin. Cf. *Mod. Philol.,* X (1912–1913), p. 522, and *Romanic Rev.,* XXXII (1941), pp. 20ff. The example in the literature associated with Prester John probably comes from French romance: see Zarncke, Leipzig *Abhandlungen, Phil.-Hist. Cl.,* VIII (1883), p. 160.

[158] See above pp. 157ff. For further material on the cycle see above pp. 24f.

[159] *Li Roman d'Alexandre par Lambert li Tors et Alexandre de Bernay,* ed. Heinrich Michelant (*Bibl. des Litt. Vereins in Stuttgart,* XIII), pp. 340ff. Most of the account appears in the *Chrestomathie de l'Ancien Français,* 12th

travelers then enjoy the entertainment afforded by the damsels and are reluctant when finally they have to leave the region. All this seems to be the case of an Otherworld journey, that of the visit to Paradise, broken up into separate units,[160] but attracting further detail of the same kind. The forest with the damsels looks like a Celtic Maidenland, but represents a separate story and almost certainly comes from the East.

Just when the detail of the bridge was added is doubtful, but the whole idea recalls the somewhat elaborate structures found in allegory and romance, not unlike, for example, the one described by Andreas Capellanus.[161] If, like the story of the trees, the bridge came from an oriental narrative, it was certainly modified in the transmission. A comparable development is found in the romance of *Partonopeus,* where an Otherworld adventure is repeated in different forms.[162] The hero goes voyaging across the sea in a rudderless boat to the country of the fairy mistress; when he gets there he enters a town and comes to a house where food is mysteriously furnished to him; (in a Middle English version) through the hall he sees a marble tower which he now regards as a mighty castle; round the wall of this is a ditch of clear water and over it a drawbridge a hundred feet in length.[163] Thus there is the sea journey leading to the house; and then within that house begins another expedition which takes the hero over the ditch into the marble castle.[164] The ditch and

---

ed., Karl Bartsch, rev. Leo Wiese, pp. 132ff., No. 36. See for the episode Paul Meyer, *Alexandre le Grand dans la Litt. fr. du Moyen Age,* II, pp. 181–182. The forest with the trees bearing the lovely damsels as fruit is found in Lamprecht's *Alexander*: see Karl Kinzel, *Lamprechts Alexander* (*Germanistische Handbibliothek,* VI), pp. 302ff., ll. 5157ff.; on the question of an oriental source, p. 497, and *Germania,* II (1857), p. 458. For the automata see *Mod. Philol.,* X (1912–1913), pp. 517–518; *Mod. Lang. Notes,* XXXV (1920), p. 133; *Publ. Mod. Lang. Assoc.,* XXXVIII (1923), pp. 436–437, n. 41, and p. 440; Spargo, *Virgil the Necromancer,* pp. 117ff. and 363ff.; Nitze, *Le Haut Livre du Graal, Perlesvaus,* I, pp. 254–255 (two men with hammers), and II, pp. 314ff.; *Huon de Bordeaux,* ed. Guessard and Grandmaison, p. 136, ll. 4562ff. (two men of copper with iron flails, see above p. 162.)

[160] Cf. *Medium Aevum,* V (1936), p. 46.

[161] Cf. pp. 197–198 above.

[162] See above, pp. 251ff.

[163] *Partonope of Blois,* ed. Bödtker. (*EETS:ES,* 109), p. 26. The bridge is not in the French (Arsenal MS): *Partonopeus,* ed. Robert, I, pp. 33–34.

[164] The town itself is of the Other World. Notice the use of crystal and

bridge are apparently a late and really unnecessary addition, which (if they represent anything more than architecture) came in all probability from some other romance. They almost serve to produce a second Otherworld scene within the larger framework of the first.

iii

Otherworld material in the romances of the Arthurian cycle is almost beyond any adequate means of estimate, and here only a few of the outstanding problems may be indicated. The examples, moreover, are so well known that it is hardly necessary to outline the descriptions or accounts of them in any detail. Only someone who has worked in this territory can guess the extent of our indebtedness to the many specialists who have been here first, or have a proper picture of the amount of scholarship, rough and roaring or fair and sweet, that metaphorically speaking has gone under the bridge these many years. On Avalon itself a whole book could probably be written, if all the controversy and all the detail were to be covered.

In the *Historia regum Britanniae* Geoffrey of Monmouth says that Arthur at the end of his life was taken to the island of Avalon for the healing of his wounds ("ad sananda uulnera sua in insulam auallonis euectus").[165] In the *Vita Merlini* he shows a picture of the "insula pomorum que fortunata uocatur," taking detail from Isidore of Seville and others regarding the Fortunate Isles of classical fame, and telling us that thither Arthur went to

---

the supernatural light (*Partonope*, ed. Bödtker, p. 23, ll. 847–849 and p. 24, ll. 881–883); this corresponds to the strange light on board ship in the French (*Partonopeus*, ed. Robert, I, p. 27, ll. 765–768):

> Et quant li jors est declinés,
> Li enfès voit moult grant clarté,
> Et quant la nuis est plus oscure,
> De tant est la clartés plus pure.

[165] *The Historia regum Britanniae of Geoffrey of Monmouth*, ed. Acton Griscom, p. 501 (xi, ii). On the problem of Avalon see *Manly Anniversary Volume*, pp. 284ff.; Paton, *Fairy Mythology*, pp. 25ff.; *Vassar Mediaeval Studies* (New Haven, 1923), pp. 3ff.; *Zeits. f. fr. Sprache und Litt.* XII (1890), pp. 240ff., and XIII (1891), pp. 106ff.; *Romania*, XXIV (1895), pp. 327ff. and 501ff.; *Mod. Lang. Notes*, XIV (1899), cols. 93ff.; *Mélanges Jeanroy*, pp. 243ff.; *Mod. Philol.*, XXVIII (1930–1931), pp. 385ff. and 395ff.; *Speculum*, XVIII (1943), pp. 303ff.; *American Philol. Assoc., Transactions*, 73, (1942), pp. 405ff.

be healed guided by Barinthus. Morgan put him in a golden bed.[166] As many scholars have observed, the "insula pomorum" is a translation of Avalon, the Celtic for "isle of apples," and in relating the idea to the Fortunate Isles, Geoffrey shows a characteristic originality which may be sometimes misunderstood for honesty. But surely it is hard to see how anyone can now suppose that Geoffrey of Monmouth was inventing the whole episode of the "passing of Arthur" and his journey by boat to the realm of Morgan the *fée*. The formula in one guise or another is too familiar in Celtic literature.

There is almost every sign that the story was an old one. In the Welsh "Spoils of Annwn," a work that could hardly be the late reflection of twelfth-century romance, we have the story of Arthur's expedition to the realms of darkness on another adventure.[167] In *Kulhwch and Olwen* from the early twelfth century we get further indication that he was somehow associated with ideas of the Other World.[168] Avalon is mentioned as early as 1130 in the *Couronnement de Louis* as a realm of gold, presumably a place well known to which everybody would understand the reference.[169] In the *Vita Gildae,* attributed to Caradoc of

[166] *The Vita Merlini*, ed. J. J. Parry, pp. 82ff. (*Univ. Illinois Studies in Lang. and Lit.*, X). Barinthus may be a figure derived from a Celtic god of the sea, according to the suggestion of Brown in *Revue celtique*, XXII (1901), pp. 339ff. On the sources of the passage see *Vassar Mediaeval Studies*, pp. 3ff.; *Romania*, XLV (1918–1919), p. 14, notes 1 and 2; *Mod. Philol.*, XXVIII (1930–1931), pp. 385ff.; *Mélanges Jeanroy*, pp. 243ff.; and Faral, *La Légende Arthurienne*, II, pp. 299ff. and 425ff.

[167] Skene, *Four Ancient Books*, I, pp. 264ff., and Loomis in *Publ. Mod. Lang. Assoc.*, LVI (1941), p. 887ff.

[168] *The Mabinogion, A New Translation*, T. P. Ellis and John Lloyd, I, p. 185 (when Arthur and his hosts came to the front of a torrent, he put his knife across in its scabbard for a bridge); I, pp. 191ff. Arthur sends Gwalchmai on the journey for Olwen, an Otherworld adventure; note also in the *Dream of Rhonabwy*, II, p. 10, Arthur's location on the island suggests the same theme. For further material on the Other World in the *Mabinogion* see, for example, the fairy mound, I, pp. 17 and 54; the scene in which Bendigaid Frân serves as a bridge over the river that has "magic quality," I, pp. 61–62; the druid mist, I, p. 79; Pwyll's visit to Arawn, I, pp. 9ff. On the date of the Kulhwch story see *Zeits. f. celt. Philol.*, XII (1918), p. 283; J. G. Evans, *The White Book Mabinogion*, p. xiv; *Romanic Rev.*, XXXII (1941), pp. 14ff.

[169] *Le Couronnement de Louis*, ed. E. Langlois, laisse xliii, (l. 1796, p. 83, and 1827, p. 84), (*SATF*, 21); ed. Langlois (*Classiques Fr. du Moyen Age*), p. 56 (l. 1795) and p. 57 (l. 1826). Cf. Warren, maintaining that Avalon was

Llancarfan, we are told how Guinevere was abducted to Glastonbury by Melwas, King of Somerset ("in aestiua regione"),[170] and restored to Arthur by the intervention of Gildas and the abbot there before he did battle for her. William of Malmesbury tells us the place was also called Avalon ("etiam insula Avallonia celebriter nominatur. . .)" [171] and from the fact that the story of the rape of Guinevere is clearly the same as that which is so familiar later in romance, perhaps too from the fact that later the legend grew of the exhumation of Arthur's body there, we may see that Glastonbury was already associated with Otherworld ideas.[172] The belief among the Bretons in Arthur's return and the familiarity of the name Avalon would persuade us at the very least that Geoffrey in his story had made an inference rather than an invention. In the *Vita Merlini* then, in borrowing from the Fortunate Isles, he did for the "insula pomorum" very

---

not merely a literary derivative from Geoffrey and Wace, *Mod. Lang. Notes*, XIV (1899), cols. 93ff. On the date see *Le Couronnement*, p. clxx (*SATF*); p. vii (*Classiques Fr.*); and *Romanic Rev.*, XXXII, pp. 19–20.

[170] In *Auctores antiq.* XIII, ed. Theodore Mommsen, *Chron. minora*, Part I, iii, p. 109, (*MGH*). For the date, not later than 1136 and perhaps much earlier, see *Speculum*, XIV (1939), pp. 350ff. and *Romanic Rev.* XXXII, pp. 6–7; cf. *Romania*, XXIV (1895), p. 330. On the story see also pp. 302ff. below.

[171] Migne, *Patr. Lat.* CLXXIX, col. 1687; cf. col. 1685. On the whole matter of Glastonbury and Avalon, reflected later in the *Perlesvaus*, see Faral, *Légende Arthurienne*, II, pp. 300ff. and 402ff.; Nitze and collab., *Perlesvaus*, II, pp. 45ff. with further references there indicated; *Romanic Review*, XXIX (1938), pp. 175ff.; *Romania*, XXIV (1895), pp. 501ff.; *Romania*, XXVII (1898), pp. 529ff.; *Speculum*, II (1927), pp. 268ff.; *Speculum*, X (1935), pp. 46ff.; *Speculum*, XI (1936), pp. 129ff.; *Speculum*, XVIII (1943), pp. 306ff.

[172] How it came to be associated is a difficult problem that may have something to do with the name. The *Vita Gildae* (*Auct. antiq.* XIII, ed Mommsen, pp. 109 and 110) interprets Glastonia as "Urbs Vitrea," and "Ynisgutrin" (cf. William of Malmesbury's "Yniswgtrin," according to Migne, *Patr. Lat.* CLXXIX, col. 1687, but "Yneswitrin" according to Faral's reading, *Légende Arthurienne*, I, p. 304) as "insula vitrea." Glass plays a large part in Otherworld architecture. Cf. Nitze, *Perlesvaus*, II, p. 152; *Speculum*, XVIII (1943), pp. 306ff.; and below p. 290, n. 182. William of Malmesbury's interpretation of "insulam Avalloniae" as "insula pomorum" (Migne, *op. cit.*, col. 1687), with his story of the orchard there, does not fully explain the use of the name, as his later reference to Avalloc shows. The appearance of the region, with the mysterious pyramids and the Tor, may also have had something to do with it. Rhŷs in his *Studies in the Arthurian Legend*, p. 330, indicates how Glastonbury could be thought of as an island; and the *Vita Gildae* speaks of the saint as arriving in a small boat (p. 109).

much the same thing as the author of the *Gesta regum Britanniae* many years later did for Avalon: this later writer took the well-known conception of Avalon and described the place with expressions only too familiar in the traditional accounts of the Earthly Paradise. Eternal spring reigns there, he said, no immoderate heat or cold; all flowers and fruits are seen, nor fail the lily and the rose. Beautiful maidens too are included: it is a Celtic Maidenland where Arthur is being healed, presented to us as if it were the garden of Eden.[173]

The fortress where Guinevere was confined when she was abducted (here by Marduc, who is Modred and corresponds to Melwas) is, with its surrounding waters, almost certainly represented in sculpture in the archivolt on the Porta della Pescheria of the cathedral at Modena. This has been dated by several archaeologists as of the early twelfth century,[174] and in that case it shows an example of an Other World of the Arthurian cycle in art, quite independent of Geoffrey's creations, at a very early period indeed. The emphasis on the water barrier in this economically simplified carving is of special interest here. In the many stories which include the abduction of Guinevere there is of course a great variety of descriptions of the realm of the abductor; and in the two which have been held to furnish the closest parallels for the version apparently represented in the sculpture,[175] the similarities in that detail are not close. In *Durmart le Galois,* when the hero seeks out the castle of Brun de Morois, he finds it surrounded for a league by a marsh and by swampy soil, a type of barrier we have found elsewhere (for example, in the *Vision of the Monk of Eynsham*), but rather different from that in the carving.[176] The town is protected by walls (there are seven

[173] *Gesta regum Britanniae,* ed. Francisque Michel, *Archaeologia Cambrensis,* 1862, p. 153, ll. 4213.

[174] The literature on the subject is considerable: see among other articles *The Art Bulletin,* VI, No. 3 (Providence, R.I., 1924), pp. 71–74; *Speculum,* X (1935), pp. 355–376; *Speculum,* XIII (1938), pp. 221–231; Loomis, *Celtic Myth and Arthurian Romance,* pp. 6–11 and *passim*; *Romanic Rev.,* XXXII (1941), pp. 22ff. On the mythological roots of the story see *Romanic Rev.,* XV (1924), pp. 266ff.

[175] *Romanic Rev.,* XV (1924), pp. 266ff.; *Zeits. f. roman. Phil.,* XXII (1898), pp. 243ff.

[176] *Li Romans de Durmart le Galois,* ed. Edmund Stengel (*Bibl. des Litt. Vereins in Stuttgart,* CXVI), p. 120, ll. 4304ff.

barriers to pass) with towers; the streets are great and broad and well paved, and all about are buildings of all kinds and gardens and fountains. After an interview with a dwarf in the master castle, the hero and Ydier, who has joined him, cross a bridge and come into a fair garden of trees and flowers where Guinevere is sitting.[177] In the adventure of the Dolorous Tower in the prose *Lancelot*,[178] an episode related to that of the abduction of Guinevere, Galeshin rides into the valley of enchantment called "Le val sans retor" or "Le val des faus amans" (protected by a wall of air) which is a place of great beauty ("vns des plus biaus vauls del monde") where knights untrue in love must stay. He comes to a vault guarded by four chained dragons, from which he escapes, although wounded, and next to a plank not a foot broad over a stream great and deep. As he attempts to cross this, one of two knights who stand there on guard strikes him down into the stream and he has to join the knights of the valley. Ywain also fails in the enterprise; but, when Lancelot arrives, he kills the dragons, causes one of the knights at the stream to fall, passes over in safety himself, and strikes down the other knight. The magic ring he wears causes the plank to vanish. Later Galeshin as well crosses over the plank; but nothing in any part of the episode suggests as close a parallel to the carving as the later detail in what is actually the Guinevere story, where the Queen and Baudemagus in a prison tower watch from the window for

[177] *Ibid.*, p. 121, ll. 4341ff.; p. 123, ll. 4399ff.; p. 126, ll. 4521ff. Note too the Castle of the Ten Maidens: the maidens sit in a garden listening to a harper, and with their ten *amies* live for pleasure, pp. 173–174, ll. 6201ff. Also see the great tree with the candles on it and the Christ Child at its top: pp. 42–43, ll. 1509ff., imitating Wauchier's continuation of *Perceval*, ll. 34414ff. as Bruce points out (*Evolution of Arthur. Rom.*, II, p. 225, n. 7: see Potvin, *Perceval le Gallois*, IV, p. 152). On the Castle of Maidens see p. 299, n. 213 below.

[178] *Le Livre de Lancelot del Lac* Part II, ed. H. Oskar Sommer (*The Vulgate Version of the Arthurian Romances*, IV), pp. 87ff. For the part under discussion see pp. 117ff. Cf. Legrand d'Aussy, *Fabliaux ou Contes*, I, pp. 156ff. In the conte Lancelot sees a kind of mist or smoke that is the surrounding wall of air (p. 160). Here the region is surrounded by mountains. On the valley here and in other romances see Paton, *Fairy Mythology*, pp. 81ff. Note too the enchanted stream, Sommer, *op. cit.*, p. 122. The valley is briefly dealt with in the *Livre d'Artus* in Sommer's *Vulgate Version of the Arthurian Romances*, VII, p. 136 (note the two roads).

her majesty's deliverer. The stream is here too (with the bridges), pretty much as in Chrétien's version.[179]

The Val sans Retour recalls in some respects the scene of the Joie de la Cort in Chrétien's *Erec,* where a knight is detained by magic until a hero arrives who can defeat him. Erec and Enid ride on their journey until they come to a castle surrounded by a wall and a deep stream ("Rade et bruianz come tanpeste").[180] They cross the drawbridge and the barriers (*lices*), and eventually they enter the garden where the stakes and the human heads are found. This garden, abounding in flowers and ripe fruits summer and winter, having every herb and spice with medicinal value, and filled with the songs of all kinds of birds, has round it no barrier except that of air ("Mur ne paliz se de l'er non"),[181] which, however, is as impenetrable as iron. People get in by a narrow entrance ("une estroite antree"), which, with the roaring stream, may suggest to us a reminiscence, direct or indirect, of the corresponding motifs in the visions.[182] Certainly it is forcing

[179] Sommer, *Le Livre de Lancelot del Lac,* Part II, p. 193 ("la planche si feble et si crollant," "lyaue qui tant estoit noire et parfonde"); pp. 199–200 (the prison, the sword bridge, and the two lions which later vanish; Lancelot crosses the sword bridge astride). A suggestion of the symbolism of death in passing over the stream is found in the earlier use of the motif, where Galeshin crosses: "Si dist a soi meisme quil quidoit bien auoir le meillour esleu dez .ij. passages. mais cestoit li pires. Car ce nest mie perilleuse chose de morir honestement" (*ibid.,* p. 131). For Lancelot's sword bridge in art see R. S. Loomis and L. H. Loomis, *Arthurian Legends in Medieval Art,* fig. 267, p. 103.

[180] *Kristian von Troyes Erec und Enide,* ed. Wendelin Foerster, (*Rom. Bibl.,* XIII), p. 149, l. 5375. Cf. the "Castiel sans Non" on a *floating island,* where Guengasonain was held captive by a *fée* in *La Vengeance Raguidel,* ed. Mathias Friedwagner, (*Raoul von Houdenc, Sämtliche Werke,* II), p. 144, ll. 5056ff. The motif of the heads on stakes occurs in a different scene earlier (p. 23, ll. 715ff.) where the castle, surrounded by a deep ditch, seems deserted.

[181] Foerster, *op. cit.,* p. 159, l. 5740. For such a barrier of air in the legend of Virgil see Loomis, *Arthurian Trad. and Chrétien de Troyes,* p. 178, and Spargo, *Virgil the Necromancer,* pp. 60ff.; note too the instance in the Val sans Retour, Sommer, *Vulgate Version of the Arthur. Rom.,* IV, p. 117.

[182] The castle, the river, and the barrier of air are not mentioned in the story of Geraint in the *Mabinogion,* where the garden is surrounded instead with a barrier of mist (see Loth, *Mabinog.,* II, p. 169). In Hartmann von Aue's *Erec* (*Hartmann von Aue Erec/Iwein,* ed. Hans Naumann and Hans Steinger, *Deutsche Lit. Sammlung, Höfische Epik* XII, p. 129, ll. 7833ff.) the castle is situated on a vast round rock, and the roaring stream is down below in a deep cleft making anyone think of Hell who looks at it; about the garden (p.

the evidence considerably to see in the river here or elsewhere merely a remnant of the Celtic ocean barrier, when, in many instances, we find it has new characteristics of its own quite unexplained by that kind of hypothesis.[183]

Related somehow to the scene of the Joie de la Cort in the *Erec* is the picture of the Other World in a group of romances which share certain important features in their plots, of which a familiar example is *La Mule sanz Frain,* and also that in another group dealing with the story of Gawain's son, as in the Middle English *Libeaus Desconus.*[184] The first group we have already considered in the examples of *Yder, La Mule* itself, and Heinrich von dem Türlin's *Diu Crône.*[185] In these the stream is notably swift or it is deep and dark. In *Hunbaut* the city of the Island King must be reached by a voyage, but by the gate of the city is a "grant fosse," over which goes a very long plank only a foot and a half wide, and from this Gawain kicks a cripple guardian of the bridge into the mud.[186] The narrow plank in

141, ll. 8702ff.) is no wall or ditch or hedge or stream or thorny barrier — Hartmann has borrowed here with some independence and knows the motifs. The two roads are in the *Mabinogion* and in Hartmann's *Erec* (Loth, *Mabinog.*, II, p. 168; Hartmann's *Erec*, p. 129, ll. 7811ff.) suggesting a common source apart from Chrétien: see Zenker in *Zeits. f. fr. Sprache und Litt.*, XLV (1919), pp. 87–88. Cf. the roads in the *Palamedes,* summarized by E. Löseth, *Le Roman en Prose de Tristan,* p. 463. On the other hand Hartmann's earlier reference to the realm of Maheloas, with the negative formula used in the description of the Isle of Glass (p. 50, ll. 1919ff.), reads like a close adaptation of Chrétien (*Erec,* ed. Foerster, p. 54, ll. 1945ff.). For Maheloas (Melwas) and the Isle of Glass cf. above pp. 230–231 and 286–287; also *Romania,* X (1881), pp. 490–491; XX (1891), p. 149; and *Zeits. f. fr. Sprache und Litt.*, XII (1890), p. 246.

[183] Cf. *Romania,* XXV (1896), p. 267; *Publ. Mod. Lang. Assoc.*, XXXIII (1918), pp. 630ff. Loomis in *Romania,* LIX (1933), pp. 557ff., does not really solve this problem. Cf. too the river in *La Mule sanz Frain* and related romances, and see p. 245 above.

[184] Cf. Philipot in *Romania,* XXV (1896), p. 269; F. Piquet, *Étude sur Hartmann d'Aue,* p. 171.

[185] Pp. 259 and 279ff. above. In *Yder* notice too the ditch forty feet wide and deep with a drawbridge: *Der Altfranzösische Yderroman,* et Gelzer, p. 108, ll. 3770ff.

[186] *Hunbaut, Altfranzösischer Artusroman des xiii Jahrh.*, ed. Jakob Stürzinger and Hermann Breuer, (*Gesells. für romanische Lit.* 35), pp. 38ff., ll. 1261ff. Cf. the deep and wide fosse and bridge in the *Chevalier à L'Epée,* ed. E. C. Armstrong, p. 12, 209ff. On the guardian cf. Loomis, *Celtic Myth and Arthur. Rom.*, pp. 105ff., who, however, deals with the "vilain" and the

La Mule sanz Frain is of iron and bends under the weight of Gawain and the mule; and here we must also note that the hero first goes through a forest of wild beasts, then by a narrow path to a valley of serpents, scorpions, and monsters breathing fire, and, crossing the bridge, reaches the turning castle with the stakes, on which (except for one) are severed heads, where there seems to be nobody at all.[187] The *terre gaste* in a different form, with no beast or birds, with the land dry and poor, and with an empty city with fallen walls and desolate palace, appears in the *Perlesvaus,* and later — apart from the beheading game but as if once associated with it in some previous story — we have the turning castle.[188] The castle too is reached by a journey through a desolate and waste place; but it is situated in a pleasant meadow land, and round it are running streams and high walls. It turns faster than the wind blows, and it is protected by copper archers with crossbows and living men that sound horns. Lions and bears are chained by the gate; there are three bridges that are lowered if assault threatens. In the group of romances thus far considered we may note that, while the turning castle and the motif of the stakes suggest Celtic origin,[189] there are definite signs of influence from the visions or the Orient in the bridge and in the river. It

"garçon" with the axe later in the story (p. 44, ll. 1464ff.). Note too the deep stream later which must be crossed by a boat that is safe only when it transports odd numbers of passengers (pp. 84ff., ll. 2870ff.).

[187] *La Mule,* ed. Orłowski, p. 160, ll. 401ff. (the bridge, "qui n'est mie plus d'un dor lee"); p. 152, ll. 129ff., and p. 159, ll. 358ff. (the forest); p. 153, ll. 168ff. and p. 159, ll. 377ff. (the perilous valley, deep and broad and very dark, and making anyone fear death who goes there); pp. 161ff., ll. 429 (the castle with dark and deep water about it, with the stakes, and turning like a mill). For the empty castle see *Yder,* p. 259 above. For the turning castle see *Diu Crône,* pp. 281–282 above.

[188] *Le Haut Livre du Graal, Perlesvaus,* Nitze and Jenkins I, p. 136, ll. 2856ff. (the *terre gaste,* found again p. 284, ll. 6657ff.). Note the two roads ll. 6637ff. Cf. the notes, II, pp. 281–283. For the turning castle see I, p. 247, ll. 5714ff.; cf. the notes, II, pp. 312ff. For other automata see the Castle of the Copper Bull, I, pp. 254ff.: two men of copper with iron mallets; I, p. 91, two men of copper with crossbows. On the *terre gaste* see the material cited by Loomis, *Arthurian Trad. and Chrétien de Troyes,* pp. 338 and 342; and by Nitze in *Mod. Philol.,* XLIII (1945–1946), pp. 58ff. Real examples in Celtic seem rare, and the motif of the arid and barren country may show some influence from the Eastern tradition. Cf. Schlauch, *Romance in Iceland,* p. 34.

[189] For the stakes see *Romanic Rev.,* IX (1918), pp. 21ff. Instances other than Celtic have been pointed out, notably the *Iliad* xviii, 176ff. Cf. p. 68 above.

is not without significance that in speaking of how horrible and cruel the river was, Païen de Maisières says the river in *La Mule* was "li fluns au diable." [190]

In three other romances related to these, *The Turke and Gowin, Gawain and the Green Knight,* and *The Grene Knight,* we have clearly a Celtic reminiscence in the use of a hollow hill as the home of the monster of the challenge. The "turk" (dwarf) leads Gowin to a hill: "the earth opened & closed againe" and there was darkness, thunder, lightning, snow, and rain.[191] In *The Grene Knight* the chapel is "under a hill." [192] *Gawain and the Green Knight* shows the chapel in a smooth mound by a fountain where a stream boils forth; the mound is overgrown with grass and has a hole in the end and on either side. Gawain strides up to the rock of the rough dwelling and hears a fierce noise; the Green Knight coming out of one of the holes arrives at the stream and hops over it on his axe.[193] Here is a strange hint that the water barrier was more important in an earlier version of the episode and that perhaps a bridge had a place there. The castle of the temptation, however, is located on a hill in a clearing, amidst trees in a meadow with a park around it; it has a bridge (drawn up), a double ditch goes to the place, and its wall with battlements and tower stands in water.[194]

The *terre gaste* and the scene including the heads on stakes are found in romances of the second group to which I made earlier reference. The first of these motifs appears in the *gaste*

[190] *La Mule,* ed Orłowski, p. 160, l. 398. Cf. Kittredge with regard to the influence of Christian and Moslem legends: *Gawain and the Green Knight,* pp. 243–244 ("The Christian idea . . . was certainly present to the mind of Païen, as his language shows," p. 244, n. 1. He goes on to suggest that the valley reveals similar influences).

[191] *Bishop Percy's Folio Manuscript,* ed. J. W. Hales and F. J. Furnivall, I, p. 93, ll. 66ff.

[192] *Ibid.,* II, p. 75, ll. 448–450. Cf. *Mod. Philol.,* XIII (1915–1916), pp. 73 and 127.

[193] *Sir Gawain and the Green Knight,* ed. J. R. R. Tolkien and E. V. Gordon, pp. 67ff., ll. 2161ff. The mound is a "berȝe."

[194] *Ibid.,* pp. 24ff., ll. 763ff. In the *Carl of Carlile* (Porkington MS) the journey to the house of the Carl is through a forest wide and broad, and a thick mist falls on the travelers: *Syr Gawayne,* ed. Sir Frederic Madden (Bannatyne Club: London, 1839), pp. 258–259.

cité, Senaudon (Snowdon), in *Le Bel Inconnu* of Renaut de Beaujeu, where the city is located between two streams ("molt bruians") and is all in ruins and apparently empty of people. A stream with a bridge over it flows before the gate. The second motif, that of the heads on stakes, is used in the episode of the Ile d'Or, where the castle is on an arm of the sea; it is surrounded by walls of white marble; within are a hundred towers of red marble; the palace is of a stone like crystal, its vault and pavement are of silver, it is illumined by a carbuncle, and twenty towers sustain the structure.[195] So far in all this, except possibly for the *gaste cité*, there is little that might not reflect Celtic literature. In the Sparrow-Hawk adventure, however, we find the castle surrounded by a stream, full of fish and used for transporting merchandise; and the place is also enclosed by ditches, great, deep, long, and broad, above which tower the high walls. Possibly in such details there is the suggestion of a different influence, and certainly there is much further along in the poem where the hero on his way to the fée's room thinks he is suddenly on a plank over a stream "Qui molt bruians et corans." He falls down to clutch the plank and is discovered by the servants holding on to the perch of the sparrow hawk.[196] The heads on stakes appear in the Middle English *Libeaus Desconus* in the Sparrow-Hawk adven-

[195] *Le Bel Inconnu*, ed. G. Perrie Williams, p. 85, ll. 2773ff., and p. 104, ll. 3387ff. (*gaste cité* and Senaudon). On the episodes with a comparison of different versions, see W. H. Schofield, *Studies on the Libeaus Desconus* (Boston, 1895), [*Harvard*] *Studies and Notes in Philol. and Lit.*, IV, pp. 36, 46, and *passim*. For a reminiscence of the actual Snowdon, in ruins between two streams, see *Speculum*, XXII (1947), pp. 520ff., especially 528ff. In the episode of the Ford Perilous notice that the "loge," made of fresh branches in Welsh fashion, is on the bank of the river. See too the Ford Perilous in the *Contes del Graal* and elsewhere: *Der Percevalroman*, ed. Alfons Hilka, pp. 380–381, ll. 8479ff., and notes, p. 765; the Didot-*Perceval*, ed. Roach, pp. 195ff. (cf. pp. 70ff.); in the *Yder* (ed. Gelzer, p. 108, ll. 3750ff., with the two roads); the fight at the ford in Celtic, Cross in *Mod. Philol.* XII (1914–1915), p. 604, n. 1; *Mod. Philol.* XLIII (1945–1946), pp. 63ff.; and on some fords in Celtic cf. Cross in the [*Kittredge*] *Anniv. Vol.*, pp. 382–383. The similarity of the *gaste cité* to that in the *Conte del Graal* shows that the stories are related.

[196] *Le Bel Inconnu*, ed. Williams, pp. 46–47, ll. 1497ff. (Sparrow-Hawk adventure); p. 149, ll. 4891ff. (the plank). Cf. the Celtic stories cited by Krappe in *Romania*, LVIII (1932), pp. 429–430. Mention should be made too of the reminiscence of Maiden Land in the "Castiel des Puceles (*Bel Inc.*, p. 166, ll. 5454ff.) ; cf. p. 299, n. 213, below.

ture.[197] The *terre gaste* is not here, except for the fact that the castle of Sinadoune is seemingly inhabited only by the minstrels. The pillars of crystal and the painted windows in the place are worthy of note; and the vanishing of the minstrels, the collapsing of the walls, the earthquake, the unlocking (opening up) of the roof, when the hero sits on the dais, suggest something of the ruined city. The Ile d'Or episode shows a palace on a river side with a bridge where the knight who crosses must lay down his arms, and where the giant Maugis waits for him. Later Maugis smites Libeaus as he lies on the river bank, and knocks him into the stream.[198] In all the romances thus far examined, then, which may be associated with Chrétien's *Erec,* in addition to the material which seems to come from Celtic (such as the combat at the ford, the motif of the heads on stakes, the mist, the chapel in the mound), there are also derivatives from the visions or from Germanic or Eastern literature (such as the forest, the roaring or rushing stream, the bridge). It would seem likely, moreover, that the combination had been made in romances of some sort rather a long time before the *Erec.* The *terre gaste,* for example, belongs to the story of disenchantment, but it may be a development in part from the desolate tracts familiar in the visions.

Related somewhat less directly to these groups of romances, but showing clear indebtedness to the *Erec, Meraugis de Portlesguez* of Raoul de Houdenc, written about 1200, introduces the episode of the Sparrow Hawk; and, like the knight in the Joie de la Cort, Gawain in this romance is held captive on an island near the Nameless City. The story includes the search of Meraugis for Gawain and the visit to the "Esplumeor Merlin," which he finds close to the sea on a very high inaccessible rock, where the twelve damsels in a meadow under a laurel tree utter prophecies. One of the damsels gives directions for approaching the place, and in following her guidance (by going to a chapel) Meraugis finds that there are three roads that here divide: the Road without

[197] *Libeaus Desconus,* ed. Max Kaluza (*Altengl. Bibl.* V), pp. 44–45, ll. 777ff.

[198] *Ibid.,* pp. 104ff., ll. 1861ff. (Sinadoune); pp. 72ff., ll. 1309ff. (Ile d'Or episode). Cf. the magnetized bridge in *Li Romans de Claris et Laris,* ed. Johann Alton (*Bibl. des Litt. Vereins in Stuttgart*), pp. 610ff., ll. 22713ff., which Laiz Hardiz can cross only by leaving his armor on the shore.

Mercy, the Road against Reason, and the third without name. Of these the first is the one that takes him to the Nameless City, which is near (*desoz*) a mountain by the sea, with many ships in its fine harbor. From here he goes over to the island by boat (somewhat reluctantly) to rescue Gawain, who has been kept there until a stronger knight can slay him and thus take over the control of the isle.[199] In all this the rock may recall the mountain setting of the Other World in stories of the Earthly Paradise and in visions, in particular perhaps the rock to which the griffon bears Huon of Bordeaux.[200] The island suggests Celtic antecedents; and as in the case of the Val sans Retour, we have doubtless a reflection here of the story better known as that in which Merlin is confined in the Other World by a *fée*.[201] Such a region also appears in the present romance in the enchanted garden where Meraugis falls under the spell and joins the caroling girls: [202] he

[199] *Meraugis von Portlesguez*, ed. Mathias Friedwagner (*Raoul von Houdenc, Sämtliche Werke*, I) , pp. 9ff. (Sparrow-Hawk episode); pp. 101ff., ll. 2633ff. (Esplumeor); pp. 106–107 (the roads); p. 108 (the city); pp. 113ff. (the isle and its tower, the journey).

[200] Cf. pp. 162–163 above. But see Nitze's fine article on the whole episode, *Speculum*, XVIII (1943) , pp. 69ff., suggesting a parallel in Pomponius Mela. The rock appears in the fragmentary MS 112 Bibl. Nationale: see *Die Abenteuer Gawains Ywains und Le Morholts mit den drei Jungfrauen*, ed. H. Oskar Sommer (*Beihefte zur Zeitschrift für romanische Philol.*, XLVII (1913), pp. 61ff.; cf. *Speculum*, XVIII, p. 77; *Medium Aevum*, II (1933), p. 209, (they are enticed into the "Roche aux Pucelles" — I would comment, in spite of "se voient en my la roche," they seem really to be "lassus" and can "tout entour eulx surveoir le pais."). Malory has the twelve damsels in a valley by a turret, all of which appear earlier in the same French manuscript (*Die Abenteuer Gawains*, pp. 3ff.; *The Works of Sir Thomas Malory*, ed. Eugène Vinaver, I, pp. 158ff.). The rock is not there, but the damsels are found caroling about a tree (Malory says "went to and fro by a tre") as if reflecting the episode of the carolers in *Meraugis* or a common source. The caroling and tower but no rock appear in the Huth *Merlin*: *Merlin*, ed. Gaston Paris and Jacob Ulrich, II (*SATF*, 56), pp. 232ff., and cf. Vinaver, *op. cit.*, III, p. 1350, 158.23.

[201] For the Celtic element see Brown in *Speculum*, XX (1945), pp. 426ff.; Lot in *Romania*, XXIV (1895), pp. 325ff.; Philipot, *Romania*, XXV (1896), pp. 266–267. The Merlin story one may follow further in Nitze's article already cited. Note that in the *Vengeance Raguidel* (ed. Friedwagner, p. 144) the "Castiel sans Non" is on a floating island and cf. the floating Maiden Land in *Diu Crône*, ed. Scholl, pp. 213ff., ll. 17354ff.

[202] *Meraugis*, ed. Friedwagner, pp. 143ff. See Paton, *Fairy Mythol.*, pp. 90ff., and p. 299, n. 213 below.

comes to a castle all of marble, wall and battlements, and at the tower gazes through the portal to where he sees the damsels singing and dancing about a pine tree. These he joins and cannot leave. In the development of the scene familiar in Chrétien's Joie de la Cort, then, it is abundantly clear that Raoul de Houdenc had access to much material outside of the *Erec*. Perhaps this conclusion is supported too when we notice the forked road leading to the Other World in the versions of the story according to the *Mabinogion* and Hartmann von Aue and the *Perlesvaus*, but not in Chrétien,[203] and see that here it is used again, though divided into three.

A very poor road, thorny and full of briars, takes the hero along its dark way through mountains, valleys, and forests, and ultimately to the pine which stands beside the spring and the stone in Chrétien's *Yvain*.[204] This avenue of approach would seem to derive from the *terre gaste*. The scene in such a journey to the Other World recalls a little what we have found in the *Mule sanz Frain*; and indeed it has been compared with that

[203] See above, pp. 289–290, n. 182, and p. 291, n. 188.

[204] *Kristian von Troyes Yvain*, ed. Wendelin Foerster, (*Romanische Bibl.* V), p. 20, ll. 760ff. An earlier reference suggests the motif of the crossroads here, p. 5, ll. 180ff. There the path leads him to a wooden tower with a palisade and a fosse deep and broad with its bridge (where the owner of the "fortress" meets him with a falcon on his wrist). In the other instance he spends the night at the castle; but the path, in both cases it would seem, is one that an adventurer takes in going to the region of the pine tree and the spring: once started on the path Yvain "ne finera tant que il voie/Le pin, qui la fontainne onbroie" (*ibid.*, p. 21, ll. 773–774). The castle he reaches first seems to be something of a reflection of an Otherworld scene, with its garden where Calogrenant talks with the charming damsel. The *Mabinogion* account in *Owein et Lunet* has a different path that goes through the loveliest valley in the world covered with trees all of equal size; it takes Kynon along a river of rushing waters ("aux eaux rapides," Loth, *Les Mabinogion*, II, p. 5), and he, as well as Owein somewhat later, crosses the stream and follows it along the other side (for Owein see Loth, *op. cit.*, II, p. 15). Here the castle is shining (Loth, II, p. 5, "un château fort etincelant, baigné par les flots"), with the stream about its walls, and in the hall four and twenty beautiful damsels (obviously a Maidenland). Cf. Walter Greiner, *Owein-Ivain*, (cf. *Zeits. f. celt. Philol.*, XII [1918], pp. 1–184), pp. 14–15 and 41–42. On the fortress and the shining castle as an Otherworld scene, cf. Brown in *Romanic Rev.*, III (1912), pp. 158ff.; *Publ. Mod. Lang. Assoc.*, XX (1905), pp. 698–699; *Mod. Philol.*, IX (1911–1912), p. 111. *Ywain and Gawain* and Hartmann von Aue's *Iwein* (*Hartmann von Aue, Iwein*, ed. Emil Henrici [*Germ. Handbibl.* VIII], pp. 16–17 and p. 50) keep fairly close to Chrétien's version.

and with a corresponding part of the *Wigalois* and the *Chevalier du Papegau.*[205] In the *Wigalois* the hero goes through a forest and then through a heavy black mist on a moor, and he comes to a bridge where he finds a turning wheel moved by a big stream and covered with swords and clubs;[206] in the *Chevalier du Papegau,* which was written much later (perhaps as late as the fifteenth century), we have parallel material in the journey through the Waste Land to the Chastel Perilleux, with a narrow road through trees and thorns, ("une chaucie, qui estoit moult estroite et serree d'arbres et d'espines, pres d'une montaigne bien haulte") with a terrible river which seemed nothing less than a hell, ("parfonde et lee, obscure et noire") and with a narrow bridge that vibrated when walked on, and a revolving knife-edged wheel.[207] A common source for these two romances would include the bridge and something like the knife-edged wheel. The turning castle of *Diu Crône* or that in the *Mule sanz Frain* comes to mind as a parallel; but perhaps closer than anything of that sort is the combination of the bridge and the wheel of fire in Redaction IV of the *Vision of Saint Paul.*[208] One may suspect then that the thorny road, the *terre gaste* of the *Yvain* and the other stories just considered, has a somewhat similar ancestry. Moreover, when we find the entrance to Laudine's castle so

[205] *PMLA*, XX (1905), pp. 692–693 and pp. 697ff.

[206] *Wigalois*, ed. Kapteyn, I, pp. 282ff., ll. 6714ff.; for the round palace with two towers and marble walls and the "grôziu sûl von êre" see. p. 297, ll. 7059ff. The palace is really a Maidenland: see p. 307, ll. 7296ff. Note earlier the river and the bridge with sixty swords, p. 275, ll. 6532ff. Another adventure of the type occurs when the hero is led on a forest path by a stag to the castle of fire (p. 180, ll. 4301ff.); a drawbridge must be crossed and he reaches a meadow without a wall but shut in by divine power (p. 193, ll. 4609ff.); the palace is walled with crystal (pp. 192–193). The purgatorial fire here and the respite in the meadow seem definitely to suggest influence from the visions. The meadow enclosed without a wall may echo the barrier of air in the Joie de la Cort (p. 289 above).

[207] *Le Chevalier du Papegau,* ed. Ferdinand Heuckenkamp, pp. 72–73. For the theory of a common source in a twelfth-century romance see Saran in Paul *u.* Braune's *Beiträge*, XXI (1896), pp. 336ff.; for the bridge especially, pp. 402ff. Cf. the bridge in *La Mule sanz Frain,* and see too the shaky one in Max Voigt, *Beiträge zur Geschichte der Visionenliteratur im Mittelalter,* (*Palaestra,* CXLVI), p. 168.

[208] See above pp. 92–93; cf. the bridge and the mill in the *Vision of Saint Galgano,* pp. 126–127 above.

narrow that two men or two horses could hardly enter together, and the passage at the gate so "estroiz" "Con se fust uns santiers batuz,"[209] where the sharp portcullis comes down, we may be tempted to see a reminiscence of the narrow bridge found in so many of the analogues,[210] combined, one may well believe, with a fantastic element derived from the Celtic.

The motif of the tree filled with birds singing in harmony yet with different notes would seem to be an inheritance ultimately from the Celtic, but one cannot be certain.[211] The episode at the town of Pesme Avanture, however, where the hero finds the meadow surrounded by large pointed stakes, seems to be a derivative from the story familiar in the Joie de la Cort of the *Erec*,[212] and there at least the motif of the heads and the stakes seems to come from Celtic. In the *Yvain* changes have been introduced, but none more startling than the detail of the annual tribute of thirty damsels from the King of the Isle of Damsels, so that the first impact of the place on the reader is that of a Maidenland. Three hundred maidens now sit with their embroidery within the enclosure of the stakes until some visitor comes to defeat the

[209] *Yvain*, ed. Foerster, p. 25, ll. 930–931.

[210] Brown has, of course, sufficiently pressed the case for Celtic origins here. For that side of the matter see his *Iwain*, pp. 75ff., with instances cited of the revolving barrier and the "active door." But when all his parallels are examined together, there is still something left unexplained, and I notice that regarding the portcullis Chrétien says it descended "Aussi con deables d'anfer" (*Yvain*, ed.. Foerster, p. 25, l. 944) as if even he recalled some of the visions at this point.

[211] *Yvain*, pp. 12–13, ll. 459ff. For the Celtie see above pp. 54–55, and Brown, *Iwain*, pp. 83ff.; Nitze in *Mod. Philol.*, III (1905–1906), p. 274, n. 2; and Kölbing in *Zeits. f. vergl. Litteraturgesch.*, XI (1897), pp. 442ff.; and cf. Foerster, *Yvain*, p. 182, note on ll. 465ft., and Bruce, *Evol. of Arthur. Romance*, II, pp. 77–78, n. 6. Note the example in the *Vision of Tundale* cited by Kölbing, *op. cit.*, and above p. 113; and also that in the D-interpolation of the Epistle of Prester John (Leipzig *Abhandlungen, Phil.-Hist. Cl.*, VII [1879], p. 923): ". . . et infra ipsas sunt totidem magnae arbores argenteae, uelut lucernae lucidissime lucentes, in quibus resident omnia genera auium aurearum, et unaquaeque habet colorem secundum genus suum, et sunt ita per autem musicam dispositae quod, quando Porus rex uolebat, omnes simul cantabant secundum suam naturam aut unaquaeque per se singulariter." Cf. also the bird Mass, above pp. 201–202.

[212] See Brown, *Iwain*, pp. 136ff.; Bruce, *Evol. of Arthur. Romance*, II, pp. 79–80; Foerster, *Yvain*, pp. 133ff., ll. 5155ff., and pp. xliiff.; Foerster, *Wörterbuch*, pp. 116*–117*.

diabolic creatures that hold them prisoner. One may be tempted to see the stakes here as merely a type of the so-called Belgian fence used to surround pastures; and the original Val sans Retour is somewhat obscured even considering the words of the porter (for example, "Que vos n'an istroiz or,"),[213] the scene in the garden, and the necessity of the combat.

At this point perhaps some word may be said regarding the fourteenth-century romance *Rigomer,* where Lancelot is detained in a Val sans Retour and rescued by Gawain in an episode that suggests the reverse of the story of Guinevere. In this romance one might almost say that all of Ireland becomes a Waste Land with its forests, swamps, and thickets. The castle is on an arm of the sea and protected by a river (a "canal" with enormously high banks) enclosing the country round. It is reached by a bridge of copper which is guarded by a serpent. Here one may hunt or joust and be entertained by the fairest women of a hundred realms. But when Lancelot rides onto the bridge, an alarm (a drumming that may be heard for two leagues and a half) is sounded and he has to fight for entry, which because of his wounds is delayed for a month. On that occasion he battles with the serpent and lays it low, although it revives and hurries

[213] *Yvain,* ed. Foerster, p. 135, l. 5217. Cf. also p. 134, ll. 5182–5183. What may correspond in the *Mabinogion* to the episode of the Castle of Pesme Avanture is the fight at the end to rescue the four-and-twenty ladies from the Black Man (Loth, *Les Mabinog.,* II, pp. 40ff.); but certainly in that case the version in the Welsh was never derived from Chrétien's. Cf. *Romanic Rev.,* III (1912), pp. 152–153; Greiner, *Owein-Ivain,* pp. 113ff.; and *Revue celtique* XXXIV (1913), pp. 339ff. Hartmann's version is fairly close to the French: *Iwein,* ed. Emil Henrici, pp. 294ff., ll. 6166ff. So is *Ywain and Gawain* (ed. Gustav Schleich, p. 76, l. 3010), which refers to the home of the ladies as Maidenland. The rescue of the ladies from the Black Man in the *Mabinogion* seems to be part of the story found also in *Yder,* ed. Gelzer, pp. 3ff., of the *chastel as puceles* and the Black Knight. Cf. too *Historia Meriadoci and De ortu Waluuanii,* ed. Bruce, pp. 89ff. and pp. lviiif. and lxxv, for the *chastel,* citing, among other references, Lufamour of Maydenelande in the Middle English *Sir Perceval.* To Bruce's examples add *Le Livre d'Artus,* ed. Sommer (*The Vulgate Version of Arthurian Romances,* VII), p. 323; and on the identification of the castle with Edinburgh see *Speculum,* XVII, (1942), pp. 250ff.; Loomis, *Arthurian Tradition and Chrétien de Troyes,* pp. 108ff.; and *Publ. Mod. Lang. Assoc.,* LXIII (1948), pp. 811ff. On the Castle of Maidens as a nunnery see Brown, *Origin of the Grail Legend,* p. 286 and references. For other castles of the sort see pp. 288, n. 177, and 293, n. 196, above, and p. 308 below.

after him; and when he at last gets into the place he learns that he, like others who cross the bridge, is a prisoner. Gawain goes to his rescue, however, and has many adventures along the way.

Here the bridge motif is introduced in a different way: he comes to a castle before which is a great swamp, and he has to cross a bridge four hundred feet broad at the start, but so narrow at the end one can hardly lead a horse over it. Beside it are spears and stakes for defense. Later we learn of another castle, where a knight tells how he and his wife were sitting on the bridge there when a great storm came up which drove many a bird and beast to its death and carried off his wife. We also come to a hollow mountain where ladies and knights, maids and squires, were having great joy, with the playing of musical instruments and with revelry of all kinds; the place seemed a kind of Paradise. Once Gawain, in leaving a castle, slips by a loose plank and falls through to a deep stream, where, however, a *fée* rescues him with a richly ornamented boat. He also comes to a castle before which runs a rapid stream to be crossed only by a bridge which must be lowered by enchantment. He sees a meadow in which the grass withers before strange knights, but not before him. At length, when he arrives at the Chateau de Rigomer the serpent humbles himself before the great hero, the adventure of the bridge is simple, and Lancelot is freed. But Gawain then comes to an island with a beautiful garden, to which one may cross by a metal bridge made by enchantment [214] and watched over by copper giants, a hundred archers and a hundred shooters of the arbalest, a further hundred with flails and a hundred more with hammers. Lancelot also comes to an

[214] Cf. the bridge of iron made by Merlin which leads off the island in the Huth *Merlin* (ed. Paris and Ulrich, II, p. 59), and which was not half a foot broad; also the plank that will not bear the weight of an armed man, *The Legend of Sir Lancelot du Lac*, Jessie L. Weston (*Grimm Library*, 12), p. 217, from the Dutch Lancelot. The sword bridge (of steel, only a foot wide) and the water bridge, according to the *Livre de Lancelot del Lac* (Sommer, *The Vulgate Version of the Arthur. Rom.*, IV, pp. 40–41), were made by Baudemagus to replace two narrow and feeble bridges, at the head of each of which had stood a powerful high tower. A throng, "trop grant plente de sergans et de chevaliers," guarded them and compelled people who crossed to remain in Gorre until rescued. See too the magnetized bridge in *Claris et Laris*, above p. 294, n. 198.

evil forest full of all sorts of wild beasts and serpents.[215] This vast conglomeration of borrowings and confusion of motifs needs little comment, except to note that its author was apparently so fascinated by the idea of the bridge he could not get away from it.

Both stories, that of the abducted lady and something like that of the Val sans Retour, are reflected in the *Historia Meriadoci* of the second quarter of the thirteenth century or later. Here Meriadoc goes to the assistance of the Emperor of Germany, whose daughter has been ravished away by Gundebald ("rex terre ex qua nemo reuertitur").[216] The hero fights Gundebald's army, driving it across a river into a thick forest (a narrow path leads out of it), which is vast and horrible and inhabited by wild beasts and strange phantasms. The next day he comes to a plain where once he went hunting but where now appears a remarkable building, a palace of marble and porphyry surrounded with a deep fosse and a wall. He enters, and in a banquet scene his hostess and all the banqueters and servants preserve silence. On leaving the palace with his men, Meriadoc again crosses a river (where many of his soldiers perish) and the more he tries to leave the forest the further into it he gets. A heavy thunderstorm makes him seek shelter, and he learns of a palace from which, he is told, no one ever has gone forth except in disgrace. After several adventures he continues on his way to seek the princess who is imprisoned in the chief city

[215] *Les Mervelles de Rigomer von Jehan*, ed. Wendelin Foerster (*Gesells. f. roman.* Lit., 19, with notes 39), the château described, pp. 84ff. (called "Melite" from Malta? p. 138, l. 4792; cf. 39, p. 195, *Erec*, l. 2358, and *Romania*, XXXIX [1910], pp. 83–86); the bridge, pp. 143ff.; the castle with the swamp, pp. 213ff.; the bridge of the storm, pp. 235ff.; the hollow mountain, pp. 241ff. (a paradise, p. 243, ll. 8275ff.); the sight of Rigomer and the garden of medicinal herbs, pp. 325ff.; the loose plank, p. 352ff.; the enchanted bridge, pp. 373f.; the safe entry of Rigomer, p. 409; the metal bridge and the giants, pp. 426ff.

[216] *Historia Meriadoci and De ortu Waluuani*, ed. J. D. Bruce, (*Hesperia Ergänzungsreihe* 2), pp. 25ff. (for the date see p. xxiv). On the episode in the forest see *ibid.*, pp. xxxii–xxxiii; on Gundebald's square island, pp. xxxiv–xxxv (comparing the island in the *Sone de Nansay*); and for square gardens and palaces of the Other World see Brown, *Origin of the Grail Legend*, pp. 358ff. (with examples in the visions, the Garden of Eden, Revelation, and the tower of the Grail castle, as well as in Celtic stories).

of Gundebald's realm. He has to take the test of all knights who would enter Gundebald's service: he must do battle with his enemy on one of the four causeways that lead to the square island in the Rhine, which is all marsh except for a space in the center reserved for a palace and its garden. The four causeways are guarded by castles, and the roads are so narrow that one person can not pass another on them. The island is known as the "terra de qua nemo reuertitur" because of the swamp which can support no living thing. Eventually Meriadoc throws his enemy into the marsh, where he is submerged.

In this strange narrative the forest (with its "strictam semitam") and its terrors seem to be an imaginative development out of the Val sans Retour and similar scenes in the visions; the island, on the other hand, is ultimately a Celtic derivative, one may suppose, with the swamp as a kind of *terre gaste* of the visions [217] and with the narrow causeways also reminiscent of the bridge and its guardian.

In view of the many versions of the story of the abduction to the Other World, it is impossible to suppose that Chrétien's *Roman de la Charrete* offered the first use of the plot known to medieval Europe, and prompted or guided by its direct or indirect influence all the rest. It was written to order before the *Yvain* and apparently he did not care enough about it to finish it himself. The realm of Meleaganz in the story has long been recognized as the Otherworld scene, and has been the subject in one way or another of many studies and much fruitful investigation.[218] Little perhaps needs to be said further, except for the

[217] Of course Bruce may be right in seeing the swamp merely as "a crude attempt . . . to rationalize the description of the marvellous island as the land from which no one returned" (*Hist. Meriadoci*, p. xxxiv). But the Otherworld marsh is a common motif, and here the language tempts one to attribute the passage to such a source: "Non herbas gignit, non arbores nec aliquid quod uitalem spiret animam" (*ibid.*, p. 44). Note that in Andreas Capellanus's account of the bridge, the hero drowns his opponent, p. 197 above.

[218] Particularly, of course, the superb study, *Lancelot and Guenevere* by T. P. Cross and W. A. Nitze, (*Mod. Philol. Monographs of the Univ. of Chicago*), with bibliographical suggestions in the notes, and now Loomis's *Arthurian Tradition and Chrétien de Troyes*, pp. 218ff., to which may be added Loomis, *Celtic Myth and Arthurian Romance*, for important details, and Brown, *Speculum*, XV (1940), pp. 3ff., and *Origin of the Grail Legend*,

undoubted fact that, although the plot as a whole is Celtic, certain details come from another source. Most important of these, it would appear, is the river over which the heroes cross the two bridges, a stream which has very special characteristics:

Et voient l'eve felenesse,
Roide et bruiant, noire et espesse,
Si leide et si espoantable
Con se fust li fluns au deable.[219]

Even more than the description of the river in the *Erec,* this passage sets the pattern for the description of many other rivers in later romances by authors other than Chrétien: "bruiant," "noire," "espoantable," how often these words are repeated in such lines! And the last line of the passage suggests that Chrétien himself perhaps had seen a typical account of one of these rivers in the visions. Only two words are omitted: "perilleuse" and "parfonde," and they occur in the very next line:

Et tant perilleuse et parfonde
Qu'il n'est riens nule an tot le monde
S'ele i cheoit, ne fust alee
Aussi com an la mer salee.[220]

These lines in turn suggest that if the poet had introduced something of the river of Hell, his source for the story as a whole was nevertheless at least ultimately Celtic with the voyage over the sea. If this is not pressing conjecture too far, we may then read a similar process into the history of the two bridges. The submerged plank only a foot and a half wide recalls similar planks in the visions, and the sword bridge offers the narrowness of the bridge of judgment; but both have been modified by the Celtic imagination.[221] The original story would then have

---

pp. 99ff. See, too, the reviews by Webster in *Mod. Lang. Notes,* XLVI (1931), pp. 53ff., and Krappe, *Revue celtique,* XLVIII (1931), pp. 94ff.

[219] Lines 3023–3026, *Der Karrenritter* (*Lancelot*) *und Das Wilhelmsleben* (*Guillaume d'Angleterre*), ed. Wendelin Foerster, (*Christian von Troyes Sämtliche Erhaltene Werke,* IV), p. 107.

[220] *Ibid.,* p. 108, ll. 3027–3030.

[221] Cf. the sword bridge in the vision of Gunthram, pp. 73–74 above; the

shown a trip over the sea to the abductor's Other World, which in time yielded to the idea of crossing the terrible river of the visions with the bridge of souls as the means and test — an idea long known to the Celts by Chrétien's day. The two lions, which by enchantment appear to be waiting across the sword bridge, are probably the poet's own embellishment.

For these conjectures, however, the analogues to the story do not help us much. Webster's theory that Chrétien's source showed a sort of subaqueous causeway or bridge over a bog or lake, instead of the river and the water bridge,[222] is reasonable; and it is supported by the fact that in *Durmart le Galois* the castle of Brun de Morois is surrounded by a marsh,[223] as is also Gundebald's palace on the square island in the Rhine. In *Diu Crône* Arthur finds the enemy at a ford, on the other hand, and in the romance of *Durmart* the hero crosses a bridge to come into the garden where he sees Guinevere.[224] In the *Lanzelet* of Ulrich von Zatzikhoven Valerin's misty castle is protected by a wild area (*hac*) through which no one can pierce because of the snakes and vermin there.[225] In all these cases the fact of the terrible

---

bridge small as a sword in the vision outlined by Voigt in *Palaestra,* CXLVI, pp. 167–168; the sword bridge in the story of *Kulhwch and Olwen,* Loth, *Les Mabinog.,* I. pp. 215–216; and Rhŷs, *Arthurian Legend,* pp. 54ff. And see *Romanic Rev.,* IV (1913), pp. 166ff., where, however, the distinction between the bridge of judgment and the bridge as a test has in my opinion a doubtful validity when it comes to distinguishing between sources; also Loomis, *Arthurian Tradition and Chrétien de Troyes,* pp. 222ff. Cf. E. Willson, *The Middle Eng. Legends of Visits to the Other World,* pp. 28ff. For the water bridge cf. *Mod. Lang. Rev.,* XXVI (1931), pp. 69ff. For the sword bridge in art see Loomis, *Arthur. Leg. in Med. Art,* pp. 70–71 and figs. 136 and 137. On the lions, cf. Brown, *Origin of the Grail Legend,* p. 95.

[222] *Mod. Lang. Rev.,* XXVI (1931), p. 70.

[223] See above p. 287.

[224] See above, pp. 280 and 288.

[225] *Lanzelet,* ed. K. A. Hahn, p. 118, ll. 5036ff. For the date cf. G. Ehrismann, *Gesch. der deutschen Lit. bis zum Ausgang des Mittelalters,* II, 2, 2, p. 4, (not long after 1194); *Der Lanzelet,* Werner Richter, (*Deutsche Forschungen* 27), pp. 270ff. (after 1200). There are plenty of rivers and bridges if we look elsewhere for them. In the *Lanzelet* one should note also the Maidenland, where the ladies are dressed in silk and satin, their land during the whole year in bloom, their castle fast on a crystal rock round as a ball with a strong wall and a portal of adamant: pp. 5–6; the dwelling of Mabuz, Schatel le Mort, on a smooth plain in a beautiful land, a stream about it, and a bridge which deprives one of courage: pp. 83ff.; Iweret's palace all

river "noire" and "bruiant" in the *Roman de la Charrete* (recalling perhaps that in the *Erec*) is still unexplained unless we suppose that Chrétien himself added it, preferring it to the marsh and because of the marsh motif remembering some hideous stream he had come across in the visions. Such a combination of sources might account for the strange phenomenon of the two bridges at this point.[226]

This hypothesis may seem the more likely when we notice that in the *Lanzelet*, not in the immediate neighborhood of Valerin's castle but at least entered during the journey of the hero and his companions to get help for the rescue of the queen, there is the Shrieking Moss, a place to which no horse could come, with lake and a stream from which no animal would drink, with square fish, and sometimes hot water, and giving forth a yell which causes the death of any creature. In the Moss is the house of Dodines on a rock. A Spraying Bridge (*stiebenden stege*) takes them over the river (the water is great and deep and runs swiftly), and they come to the misty lake where the dwelling of Malduc waits them wrapped in mist.[227] To this a bridge, invisible except through the aid of Malduc's daughter, leads over the water. There is enough mist in this whole picture to indicate Celtic sources. If ultimately this swamp came from the visions, it was clearly subjected to a marvelous transformation along the way by the Celtic imagination. From some such description as this Chrétien may have taken the episode of the water bridge. The idea may be regarded as implicit in the scene of the ford and just possibly in that of the invisible bridge. For the black and rushing stream, however, and the sword bridge too, the poet apparently found suggestions elsewhere. A detail like the hedge infested with serpents around Valerin's castle may

---

decorated with marble, onyx, and gold: p. 96, ll. 4091ff.; the island of beautiful women called Thîle, where the days are shorter in winter and longer in summer than here: p. 187, ll. 7994ff.

[226] Yet perhaps I should mention here the two bridges (which, swung by chains, represent a totally different arrangement) in the approach to the Grail Castle in *Diu Crône*, ed. Scholl, p. 179, ll. 14586ff.

[227] *Lanzelet*, ed. Hahn, pp. 165ff., ll. 7040ff.; Webster, *Mod. Lang. Rev.*, XXVI, pp. 71–73. For somewhat analogous scenes cf. Richter, *op. cit.*, pp. 75–76.

have reminded him of a bridge guarded by serpents like that over the boiling stream in the vision of Louis of France.[228] At any rate, although some region like the Plain of Ill Luck and the glen (with the narrow path frequented by monsters) in the *Wooing of Emer* may be related in some general way to the Shrieking Moss, we can hardly find the active Bridge of the Cliff in that story a likely antecedent for the invisible bridge or for either of the bridges in the *Charrete*.[229]

Further material from the Other World appears in Chrétien's poem in the castle of the perilous bed, which is a tower on a high rock descending in a precipice to a meadow (ll. 425ff.); in the castle of the temptation, by a river and furnished with a drawbridge, where the meal is served, but no retainers appear (ll. 986ff.); in the region of the Val sans Retour (ll. 2100ff. and cf. l. 1948); in the stony passage, through which only one horse can go at a time and two men cannot pass abreast (ll. 2170ff.); and the tower for the imprisonment of Lancelot (ll. 6132ff.). The stony passage is like the narrow paths we have encountered before, in the *Yvain*, for example,[230] except that it has a wooden tower in the middle for a guard; and one is tempted to find evidence in both scenes for an earlier version with the narrow bridge at this point of the story, which was later pushed along to where Chrétien introduced it. The imprisonment of Lancelot, a kind of reversal, as I have said, of the abduction of Guinevere, is effected in a stone tower on an island in an arm of the sea. Only one small window is left open in the structure. As with the scene in *Meraugis de Portlesguez* one may guess that, except

228 ". . . diuersi coloris serpentes drachonesque astabant undique circumcircha ac alie fere multe [ignem] ad ethera emitentes palusque plurime picis fortiter bulientis hominibus mulieribusque plene ibidem site erant fortitissime uociferantium ululantiumque. Sub ponte aqua fortiter bulientis fluminis uelocissime decurebat, in quo crudelissime bestie defluebant, que uolentem ad pontem accedere rapiebant et in fluuio submergebant," *Palaestra*, CXLVI, p. 235.

229 See above pp. 48ff.; Cross and Nitze, *Lancelot and Guenevere*, p. 75; *Romanic Rev.*, IV, p. 179, n. 25, (stressing the fact that when leaped on the bridge in the Book of Fermoy [*Rev. celtique*, XXIX, 1908, p. 119] became narrow and sharp); Brown, *Origin of the Grail Legend*, pp. 49–50 and note 36.

230 See above pp. 297f. Note the falling portcullis there and also here (ll. 2341ff.); cf. Cross and Nitze, *op. cit.*, pp. 73–74 ("the Passage of Stones — a kind of giant's causeway").

Morgan Library MS. 806. *Courtesy of the Pierpont Morgan Library*

THE SWORD BRIDGE

as such fortress islands were actually used in the Middle Ages for prisons, this detail comes from the Celtic.[231]

iv

The story of the Holy Grail itself is unrelated to that of the fairy mistress, that of the abduction of Guinevere, or that of the Val sans Retour. It is outstanding perhaps because of the fact that in its different versions it embodies to a greater or less degree the idealism of the period; and whether or not it shows at times a sentimental religiosity, or whether it is at some times more Christian than at others, it has always through its symbolic possibilities a powerful imaginative appeal. In medieval romance its position is comparable, therefore, to that which Dante's account of the Other World occupies in the field of allegory; and its influence on subsequent literature, though far less, is not without similar significance.

In Chrétien's *Contes del Graal* we find ourselves almost at once in the "gaste forest soutainne" [232] where the young hero sees the knights and thinks that they are angels. This is just one form of the *terre gaste,* if we take as pertinent the story in the *Elucidation* telling of the damsels who lived in wells, and of the violation of one of them by King Amangons,[233] and describing how the country wasted away thereafter:

> Li roiaumes si agasti
> K'ains puis n'i ot arbre fuelli;
> Li pré e les flor[s] essecierent
> Et les aiges apeticierent . . .[234]

When Perceval goes forth to his initial great experience, the birds are singing and the grass seems fairly fresh and green in

[231] See above pp. 294–295. Notice that Malduc's daughter helps Arthur to get away from the misty island in the *Lanzelet,* and here Meleaganz' sister aids Lancelot in his escape (ll. 6639).

[232] *Der Percevalroman (Li Contes del Graal),* ed. Hilka, pp. 4 and 17. Brown in *Mod. Philol.,* XXII (1924–1925), p. 122, takes "soutainne" as "under the earth." On the *gaste forest* and the *terre gaste* in general see p. 291, n. 188, and p. 293, n. 195, above.

[233] *Der Percevalroman,* ed. Hilka, pp. 418–419. Cf. the notes on ll. 29 and 32, p. 783. See Brown, *Origin of the Grail Legend,* pp. 422ff.

[234] *Der Percevalroman,* p. 419, ll. 95–98. The *Bliocadran Prologue* goes on

the region where he encounters the knights, but we find the *terre gaste* definitely indicated outside the walls of the Castle of Belrepeire. Here the land is dry, the streets deserted, the houses in ruin, the mills no longer turning, and no food available.[235] A bridge has to be crossed here so weak that one hardly thinks it will bear one safely over. The terrible river is not here, however, but, strangely enough, we do find it surrounding Gornemant's castle. It is a crossbow shot in width; it roars along ("bruit"), it is deep and black and swifter than the Loire.[236] Over it is a powerful and high bridge made of stone and of what would appear to be a mixture like concrete (sand and "chauz"). In the middle is a tower with a drawbridge. Another castle, near a forest and girt by a great river, appears much later in the poem where Gawain finds the damsel under an elm in the meadow.[237] In the same scene there is a plank used as a bridge.[238] The terrible river itself appears again not long after this episode, when Gawain rides "Par forez gastes et soutainnes" to the banks of a deep stream so broad that no one could shoot across with slingshot or crossbow. On the other side on a cliff is the marble castle of maidens on a conspicuous rock. Eventually Gawain crosses over by the ferryman's boat.[239] The castle itself he visits the next day; the palace entrance is high, the portals rich and fair; one gate is of ivory and one of ebony,[240] well carved and adorned with gold and precious stones. Within is the Perilous Bed, an excellent motif as here developed, one would think, to appear in this setting of Maidenland. Along with the other

---

with the story of Perceval's father and how he was killed near the *Gaste Fontaine*, *ibid.*, p. 433, l. 123.

[235] *Ibid.*, pp. 75ff., ll. 1699ff.

[236] *Ibid.*, pp. 57ff., ll. 1305ff. For the reference to the Loire Hilka compares *Mule sanz Frain*, l. 392 (*ibid.*, p. 647, n. 1316).

[237] Pp. 297ff., ll. 6664ff.

[238] Pp. 300–301, ll. 6726ff. Cf. Brown, *Origin of the Grail Legend*, p. 136.

[239] Pp. 323ff., ll. 7224ff. On the river (as all that remains of the sea in the Celtic) cf. Loomis, *Romania*, LIX (1933), pp. 557ff., admitting contamination in the transmission of the stories, a point that is clear in those which have the bridge or the causeway. On the palace cf. the notes in the *Percevalroman*, ed. Hilka, p. 757. See too Brown, *Origin of the Grail Legend*, pp. 132 ff. and *passim.*; Loomis, *Celtic Myth and Arthurian Romance*, pp. 165ff.; Loomis, *Arthurian Trad. and Chrétien de Troyes*, pp. 448ff.; and p. 299, n. 213 above.

[240] Cf. the gates of horn and ivory in the *Aeneid*, see above pp. 21–22.

ornaments the bed has carbuncles on the posts, which shed as much light as four tapers. The windows of the palace are painted with the richest of colors and the best that one can imagine. Thus Otherworld material of different kinds is scattered through the whole poem, the dark river here and the bridge there, attached to various scenes (as in the case of Gornemant's castle, where Otherworld associations are slight) as if consistency no longer mattered or had meaning to the poet.[241]

One may be cautious, therefore, in seeing much significance in the arrangement of the details of the Grail Castle and its surroundings. The poet has, however, clearly taken special pains with it. As Perceval approaches, we are told, he comes to a rough and deep stream ("roide et parfonde") below a height (*angarde*). A rock stops him from going along the shore, but he sees the men in the boat and gets directions from them. The stream, the fisherman tells him, has no bridge or ford. He must get over the rock and then he will see a place to lodge. When he has followed their advice and stands on a hill (*pui*), he does see a valley where there is a tower of dark stone with two turrets, and then he makes out the hall and the *loges* of the castle. It has a drawbridge, which is down and which he can cross. Within the castle in a square hall he sees the "bel prodome" and the sword, the lance, and the grail. On his way out he has trouble at the drawbridge where somebody raises the bridge and his horse leaps across with him just in time.[242] In the whole description we may note that we do not have an extreme form of the Otherworld setting. The river around Gornemant's castle shows its origin much more clearly; the *terre gaste* and the bridge at Belrepeire

[241] Note the motif of the hill and the damsel, p. 211, ll. 4705ff.; also the tree stripped of leaves and the damsel, pp. 290–291; also the Ford Perilous, pp. 380ff. (cf. above p. 293, n. 195).

[242] *Ibid.*, pp. 133ff., ll. 2985ff. For the leap at the bridge see p. 153, ll. 3402ff., and cf. above p. 50, n. 50. The episode is like that of the falling portcullis in the *Yvain*, the experience of a sudden obstacle at the entrance to the Other World; and, coincidence or not, it does a little suggest the Celtic use of the bridge. Cf. that in Wauchier's continuation, ll. 28825ff. (*Perceval*, ed. Potvin, IV, pp. 286ff.); and for further comment see Hilka's note, *Percevalroman*, p. 674, 3065ff.; *Publ. Mod. Lang. Assoc.*, XXIV (1909), pp. 375–376; and Paton, *Fairy Mythology*, p. 85, n. 3 (on "dangerous bridges," the one she refers to as *Perc.*, ll. 28411, is really the bridge of glass).

have far more definite qualities of the approach to the eery country. In fact the Grail castle and its landscape might seem to have been taken from the description of almost any medieval stronghold of the sort, with a river near by and a drawbridge over its moat, except for the fact that at this late date no serious scholar is likely to have much doubt that at least in part it is a development of another kind.[243] In the poem in general only the terrible river, the bridge motif, and the waste land, show clearly some influence of a tradition from the visions or the Orient; the Grail castle, on the other hand, could be almost purely Celtic except for the stream, which, however, does not serve as a barrier.

In the Pseudo-Wauchier continuation, the castle has a different setting and is reached by a long and wide causeway darkened by overhanging branches of trees and running out into the sea.[244] But this idea seems not to be sustained later in the Wauchier continuation, where Perceval comes to a river "Moult roide et moult fort et moult fière." [245] It is too wide to cross ("Si estoit si lars li rivages"), except by boat. Here, he remembers, he found the Fisher King. Eventually boatmen take him over the stream and the master pilot shows him the road to the King's castle. This is clearly a reminiscence of Chrétien. So too, it would seem, is the description in the Didot *Perceval*, where as the hero rides along he comes to a very beautiful meadow and a river (in

[243] The literature on the subject is vast, but one should certainly consult Nitze, *The Castle of the Grail — an Irish Analogue*, in *Studies in Honor of A. Marshall Elliott*, I, pp. 19ff.; Brown, *Origin of the Grail Legend*, pp. 116ff. and 358ff.; Loomis, *Celtic Myth and Arthur. Romance*, pp. 158ff., and "'Chastiel Bran,' 'Dinas Bran,' and the Grail Castle," in *A Miscellany of Studies in Romance Languages and Literatures*, pp. 342ff. Brown's theory (*op. cit.*, p. 117) that the "Castle of Maidens occurs five times" in the poem, in other words that the Otherworld pattern of that motif was thus distributed in the several castles, would serve to explain the scattering of that material in such a way.

[244] *Perceval*, ed. Potvin, III, pp. 362ff., ll. 19961ff. Brown finds it "a euhemerization of a castle beneath the waves" [*Kittredge*] *Anniversary Papers*, p. 247. Note the causeway and the entry between two rocks in *Sone de Nansay* (*Sone von Nausay*, ed. Goldschmidt, ll. 4331ff). On the *Sone de Nansay* see *Zeits. f. d. Alt.*, XLIV (1900), pp. 327ff.; *Romania*, XXXV (1906), p. 564; *Romania*, XLIII (1914), pp. 403ff.

[245] *Perceval*, IV, p. 73, l. 22296. Cf. V, p. 139, ll. 34611ff.

this case "molt bele") with a windmill. In the river is a boat with three men. One of these, it appears, the Fisher King, calls to him and gives him directions to get to his dwelling. Perceval rides on along the river until he sees the top of a tower between two mountains, and finally he comes to the castle where he finds the river flowing round it. The drawbridge is down and he enters.[246] All this seems to be really a borrowing, although the terrible river is now "bele" and we have the mill introduced as if the scene depends ultimately on a much modified description of the river and the wheel barrier we have found elsewhere.[247] Dependent rather on the Didot *Perceval* than on Chrétien, the scene in the *Perlesvaus* shows the river (*clere et large*) in a fair meadow (*molt bele*), the boat with two knights and another knight lying prone (and a different one, apparently, who is fishing), and the Grail castle beyond a mountain round which the river has its course.[248] In both of the prose works a forest lies beyond the meadow, and that in this story may quite possibly represent the Waste Land.[249] The most striking change in the *Perlesvaus*, however, is in the addition of three bridges: one a bow shot in length and not more than a foot in breadth called the "Bridge of the Needle" ("le Pont del Aguille"); one feeble and thin, a bridge of ice; and one with columns of marble all about.[250] The first bridge gets broader when Gawain rides on it, and the feeble one is stronger. We are now told that there are three streams here of which one is certainly "grant et parfonde

[246] The Didot-*Perceval*, ed. William Roach, pp. 205–206. Cf. pp. 80ff. ("all clearly borrowed from Chrétien"); but see J. L. Weston, *The Legend of Sir Perceval* (*The Grimm Library*), II, pp. 215ff.

[247] See above, p. 297.

[248] *Perlesvaus*, ed. Nitze and Jenkins, I, pp. 166–167, ll. 3626ff. Cf. *ibid.*, II, p. 91. For the landscape see also I, p. 91, ll. 1689–1690. Here we learn that the castle is surrounded with a great wall; a lion is chained to the wall at the entry; two automata, men of copper with crossbows, guard the place.

[249] Cf. the motif clearly marked, *ibid.*, I, pp. 122–123, ll. 2528ff., and p. 136, ll. 2856ff. See II, pp. 244–245.

[250] *Ibid.*, I, pp. 113ff., ll. 2289ff. Cf. II, pp. 100 and 261–262. This scene, like all the rest, appears again in the Welsh *Y Seint Greal* (*Selections from the Hengwrt MSS*, ed. Robert Williams, I, pp. 594–595). Here the second and third bridges seem to be of ice. The first here is called the "Bridge of the Eel." See Rhŷs, *Arthurian Legend*, pp. 56, 59, and 276. One may suspect that the *Perlesvaus* should read "Pont del Anguille."

et rade." The whole scene suggests a combination of material from the visions and from the Celtic.[251]

The corresponding scene of river and castle in *Diu Crône* was hardly taken from Chrétien, but it is not wholly unlike what he describes, a fact suggesting that there was a common ancestor for the idea of the terrible river and the bridge along with the Grail castle. According to Heinrich's poem, Gawain passes through a Waste Land, has various experiences, and approaching the Grail castle comes to a stream in which he is almost lost, although he is rescued by a *fée*. In front of the castle are two bridges hung from chains; and when Gawain climbs on the first it is lowered so that he can enter. The ditch round the place is so wide one cannot call across it, and the castle has four high towers and two portals.[252] Here the differences from the account in the *Contes del Graal* do not seem to be changes introduced into the framework of the French story so much as variations that come from a common original. Almost as remote from Chrétien in some respects is the corresponding scene in Wolfram's *Parzival*. In Book V we read how the hero has ridden over fallen trees and swamp (*mos*) when, at evening, he comes to a lake (*se*) in which fishermen have anchored. One of these tells

[251] With the bridge of ice compare Wauchier's glass bridge two and a half feet broad, *Perceval*, ed. Potvin, IV, pp. 273–276, ll. 28411ff. The river here is "rade et pérellouse/Et moult parfonde et mervellouse" and, seen through the glass, rushes like a tempest. Note the bridge of ice in the *Voyage of Maeldúin*, p. 32 above, and other Celtic bridges, pp. 52f. above.

[252] *Diu Crône*, ed. Scholl, p. 173, ll. 14110ff., the Waste Land (neither grass nor corn grows there); pp. 177ff., ll. 14410ff., the stream, the castle, the bridges. In *Sone de Nansay* the castle has four towers (ed. M. Goldschmidt, *Bibl. des Litt. Vereins in Stuttgart*, CCXVI, ll. 4381ff.) There is considerable Otherworld material in *Diu Crône*: see the river barrier in the deep mountain stream with rolling rocks on the approach to Amurfina's home, pp. 98ff., ll. 7964ff.; the palace with crystal wall on a rock, ll. 14267ff.; the house of Frau Saelde, p. 192, ll. 15664ff. (all jewels and crystal, with a carbuncle to light the place); the floating island which is Maiden Land and which acts like a ferry for Gawain, pp. 213ff., ll. 17354ff. (cf. p. 289, n. 180, above; and the Turning Island in *Lestoire del Saint Graal*, in *The Vulgate Version of the Arthurian Romances*, ed. Sommer, I, pp. 114ff.); the wonderful castle on a high mountain by a broad river, pp. 247–248, ll. 20102ff.; the experience of Gawain and his companions, covered over by a mountain, when they see the stream in which the knight and the damsel are pulled along in a boat by a swan, pp. 325ff., ll. 26367ff.; the mountain, forest, river, and bridge (covered by the stream when it overflows), pp. 339ff., ll. 27489ff.

him to ride to the end of the cliff, and then when he reaches the moat to call for the lowering of the drawbridge. Parzival takes the right path and carries out the instructions. The castle, he finds, has many towers and many palaces.[253] It stands there as if it was turned on a lathe, round and smooth. The general outline of all this seems close to the French, but the region of the fallen trees and the swamp, a kind of Waste Land, and the lake too, happen to find a much closer parallel in the *Peredur*. In the Welsh the hero comes to a great desert forest at the edge of which is a lake.[254] Here are the venerable man and his attendants who are fishing in the lake. On the other side is a castle where Peredur spends the night. The next day he goes forth; again he comes to a deserted wood; and at its edge is a meadow and the castle where the bleeding lance and the salver are shown to him. Here the details of the setting seem spread over two episodes; but in both the *Peredur* and in Wolfram we have the Waste Land and the lake, and these in both stories are entirely independent of anything that has to do with the *gaste citée* at Pelrapeir[255] or (whichever may be its equivalent) the Welsh castle of many towers or that of the nine sorceresses.[256] In other words, one may

[253] *Wolframs von Eschenbach Parzival und Titurel*, ed. Ernst Martin, (*Germanistische Handbibl.* IX, 1–2), I, pp. 79–80, 224, ll. 19ff. That it is "round and smooth" we infer from "Si stuont reht als si wære gedræt" (226, l. 15). See the translation *ibid.*, II, p. 210 (226, l. 16). Cf. Sister Mary A. Rachbauer, *Wolfram von Eschenbach*, Cath. Univ. *Studies in German*, IV), pp. 134 ff.

[254] Loth, *Les Mabinogion*, II, pp. 56ff. Further Otherworld material appears in the Round Valley, *ibid.*, II, pp. 77–78; the valley and river with white sheep on one side and black sheep on the other, II, pp. 87–88; the lofty mountain and castle with the prisoner maiden, II, p. 97.

[255] *Parzival*, ed. Martin, I, pp. 64ff., 183, ll. 19ff. (confined mostly to hunger); the swinging bridge without a rope, *ibid.*, I, p. 63, 181, ll. 3ff. If there is an implication of Celtic influence in this argument, I should not dispute the evidence for oriental material in the *Parzival*: for example, in the details of the Schastel Marveile, see Paul Hagen, *Der Gral*, (*Quellen und Forschungen*, 85,) p. 5; cf. Brown, *Origin of the Grail Legend*, p. 193; the shining pillar, *Parzival*, ed. Martin, p. 209, 589, ll. 5ff., and Prester John, ed. Zarncke, Leipzig *Abhandlungen, Phil.-Hist. Cl.*, VII (1879), p. 919, 67ff.; and on columns in general, see above pp. 32, 35, 149, 176 n. 3, 208, etc., and cf. *Publ. Mod. Lang. Assoc.*, XXXIII (1918), p. 626.

[256] Loth, *Les Mabinog.*, II, pp. 62ff. (the castle of many towers, reached through a desert wood, vegetation grows high at its entrance); *ibid.*, II, pp. 69ff. (the nine sorceresses).

here suspect that Wolfram and the author of *Peredur* had access to some other tradition than that of the *Contes del Graal.*

When the evidence is so necessarily tenuous in this whole problem, it may be rash to leap to any conclusions at all, but one or two would seem sufficiently secure to be formulated. One is that Chrétien himself knew the motif of the terrible river and the bridge, and used it from time to time in his works where he thought it effective. We cannot be sure then that he introduced it in any particular story because it was in that particular source, and yet when we find it in early analogues we may suspect that such is the case. Another is that material from Chrétien was spread by imitation among various writers, who, however, seem to have had access to other forms of the Grail story as well. In view of the variety here and the apparent lines of direct influence it seems folly any longer to hold that Chrétien's version was the first. It is clear too that if the early Celtic narrative that lies behind the Grail quest included a voyage over the sea to the Grail castle,[257] the river was introduced later and with it the bridge from vision literature, whether in Celtic documents or others before Chrétien. The influence of vision literature and perhaps too an inheritance from the Germanic seem extensive in these matters, and also in the motif of the dark valley or swampy region and probably too in the Waste Land.

By the thirteenth century it is clear that Otherworld material has become so widely known and so generally used that the motifs have become mixed in character at times and traces of the origin are almost entirely obscured. This is true of much that may be found in the Vulgate prose romances, for example in the deserted valley, the island of high rock, the bird motif, the mist, the mountain, the stream, and the black cloud and the dark valley, all in the *Estoire del Saint Graal.*[258] Or take the adven-

[257] In late versions of the story note Lancelot's approach by boat in the *Aventures del Saint Graal*, ed. Sommer, *Vulgate Version of the Arthurian Romances*, VI, p. 178; *Selections from the Hengwrt MSS*, ed. Robert Williams, I, *Y Seint Greal*, p. 535; Perceval departs in a boat at the end of the *Perlesvaus*, ed. Nitze and Jenkins, I, p. 408; in *Sone de Nansay*, the castle is on an island, ed. M. Goldschmidt, ll. 4327ff.

[258] *Vulgate Version of Arthurian Romances*, ed. Sommer, I, pp. 150ff.

ture of the "gaste capele" in the *Chevaliers as Deus Espees,* where the damsel rides on a mule through the forest and by thorns and bushes, into a dark rocky region where bears and lions roar, a heavy storm blows, and a broad flame shoots up in front of her apparently to the sky, suggesting a confused form of the *terre gaste* and certainly an Otherworld neighborhood. Later we have the island motif, the ship that conveys a lamenting throng, and the Vale Perilous hard to enter.[259] This sort of general combination is what became the heritage for a later period. In Christopher Middleton's *Chinon of England,* for example, we have the cave of the woman-faced serpent, the dark forest, the flight motif, and the cloven rock hiding Cassiopeia, and closing to shut her from sight.[260] The various elements are now stage properties for romance, to be shifted about at will. How much is traditional and how much is new invention it would often be hard to say.

On the other hand, a remarkably consistent picture of an Otherworld scene, in which the traditional elements can be established with some ease, is found in *Arthur of Little Britain,* a prose romance translated by Lord Berners from the fourteenth-century French.[261] Here the Castle of Porte Noyre, "ordeyned by proserpyne, who was on of the quenes of the fayry," shows many of the familiar motifs:

(deserted valley); pp. 89ff. (island of high rock); pp. 117ff. (bird motif); p. 109 (mist); pp. 149 and 165 (mountain); pp. 219–220 (the stream and valley). Does the floating turning island here (pp. 114ff.) derive from a floating Maidenland like that in *Diu Crône* or from the turning castle, or from both? Note (p. 116), no vegetation or animals could live there and "toutes les fois que li firmamens tourne lille tourne ausi. . . ."

[259] *Li Chevaliers as Deus Espees,* ed. Wendelin Foerster, pp. 16ff., ll. 441ff.; pp. 22ff. (the forest and rocks); p. 89, ll. 2798ff. (the realm of the Isles); p. 132 (the Castel du port with waste lands all around); p. 196, ll. 6316ff. (the ship); p. 360, ll. 11680ff. (the Vale Perilous).

[260] *The Famous Historie of Chinon of England,* ed. W. E. Mead, (*EETS,* 65), pp. 23ff. (cave, cf. p. 26); p. 25 (deep, dark valley with serpents); pp. 40–41 (flight); pp. 47ff. (the rock with company of fair creatures).

[261] I have used the copy in the Henry E. Huntington Library: "The Hystory of the moost noble and valyaunt knyght Arthur of lytell brytayne, translated out of frensche into englushe by the noble Johan bourghcher knyght lorde Barners, newly Imprynted." See Loomis, *Celtic Myth and Arthur. Romance,* pp. 172ff. For the Castle of Porte Noyre see ff. xiv vo. and xlv vo.

A great river ran around the castle with banks so high the water could hardly be seen. It ran so "rudely" that whoever entered it perished. It was blacker than "smythy Water" and "smelled abhomynably." It was full of sharp rocks swarming with vermin. Adjoining the river were mountains too high to climb and so bare and hard the birds could get no sustenance. Among them was a passage the width of a chariot and defended at places with barbicans; and below the mountains was a great and foul marsh into which no one could go without perishing, but a passage the width of a spear led through it with thirty drawbridges. So the castle was protected by the circle of marsh, then that of the mountains, and then that of the river, and it also had double walls of chalk and sand reinforced with bars and crampons of iron and steel fixed in lead. A hundred towers were there chained and knit together with iron. And before the gates of the castle and a little higher on the hill were palace, halls, and chambers with strong battlements. On Mount Perilous, on the side of which the castle was located, was a rich pavilion with a gold eagle in the top.

When Arthur visited the place he first came to the river hideous "depe and perfound," where the water "rored and brayed" and ran so swiftly none could pass without drowning. He followed a path along the bank, and then at high noon he came to a "streyght waye" between two mountains and found a narrow bridge over the river. A causeway of stone took him over the marsh. At the castle bridge he met twelve knights, six at each end, and at the gate twelve more holding axes and maces. The bulwarks were guarded by men with crossbows. After battling his way into the place, Arthur entered the palace, which was set with images of fine gold and windows of amber. Here was a chamber the richest ever seen, painted with gold and azure and displaying in fresh colors how God did create the sun and the moon. In the roof were all the seven planets wrought with gold and silver and the constellations marked with carbuncles and precious stones, which shone by day and night. Here were wonderful beds, and one in particular set with gold and precious stones and with pipes at the corners to convey perfume. At the head of the bed was an image of gold with an ivory bow and arrow of silver; at each corner an image of gold with a horn of silver. When Arthur lay on the bed, he was threatened by lions, and the images blew their horns and the bowman shot his bow. Terrible things happened including the appearance of a giant clad in a serpent skin, and the entrance of a burning spear that had to be dodged. The palace revolved like a wheel and Arthur embraced in his arms the images of gold at the head of the bed which did not move. Later he went along a dark gallery to the pavilion on Mount Perilous and encountered two men of copper with flails.

In all this we recognize the familiar barriers in the mountains, the marsh, and the river. The little narrow bridge and the drawbridge of the castle with its defenders represent the same motif, and when the defenders fall, we discover they fall "into the river." The rich chamber with the illumination of the carbuncles is nothing very new.[262] The turning castle in various ways recalls the scene in the *Pèlerinage de Charlemagne,* where we find the youths with horns, and similar material in *Diu Crône* and the *Mule sanz Frain.*[263] It also shows certain points of resemblance to the Grail castle as we see it in Chrétien's poem and the Didot *Perceval;* but in contrast to the description of the setting in those works the curious fact is that in *Arthur of Little Britain* with each motif the values are much intensified. The mountains are higher, the marsh is fouler, the river more stinking than we remember they were in earlier accounts. It seems almost as if this author had freshly consulted the visions and mythological documents himself.

The romances then show a considerable use of Otherworld motifs with derivatives apparently from every source. The voyage appears in the lay of *Guigemar,* and also in such romances as *Partonopeus, Florimont,* and *Floriant et Florete.* The island, both in forms remote and in others near at hand, is familiar in the many instances of Avalon, in the Nameless City of *Meraugis de Portlesguez* and in the *Vengeance Raguidel.* The river barrier is used over and over again, as for example in the lays of *Guingamor, Lanval,* and *Graelent,* and the romances *Erec, Lancelot,* and the *Contes del Graal* of Chrétien de Troyes. When it is described as roaring and deep, in a word when it is what we have called the terrible river, it seems to go back to the motif in the visions and in Eastern literature or that in Old Norse. When

[262] Cf. the chamber of Prester John in a fourteenth-century account, Leipzig *Abhandlungen, Phil.-Hist. Cl.,* VII (1879), p. 167, § 35: "Et ibi prope est dormitorium presbiteri Iohannis, mirae pulchritudinis . . . . et ibidem est sol et luna cum septem speris planetarum, tenentes cursus suos ut in coelo, et hoc est artificialiter factum." On the automata see Loomis, *op. cit.,* p. 175, and above pp. 282f., n. 159.

[263] See above, pp. 277ff.

it is less fearsome, one is tempted to see it as merely a substitute for the stream with a ford or the more extensive water barrier from Celtic, but even in such a case one can hardly be sure. Oriental influence was easily available, as one may see from the story in the *Historia septem sapientum* and the motifs in *Floire et Blanceflor*. The same thing may be said of the bridge. The active forms suggest Celtic transmission, and yet one may see possibilities of a different source in the story quoted earlier from William of Malmesbury or that in the *Disciplina clericalis*. On the whole, the evidence for the borrowing of both bridge and stream from the tradition of the visions, which had great popularity in the twelfth century, is considerable.

The motif of the Other World on top of the mountain is apparently rather less extensive here than in allegory. Something like it may appear in the location of the Grail castle and Wolfram's Munsalvæsch. The hollow hill, as derived from the Celtic, is found in the dialogue of the *Cristenmon and a Jew*, the story of the *Adulterous Falmouth Squire*, *Gawain and the Green Knight*, and elsewhere. The cave motif or the hollow mountain seems rather more widely spread, as in the stories of William of Malmesbury, Walter Map, Giraldus Cambrensis, and others. Mount Etna becomes the scene at times, and perhaps was the setting for a story that lies behind the romances of *Guerino*, *La Salade*, and *Melusine*. In general, this idea seems closer to the motif as we find it in Germanic literature than it does to anything Celtic or the wider underground realm of Hades.

The Waste Land motif takes several forms. Sometimes it is the wild forest, as in the *Gaste Forest* of the *Contes del Graal* or in a similar scene in *Brun de la Montaigne*; sometimes it is a devastated region as in the *Contes del Graal* (in the country about Belrepeire) and in the *Perlesvaus*; and sometimes it seems to appear in the swampy tracts that serve as obstacle to the hero's approach to an Otherworld castle. Probably it derives from more than one source, the visions in one instance and a Celtic equivalent in another. The swamp in *Arthur of Little Britain* with its pools of water, as if, the author says, it were an arm of the sea, may go back to something like the Shrieking Moss of the *Lanzelet* with its lakes and causeway, and both may represent an earlier ocean scene replaced in part by a similar region familiar in the visions. It may also presumably have a reminiscence of marshy land at Glastonbury in the rainy season, or of some other actual scene.[264] The dark valley "sans Retour" seems to suggest a development from the visions or from Old Norse. On the other hand, one may not trace these borrowings with too much confidence, for coincidence may obviously have a part in all these imaginary scenes. But even if in such parallels we have nothing more than the operation of chance, the examples are so numerous that we can learn something here about the human imagination and symbolism as well as about romantic literature.

The problem of sources must always be more complicated than a general survey can indicate. The possibility that an author has added a completely new element out of sheer inventiveness must be especially great in the field of medieval romance, and the chances that this will happen to duplicate something already familiar are considerable. Browning's *Childe Roland to the Dark Tower Came* gives us a complete journey to the Other World: the "sudden little river" is here with its "black eddy"; here too is a bit of "stubbed ground, once a wood," and then a marsh; a bird to serve as guide; the two hills and the mountains; and the round squat tower, where Roland blows the horn. Is the poem actually based on a tower and a painting Robert Browning saw? Or if so, was the painting in turn based on old stories and old motifs which derive, like the poem's title, from the tradition we have been following? The case is clear with another poetic work, T. S. Eliot's *Waste Land*, for there the dryness and the rocks are certainly taken from the *terre gaste* of the Grail stories, as the author himself has told us. If then allegory and romance represent frequently the debris of old religions, we see here the interesting return from such aridity to the religious point of view in Eliot's *Ash Wednesday*, where we find the Otherworld garden along with the desert, the ladder, and the fountain.

[264] Cf. the suggestion that the *Sone de Nansay* reflects Norse scenery, (*Romania*, XXXV [1906], p. 564). Cf. too the "point perilous" in *Libeaus Desconus*, ed. Kaluza, ll. 202 and 306, and J. A. Robinson, *Two Glastonbury Legends*, pp. 1ff. and 25–27 (the French has the Ford Perilous); Loomis on the Grail Castle in *Misc. of Studies*, p. 350; also p. 263, n. 104 above.

CONCLUSION

IN THE PAGES PRECEDING we have taken many journeys to the mysterious realm, and "many goodly states and kingdoms seen." When we follow one account with another, in which there is such profusion of detail, however, it cannot be denied that an element of monotony creeps in almost inevitably from the sheer fact of repetition. This is the country, we read, that inspired some of the poetry of Spenser and Milton and attracted even Christopher Columbus in his excursion to the new world. Even so, while the accounts show a great variety, they have yet a marked similarity in their method of telling. The same motifs are there time after time; and perhaps after a while our wonder wears thin as we see the island, the hill, the mountain, the river, and all the other familiar patterns of scenery. Perhaps there is some advantage in getting to know the geography of the Other World so well, but some of the novelty will be missing when we visit the place in this or another life.

Almost all the possible motifs were present in the literature of oriental and classical mythology. The island receives rather more emphasis in Greek and Roman culture; and perhaps, the mountain, certainly the river and the bridge, play a greater part in Eastern religion. In particular the river, black and gloomy with fetid water, receives a special quality in the Persian and Moslem accounts that makes it easier to identify, even when we find it later flowing less conspicuously in the West. The bridge too, guarded by dogs, and narrow for the wicked but growing broader for the righteous, has a character that stays with it in a different context. The lower world, familiar especially in Egyptian culture and in the conception of Hades or Avernus, is a vaguer idea but may be seen in the Gilgamesh Epic and perhaps too in the hollow mountain found sometimes in Greek references to Olympus. All this material from the East was transmitted in the vision literature of the Middle Ages, where we find notably the mountain, the river, the bridge, the lower world, and the deep dark valley or marshy tract; and in the description of the Earthly Paradise, where we have the island, the mountain, and the garden with four rivers.

A rather different tradition presents itself in Celtic literature, but here we have characteristically the island and the hollow hill. In addition we find Under-the-Wave Land and also several active bridges, which, however, apparently from the play of the Celtic imagination, differ enough from one another to escape from any precise category. In Old Norse, on the other hand, there are: the lower-world realm of Hel, the mountain sometimes found hollow, the river identified by its terrible quality, perhaps in the appearance of mist or fire, the great bridge spanning its breadth, the barrier of fire, and the gloomy forest. Both Celtic and Old Norse show the barrier of mist; and it is probably doubtful whether the cave motif in the twelfth century derives from the hollow hill of the Celts, the hollow mountain of Old Norse, the realm of Hel, or the lower world in Eastern literature.

The journey to the Other World may be taken on foot or on horseback or muleback, with a guide like the Archangel Michael or the eagle of the *House of Fame*. It is often a voyage like that of Odysseus, that of Bran, and again that of Saint Brendan, and the journeys to the Earthly Paradise. Behind all this may lie the actual excursions of missionaries to remote places, or again the idea of the funeral barge as it is reflected in *Beowulf*, in the story of Arthur, and perhaps in that of Elaine. Boat burial is itself a reflection of the folklore motif. Sometimes the journey is a flight, like that with wings or a car in the *Rig Veda*, the ascent through the spheres of Scipio Africanus, or the trip in the chariot of griffons of Alexander the Great. Occasionally a ladder or some steps may be required as in the *Vision of Perpetua* or the story of Gunthelm. Crossing the barrier to the strange country may sometimes suggest the risk of death as in Gawain's and Lancelot's experiences at the river and also in the whole idea of the *Val sans Retour*.[1] The return sometimes involves an awareness of the

[1] Note the curious symbolism, suggesting the span of life, in the bridge of forty-five planks with the leopard and the serpent in the *Livre de Lancelot* (ed. Sommer, *The Vulgate Version of the Arthur. Rom.*, IV, pp. 23ff.).

great passage of time during the period spent in the Other World, as in the *Voyage of Bran* and the *Pantheon* of Godfrey of Viterbo.

In tracing the history of any one of the different elements, it is easier to point out difficulties in the interpretation of evidence than it is to establish clear indebtedness. The phrasing of the descriptions falls sometimes into the use of formulae, like the negative expression such as "There shall be no night" – no ice, no snow, no excessive heat – or the recurrent adjectives for the river "rushing," "roaring," "black," and "deep," which suggest proof of immediate borrowing but, as we have seen, are common enough to spring from coincidence or general use. Furthermore, it is always possible that the author of some account in particular has turned to local scenery for fresh detail, as one may suspect that the gardens familiar in the literature of Courtly Love were reinforced, or as the landscape at Glastonbury may have influenced medieval romance. Free invention, too, based on similar elements in human psychology, may explain some resemblances. Yet when due allowance is made for all these very real factors, there are still so many cases indicating a common use of material (and the formation of special traditions with a consequent interplay of influence) that some attempt at an analysis and classification seems justified.

The island motif is all but universal, and, perhaps because of Celtic influence, appears even in the Germanic tradition. In European literature, on the whole, one would expect to find it probably as a heritage from the Celts, especially when a story such as that of Huon of Bordeaux has to do with a succession of visits to a number of different regions somewhat in the manner of the Irish *imram*. But with the spreading of classical influence one must depend for certainty in such matters on other features of the plot. The hollow hill, it would seem, almost certainly comes from the Celts, and may reappear somewhat transformed and extended in the idea of the hollow mountain. For the most part, however, the mountain itself, whether its Other World is hidden within or lifted to the skies at its top, would seem to derive from Old Norse or the visions and the literature from the

East. It is found again and again in allegory; and as what may be called a natural symbol for the inaccessible and the difficult (as indeed the island is too) it may of course be only the subject of free invention. Sometimes it appears with more than one peak; sometimes it is situated only in the neighborhood of the Other World as if surviving only as a reminiscence. Sometimes too a well-known mountain like Stromboli or Etna, stirred people to the creation of legends only in small part, if at all, dependent on the Otherworld tradition. The river is another natural symbol (for there is usually in life "one more river to cross") and may come from the everyday experience of travelers or from some castle's moat; but when it shows the special and terrifying characteristics it has, for example, in the *Livre du Cuer d'Amours Epris* of the King René or in the *Mule sanz Frain* we may well believe that it comes from the visions and from Eastern literature. The river in this guise seems rather commoner in romance than in allegory, where in most cases the stream flows along rather pleasantly as if it issued from the garden of the *Roman de la Rose*.

The bridge may derive in some forms from the Celtic, but when we find it crossing the terrible river it is almost certainly borrowed, directly or ultimately, from another tradition. When its narrowness is emphasized, we may properly assume, I believe, that it comes from the type of bridge known to Gregory the Great or Gregory of Tours. When, moreover, we are told that it became broader as the hero set foot upon it, as was the case with the "Bridge of the Needle" in the *Perlesvaus*, we may be sure that the tradition of this motif not only goes back to one Gregory or the other, but was amplified by fresh contacts somewhere along the line directly or indirectly with Eastern culture. The active bridge, on the other hand, may well come from early Celtic documents or storytelling; and one may add that, since the visions appeared also in Irish, the oriental type of bridge became Celtic property too at least by the eleventh century in the *Vision of Adamnán* (where we have the broadening type as also in the *Legend of Saint Patrick's Purgatory*). In Irish too the ford and the causeway over swampy land made the transition easy to the ordinary type of bridge, which in turn might derive something from the visions or Germanic ideas or from the East,[2] but as an element in the plot went back to Celtic origins. The drawbridge of any castle could also replace such a structure or be subject to the same change.

The castle or palace of the Other World is not easy to identify. It often shows splendor, especially in the use of crystal (a favorite building material in this realm) and in that of the carbuncle for illumination. It is of course jeweled, and it often has powerful walls and frowning towers, of which in the case of Grosseteste's *Chasteau d'Amour* and the Grail castle with *Diu Crône* and the *Sone de Nansay* there are four. It is decorated with columns or may have, as in Wolfram's *Parzival* and in the *Minneburg,* a remarkable pillar. Sometimes it turns round like a mill, a trick that apparently comes from the Celtic, but in the general idea may be assisted by the wheel or mill sometimes found in association with the bridge. Its inhabitants may be chiefly women, in the form known as Maidenland, a motif probably from the Celtic rather than from Moslem ideas of Paradise since usually it is found along with other features from the Irish. The castle may also be empty of all dwellers if it is under some particular spell. Its garden will often have a special fruit tree and also a fountain, and the fruit or the water has sometimes the power to restore youth. There the birds furnish music heard particularly in early Celtic accounts and borrowed later, probably from that source, in the allegories.

The castle is often protected by a moat that takes some of its characteristics from the river barrier, and it may also be situated near a marshy tract or by the Waste Land. This *terre gaste* may come from desolate regions known to the Celts or from the dark valley of the Norse or from a similar territory in the visions. It is considerably used in the so-called deserts of love in the allegories and is perhaps best known in the devastated country of the stories of the Grail. How far it is the creation of human psychology in terms of allegory and how far it is taken from tradition

[2] It too is a common inheritance. See examples of the Soul Bridge cited by J. G. Frazer, *The Belief in Immortality and the Worship of the Dead,* I, p. 350 (the Solomon Islands); pp. 27f. (the Maoris). Cf. Hastings, *Encyclopaedia, s. v.* bridge.

and folklore is the problem of each special instance and extremely difficult to decide. A narrow path like that familiar in the visions leads through such regions to the castle or territory; on the other hand, it may be a difficult passage between threatening rocks or a gate such as Yvain found at Laudine's palace, or there may be two roads with obvious biblical or Eastern inheritance, one of which is the "strait and narrow" way such as William the Clerk described in his *Besant de Dieu*. Sharp contrasts are sometimes introduced in the account of the scenery along the road, that of cold and heat perhaps; and contrast is used extensively from time to time in several of the elements in the allegory of Lady Fortune to convey the idea of good and bad fortune. Indeed, it is impossible here to give an adequate survey of all the details in these many descriptions or of all the Otherworldly devices used.

In the present review in general, however, one fact, I think, becomes increasingly clear. That is the very considerable use of material from the East, transmitted by the visions perhaps or even by Celtic stories or other documents, in the whole field of medieval allegory and romance. The cumulative effect of the number of instances we have examined contributes a powerful argument for the extent of that influence, which is not offset, it would seem, by the possibility of coincidence or fresh invention. We may also notice the extensive introduction of Otherworld motifs into the works of Chaucer, Boccaccio, and Dante. A medieval writer apparently could not escape from the necessity of going on one of these marvelous journeys at least once. Chaucer uses the mountain, the turning castle, the garden, the flight, and other details. Boccaccio has the palace, the garden, and the flight. There is really nothing that Dante leaves out. He has the descent to the lower world, the voyage to an island, the ascent of the mountain, and the journey through the spheres. He may even be said to have the terrible river, the one over which Charon ferries souls, although that comes from the classics and the bridge is here missing; the pleasant one, again from the classics, is in the Earthly Paradise. His most amazing achievement, however, is the success with which he conveys by symbolism a heaven of spiritual delights.

For as we survey through the centuries the number of gardens with their flowery meadows, the palaces with all the lustre of their precious stones, there is pathos in the thought that these truly are the stuff that human dreams are "made on" and the nobility of aspiration has come only to this. Moreover, in many of these accounts we find the human element of fear and risk presented in the peril of the barriers, the devastation that has swept over the land, and the spell under which the splendor of the scene has had to be diminished at least until the hero arrives who can save the realm by beheading somebody. Perhaps it is the descendant of the new sun god who defeats the god of the dying year, a deity whose dwelling turns with the firmament on high. Or perhaps the remote country is reached only by crossing the river of death. But at least we may say that as origins have become obscured and only the general notion of an Other World is left, the familiar pattern of the story shows us a final release of the baneful spell and the Grail is there.

BIBLIOGRAPHY

BIBLIOGRAPHY

CSEL	:	Corpus scriptorum ecclesiasticorum Latinorum
EETS	:	Early English Text Society. ES : Extra Series
MGH	:	Monumenta Germaniae historica
PMLA	:	Publications of the Modern Language Association
SATF	:	Société des Anciens Textes Français
SPCK	:	Society for Promoting Christian Knowledge

Abraham, The Testament of, trans. W. A. Craigie, in *The Ante-Nicene Fathers,* ed. Allan Menzies, vol. IX, 5th ed., pp. 183 ff. New York, 1906.

Abraham, The Testament of, ed. M. R. James, Cambridge, 1892 (*Texts and Studies,* II:2).

Acart de Hesdin, Jehan, *La Prise Amoureuse,* ed. Ernst Hoepffner, Dresden, 1910 (*Gesellschaft für Romanische Literatur,* 22).

Ackermann, Elfriede, *Das Schlaraffenland in German Literature and Folksong,* Chicago, 1944.

Acta Sanctorum, begun by J. Bollandus, I, 1643 and seq.

Addison, Joseph, Selections from the Writings of, ed. Barrett Wendell and C. N. Greenough, [1905] (*Athenaeum Press Series*).

Adulterous Falmouth Squire, The, in *Political, Religious, and Love Poems,* ed. Frederick Furnivall, London, 1866 (*EETS,* 15).

Æneas Sylvius, *Opera omnia,* Basel, 1571.

Aimon von Varennes : Florimont, ein Altfranzösischer Abenteuerroman, ed. Alfons Hilka, Göttingen, 1932 (*Gesellschaft für Romanische Literatur,* 48).

Aislinge Meic Conglinne, The Vision of Mac Conglinne, a Middle Irish Wonder Tale, ed. Kuno Meyer with an introduction by W. Wollner, London, 1892.

Alain de Lille, The Anticlaudian of, trans. William H. Cornog, Philadelphia, 1935.

Alexander, The Prose Life of, ed. J. S. Westlake, London, 1913 for 1911, (*EETS,* 143).

Alexanderroman des Archpresbyters Leo, Der, ed. Friedrich Pfister, Heidelberg, 1813.

Alexandre, Roman d', see *Roman.*

Alger, W. R., *The Destiny of the Soul. A Critical History of the Doctrine of a Future Life,* 10th ed., Boston, 1880.

Allen, J. Romilly, *Early Christian Symbolism in Great Britain and Ireland, Before the Thirteenth Century,* London, 1887 (*The Rhind Lectures in Archaeology* for 1885).

Allen, Philip Schuyler, and Howard Mumford Jones, *The Romanesque Lyric,* Chapel Hill, [N.C.], 1928.

Amadas et Ydoine, Roman du XIIIe Siècle, ed. John R. Reinhard, Paris, 1926 (*Classiques Français du Moyen Age,* 51).

Ambrosii, Sancti, Opera, part I, *De Paradiso, Leipzig,* 1897 (*CSEL,* XXXII:1).

Ampère, J.-J., *Histoire Littéraire de la France avant la douzième Siècle,* vol. III, Paris, 1839.

Analecta hymnica medii aevi, ed. G. M. Dreves, vol. I, Leipzig, 1886.

Ancona, Alessandro d', *Scritti Danteschi, I Precursori di Dante,* Florence [1912–1913].

Ancona, A. d', and O. Bacci, *Manuale della Letteratura Italiana,* 5 vols., Florence, 1904.

Anderson, Andrew R., *Alexander's Gate, Gog and Magog, and the Inclosed Nations,* Cambridge [Mass.], 1932.

Andreae Capellani regii Francorum, De Amore Libri Tres, ed. E. Trojel, Copenhagen, 1892.

Andreas Capellanus, The Art of Courtly Love, ed. John J. Parry, N. Y., 1941 (*Records of Civilization, Sources and Studies,* XXXIII).

Antiquarian Repertory, The: A Miscellany, Intended to Preserve and Illustrate Several Valuable Remains of Old Times, Adorned with Elegant Sculptures, vol. III, London, 1780.

Apokalypsen, Die, des Esra und des Baruch, trans. Bruno Violet and Hugo Gressmann, Leipzig, 1924 (*Die Griechischen Christlichen Schriftsteller der ersten drei Jahrhunderte*).

Apuleius, The Golden Ass, Being the Metamorphoses of Lucius Apuleius, trans. W. Adlington, revised by S. Gaselee, London, 1925 (*Loeb Library*).

Arabian Nights' Entertainments, The Thousand and One Nights, Commonly Called The, trans. E. W. Lane, ed. Edward S. Poole, 2 vols., London, 1912.

Arber, Edward, ed., *The Dunbar Anthology. 1401–1508* A.D., London, 1901 (*British Anthologies,* I).

Arbois de Jubainville, H. d', *Le Cycle Mythologique irlandais et la Mythologie celtique, Cours de Littérature celtique,* vols. II and IV, Paris, 1884, 1889.

Ardâ-Vîrâf, The Book of. The Pahlavî Text prepared by Destur Hoshangji Jamaspji Asa, ed. Martin Haug and E. W. West, Bombay and London, 1872.

Ariosto, Lodovico, *Rime e Satire,* Florence, 1824.

Arras, Jehan d', *Melusine,* ed. Ch. Brunet, Paris, 1854 (*Bibliothèque Elzevirienne*).

Arthur of Little Britain, see *Bourghcher.*

Asín Palacios, Miguel, *La Escatologia Musulmana en la Divina Comedia,* Madrid, 1919.

Asín Palacios, Miguel, *Islam and the Divine Comedy,* trans. and abridged by Harold Sunderland, London, 1926.

Ásmundarson, V., *Fornaldarsögur Northrlanda,* III, Reykjavik, 1889.

Assyrian and Babylonian Literature, Selected Translations, New York, 1901 (*The World's Great Books*).

Athanasius, *Opera omnia,* vol. II: *Quaestiones ad Antiochum,* Padua, 1777.

Atharva-Veda Saṁhitā, trans. W. D. Whitney, Cambridge, 1905 (*Harvard Oriental Series,* VII).

Athenaeus: The Deipnosophists, trans. C. B. Gulick, London and N. Y., 1927 sqq. (*Loeb Library*).

Atkinson, R. and J. H. Bernard, *The Irish Liber Hymnorum,* 2 vols., London, 1898 (*Henry Bradshaw Society,* XIII).

Augustini, Sancti Aurelii, Episcopi, De civitate Dei, Libri XXII, ed. Emanuel Hoffmann, 2 vols., Prague, Vienna and Leipzig, 1899, 1900 (*CSEL,* XXXX:1,2).

Augustini, Sancti Aurelii, De genesi ad litteram Libri duodecim, Part I, ed. Joseph Zycha, Prague, Vienna and Leipzig, 1894 (*CSEL,* XXVIII:1).

Avitus, *De mundi initio,* ed. R. Peiper, in *Auctores antiquissimorum,* vol. VI, ii, pp. 203ff. Berlin, 1883 (*MGH*).

Ayenbite of Inwyt, see *Dan Michel's Ayenbite.*

Baehrens, Emil, *Poetae Latini minores,* vol. III, Leipzig, 1881 (*Bibliotheca scriptorum Graecorum et Romanorum Teubneriana*).

Barbazan, Étienne, and D. M. Méon, eds., *Fabliaux et Contes des Poètes François des XI, XII, XIII, XIV et XVe Siècles, tirés des meilleurs Auteurs,* 4 vols., Paris, 1808.

Barberino, Andrea Da, *Guerino detto Il Meschino,* etc., Venice, 1816.

Baring-Gould, Sabine, *Curious Myths of the Middle Ages,* Boston, 1867.

Bartholomew Anglicus, *De Proprietatibus Rerum,* ed. Wynken de Worde, trans. John Trevisa, 1426.

Bartholomew Anglicus, *De Proprietatibus Rerum,* Nuremberg, 1492, Hain-Copinger * 2510, Proctor 2073.

Barto, P. S., *Tannhäuser and the Mountain of Venus,* Oxford, 1916.

Bartsch, Karl, *Chrestomathie de l'ancien Français,* 12th ed., revised by Leo Wiese, Leipzig, 1927.

Bartsch, Karl, *Chrestomathie provençale* (*X^e^–XVe Siècles*), 6th ed., revised by E. Koschwitz, Marburg, 1904.

Baruch, the Apocalypse of, trans. W. R. Morfill, in *Apocrypha anecdota,* ed. M. R. James, 2nd series, Cambridge, 1899 (*Texts and Studies,* V).

Baruch, The Apocalypse of, translated from the Syriac, ed. R. H. Charles, London, 1896.

Basilii, Sancti Patris Nostri, Caesareae Cappadociae Archiepiscopi opera omnia que exstant, vol. I, Paris, 1839.

Baudoin de Condé et de son Fils Jean de Condé, Dits et Contes de, ed. Auguste Scheler, 3 vols., Brussels, 1866–1867.

Baudoin de Sebourc, Li Romans de, Valenciennes, 1841.

Becker, E. J., *A Contribution to the Comparative Study of the Medieval Visions of Heaven and Hell,* Baltimore, 1899.

[Bede] *Baedae opera historica, Ecclesiastical History of the English Nation Based on the Version of Thomas Stapleton,* 1565, 2 vols., trans. J. E. King, London, New York, 1930 (*Loeb Library*).

[Bede] *Venerabilis Baedae Historiam Ecclesiasticam Gentis Anglorum* etc., ed. Charles Plummer, 2 vols., Oxford, 1896.

Bellows, Henry A., trans., *The Poetic Edda,* American Scandinavian Foundation, New York and London, 1923.

Benedeit, The Anglo-Norman Voyage of Saint Brendan by, ed. E. G. R. Waters, Oxford, 1928.

Bernard of Clairvaux, *Genuina sancti doctoris opera,* Paris, 1719.

Bernard of Clairvaux, *Opera genuina,* vol. III, Lyons and Paris, 1854.

Bernard Silvester, *De mundi uniuersitate*, ed. C. S. Barach and J. Wrobel, 2 vols., Innsbruck, 1876.

Bett, Henry, *Joachim of Flora*, London [1931].

Beues of Hamtoun, The Romance of Sir, ed. Eugen Kölbing, parts I and III, London, 1885, 1894 (*EETS:ES*, 46, 65).

[Bevis] *Boeve de Haumtone, Der anglonormannische*, ed. Albert Stimming, Halle, 1899 (*Bibliotheca Normannica*, H. Suchier, VII).

[Bevis] *Bueve de Hantone, Der Festländische*, ed. Albert Stimming, vol. I, Dresden, 1910 (*Gesellschaft für romanische Literatur*, 25).

Bjarnason, Björn, *Sturlunga Saga* (*Fyrsta Bindi*), Reykjavik, 1908 (*Islendinga Sögur*, 42).

Bò, Eugenia dal, *La Visione nell' Arte Medievale*, Naples, 1892.

Boccaccio, Giovanni, Opere Volgari di, vols. V, XIV, XV, Florence, 1828, 1833.

Boccaccio, Giovanni, Teseida, ed. Salvatore Battaglia, Florence, 1938 (*Autori Classici e Documenti di Lingua Pubblicati dalla R. Accademia Della Crusca*).

Bo̊ll, Lawrence Leo, *The Relation of the Diu Krône of Heinrich von dem Türlin to La Mule sanz Frain, A Study in Sources*, Washington, D.C., 1929 (*Catholic University of America, Studies in German*, II).

Bonaventurae, S., S. R. E. Cardinalis, Opera omnia, ed. A. C. Peltier, vol. III: *Librum Sententiarum*, Paris, 1865.

Bond, Francis, *Wood Carvings in English Churches*, London, 1910.

Boniface, Saint, The English Correspondence of: Being for the Most Part Letters Exchanged between the Apostle of the Germans and his English Friends, trans. Edward Kylie, London, 1911 (*The King's Classics*).

Boniface, St., *Epistolae* III, *Epistolae Merovingici et Karolini*, ed. Ernst Dümmler, I, pp. 252ff., Berlin, 1892 (*MGH*).

Boniface, Saint, The Letters of, trans. Ephraim Emerton, New York, 1940 (*Records of Civilization: Sources and Studies* XXXI).

Bonifatius, Die Briefe des heiligen, ed. Michael Tangl, Leipzig (*Die Geschichtschreiber der Deutschen Vorzeit* XCII [1912]).

Bonifatius, Die Briefe des heiligen, und Lullus, ed. Michael Tangl, in *Epistolae Selectae*, I, Berlin, 1916 (*MGH*).

Book of Vices and Virtues, The, A Fourteenth Century English Translation of the Somme le Roi of Lorens d'Orleans, ed. Francis W. Nelson, London, 1942 (*EETS,* 217).

Boswell, C. S., *An Irish Precursor of Dante, A Study on the Vision of Heaven and Hell ascribed to the Eighth-century Irish Saint Adamnán, with Translation of the Irish Text,* London, 1908 (*Grimm Library,* 18).

Bourchier, Sir John, Lord Berners, *The Boke of Duke Huon of Burdeux,* ed. S. L. Lee, in *The English Charlemagne Romances,* parts VII and VIII, London, 1882, 1883 (*EETS:ES,* 40, 41).

Bourghcher, Johan, knyght lorde Barners, The Hystory of the moost noble and valyaunt knyght Arthur of lytell brytayne, translated out of frensche into englishe by the noble, newly Imprynted [London, 1555?].

Bozon, Nicole, Les Contes Moralisés de, ed. Lucy T. Smith and Paul Meyer, Paris, 1889 (*SATF,* 15).

Bran, Son of Febal, to the Land of the Living, The Voyage of, see *Meyer, Kuno.*

Brandes, H., *Visio Sancti Pauli, Ein Beitrag zur Visionslitteratur mit einem Deutschen und zwei Lateinischen Texten,* Halle, 1885.

Braz, Anatole Le, *La Légende de la Mort chez les Bretons Armoricains,* 3rd ed., Paris, 1912.

Breul, Karl, ed., *The Cambridge Songs, A Goliard's Song Book of the XIth Century,* Cambridge, [Eng.,] 1915.

Brotanek, Rudolf, *Die Englischen Maskenspiele,* Vienna and Leipzig, 1902 (*Wiener Beiträge,* XV).

Brown, A. C. L., *Iwain, A Study in the Origins of Arthurian Romance,* Boston, 1903. In [*Harvard*] *Studies and Notes in Philology and Literature,* VIII.

Brown, A. C. L., *The Origin of the Grail Legend,* Cambridge [Mass.], 1943.

Browne, George Forrest, *The Venerable Bede, His Life and Writings,* London, 1919 (*SPCK*).

Bruce, James Douglas, *The Evolution of Arthurian Romance from the Beginnings down to the Year 1300,* 2 vols., 2nd ed., Baltimore and Göttingen, 1928 (*Hesperia, Ergänzungsreihe,* VIII and IX).

Brun de la Montaigne, Roman d'Aventure, ed. Paul Meyer, Paris, 1875 (*SATF,* 16).

Budge, E. A. Wallis, trans., *The Alexander Book in Ethiopia, The Ethiopic Versions of Pseudo-Callisthenes, The Chronicle of Almakîn, The Narrative of Joseph Ben Gorion, And a Christian Romance of Alexander,* London, 1933.

Budge, E. A. Wallis, ed., *The History of Alexander the Great, Being the Syriac Version of the Pseudo-Callisthenes,* Cambridge [Eng.], 1889.

Bugge, Sophus, *The Home of the Eddic Poems with Especial Reference to the Helgi-Lays,* trans. W. H. Schofield, rev. ed., London, 1899 (*Grimm Library,* 11).

Burkitt, F. Crawford, *Jewish and Christian Apocalypses,* The British Academy, London, 1914 (*The Schweich Lectures,* 1913).

Burnt Njal, The Story of, trans. G. W. Dasent, 2 vols., Edinburgh, 1861.

Cabrol, Fernand, and Henri Leclerq, *Dictionnaire d'Archéologie Chrétienne, et de Liturgie,* vol. XIII, Paris, 1937.

Caesarius of Heisterbach, *Dialogus Miraculorum,* ed. Joseph Strange, 2 vols., Cologne, Bonn, and Brussels, 1851.

Caesarius of Heisterbach, The Dialogue on Miracles by, trans. H. von E. Scott and C. C. Swinton Bland, introd. by G. G. Coulton, 2 vols., London, 1929.

Campbell, John F., *Popular Tales of the West Highlands,* London, 1890.

Campbell, John G., *Superstitions of the Highlands and Islands of Scotland,* Glasgow, 1900.

Cancellieri, Francesco, *Osservazione intorno alla questione promossa dal Vannozzi dal Mazzocchi dal Boltari especialmente dal P. Abato D. Giuseppe Giustino di Costanzo sopra l'Originalità della Divina Commedia di Dante,* Rome, 1814.

Carver, Marmaduke, *A Discourse of the Terrestrial Paradise,* London, 1666.

Castel of Love, in *The Minor Poems of the Vernon MS,* part I, ed. Carl Horstmann, London, 1892 (*EETS,* 98).

Castro, Adolfo de, *Curiosidades bibliográficas, Collecion escogida de Obras raras de Amenidad y Erudicion con Apuntes biográficos de los diferentes Autores,* Madrid, 1871 (*Biblioteca de Autores Españoles,* 36).

Caterina da Siena, Le Lettere di S., ed. Niccolò Tommaseo and Piero Misciatelli, vol. IV, Siena, 1913.

Caterina da Siena, Santa, Libro della Divina Dottrina volgarmente detto Dialogo della divina Provvidenza, ed. Matilde Fiorilli, Bari, 1912 (*Scrittori d'Italia* [34]).

Caxton's Mirrour of the World, ed. Oliver H. Prior, London, 1913 for 1912 (*EETS:ES,* 110).

Chantepie de la Saussaye, P. D., *The Religion of the Teutons,* trans. Bert J. Vos, Boston and London, 1902 (*Handbooks on the History of Religions,* III).

Charles d'Orléans, Poésies, ed. Pierre Champion, 2 vols., Paris, 1923, 1927 (*Les Classiques Français du Moyen Age*).

Charles d'Orléans, Poésies Complètes de, ed. Charles d'Héricault, vol. I, Paris, 1896.

Charles of Orleans, The English Poems of, ed. Robert Steele, London, 1941 (*EETS,* 215).

Chartier, Alain, Les Œuvres de Maistre, ed. André Du Chesne Tourangeau, Paris, 1617.

Chaucer, Geoffrey, The Complete Works of, ed. F. N. Robinson, Boston and New York, 1933.

Chaucer, Geoffrey, The Complete Works of, ed. W. W. Skeat, 6 vols., Oxford, 1894–1900. Vol. VII, Supplementary vol.: *Chaucerian and Other Pieces, Oxford,* 1897.

Chaucer, Geoffrey, The Works of, Compared with the Former Editions, and Many Valuable MSS Out of Which Three Tales Are Added Which Were Never Before Printed; [etc.], ed. John Urry, London, 1721.

Chauvin, Victor, *Bibliographie des Ouvrages Arabes ou Relatifs aux Arabes publiés dans l'Europe Chrétienne de 1810 à 1885,* vol. IX, Liége and Leipzig, 1905.

Chevalier à L'Épée, Le: An Old French Poem, E. C. Armstrong, Baltimore, 1900 (Dissertation submitted to the Board of University Studies of the Johns Hopkins University for the Degree of Doctor of Philosophy, 1897).

Chevalier au Cygne, La Chanson du, in *Collection des Poètes Français du Moyen Age, première* partie, ed. Celestin Hippeau, Paris, 1874.

Chevalier du Papegau, Le, ed. Ferdinand Heuckenkamp, Halle a.S., 1897 (for 1896).

Chevaliers as Deus Espees, Li, ed. Wendelin Foerster, Halle, 1877.

Child, Francis James, ed., *The English and Scottish Popular Ballads,* 5 vols., Boston [1882–1898].

[Chrétien de Troyes] *Kristian von Troyes Erec und Enide,* ed. Wendelin Foerster, 2nd ed., Halle a.S., 1909 (*Romanische Bibliothek,* XIII).

[Chrétien de Troyes] *Kristian von Troyes, Yvain* (*Der Löwenritter*), ed. Wendelin Foerster, Halle a.S., 1891 and 1906 (*Romanische Bibliothek,* V).

Christian von Troyes, Der Karrenritter (*Lancelot*) *und das Wilhelmsleben* (*Guillaume d'Angleterre*) *von,* ed. Wendelin Foerster, Halle a.S., 1899 (*Christian von Troyes Sämtliche Erhaltene Werke,* IV).

Christian von Troyes, Der Percevalroman (*Li Contes del Graal*) *von,* ed. Alfons Hilka, Halle a.S., 1932 (*Christian von Troyes Sämtliche Werke,* V).

Christiansen, Reidar, *The Dead and the Living,* Oslo, 1946 (*Studia Norvegica* I:2).

Cicero: De re publica, De legibus, trans. C. W. Keyes, London, 1928 (*Loeb Library*).

Claris et Laris, ed. Johann Alton, Tübingen, 1884 (*Bibl. des Litt. Vereins in Stuttgart,* CLXIX).

Claudian, trans. Maurice Platnauer, 2 vols., Cambridge [Mass.], 1922 (*Loeb Library*).

Clene Maydenhod, ed. Frederick J. Furnivall, London, 1867 (*EETS,* 22).

Coli, Edoardo, *Il Paradiso Terrestre Dantesco,* Florence, 1897 (*Pubblicazioni del R. Instituto di Studi Superiori Pratici e di Perfezionamento in Firenze, Sezione di Filosofia e Lettere*).

Collin de Plancy, J. A. S. C., *Légendes de l'Autre Monde,* Paris [1862].

Comparetti, Domenico, ed. *Novelline Popolari Italiane,* 4 vols., Rome, Turin, Florence, 1875–1891 (*Canti e Racconti del Popolo Italiano,* VI).

Comparetti, Domenico, *Researches Respecting the Book of Sindibâd,* London, 1882 (*Publications of the Folk-Lore Society,* IX).

Cornelius, Roberta D., *The Figurative Castle, A Study in the Mediaeval Allegory of the Edifice with Especial Reference to Religious Writings,* Bryn Mawr, 1930.

Coulton, G. G., *Life in the Middle Ages,* 4 vols., Cambridge, 1929 (*The Cambridge Anthologies*).

Couronnement de Louis, Le, ed. Ernest Langlois, Paris, 1920 (*Les Classiques Français du Moyen Age,* 22).

Couronnement de Louis, Le, ed. E. Langlois, Paris, 1888 (*SATF,* 21).

Court of Sapience, The, ed. Robert Spindler, Leipzig, 1927 (*Beiträge zur Engl. Philol.*).

Cowardin, S. P., Jr., *On an Episode in the Middle English Metrical Romance of Guy of Warwick,* diss. unpubl., Harvard University, 1930.

Cross, Tom Peete, and Clark H. Slover, *Ancient Irish Tales,* New York, 1936.

Cross, Tom Peete, and William A. Nitze, *Lancelot and Guenevere, A Study on the Origins of Courtly Love,* Chicago [1930] (*Modern Philology Monographs of the University of Chicago*).

Culex, Vergilius Maro, Appendix Vergiliana, ed. Robinson Ellis, Oxford [1907], (*Scriptorum classicorum bibliotheca Oxoniensis,* 30).

Cumont, Franz, *After Life in Roman Paganism,* New Haven, 1922.

Cursor Mundi (*The Cursor o the World*). *A Northumbrian Poem of the XIVth Century, In Four Versions, Two of Them Midland,* ed. Richard Morris, 2 parts bound as 1, London, 1874, 1875 (*EETS,* 57, 59).

Cyprian, Bishop of Carthage, The Writings of, trans. Robert E. Wallis, vol. I, *Epistles and Some of the Treatises,* Edinburgh, 1868 (*Ante-Nicene Christian Library*).

Cypriani, S. Thasci Caecilii, Opera omnia, ed. W. Hartel, Vienna, 1871 (*CSEL,* III:3).

Cypriani Galli Poetae Heptateuchos accedunt de Sodoma et Iona et ad Senatorem Carmina et Hilarii quae feruntur in Genesin, de Maccabaeis atque de Evangelio, ed. R. Peiper, Prague, Vienna, Leipzig, 1881 (*CSEL,* XXIII).

Damoisele a la Mule, La, ed. Boleslas Orłowski, Paris, 1911.

Dan Michel's Ayenbite of Inwyt, or, Remorse of Conscience, ed. Richard Morris, London, 1866 (reprinted, 1888) (*EETS,* 23).

Dana, H. W. L., *Medieval Visions of the Other World,* diss. unpubl., Harvard University, 1910.

Dante Alighieri, La Divina Commedia di, ed. C. H. Grandgent, revised edition, New York [1933].

De la Mare, Walter, *Desert Islands and Robinson Crusoe,* New York, 1930.

Delitzsch, Friedrich, *Wo lag das Paradies?* Leipzig, 1881.

Deschamps, Eustache, Œuvres Complètes de, ed. Le Marquis de Queux de Saint-Hilaire and G. Raynaud, 11 vols., Paris, 1878–1903 (*SATF,* 24–34).

Didot *Perceval, The, according to the Manuscripts of Modena,* ed. William Roach, University of Pennsylvania Press, Philadelphia, 1941.

Didron M., *Christian Iconography; or the History of Christian Art in the Middle Ages,* trans. E. J. Millington, 2 vols., London, 1851.

Dillmann, August, *Die Genesis,* ed. August Knobel, Leipzig, 1875.

Dillon, Myles, ed., *Serglige con Culainn,* Columbus, 1941.

Diodorus of Sicily, trans. C. H. Oldfather, vols. I and II of a projected 10-vol. ed., London and New York, 1933, 1935 (*Loeb Library).*

Dods, Marcus, *Forerunners of Dante, An Account of Some of the More Important Visions of the Unseen World, from the Earliest Times,* Edinburgh, 1903.

Dolopathos, Li Romans de, ed. [J.] Charles Brunet and Anatole de Montaiglon, Paris, 1856 (*Bibliothèque Elzevirienne*).

Doon de la Roche, ed. Paul Meyer and Gédéon Huet, Paris, 1921 (*SATF,* 46).

Dottin, Georges, *Manuel pour Servir à l'Étude de l'Antiquité Celtique,* 2nd edition, Paris, 1915.

Douglas, Gavin, Bishop of Dunkeld, The Poetical Works of, ed. John Small, 4 vols., Edinburgh and London, 1874.

Draumkvæde, A Norwegian Visionary Poem from the Middle Ages, ed. Knut Liestøl, Oslo, 1946 (*Studia Norvegica,* I [1946] 3).

Duckett, Eleanor S., *Latin Writers of the Fifth Century,* New York, 1930.

Du Méril, Édélestand, *Poésies populaires Latines antérieures au douzième Siècle,* Paris, 1843.

Du Méril, Édélestand, *Poésies populaires Latines du Moyen Age,* Paris, 1847.

Dümmler, E., *Poetae Latini aevi Carolini,* I, Berlin, 1881 (*MGH*).

Dunbar, William, *The Goldyn Targe,* in *The Poems of William Dunbar,* ed. John Small, vol. II, Edinburgh and London, 1893 (*Scottish Text Society,* 16).

Dunn, J., *The Ancient Irish Epic Tale Táin Bó Cúalange,* etc., London, 1914.

Durmart le Galois, Li Romans de, ed. Edmund Stengel, Tübingen, 1873 (*Bibl. des Litt. Vereins in Stuttgart,* CXVI).

Dutt, Manatha Nath, *A Prose English Translation of Markandeya Purana,* Calcutta, 1897.

Eddica Minora, ed. Andreas Heusler and Wilhelm Ranisch, Dortmund, 1903.

Eger and Grime, ed. James R. Caldwell, Cambridge [Mass.], 1933 (*Harvard Studies in Comparative Literature*, IX).

Ehrismann, Gustav, *Die Mittelhochdeutsche Literatur*, vol. II 2.2 in *Geschichte der Deutschen Literatur bis zum Ausgang des Mittelalters*, 4 vols., Munich, 1918–1935 (*Handbuch des Deutschen Unterrichts*, VI).

Elene, Phoenix, and Physiologus, The Old English, ed. Albert S. Cook, Yale University Press, New Haven, 1919.

Elias, Die Apokalypse des, ed. Georg Steindorff, in *Texte und Untersuchungen zur Geschichte der Altchristlichen Literatur*, ed. Oscar von Gebhardt and Adolf Harnack, neue folge II, 2 vols., Leipzig, 1899.

Ellis, Hilda R., *The Road to Hel, A Study of the Conception of the Dead in Old Norse Literature*, Cambridge [Eng.], 1943.

Enoch, Book of, ed. R. H. Charles, London, 1917 (*SPCK*).

Enoch, The Book of, translated from Professor Dillmann's Ethiopic Text, ed. R. H. Charles, Oxford, 1893.

Enoch, The Book of the Secrets of, trans. W. R. Morfill, ed. R. H. Charles, Oxford, 1896.

Enrrique Fi de Oliua, Historia de, Madrid, 1871 (*La Sociedad de Bibliófilas Españolas*).

Ere-Dwellers, The Story of the, (*Eyrbyggia Saga*), trans. William Morris and Eiríkr Magnússon, London, 1892 (*The Saga Library*, II).

Eríks Saga Vídförla (*Eric the Far Traveller*), in *Fláteyjarbók*, ed. G. Vigfússon and C. R. Unger, vol. I, Christiania, 1860.

Eríks Saga Vídförla (*Eric the Far Traveller*), in *Fornaldarsögur Norðrlanda*, vol. III, ed. C. C. Rafn, Copenhagen, 1830 (revised by Valdimar Ásmundarson, Reykjavik, 1889).

Ernst, Lorenz, *Floire und Blantscheflur, Studie zur vergleichenden Literaturwissenschaft*, Strassburg, 1912 (*Quellen und Forschungen*, 118).

Esclarmonde, ed. M. Schweingel, Marburg, 1889 (*Ausg. und Abhandlungen*, LXXXIII).

Esra-Apocalypse (*IV: Esra*), *Die*, ed. Bruno Violet, part I, Leipzig, 1910.

Étienne de Bourbon, Anecdotes Historiques, Légendes et Apologues, tirés du Recueil inédit d', ed. A. Lecoy de la Marche, Paris, 1877.

Étienne de Rouen, The Draco Normannicus of, in *Chronicles of the Reigns of Stephen, Henry II, and Richard I,* vol. II, ed. Richard Howlett, London, 1885 (*Rolls Series,* LXXXII:2).

Exeter Book, The, ed. George P. Krapp and E. van K. Dobbie, New York, 1936.

Ezra, The Fourth Book of, ed. R. L. Bensly, introd. M. R. James, Cambridge, 1895 (*Texts and Studies,* III:2).

Ezra, The Apocalypse of (II:Esdras III–XIV), trans. G. H. Box, with text, London, 1917 (*SPCK*).

Ezra-Apocalypse, The, Being Chapters 3–14 of the Book Commonly Known as Ezra (or II Esdras), ed. George H. Box, London, 1912.

Fablel dou Dieu d'Amours, Li, ed. Achille Jubinal, Paris, 1834.

Faral, Edmond, *La Légende Arthurienne,* 3 vols., Paris, 1929. (*Bibliothèque de l'École des Hautes Études*).

Faust-Book of 1592, The English, ed. H. Logeman, Ghent and Amsterdam, 1900 (*Recueil de Travaux, Université de Ghent,* fascicule 24).

Faust, Das Volksbuch vom Doktor, ed. Josef Fritz, Halle, 1914.

Faust, Das Volksbuch vom Doktor, ed. Robert Petsch, Halle a.S., 1911 (*Neudrucke deutscher Litteraturwerke des XVI. und XVII. Jahrhundert*).

Faust, George P., *Sir Degare, A Study of the Texts and Narrative Structure,* Princeton, 1935 (*Princeton Studies in English,* 11).

Félice, Philippe de, *L'Autre Monde, Mythes et Légendes, Le Purgatoire de saint Patrice,* Paris, 1906.

Ferumbras, Sir, ed. Sidney J. Herrtage, in *The English Charlemagne Romances,* part I, London, 1879 (*EETS:ES,* 34).

Fierabras, Chanson de Geste, ed. Auguste Kroeber and G. Servois, Paris, 1860 (*Anciens Poètes de la France,* IV).

Filippini, Enrico, *La Materia del Quadriregio,* Menaggio, 1905.

Fláteyjarbók, G. Vigfússon and C. R. Unger, Christiania, 1889.

Fleck, Konrad, *Flore und Blanscheflur,* ed. Wolfgang Golther in *Deutsche National-Litteratur,* ed. Joseph Kürschner, vol. IV, 2, Berlin and Stuttgart [n.d.].

Fled Bricrend, The Feast of Bricriu, ed. George Henderson, London, 1899 (*Irish Texts Society,* II).

Floire et Blanceflor, Poèmes du XIIIe Siècle, ed. Édélestand du Méril, Paris, 1856.

Floriant, ed. Harry F. Williams, Ann Arbor [Mich.], 1947 (*University of Michigan Publications, Language and Literature*, XXIII).

Floriant et Florete, A Metrical Romance of the Fourteenth Century, ed. Francisque Michel, Edinburgh, 1873 (*Roxburghe Club*).

Floris and Blauncheflur, ed. Emil Hausknecht, Berlin, 1885 (*Sammlung Englischer Denkmäler*, V).

Foerster, Wendelin, *Kristian von Troyes, Wörterbuch zu seinen sämtlichen Werken*, Halle a.S., 1914 (*Romanische Bibliothek*, XXI).

Fornaldarsögur Norđrlanda, see Rafn, C. C., and V. Ásmundarson.

Frazer, J. G., *The Belief in Immortality and the Worship of the Dead*, vol. I, London, 1913.

Fregoso, Antonio Phileremo, *Dialogo di Fortuna*, Venice, 1531.

French, Walter Hoyt, and Charles Brockway Hale, eds., *Middle English Metrical Romances*, New York, 1930.

Frezzi, Federigo, *Il Quadriregio*, ed. Enrico Filippini, Bari, 1914 (*Scrittori d'Italia*, 65).

Friedel, V.-H. and Kuno Meyer, *La Vision de Tondale*, Paris, 1907.

Friedel, V.-H. and Kuno Meyer, *Versions inédites de la Vision de Tondale*, Paris, 1899.

Froissart, John, *Chronicles of England, France, and Spain, and Adjoining Countries, from the Latter Part of the Reign of Edward II to the Coronation of Henry IV*, trans. Thomas Johnes, New York, 1880.

Froissart, Œuvres de, Poésies, ed. A. Scheler, 3 vols., Brussels, 1870–1872.

Gardner, Edmund G., *The Arthurian Legend in Italian Literature*, London [1930].

Gaselee, Stephen, ed., *The Oxford Book of Medieval Latin Verse*, Oxford, 1928.

Gautrekssaga, Die, ed. Wilhelm Ranisch, Berlin, 1900 (*Palaestra*, 11).

Gawain, Sir, and the Green Knight, ed. J. R. R. Tolkien and E. V. Gordon, Oxford, 1925.

Gawayne, Sir, A Collection of Ancient Romance Poems by Scotish and English Authors Relating to that Celebrated Knight of the Round Table, ed. Sir Frederick Madden, 1839 (*Bannatyne Club*).

Gebhardt, Oscar von, and Adolf Harnack, *Texte und Untersuchungen zur Geschichte der Altchristlichen Literatur*, n.f., II, Leipzig, 1899.

Genesis, Die ältere, ed. F. Holthausen, Heidelberg and New York, 1914 (*Alt-und Mittelenglische Texte*).

Geoffrey of Monmouth, The Historia Regum Britanniae of, ed. Acton Griscom, London, New York, Toronto, 1929.

Gervase of Tilbury, *Otia Imperialia,* in *Scriptores rerum Brunsuicensium illustrationi inseruientes, Antiqui omnes et religionis Reformatione priores,* ed. G. W. Leibniz, vol. I, Hanover, 1707.

Gervasius von Tilbury, Otia Imperialia, Des, ed. Felix Liebrecht, Hanover, 1856.

Gesta Dagoberti I, ed. Bruno Krusch, *Scriptores rerum Merovingicarum,* vol. II, pp. 401ff., Hanover, 1888 (*MGH*).

Gesta Romanorum, ed. Hermann Oesterley, Berlin, 1872.

Gesta Romanorum, The Early English Versions of the, ed. Sidney J. H. Herrtage, London, 1879 (*EETS:ES,* 33).

Giraldi Cambrensis Opera, vol. VI: *Itinerarium Kambriae,* ed. James F. Dimock, London, 1868 (*Rolls Series,* XXI:6).

Giraldus Cambrensis, The Itinerary through Wales and the Description of Wales by, ed. W. L. Williams and trans. R. C. Hoare, London and New York, 1912 (*Everyman's Library*).

Glæsisvellir (*The Realm of the Glittering Plains*) in *Fornmanna Sögur,* III, Copenhagen, 1827.

Godefroid de Bouillon, in *Collection des Poètes Français du Moyen Age,* deuxième partie, ed. Celestin Hippeau, Paris, 1877.

Godfrey of Saint Victor, *Fons Philosophie, Poème inédit du XII Siècle,* ed. M. A. Charma, Caen, 1869 (*Mémoires de la Société des Antiquaires de Normandie,* XXVII).

Godfrey of Viterbo, *Pantheon,* in *Germanicorum scriptorum,* etc., ed. J. Pistorius, 3rd. ed., B. G. Struve, II, Ratisbon, 1726.

Golther, Wolfgang, *Handbuch der Germanischen Mythologie,* Leipzig, 1895.

Gonzalo de Berceo, La Vida de Santo Domingo de Silos par, ed. John D. Fitz-Gerald, Paris, 1904 (*Bibliothèque de l'École des Hautes Études,* Fascicule CXLIX).

Gorra, E., *Studi di Critica Letteraria,* Bologna, 1892.

Gower, John, The Complete Works of, ed. G. C. Macaulay, 4 vols., Oxford, 1899–1902.

Graf, Arturo, *Miti, Leggende e Superstizioni del Medio Evo,* Turin, 1925.

Graf, Arturo, *Roma nella Memoria e nella Immaginazioni del Medio Evo,* Turin, 1923.

Grandgent, C. H., *The Power of Dante,* Boston, 1918.

Gregorii episcopi Turonensis Historia Francorum, ed. W. Arndt, in *Gregorii Turonensis Opera, Scriptores rerum Merovingicarum,* vol. I, pp. 1ff., Hanover, 1885 (*MGH*).

Grégoire de Tours, Histoire des Francs, Texte de Manuscrits de Corbie et de Bruxelles, ed. H. Omont and G. Collon, new edition by R. Poupardin, Paris, 1913 (*Collection de Textes pour servir à l'étude et à l'enseignement de l'histoire*).

Gregory, Bishop of Tours, History of the Franks by, ed. and trans. Ernest Brehaut, New York, 1916 (*Records of Civilization: Sources and Studies* [II]).

Gregory of Tours, The History of the Franks, by, ed. O. M. Dalton, 2 vols., Oxford, 1927.

Gregory, St., surnamed the Great, The Dialogues of, ed. Edmund G. Gardner, London, 1906.

Greiner, Walter, *Owein-Ivain,* Halle a.S., 1917.

Grettir the Strong, The Saga of, A Story of the Eleventh Century, trans. G. A. Hight, London and New York [1914] (*Everyman's Library*).

Grettir the Strong, The Story of, trans. Eiríkr Magnússon and William Morris, London, 1869, new ed. 1900.

Griffis, William E., *The Religions of Japan from the Dawn of History to the Era of Méiji,* 4th ed., revised, New York, 1904.

Grimes, E. M., ed., *The Lays of Desiré, Graelent and Melion,* New York, 1928 (*Institute of French Studies*).

Grimm, Jakob, *Deutsche Mythologie,* 4 vols., 4th ed., Berlin, 1876.

Grimm, Jakob, *Deutsche Mythologie* (Teutonic Mythology), trans. James Stallybras, London, 1880 (vol. I), 1883 (vols. II, III), 1888 (vol. IV).

Griswold, Hervey DeWitt, *The Religion of the Rigveda,* Oxford, London, and Bombay, 1923 (*The Religious Quest of India*).

Gröber, Gustav, *Grundriss der Romanischen Philologie,* IV, *Geschichte der Mittelfranzösischen Literatur,* II, Berlin and Leipzig, 1937.

Grosseteste, Robert, Le Château d'Amour de, ed. J. Murray, Paris, 1918.

Grosseteste, Robert, Bishop of Lincoln, Castel off Loue (*Chasteau d'Amour, or Carmen de Creatione Mundi*), *An Early English Translation of an Old French Poem by,* ed. Richard Francis Weymouth, London and Berlin, 1864.

Grosseteste, Robert, Bishop of Lincoln, The Writings of, ed. S. Harrison Thomson, Cambridge [Eng.], 1940.

Guérin, Paul, ed., *Les Petits Bollandistes, Vies des Seints,* 7th ed., vol. I, Bar-le-Duc, 1874.

Guillaume de Deguileville, Le Pélerinage de l'Ame de, ed. J. J. Stürzinger, London, 1895 (*Roxburghe Club*).

Guillaume de Deguileville, Le Pélerinage de Vie Humaine de, ed. J. J. Stürzinger, London, 1893 (*Roxburghe Club*).

Guillaume de Deguileville, Le Pélerinage Jhesucrist de, ed. J. J. Stürzinger, London, 1897 (*Roxburghe Club*).

Guillaume de Guilleville, *Le Rommant des Trois Pélerinages,* c. 1500.

Guillaume de Lorris and Jean de Meun, *Le Roman de la Rose,* ed. E. Langlois, 5 vols., Paris, 1914–1924 (*SATF,* 108:1–5).

Guillaume de Machaut, Œuvres de, ed. Ernest Hoepffner, 3 vols., Paris, 1908–1921 (*SATF,* 45).

Gummere, Francis B., *Founders of England,* with supplementary notes by F. P. Magoun, New York, 1930.

Guy of Warwick, Nach Coplands Druck, ed. Gustav Schleich, Leipzig, 1923 (*Palaestra,* 139).

Guy of Warwick, The Romance of; The Second or Fifteenth-Century Version, ed. Julius Zupitza, London, 1875–76 (*EETS:ES,* 25–26).

Guy of Warwick, The Romance of, ed. Julius Zupitza, part III, London, 1891 (*EETS:ES,* 59).

Haase, Friedrich Karl, *Die Altenglischen Bearbeitungen von Grosseteste's Chasteau d'Amour verglichen mit der Quelle,* Halle a.S., 1889.

Hagen, Paul, *Der Gral,* Strassburg, 1900 (*Quellen und Forschungen,* 85).

Hales, John W., and F. J. Furnivall, eds., *Bishop Percy's Folio Manuscript,* 3 vols., London, 1867, 1868.

Hall, Edward, Chronicles, etc., London, 1809.

Hamel, A. G. van, *Immrama,* Dublin, 1941 (*Mediaeval and Modern Irish Series,* X).

Hammond, E. P., *English Verse between Chaucer and Surrey,* Durham, N. C., 1927 (*Duke Univ. Publ.*).

Hardiman, James, *Irish Minstrelsy, or Bardic Remains of Ireland,* 2 vols., London, 1831.

Hare, Henry, *The Situation of Paradise Found Out,* London, 1683.

Harper, R. F., *Introduction to Assyrian and Babylonian Literature, Selected translations,* New York, 1901 (*The World's Great Books*).

Hartland, Edwin Sidney, *The Science of Fairy Tales, An Inquiry into Fairy Mythology*, 2nd ed., London, 1925.

Hartmann von Aue Erec/Iwein, ed. Hans Naumann and Hans Steinger, Leipzig, 1933 (*Deutsche Literatur Sammlung Höfische Epik*, III).

Hartmann von Aue, Iwein, der Ritter mit dem Löwen, 2 vols., ed. Emil Henrici, Halle, 1891 and 1893 (*Germanistische Handbibliothek*, VIII, 1, 2).

Hastings, James, *Encyclopaedia of Religion and Ethics*, New York, 1908 sqq.

Hawes, Stephen, The Pastime of Pleasure by, ed. William E. Mead, London, 1928 for 1927 (*EETS*, 173).

Heinrîch von dem Türlîn, Diu Crône von, ed. G. H. F. Scholl, Stuttgart, 1852 (*Bibl. des Litt. Vereins in Stuttgart*, XXVII).

Henderson, George, *Survivals in Belief among the Celts*, Glasgow, 1911.

Henryson, The Poems of, ed. G. Gregory Smith, vol. III, Edinburgh and London, 1908 (*Scottish Text Society*, 64).

Hermannsson, Halldór, *Bibliography of the Icelandic Sagas and Minor Tales*, New York, 1908 (*Islandica, An Annual Relating to Iceland and the Fiske Icelandic Collection in Cornell University*, ed. George W. Harris, I).

Hernando del Castillo, "Una Quexa que dé su Amiga ante el Dios de Amor", in *Cancionero General de Hernando del Castillo*, vol. II, Madrid, 1882 (*Sociedad de Bibliofilos Españoles*, XXI).

Herrad von Landsberg, Hortus Deliciarum, ed. A. Straub and G. Keller, Strasburg, 1901.

Hervarar Saga ok Heidreks, ed. Sophus Bugge, Christiania, 1873 (*Norr. Skrifter*, XVII).

Hesiod: The Homeric Hymns and Homerica, trans. H. G. Evelyn-White, London and New York, 1914 (*Loeb Library*).

Heuzey, L., *Le Mont Olympe et l'Acarnanie*, Paris, 1860.

Hibbard, Laura, *see* Laura Hibbard Loomis.

Higden, Ranulph, *Polychronicon, together with the English Translations of John Trevisa and of an Unknown Writer of the Fifteenth Century*, ed. Churchill Babington, vol. I, London, 1865 (*Rolls Series*, XLI).

Highbarger, E. L., *The Gates of Dreams, An Archaeological Examination of Vergil, Aeneid VI, 893–899*, Baltimore, Johns Hopkins

Press, 1940 (*The Johns Hopkins University Studies in Archaeology*, no. 30).

Hillebrandt, Alfred, *Lieder des Ṛgveda*, Göttingen and Leipzig, 1913 (*Quellen der Religions-Geschichte*).

Hilton, James, *Lost Horizon*, Hawthornden Prize ed., New York, 1934.

Histoire Littéraire de la France, vol. XXX, Paris, 1888.

Historia Meriadoci and De ortu Waluuanii, Two Arthurian Romances of the Thirteenth Century in Latin Prose, ed., J. Douglas Bruce, Göttingen and Baltimore, 1913 (*Hesperia, Ergänzungsreihe*, II).

Historia septem sapientum, ed. Alfons Hilka, Heidelberg, 1912 (*Sammlung mittellateinischer Texte*, 4,1).

History of the Holy Rood-Tree, A Twelfth Century Version of the Cross-Legend . . . and a Middle English Compassio Mariae, ed. Arthur S. Napier, London, 1894 (*EETS*, 103).

Hollander, Lee M., *Old Norse Poems, The Most Important Non-Skaldic Verse not Included in the Poetic Edda*, New York, 1936.

Hollander, Lee M., trans., *The Poetic Edda*, Austin, Texas, 1928.

Homer, The Odyssey of, trans. George Herbert Palmer, Boston and New York, 1891.

Homilies of the Anglo-Saxon Church, The. The First Part, containing the Sermones Catholici, or Homilies of Aelfric, ed. Benjamin Thorpe, 2 vols., London, 1844, 1846 (*Aelfric Society Publications* 1–4, 6–7).

Hopkins, Edward Washburn, *The Religions of India*, Boston and London, 1895 (*Handbooks on the History of Religions*, vol. I).

Horace: Odes and Epodes, ed. Paul Shorey, Boston, 1901.

Horn et Rimenhild, Recueil de ce qui reste des Poëmes relatifs à leurs Aventures, ed. F. Michel, Paris, 1845 (*Bannatyne Club*, 80).

Horstmann, C., *The Minor Poems of the Vernon MS*, London, 1892 (*EETS*, 98).

Horstmann, C., *Sammlung altenglischer Legenden*, first series, Heilbronn, 1878.

Huber, P. M., *Beitrag zur Visionsliteratur und Siebenschläferlegende des Mittelalters*, 2 vols., Matten, 1902–1903.

Hueline et Aiglantine, ed. D. M. Méon, *Nouveau Recueil de Fabliaux et Contes*, vol. I, Paris, 1823.

Hull, E., *The Cuchullin Saga in Irish Literature*, London, 1898 (*Grimm Library*, 8).

Hunbaut, Altfranzösischer Artusroman des xiii Jahrhunderts, ed. Jakob Stürzinger and Hermann Breuer, Dresden, 1914 (*Gesellschaft für romanische Literatur,* 35).

Huon de Bordeaux, Chanson de Geste, ed. F. Guessard and C. Grandmaison, Paris, 1860 (*Les anciens Poètes de la France,* V).

Huon of Burdeux, The Boke of Duke, see Bourchier.

[Huth] *Merlin, Roman en Prose du xiiie Siècle publié avec la Mise en Prose du Poème de Merlin de Robert de Boron d'après le Manuscrit appartenant à M. Alfred H. Huth,* 2 vols., Paris, 1886 (*SATF,* 55, 56).

Hyde, Douglas, ed. and trans., *Adventures of the Children of the King of Norway* and *Lad of the Ferule,* London, 1899 (*Irish Texts Society,* I).

Ingersoll, Ernest, *Birds in Legend, Fable, and Folklore,* New York, 1923.

Irenaei contra omnes haereses libri quinque, S., ed. A. Stieren, vol. I, Leipzig, 1853.

Iselin, Ludwig Emil, *Der Morgenländische Ursprung der Grallegende,* Halle, 1909.

Isidori Hispalensis Episcopi etymologiarum siue originum libri XX, ed. W. M. Lindsay, 2 vols., Oxford, 1911 (*Scriptorum classicorum bibliotheca Oxoniensis* 32, 33).

Jackson, A. V. Williams, *Zoroastrian Studies: The Iranian Religion and Various Monographs,* New York, 1928 (*Columbia Univ. Indo-Iranian Studies,* XII).

Jacobs, Joseph, ed., *Barlaam and Josaphat, English Lives of Buddha,* London, 1896 (*Bibliothèque de Carabas,* X).

Jacques de Vitry, Exempla or Illustrative Stories from the Sermones Vulgares of, ed. Thomas F. Crane, London, 1890 (*Publications of the Folk-Lore Society,* XXVI).

Jaffé, P., ed., *Bibliotheca rerum Germanicarum,* vol. III: *Monumenta Moguntina,* Berlin, 1866.

James I of Scots, *The Kingis Quair, Together with A Ballad of Good Counsel,* ed. W. W. Skeat, Edinburgh and London, 1911 (*Scottish Text Society,* n.s. 1).

James, M. R., The Apocryphal New Testament, Oxford, 1924 [impression of 1926].

Janer, F., *Poetas Castellanos ant. al Siglo XV,* Madrid, 1905 (*Bibl. de Autores Españoles,* 57).

Jardin de Plaisance et Fleur de Rethorique, Le, Reproduction en Fac-Similé de l'Édition publiée par Antoine Vérard vers 1501, Paris, 1910 (*SATF*, 51).

Jastrow, Morris, Jr., *Hebrew and Babylonian Traditions,* New York, 1914.

Jastrow, Morris, Jr., *The Religion of Babylonia and Assyria,* Boston, 1898.

Jaufre, ed. Hermann Breuer, Göttingen, 1925 (*Gesellschaft für romanische Literatur,* 46).

Jean d'Arras, compiler, *Melusine,* ed. A. K. Donald, part I, London, 1895 (*EETS:ES,* 68).

Jean d'Arras, Melusine, La Légende de, ed. Jean Marchand, Paris [1927].

Jenkins, T. A., *The Espurgatoire Saint Patriz of Marie de France* (*Investigations Representing the Departments of Romance Languages,* etc.), 1st series, VII, Chicago, 1903.

Jente, R., *Die Mythologischen Ausdrücke im Altenglischen Wortschatz,* Heidelberg, 1921 (*Anglistische Forschungen,* 56).

Jeremias, Alfred, *The Babylonian Conception of Heaven and Hell,* trans. J. Hutchinson, London, 1902 (*The Ancient East,* IV).

Jeû, The Book of, in *Texte und Untersuchungen zur Geschichte der Altchristlichen Literatur,* vol. VIII, ed. Oscar von Gebhardt and Adolf Harnack, Leipzig, 1892.

Jewish Encyclopaedia, The, New York, 1901–1906.

Joachim of Flora, *Visio de Gloria Paradisi,* in *Expositio magni Prophete Abbatis Joachim in Apocalipsim,* Venice, 1527.

Ioannis Damasceni, S., Opera omnia, vol. I, Paris, 1712.

John Damascene, Saint, Barlaam and Ioasaph, trans. G. R. Woodward and H. Mattingly, London, 1914 (*Loeb Library*).

John of Salisbury, The Frivolities of Courtiers and Footprints of Philosophers, Being a Translation of the First, Second, and Third Books and Selections from the Seventh and Eighth Books of the Policraticus of, ed. Joseph B. Pike, Minneapolis and London [1938].

Joinville, Jean Sire de, Histoire de Saint Louis par, ed. M. Natalis de Wailly, Paris, 1868.

Joinville, Jean Sire de, The History of St. Louis, ed. M. Natalis de Wailly, trans. Joan Evans, Oxford, 1938.

Jónsson, Finnur, *Edda Snorra Sturlusonar*, Reykjavík, 1907.

Jónsson, Finnur, *Den Norsk-Islandske Skjaldedightning*, 2 vols., Copenhagen, 1908.

Jorgensen, Johannes, *Saint Catherine of Siena,* trans. Ingeborg Lund, London, New York, and Toronto, 1938.

Josephus, trans. H. St. John Thackeray, in *Jewish Antiquities,* vol. IV, London and New York, 1930 (*Loeb Library*).

Joyce, P. W., *Old Celtic Romances,* London, 1894.

Juan Alfonso de Baena, El Cancionero de, ed. P. J. Pidal, Madrid, 1851.

Jubinal, A., *Jongleurs et Trouvères, ou Choix de Saluts, Épitres, Rêveries et autres Pièces légères des XIIIe et XIVe Siècles,* Paris, 1835.

Jubinal, A., *Mystères inédits du quinzième Siècle,* 2 vols. in 1, Paris, 1837.

Justini Philosophi et Martyris opera quae exstant omnia, Paris, 1742.

Kålund, K., ed., *Sturlunga Saga,* 2 vols., Copenhagen and Christiania, 1906, 1911.

Karlamagnus Saga ok Kappa Hans, ed. C. R. Unger, Christiania, 1860.

Karls des Grossen Reise nach Jerusalem und Constantinopel, ed. Eduard Koschwitz and Gustav Thurau, 6th printing, 5th ed., Leipzig, 1913 (*Altfranzösische Bibliothek,* II).

Keith, Arthur Berriedale, *The Religion and Philosophy of the Veda and Upanishads,* Cambridge [Mass.], 1925. (*Harvard Oriental Series,* XXXI and XXXII).

Kildare-Gedichte, Die, Die ältesten Mittelenglischen Denkmäler in Anglo-Irischer überlieferung, ed. W. Heuser, Bonn, 1904 (*Bonner Beiträge zur Anglistik,* XIV).

King, Georgiana G., *The Way of Saint James,* 3 vols., New York and London, 1920 (*Hispanic Notes and Monographs*).

King Horn, A Middle-English Romance, ed. Joseph Hall, Oxford, 1901.

Kinkel, Gottfried, *Epicorum Graecorum Fragmenta,* Leipzig, 1877.

[*Kittredge*] *Anniversary Papers,* Boston and London, 1913.

Kittredge, George Lyman, *A Study of Gawain and the Green Knight,* Cambridge, 1916.

[*Klaeber*] *Studies in English Philology, A Miscellany in Honor of Frederick Klaeber,* ed. Kemp Malone and Martin B. Ruud, Minneapolis, 1929.

Klint, Eric, *Exercitium Academicum de situ Paradisi Terrestris,* Uppsala, 1714.

Kong Olger Danske's Kronicke, in *Christiern Pedersens Danske Skrifter,* vol. V, Copenhagen, 1856.

Krapp, George P., *The Legend of Saint Patrick's Purgatory: Its Later Literary History,* Baltimore, 1900.

Krappe, Alexander Haggerty, *Balor with the Evil Eye, Studies in Celtic and French Literature* [New York], 1927 (*Columbia University Institut des Études Françaises*).

Krappe, Alexander Haggerty, *The Science of Folk-Lore,* New York, 1930.

Kuhn, Ernst, *Barlaam und Joasaph,* in *Abhandlungen der Königl. Bayer. Akad. der Wissenschaften, Philos.-Philol. Cl.,* XX, Munich, 1897.

Kuhnmuench, Otto J., *Early Christian Latin Poets from the Fourth to the Sixth Century,* Chicago, 1929.

Laisrén, Vision of, ed. Kuno Meyer, in *Otia Merseiana,* vol. I, 1899.

Lambert Li Tors, see *Roman d'Alexandre.*

Lamprechts Alexander, ed. Karl Kinzel, Halle a.S., 1884 (*Germanistische Handbibliothek,* VI).

Landau, Marcus, *Hölle und Fegfeuer in Volksglaube, Dichtung und Kirchenlehre,* Heidelberg, 1909.

[*Landnámabók*] *Íslendingabók . . . og Landnámabók,* V. Ásmundarson, Reykjavík, 1909 (*Íslendinga Sögur,* I).

Langdon, Stephen Herbert, *Mythology of All Races,* vol. V: *Semitic,* Boston, 1931.

Langlois, Ernest, *Origines et Sources du Roman de la Rose,* Paris, 1891 (*Bibliothèque des Écoles Françaises d'Athènes et de Rome,* part 58).

Larminie, William, *West Irish Folk-Tales and Romances,* London, 1893 (*Camden Library*).

La Sale, Antoine de, Le Paradis de la Reine Sibylle, ed. Fernand Desonay, Paris, 1930.

La Salle, Antoine de, Sa Vie et ses Ouvrages . . . Du Paradis de la Reine Sibylle, etc., ed. Joseph Nève, Paris and Brussels, 1903.

Latini, Brunetto, Li Livres dou Tresor par, ed. P. Chabaille, Paris, 1863 (*Collection de Documents inédits sur l'Histoire de France,* première série, *Histoire littéraire*).

Latini, Brunetto, Il Tesoro di, volgarizzato da Bono Giamboni, ed. P. Chabaille, vol. II, Bologna, 1877.

Latini, Ser Brunetto, Il Tesoretto e il Favoletto di, ed. G. Batista Zannoni, Florence, 1824.

Leach, Henry Goddard, *Angevin Britain and Scandinavia,* Cambridge [Mass.], 1921 (*Harvard Studies in Comparative Literature,* VI).

Leahy, A. H., *Heroic Romances of Ireland,* vol. I, London, 1905.

Le Bel Inconnu see Renaut de Beaujeu.

Lebor na Huidre, Book of the Dun Cow, ed. R. I. Best and Osborn Bergin, Dublin, 1929.

Lecoy de la Marche, A., *Anecdotes Historiques, Légendes et Apologues, tirés du Recueil inédit d'Étienne de Bourbon,* Paris, 1877.

Legrand D'Aussy, P. J. B., *Fabliaux ou Contes du XIIe et du XIIIe Siècle,* 4 vols., Paris, 1779.

Legrand D'Aussy, P. J. B., *Fabliaux ou Contes du XIIe et du XIIIe Siècle,* vol. I, 3rd ed., Paris, 1829.

Leibniz, G. W., *Scriptores rerum Brunsuicensium,* I, Hanover, 1707.

Leonard, William Ellery, *Gilgamesh, Epic of Old Babylonia,* New York, 1934.

Libeaus Desconus, die Mittelenglische Romanze vom Schönen unbekannten, ed. Max Kaluza, Leipzig, 1890 (*Altenglische Bibliothek,* V).

"Little Flowers" and the Life of St. Francis, with the "Mirror of Perfection," The, trans. T. Okey, Robert Steele, and E. Gurney Salter, London, 1923 (repr. of 1910 ed., *Everyman's Library*).

Lombard, Peter, *Ad claras aquas,* vol. I, 2nd ed., 1916.

Lommatzsch, Erhard, ed., *Le Lai de Guingamor, Le Lai de Tydorel,* Berlin, 1922 (*Romanische Texte,* 6).

[Loomis] Gertrude Schoepperle, *Tristan and Isolt, A Study of the Sources of the Romance,* 2 vols. in 1, Frankfurt and London, 1913 (*New York University Ottendorfer Memorial Series of Germanic Monographs,* 6–7).

[Loomis] Laura A. Hibbard, *Mediaeval Romance in England, A Study of the Sources and Analogues of the Non-Cyclic Metrical Romances,* New York, 1924 (*Wellesley Semi-Centennial Series,* I).

Loomis, Roger Sherman, *Arthurian Tradition and Chrétien de Troyes*, New York, 1949.

Loomis, Roger Sherman, *Celtic Myth and Arthurian Romance*, New York, 1927.

Loomis, Roger Sherman, *"Chastiel Bran, Dinas Bran," and the Grail Castle*, in *A Miscellany of Studies in Romance Languages and Literatures in Honour of L. E. Kastner*, Cambridge [Eng.], 1932.

Loomis, Roger Sherman, and Laura Hibbard, *Arthurian Legends in Medieval Art*, London and New York, 1938 (*Monograph Series of the Modern Language Association of America*).

Lopez de Mendoza, Dom Iñigo, Marques de Santillana, Obras de, ed. José Amador de los Rios, Madrid, 1852.

Lorenzo de' Medici, Il Magnifico, Opere, ed. Attilio Simioni, vol. I, Bari, 1913 (*Scrittori d'Italia*, 54).

Löseth, E., *Le Roman en Prose de Tristan, Le Roman de Palamède et la Compilation de Rusticien de Pise*, Paris, 1890.

Loth, J., *Les Mabinogion*, 2 vols., Paris, 1889; also vol. I, Paris, 1913; (*Cours de Littérature Celtique*, III and IV).

Lovejoy, A. O., and George Boas, *Contributions to the History of Primitivism, Primitivism and Related Ideas in Antiquity*, Baltimore, 1935 (*A Documentary History of Primitivism and Related Ideas*, I).

Lucian, *True History*, in *Lucian*, trans. A. M. Harmon, vol. I, London, 1913 (*Loeb Library*).

Ludwig, A., *Der Rigveda; oder die heiligen Hymnen der Brâhmana*, vol. II, Prague, 1876.

Lungo, I. del, ed., *Leggende del Secolo XIV*, 2 vols., Florence, 1863.

Lydgate, John, *The Assembly of Gods or The Accord of Reason and Sensuality in the Fear of Death*, ed. Oscar L. Triggs, London, 1896 (*EETS:ES*, 69).

Lydgate, John, The Minor Poems of, ed. Henry Noble MacCracken and Merriam Sherwood, part II: *Secular Poems*, London, 1934 (*EETS*, 192).

Lydgate, John, *The Pilgrimage of the Life of Man, Englisht by John Lydgate, A.D. 1426, from the French of Guillaume de Guileville, A.D. 1330, 1355*, ed. Katharine B. Locock, part III, London, 1904 (*EETS:ES*, 92).

Lydgate's Reson and Sensuallyte, ed. Ernst Sieper, parts I and II, London, 1901, 1903 (*EETS:ES,* 84, 89).

Lydgate's Temple of Glas, ed. J. Schick, London, 1891 (*EETS:ES,* 60).

"Lyke-Wake Dirge, A," in *The Oxford Book of English Verse,* ed. Arthur Quiller-Couch, Oxford, 1908.

Mabinogion, The, A New Translation, trans. T. P. Ellis and John Lloyd, 2 vols., Oxford, 1929.

MacCulloch, J. A., *Early Chrsitian Visions of the Other-World,* Edinburgh, 1912.

MacCulloch, J. A., *The Harrowing of Hell, a Comparative Study of an Early Christian Doctrine,* Edinburgh, 1930.

MacCulloch, J. A., *Medieval Faith and Fable,* with a foreword by Sir J. G. Frazer, London, 1932.

MacCulloch, J. A., *The Mythology of All Races,* vol. II: *Eddic,* Boston, 1930.

MacCulloch, J. A., *The Religion of the Ancient Celts,* Edinburgh, 1911.

MacDonald, D. B., *The Religious Attitude and Life in Islam,* Chicago, 1912.

MacDonald, K. S., and John Morrison, eds., *The Story of Barlaam and Joasaph: Buddhism and Christianity,* Calcutta, 1895.

MacInnes, D., *Folk and Hero Tales,* London, 1890 (*Folk-Lore Society,* XXV).

MacKensen, L., ed., *Handwörterbuch des Deutschen Märchens,* Berlin, 1904–1940.

Mackenzie, Donald A., *Egyptian Myth and Legend,* London, 1913.

Mackenzie, Donald A., *Myths of Babylonia and Assyria,* London [no date].

McColley, Grant, *Paradise Lost, An Account of its Growth and Major Origins, with a Discussion of Milton's Use of Sources and Literary Patterns,* Chicago, 1940.

Magoun, Francis P., *The Gests of King Alexander of Macedon,* Cambridge [Mass.], 1929.

Malory, Sir Thomas, The Works of, ed. Eugène Vinaver, 3 vols., Oxford, 1947.

Mandeville's Travels, Translated from the French by Jean d'Outremeuse, ed. P. Hamelius, vol. I, London, 1919 (*EETS,* 153).

Manly Anniversary Studies in Language and Literature, The, Chicago, 1923.

Mannhardt, Wilhelm, *Wald- und Feldkulte,* ed. W. Heuschkel, vol. I: *Der Baumkultus der Germanen und ihrer Nachbarstämme Mythologische untersuchungen,* Berlin, 1904.

Map, Walter, De nugis curialium, ed. M. R. James, Oxford, 1914 (*Anecdota Oxoniensia, Mediaeval and Modern Series,* XIV).

[Map] *Master Walter Map's Book De Nugis Curialium* (*Courtiers' Trifles*), trans. Frederick Tupper and M. B. Ogle, New York, 1924.

Marco Polo the Venetian concerning the Kingdoms and Marvels of the East, The Book of Ser, trans. Sir Henry Yule, 3rd ed., revised by Henri Cordier, 2 vols., London, 1903.

Marie de France, Die Lais der, ed. Karl Warnke, 3rd ed., Halle a.S., 1925 (*Bibliothéca Normannica,* III).

Marie de France, Lais, ed. Alfred Ewert, Oxford, 1944.

Marvels of Britain in *Auctores antiquissimi, XIII,* 1 (*Chronica Minora,* III, 1) pp. 213ff., ed. T. Mommsen, Berlin, 1894 (*MGH*).

Maspero, G., *The Dawn of Civilization — Egypt and Chaldea,* ed. A. H. Sayce, trans. M. L. McClure, 3rd ed., London, 1897.

Maundevil, The Buke of, ed. G. F. Warner, London, 1889 (*Roxburghe Club*).

Maynadier, G. H., *The Wife of Bath's Tale, Its Sources and Analogues,* London, 1901 (*Grimm Library,* 13).

Mélanges de Linguistique et de Littérature offerts à M. Alfred Jeanroy, Paris, 1928.

Meyer, Kuno, ed. and trans., *The Voyage of Bran Son of Febal to the Land of the Living . . . With an Essay upon the Irish Vision of the Happy Otherworld and the Celtic Doctrine of Rebirth,* by Alfred Nutt, 2 volumes, London, 1895 and 1897 (*Grimm Library,* 4, 6).

Meyer, Kuno, trans., see *Wooing of Emer.*

Meyer, Paul, *Alexandre le Grand dans la Littérature française du Moyen Age,* 2 vols., Paris, 1886.

Meyer, W., *Die Geschichte des Kreuzholzes,* in *Abhandlungen der Königl. Bayer Akad. der Wissenschaften, Philos.-Philol. Cl.,* XVI, 2, Munich, 1882.

Meyer, W., *Vita Adae et Evae,* in *Abhandlungen der Königl. Bayer. Akad. der Wissenschaften, Philos.-Philol. Cl.,* XIV, 3, Munich, 1878.

Middleton, Christopher, The Famous Historie of Chinon of England by, ed. William E. Mead, London, 1925 for 1923 (*EETS,* 165).

Migne, J. P., ed., *Patrologiae cursus completus: Patrologia Latina*, 221 vols., Paris, 1844–1864.

Migne, J. P., *Patrologiae cursus completus, Series Graeca et Orientalis*, 81 vols., Paris, 1856–1867.

Migne, J. P., ed., *Patrologiae cursus completus; Series Graeca, trans. Lat.*, 161 vols., Paris, 1857–1866.

Mills, L. H., *Avesta Eschatology Compared with the Books of Daniel and Revelations*, Chicago, 1908.

Mogk, E., *Bergkult*, in *Reallexicon der germanischen Altertumskunde* etc., ed. Johannes Hoops, vol. I, pp. 255–256, Strasburg, 1911–1913.

Mone, F. J., *Lateinische Hymnen des Mittelalters*, vol. I, Freiburg, 1853.

[Monk of Eynsham], *Visio Monachi de Eynsham*, in *Analecta Bollandiana*, vol. XXII, Paris and Brussels, 1903 (*Société Générale de Librairie Catholique*).

Morel, P. G., *Lateinische Hymnen des Mittelalters*, New York, 1868.

Morison, Samuel Eliot, *Admiral of the Ocean Sea, A Life of Christopher Columbus*, 2 vols., Boston, 1942.

Morris, Richard, ed., *Legends of the Holy Rood; Symbols of the Passion and Cross-Poems*, London, 1871 (*EETS*, 46).

Mosis Bar-Cepha Syri, Maxima bibliotheca veterum patrum et antiquorum scriptorum, vol. XVII, Leyden, 1677.

Müller, C., ed., *Pseudo-Callisthenes* (appended to Fr. Dübner's ed. of *Arrian*), Paris, 1877.

Müller, W. Max, *The Mythology of All Races*, vol. XII: *Egyptian*, Boston, 1918.

Munch, Peter A., *Norse Mythology*, revised by Magnus Olsen and translated by S. B. Hustvedt, New York and London, 1926 (*The American-Scandinavian Foundation*).

Muratori, L. A., *Rerum Italicarum scriptores*, Milan, 25 vols., 1723–1751, 1748–1770.

Mussafia, Adolfo, *Sulla Visione di Tundalo*, in *Sitzungsberichte der philosophisch-historischen Classe der Kaiserlichen Akademie der Wissenschaften*, vol. 67, pp. 157ff., Vienna, 1871.

Naumann, Hans, *Primitive Gemeinschaftskultur*, in *Beiträge zur Volkskunde und Mythologie*, Jena, 1921.

Neckam, Alexander, *De naturis rerum,* Book II, and *De Laudibus divinae sapientiae,* ed. Thomas Wright, London, 1863 (*Rolls Series,* XXXIV).

Neckel, Gustav, ed., *Edda, die Lieder des Codex Regius nebst Verwandten Denkmälern,* vol. I: Text, Heidelberg, 1914 (*Germanische Bibliothek,* ed. Wilhelm Streitberg, IX).

Neilson, William Allan, *The Origins and Sources of the Court of Love,* Boston, 1899 ([*Harvard*] *Studies and Notes in Philology and Literature,* VI).

[Nennius], *Historia Britonum,* ed. T. Mommsen, in *Auctores antiquissimi,* vol. XIII, 1, (*Chronica Minora,* III, 1,) pp. 111ff., Berlin, 1894 (*MGH*).

Nennius's "History of the Britons" etc., trans. A. W. Wade-Evans, London [1938] (*SPCK*).

Nevill, William, The Castell of Pleasure by, ed. Roberta D. Cornelius, London, 1930 for 1928 (*EETS,* 179).

Nicole de Margival, Le Dit de la Panthère d'Amours par, ed. Henry A. Todd, Paris, 1883 (*SATF,* 77).

Nitze, William Albert, "The Castle of the Grail – An Irish Analogue," in *Studies in Honor of A. Marshall Elliott,* vol. I, pp. 19–51, Baltimore [1911].

Norris, E., *The Ancient Cornish Drama,* 2 vols., Oxford, 1859.

Nutt, Alfred, *Irish Vision of the Happy Otherworld,* see Kuno Meyer, *The Voyage of Bran,* etc.

O'Grady, Standish H., ed. and trans., *Silva Gadelica* (*i–xxxi*), *A Collection of Tales in Irish,* 2 vols., London, 1892.

Óláf Tryggvason, Saga of, in *Fornmanna Sögur,* III, Copenhagen 1827.

Oldenberg, Hermann, *Die Religion des Veda,* Berlin, 1894.

Olrik, Axel, *The Heroic Legends of Denmark,* trans. L. M. Hollander, New York, 1919 (*Scandinavian Monographs,* IV).

Oracula Sibyllina, Die, ed. Joh. Geffcken, Leipzig, 1902.

Oracula Sibyllina, Sibyllinischen Weissagungen vollstaendig Gesammelt, ed. Joseph Henry Friedlieb, Leipzig, 1852.

Orfeo, Sir, Ein Englisches Feenmärchen aus dem Mittelalter, ed. Oscar Zielke, Breslau, 1880.

Origen, *De principiis,* in *The Ante-Nicene Fathers,* ed. Alexander Roberts and James Donaldson, revised by A. Cleveland Coxe, vol. IV, pp. 239ff., Buffalo, 1885.

Os, Arnold B. van, *Religious Visions. The Development of the Eschatological Elements in Medieval Religious Literature,* Amsterdam, 1932.

Ovid, Metamorphoses, trans. Frank J. Miller, 2 vols., Cambridge [Mass.], 1929 (*Loeb Library*).

Owst, G. R., *Literature and Pulpit in Medieval England, A Neglected Chapter in the History of English Letters and of the English People,* Cambridge [Eng.], 1933.

Ozanam, A. F., *Documents inédits pour servir a l'Histoire littéraire depuis le VIII*[e] *Siècle jusqu'au XIII*[e]*, avec des Recherches sur le Moyen Age Italien,* Paris, 1850.

Ozanam, A. F., *Les Poëtes Franciscains en Italie au treizième Siècle,* in *Œuvres Complètes de A. F. Ozanam, avec une Préface par M. Ampère,* 6th ed., vol. V, Paris, 1882.

Pahlavi Texts, Part I, *The Bundahis, Bahman Yast, and Shâyast Lâ-Shâyast,* trans. E. W. West, Oxford, 1880 (*Sacred Books of the East,* V).

Pahlavi Texts, Part II, *The Dâdistân-î Dînîk and the Epistles of Mânûskîhar,* trans. E. W. West, Oxford, 1882 (*Sacred Books of the East,* XVIII).

Panzer, Friedrich, *Studien zur Germanische Sagengeschichte,* vol. I: *Beowulf,* Munich, 1910.

Paris, Gaston, *Légendes du Moyen Age: Roncevaux, Le Paradis de la Reine Sibylle, La Légende du Tannhäuser, Le Juif Errant, Le Lai de l'Oiselet,* 4th ed., Paris, 1912.

Parlement of the Thre Ages, The, ed. Israel Gollancz, London, 1897 (*Roxburghe Club*).

Partenay, see *Romans.*

Partonope of Blois, The Middle-English Versions of, ed. A. Trampe Bödtker, London, 1912 for 1911 (*EETS:ES,* 109).

Partonopeus de Blois, ed. A. C. M. Robert, 2 vols., Paris, 1834.

Passerini, G. L., ed., *I Fioretti del Glorioso Messere Santo Francesco e de' Suoi Frati,* 4th ed., Florence [1905].

Patch, Howard Rollin, *The Goddess Fortuna in Mediaeval Literature,* Cambridge [Mass.], 1927.

Patch, Howard Rollin, *The Tradition of Boethius, A Study of His Importance in Medieval Culture,* New York, 1935.

Paton, Lucy A., *Studies in the Fairy Mythology of Arthurian Romance*, Boston, 1903 (*Radcliffe College Monographs*, 13).

Paul the Deacon, History of the Langobards by, trans. William Dudley Foulke, University of Pennsylvania [Department of History], Philadelphia, 1907.

Paul, The Vision of, trans. Andrew Rutherfurd, in *The Ante-Nicene Fathers*, ed. Alexander Roberts and James Donaldson, revised by A. Cleveland Coxe, vol. IX, New York, 1906, Supplt., ed. Allan Menzies, pp. 149ff.

Paulus Diaconus, *Historia Langobardorum*, ed. L. Bethmann and G. Waitz, in *Scriptores rerum Langobardicarum et Italicarum, s. vi–ix*, pp. 12ff., Hanover, 1878 (*MGH*).

Pausaniae descriptio Graeciae, ed. J. H. C. Schubart, vol. II, Leipzig, 1883 (*Teubner Text*).

Pausanius's Description of Greece, trans. with commentary by J. G. Frazer, vol. V, London, 1898.

Pavry, Jal Dastur Cursetji, *The Zoroastrian Doctrine of a Future Life, From Death to the Individual Judgment*, New York, 1926 (*Columbia University Indo-Iranian Series*, II).

Paz y Mélia, A., *Opúsculos Literarios*, Madrid, 1892 (*Soc. de Bibl. Españoles*, XXIX).

Pearl, The, A Middle English Poem, ed. C. G. Osgood, Boston and London, 1906 (*Belles-Lettres Series*, Section II, *Middle English Literature*).

Perceval le Gallois, ou Le Conte du Graal, ed. Ch. Potvin, vols. III and IV, Mons, 1866, 1868.

[*Perlesvaus*], Nitze, W. A., and T. A. Jenkins, eds., *Le Haut Livre du Graal, Perlesvaus*, vol. I, Chicago, 1932 (*Modern Philology Monographs of the University of Chicago*).

[*Perlesvaus*], Nitze, W. A., and collaborators, *Le Haut Livre du Graal, Perlesvaus*, vol. II, Chicago, 1937 (*Modern Philology Monographs of the University of Chicago*).

Peter, The Revelation of, trans. Andrew Rutherfurd, in *The Ante-Nicene Fathers*, ed. Allan Menzies, vol. IX, pp. 141ff., 5th ed., New York, 1906.

Petrarca, F., I Trionfi di, Testo critico, ed. Carl Appel, Halle a.S., 1902.

Petrarcas, Francesco, Die Triumphe, ed. Carl Appel, Halle a.S., 1901.

Petrus Alfonsi, Die Disciplina Clericalis des, ed. Alfons Hilka and Werner Söderhjelm, Heidelberg, 1911 (*Sammlung mittellateinischer Texte,* 1).

Philippe de Remi, Sire de Beaumanoir, Œuvres Poétiques de, ed. Hermann Suchier, 2 vols., Paris, 1884, 1885 (*SATF,* 82, 83).

Philo, *On the Creation,* in *Philo,* ed. F. H. Colson and G. H. Whitaker, vol. I, London and New York, 1929 (*Loeb Library*).

Photius, *Æthiopus,* in *Epicorum Graecorum fragmenta,* ed. G. Kinkel, Leipzig, 1877.

Photius, *Epitome of Ecclesiasticae Historiae,* see *Sozomen,* ed. E. Walford.

Photius, *Epitome,* of Philostorgius's *Ecclesiasticae Historiae, Libri XII,* trans. into Latin, by J. Gothofredus, Geneva, 1642.

Pinchin, Edith F., *The Bridge of the Gods in Gaelic Mythology,* London, 1934.

Piquet, F., *Étude sur Hartmann d'Aue,* Paris, 1898.

Piquet, F., *L'Originalité de Gottfried de Strasbourg dans son Poème de Tristan et Isolde,* Lille, 1905 (*Travaux et Mémoires de l'Université de Lille,* I, 5).

Plato, trans. Harold North Fowler, vol. I: *Euthyphro, Apology, Crito, Phaedo, Phaedrus,* London, New York, 1928; first printed, 1914 (*Loeb Library*).

Plato, The Republic, trans. by Paul Shorey, 2 vols., London and New York, 1930 and 1935 (*Loeb Library*).

Plummer, Charles, ed. and trans., *Bethada Náem nÉrenn, Lives of Irish Saints,* 2 vols., Oxford, 1922.

Plummer, Charles, *Vitae Sanctorum Hiberniae,* 2 vols., Oxford, 1910.

Plutarch, "Concerning Such Whom God Is Slow to Punish," trans. John Philips, in *Plutarch's Morals. Translated from the Greek by Several Hands,* introd. Ralph Waldo Emerson, ed. William Goodwin, vol. IV, New York, 1905 (*The Writings of Plutarch,* vol. IX : *Miscellanies,* The Athenaeum Society).

Plutarch's Lives, trans. Bernadotte Perrin, vol. VIII: *Sertorius,* etc., London and New York, 1919 (*Loeb Library*).

Pollard, A. F., *Tudor Tracts, 1532–1538,* vol. VIII of *Arber's English Garner,* Westminster, 1903.

Pomponius Mela, *De situ orbis,* vol. I, Leipzig, 1807.

Portugal, el Condestable de, "Sátira de Felice é Infelice Vida," in *Opúsculos Literarios de los Siglos XIV à XVI*, ed. A. Paz y Mélia, Madrid, 1892 (*Sociedad de Bibliófilos Españoles*, XXIX).

Post, Chandler R., *Mediaeval Spanish Allegory*, Cambridge [Mass.], 1915 (*Harvard Studies in Comparative Literature*, IV).

Priester Johannes, Der, see Zarncke, Friedrich.

Prise de Defur and Le Voyage d'Alexandre au Paradis Terrestre, La, ed. Lawton P. G. Peckham and Milau S. La Du, Princeton and Paris, 1935 (*Elliott Monographs in the Romance Languages and Literatures*, 35).

[Proba, Falconia], *Probae Cento*, in *Poetae Christiani minores*, ed. C. Schenkl, part I, Vienna, 1888 (*CSEL*, XVI).

Procopius, History of the Wars, Books VII (continued) and VIII, trans. H. B. Dewing, vol. V, London, 1928 (*Loeb Library*).

[Prudentius] *Aurelii Prudentii Clementis, Carmina*, ed. G. Bergman, Vienna and Leipzig, 1926 (*CSEL*, LXI).

Pschmadt, Carl, *Die Sage von der verfolgten Hinde*, Greifswald diss., Greifswald, 1911.

Quatrefoil of Love, The, ed. Israel Gollancz and Magdalene Weale, London, 1935 for 1934 (*EETS*, 195).

Rabelais, François, Œuvres de, ed. Abel Lefranc, Paris, 1912–1922.

Rabelais, The Works of, Faithfully Translated from the French, London — Chatto and Windus, [no date].

Raby, F. J. E., *A History of Christian-Latin Poetry. From the Beginnings to the Close of the Middle Ages*, Oxford, 1927.

Raby, F. J. E., *A History of Secular Latin Poetry in the Middle Ages*, 2 vols., Oxford, 1934.

Rachbauer, Sister Mary Aloysia, *Wolfram von Eschenbach, A Study of the Relation of the Content of Books III — VI and IX of the Parzifal to the Crestien Manuscripts*, Washington, 1934 (*Catholic University of America, Studies in German*, IV).

Rafn, C. C., *Fornaldarsögur Norðrlanda*, III, Copenhagen, 1830.

Ragozin, Zénaïde A., *The Story of Chaldea, From the Earliest Times to the Rise of Assyria*, New York, 1890.

Ralph of Coggeshall, *Chronicon Anglicanum*, ed. Joseph Stevenson, London, 1875 (*Rolls Series*, LXVI).

Ranisch, Wilhelm, and Andreas Heusler, eds., *Eddica minora*, Dortmund, 1903.

[Raoul von Houdenc], *Meraugis von Portlesguez,* ed. Mathias Friedwagner, Halle a.S., 1897 (*Raoul von Houdenc, Sämtliche Werke,* I).

[Raoul von Houdenc], *La Vengeance Raguidel,* ed. Mathias Friedwagner, Halle a.S., 1909 (*Raoul von Houdenc, Sämtliche Werke,* II).

Reinhard, John Revell, *The Old French Romance of Amadas et Ydoine, An Historical Study,* Durham, N.C., 1927 (*Duke University Publications*).

Renaut de Beaujeu, *Le Bel Inconnu, Roman d'Aventures,* ed. G. Perrie Williams, Paris, 1929 (*Les Classiques Français du Moyen Age,* XXXVIII).

René, Roi, Œuvres complètes du, ed. Le Compte de Quatrebarbes, vol. III, Angers, 1846.

Renier, R., *Memorie della Reale Accademia delle Scienze di Torino, Morali, Storiche e Filologiche,* 2nd series, XLI, Turin, 1891.

Revelation to the Monk of Evesham, 1196, The, Carefully Edited from the Unique Copy, now in the British Museum, of the Edition Printed by William de Machlina about 1482, ed. Edward Arber, Westminster, 1869 (*English Reprints*).

Rhŷs, John, *Celtic Folklore, Welsh and Manx,* 2 vols., Oxford, 1901.

Rhŷs, John, *Studies in the Arthurian Legend,* Oxford, 1891.

Richter, Werner, *Der Lanzelet des Ulrich von Zazikhoven,* Frankfurt, 1934 (*Deutsche Forschungen* 27).

Rigomer von Jehan, Les Mervelles de, Altfranzösischer Artusroman des xiii. Jahrhunderts, vol. I, text, ed. Wendelin Foerster, Dresden, 1908; vol. II, notes, ed. Hermann Breuer and Wendelin Foerster, Dresden, 1915 (*Gesellschaft für romanische Literatur,* 19, 39).

Robinson, J. A., *The Passion of S. Perpetua,* Cambridge, 1891 (*Texts and Studies* I, 2).

Robinson, J. A., *Two Glastonbury Legends: King Arthur and St. Joseph of Arimathea,* Cambridge, 1926.

Rogeri de Wendover, Chronica, sive flores historiarum, ed. Henry O. Cox, 4 vols., London, 1841–1844 (*English Historical Society Publications,* III, IX, X, XI).

Roger of Wendover's Flowers of History, Comprising the History of England from the Descent of the Saxons to A.D. 1235. Formerly Ascribed to Matthew Paris, trans. J. A. Giles, 2 vols., London, 1849.

Rohde, Erwin, *Der Griechische Roman und seine Vorläufer*, Leipzig, 1900.

Rohde, Erwin, *Psyche, The Cult of Souls and Belief in Immortality among the Greeks*, trans. W. B. Hillis, New York, 1925.

Rohde, Erwin, *Psyche; Seelencult und Unsterblichkeitsglaube der Griechen*, 2 vols. in 1, Tübingen and Leipzig, 1903.

Róheim, Géza, *Animism, Magic, and the Divine King*, London, 1930.

Roman d'Alexandre par Lambert li Tors et Alexandre de Bernay, Li, ed. Heinrich Michelant, Stuttgart, 1846 (*Bibl. des Litt. Vereins in Stuttgart*, XIII).

Romans of Partenay, The, or of Lusignen : Otherwise known as The Tale of Melusine, ed. Walter W. Skeat, London, 1866 (*EETS*, 22).

Rudolf von Ems, Die Quellen zum Alexander des, ed. O. Zingerle, Breslau, 1885 (*Germanistische Abhandlungen*).

Rüegg, August, *Die Jenseitsvorstellungen vor Dante und die übrigen literarischen Voraussetzungen der "Divina Commedia,"* 2 vols., Einsiedeln and Cologne [1945].

Rutebeuf, Trouvère du XIIIe Siècle, Œuvres complètes de, ed. Achille Jubinal, 3 vols., new ed., Paris [1874–1875].

Rydberg, Viktor, *Teutonic Mythology, Gods and Goddesses of the Northland*, trans. Rasmus B. Anderson, London, 1906.

Sabatier, Paul, ed., *Actus Beati Francisci et Sociorum Eius*, Paris, 1902 (*Coll. d'Études de Documents sur l'Histoire Religieuse et Littéraire du Moyen Age*, IV).

Santillana, Marques de, see Lopez de Mendoza.

Saxo Grammaticus, The First Nine Books of the Danish History of, trans. Oliver Elton, introd. by Fred. York Powell, London, 1894 (*Publications of the Folk-Lore Society*, XXXIII).

Schanz, Martin von, *Geschichte der Romischen Litteratur bis zum Gesetzgebungswerk des Kaisers Justinian*, IV, 2, Munich, 1920 (*Handbuch der Klassischen Altertums-Wissenschaft*, ed. Iwan von Müller, VIII).

Scheer, Eduardus, *Lycophronis Alexandra*, 2 vols., Berlin, 1908.

Scherman, Lucian, *Materialien zur Geschichte der Indischen Visionslitteratur*, Leipzig, 1892.

Schirmer, Gustav, *Zur Brendanus-Legende*, Leipzig, 1888.

Schlauch, Margaret, *Romance in Iceland*, Princeton, 1934 (*American Scandinavian Foundation*).

Schmeller, J. A., ed., *Carmina Burana, Lateinische und Deutsche Lieder und Gedichte einer Handschrift des XIII. Jahrhunderts aus Benedictbeuern,* Breslau, 1904.

Schmidt, Carl, ed., *Koptisch-Gnostische Schriften,* I, Leipzig, 1905.

Schoepperle, Gertrude, see Gertrude Schoepperle Loomis.

Schofield, William H., *The Lay of Guingamor,* Boston, 1896 ([*Harvard*] *Studies and Notes in Philology and Literature,* V).

Schofield, William H., *Mythical Bards and The Life of William Wallace,* Cambridge [Mass.], 1920 (*Harvard Studies in Comparative Literature,* V).

Schofield, William H., *Studies on the Libeaus Desconus,* Boston, 1895 ([*Harvard*] *Studies and Notes in Philology and Literature,* IV).

Schultz, Alwin, *Das höfische Leben zur Zeit der Minnesinger,* 2 vols., Leipzig, 1889.

Sébillot, Paul, *Le Folk-Lore de France,* 3 vols., Paris, 1904–1906.

Servius Honoratus, Maurus, *In Aeneidos libros Comentarii,* in *Commentarii in Virgilium Serviani,* etc., vol. I, Göttingen, 1826.

Servius Honoratus, Maurus, *Servii Grammatici qui feruntur in Vergilii Aeneidos Libros I–III,* ed. George Thilo, Leipzig, 1878.

Severus, Sulpicius, Libri qui supersunt recensuit et Commentario critico, ed. Charles Halm, Vienna, 1866 (*CSEL,* I).

Seymour, St. John D., *Irish Visions of the Other-World,* London, 1930 (*SPCK*).

Shea, David, and Anthony Troyer, *The Dabistan or School of Manners,* 2 vols., Paris, 1843.

Shea, David, and Anthony Troyer, *The Dabistan or School of Manners,* reprinted in *Universal Classics Library,* vol. VI: *Oriental Literature,* Washington and London [1901].

Shepherd of Hermas, The in *The Apostolic Fathers,* vol. II, pp. 1ff., ed. Kirsopp Lake, London, 1913 (*Loeb Library*).

Sidonius, Poems and Letters, with an English Translation, trans. W. B. Anderson, 2 vols., Cambridge [Mass.], 1936 (*Loeb Library*).

Sieper, Ernst, *Les Echecs Amoureux,* Weimar, 1898 (*Litterarhistorische Forschungen,* IX).

Silverstein, Theodore, *Did Dante Know the Vision of Saint Paul?* Boston, 1937 ([*Harvard*] *Studies and Notes in Philology and Literature,* XIX).

Silverstein, Theodore, *Visio Sancti Pauli, the History of the Apocalypse in Latin, together with Nine Texts,* ed. Kirsopp Lake and Silva Lake, London, 1935 (*Studies and Documents,* IV).

[Simeon of Durham], *Symeonis Monachi Opera Omnia,* ed. Thomas Arnold, 2 vols., London, 1882, 1885 (*Rolls Series,* LXXV).

Siuts, Hans, *Jenseitsmotive im Deutschen Volksmärchen,* Leipzig, 1911 (*Teutonia,* XIX).

Skene, William F., *The Four Ancient Books of Wales, containing the Cymric Poems attributed to the Bards of the Sixth Century,* 2 vols., Edinburgh, 1868.

Smyser, H. M., and F. P. Magoun, Jr., trans., *Survivals in Old Norwegian,* Baltimore, 1941 (*Connecticut College Monographs,* I).

Söderhjelm, Werner, "Antoine de la Sale et la Légende de Tannhäuser," in *Mémoires de la Société néo-philologique à Helsingfors,* vol. II, Helsingfors, 1897.

Sommer, H. Oskar, ed., *Die Abenteuer Gawains Ywains und Le Morholts mit den drei Jungfrauen, aus der Trilogie (Demanda) des Pseudo-Robert de Borron Die Fortsetzung des Huth-Merlin,* Halle a.S., 1913 (*Beihefte zur Zeitschrift für Romanische Philologie,* XLVII).

Sommer, H. Oskar, ed., *The Vulgate Version of the Arthurian Romances,* vol. I: *Lestoire del Saint Graal,* Washington, 1909; vol. IV: *Le Livre de Lancelot del Lac,* part II, Washington, 1911; vol. VI: *Les Aventures ou la Queste del Saint Graal* and *La Mort le Roi Artus,* Washington, 1913, vol. VII Supplement: *Livre d'Artus,* Washington, 1913.

Sone von Nausay, ed. Moritz Goldschmidt, Tübingen, 1899 (*Bibliothek des Litt. Vereins in Stuttgart,* CCXVI).

Sozomen, The Ecclesiastical History of, Comprising a History of the Church, from A.D. 324 to A.D. 440, Translated from the Greek: with a Memoir of the Author — Also the Ecclesiastical History of Philostorgius, as Epitomized by Photius, Patriarch of Constantinople, trans. Edward Walford, London, 1855.

Spargo, John Webster, *Virgil the Necromancer,* Cambridge [Mass.], 1934 (*Harvard Studies in Comparative Literature,* X).

Speculum Regale, ed. O. Brenner, Munich, 1881.

Speculum Regale, trans. L. M. Larson, New York, 1917 (*American Scandinavian Foundation*).

Statius, *Thebaid V–XII,* in *Statius,* trans. J. H. Mozley, vol. II, London and New York, 1928 (*Loeb Library*).

Stevenson, George, ed., *Pieces from the Makculloch and the Gray MSS together with the Chepman and Myllar Prints,* Edinburgh and London, 1918 (*Scottish Text Society,* 65).

Stjerna, Knut, *Essays on Questions Connected with the Old English Poem of Beowulf,* trans. John R. Clark Hall, Coventry, 1912.

Stokes, Whitley, see Windisch, Ernst, *Irische Texte.*

Strömback, Däg, "Om Draumkvaedet och dess Källor," *ARV, Tidskrift för Nordisk Folkminnesforskning,* 1946.

Stuart, Donald C., *Stage Decoration in France in the Middle Ages,* New York, 1910 (*Columbia University Studies in Romance, Philology, and Literature*).

Sturlunga Saga, including the Islendinga Saga of Lawman Sturla Thordsson and other works, ed. Gudbrand Vigfusson, 2 vols., Oxford, 1878.

Sturluson, Snorri, The Prose Edda by, trans. Arthur G. Brodeur, New York and London, 1916 (*The American-Scandinavian Foundation*).

Sypherd, W. O., *Studies in Chaucer's House of Fame,* London, 1907 for 1904 (*Chaucer Soc.,* second series, 39).

Talmud, The Babylonian, Seder Neziḳin, trans. Izhac Epstein, 24 vols., London, 1935.

Tamassia, Nino, *S. Francesco d'Assisi e la sua Leggenda,* Padua and Verona, 1906.

Terry, Milton S., *The Sibylline Oracles, Translated from the Greek into English Blank Verse,* New York, 1890.

Tertullian, *The Apology,* in *The Ante-Nicene Fathers,* ed. Alexander Roberts and James Donaldson, revised by A. Cleveland Coxe, vol. III, Buffalo, 1885.

Tertullian: Apology, De Spectaculis, trans. T. R. Glover, G. R. Rendall, W. C. A. Kerr, London and New York, 1931 (*Loeb Library*).

[Tertullian] *Quinti Septimi Florentis Tertulliani Apologeticum secundum utramque libri recensionem, Tertulliani editionis,* part II, ed. Henry Hoppe, vol. I, Vienna, Leipzig, 1939 (*CSEL,* LXIX).

Theodulph of Orleans, in *Poetae Latini Medii Aevi, Poetae Latini aevi Carolini,* ed. E. Dümmler, vol. I, pp. 437ff., Berlin, 1881 (*MGH*).

Thesaurus patrum flores doctorum, vol. V, Paris, 1824.

Thomas Aquinas, Saint, *Summa Theologica, pars prima, a quaestione L ad Quaestionem CXIX,* in *Sancti Thomae Aquinatis Opera omnia iussu Impensaque Leonis XIII P.M. edita,* vol. V, Rome, 1889.

Thomas Aquinas, St., The "Summa Theologica" of, Part I, Q.Q. LXXV.–CII. Literally Translated by Fathers of the English Dominican Province, 2nd and revised ed. [vol. IV], London, 1922.

Thomas of Erceldoune, The Romance and Prophecies of, ed. James A. H. Murray, London, 1875 (*EETS,* 61).

Thomas of Erceldoune called the Rhymer, ed. Alois Brandl, in *Sammlung Englischer Denkmäler in Kritischen Ausgaben,* vol. II, Berlin, 1880.

Thompson, Stith, *Motif-Index of Folk-Literature, a Classification of Narrative Elements in Folk-Tales, Ballads, Myths, Fables, Mediaeval Romances, Exempla, Fabliaux, Jest-Books, and Local Legends,* 5 vols., Bloomington, Ind., 1932–1936 (Studies nos. 96ff., in *Indiana University Studies,* vols. XIXff.).

Thoms, William J., ed., *Early English Prose Romances,* London, 1858.

Thorpe, Benjamin see *Homilies.*

Thorsten Oxfoot, The Tale of, in *Fornmanna sögur eptir gomlum Handritum,* III, Copenhagen, 1827.

Thorsten Oxfoot, The Tale of, ed. and trans. Gudbrand Vigfússon and F. York Powell, in *Origines Islandicae, A Collection of the More Important Sagas and Other Native Writings Relating to the Settlement and Early History of Iceland,* vol. II, Oxford, 1905.

Thurneysen, Rudolf, *Die irische Helden- und Königsage bis zum siebzehnten Jahrundert,* Halle a.S., 1921.

Thurneysen, Rudolf, *Zwei Versionen der mittelirischen Legende von Snedgus und Mac Riagla, Programm zur Feier des Geburtstags . . . Univ. zu Freiburg i. Br.,* Halle, 1904.

Tischendorf, L. F. C., *Apocalypses Apocryphae,* Leipzig, 1866.

Toy, Crawford Howell, *Introduction to the History of Religions,* Boston, 1913.

Trissino, G. G., *L'Italia Liberata da' Goti,* ed. A. Antonini, 3 parts [Paris], 1729.

Twining, Louisa, *Symbols and Emblems of Early and Mediaeval Christian Art,* London, 1852.

Tylor, Edward B., *Primitive Culture. Researches into the Development of Mythology, Philosophy, Religion, Language, Art, and Custom*, 2 vols. in 1, 7th ed., New York, 1924.

Ulrich von Zatzikhoven, Lanzelet. Eine Erzählung von, ed. K. A. Hahn, Frankfurt a.M., 1845.

Unger, C. R., *Heilagra Manna Søgur*, 2 vols., Christiania, 1877.

Ungnad, Arthur, *Gilgamesch-Epos und Odyssee*, Breslau, 1923 (*Kulturfragen*, 4/5).

Ungnad, Arthur, and Hugo Gressman, *Das Gilgamesch-Epos*, Göttingen, 1911.

Unwerth, W. von, *Untersuchungen über Totenkult und Ódinnverehrung bei Nordgermanen und Lappen*, etc., Breslau, 1911 (*Germanistische Abhandlungen*, 37).

[Valerius] *Valeri, Iuli, Alexandri Polemi Res Gestae Alexandri Macedonis Translatae ex Aesopi Graeco*, ed. Bernard Kuebler, Leipzig, 1888.

Vassar Mediaeval Studies, ed. Christabel Forsyth Fiske, New Haven, 1923.

[Veda] *Atharva-veda Sámhitā*, trans. W. D. Whitney, Cambridge [Mass.], 1905 (*Harvard Oriental Series*, VII).

[Veda] *The Rigveda: The Oldest Literature of the Indians*, ed. Adolf Kaegi, trans. R. Arrowsmith, Boston, 1886.

Venus la Deesse d'Amor, De, ed. Wendelin Foerster, Bonn, 1880.

Victoris, Claudii Marii, Alethia et Probae Cento, ed. C. Schenkl, in *Poetae Christiani minores*, part I, Vienna, Prague, and Leipzig, 1888 (*CSEL*, XVI).

Vigfússon, Gudbrand, and Powell, F. York, eds. and trans., *Origines Islandicae, A Collection of the More Important Sagas and Other Native Writings Relating to the Settlement and Early History of Iceland*, Oxford, 1905.

Vincent of Beauvais, *Speculum Historiale*, Venice, 1591.

Vincent of Beauvais, *Speculum Maius*, in *Bibliotheca Mundi seu Speculi Maioris*, vol. IV, Douai, 1624.

Viollet-le-Duc, M., *Dictionnaire Raisonné de l'Architecture Française du XIe au XVIe Siècle*, vol. V, Paris, 1868.

Virgil, vol. I: *Eclogues, Georgics, Aeneid i–vi*, ed. H. Rushton Fairclough, revised ed., London and Cambridge [Mass.], 1938 (*Loeb Library*).

Visio Wettini, in *Poetarum Latinorum medii aevi,* vol. II: *Poetae Latini aevi Carolini,* ed. Ernst Dümmler, Berlin, 1884 (*MGH*).

Vita Gildae in *Auctores antiquissimi,* XIII, 1 (*Chronica Minora,* III, 1), pp. 91ff., ed. T. Mommsen, Berlin, 1894 (*MGH*).

Vita Merlini, ed. J. J. Parry, Urbana, Illinois, 1925 (*University of Illinois Studies in Language and Literature,* X).

Vita S. Anskarii, ed. D. C. F. Dahlman, in *Scriptores,* II, Hanover, 1829 (*MGH*).

Voigt, Max, *Beiträge zur Geschichte der Visionenliteratur im Mittelalter,* Leipzig, 1924 (*Palaestra,* 146).

Voyage of Bran, see Meyer, Kuno.

Vries, Jan de, *Altgermanische Religionsgeschichte,* 2 vols., Berlin and Leipzig, 1937 (Paul's *Grundriss der german. Philol.,* 12:1–2).

Waddell, Helen, *Medieval Latin Lyrics,* London, 1929.

Wagner, Albrecht, *Visio Tnugdali Lateinisch und Altdeutsch,* Erlangen, 1882.

Wahlund, Carl W., *Die Altfranzösische Prosaübersetzungen von Brendans Meerfahrt,* Uppsala, 1900.

Walsingham, Thomas, *Historia Anglicana,* ed. Henry Thomas Riley, vol. I, London, 1863 (*Rolls Series,* XXVIII:1).

Ward, H. L. D., *Catalogue of Romances in the Department of Manuscripts in the British Museum,* vol. II, London, 1893.

Wartburgkrieg, Der, Karl Simrock, Stuttgart and Augsburg, 1858.

Watriquet de Couvin, Dits de, ed. A. Scheler, Brussels, 1868.

Wattenbach, W., *Deutschlands Geschichtsquellen im Mittelalter bis zur Mitte des dreizehnten Jahrhunderts,* 3 vols., Berlin, 1885.

Wensinck, A. J., *The Muslim Creed, Its Genesis and Historical Development,* Cambridge [Eng.], 1932.

Wentz, W. Y. Evans, *The Fairy Faith in Celtic Countries,* London, 1911.

Weston, Jessie L., *The Legend of Sir Lancelot du Lac,* London, 1901 (*Grimm Library,* 12).

Weston, Jessie L., *The Legend of Sir Perceval, Studies upon its Origin, Development, and Position in the Arthurian Cycle,* 2 vols., London, 1909 (*Grimm Library,* 17, 19).

White Book Mabinogion, The, ed. John G. Evans, Pwllheli, 1907.

Wigalois, der Ritter mit dem Rade, ed. J. M. N. Kapteyn, vol. I: Text,

Bonn, 1926 (*Rheinische Beiträge und Hülfsbücher zur Germanischen Philologie und Volkskunde*, IX).

William of Malmesbury, *De gestis regum Anglorum*, vol. I, ed. William Stubbs, London, 1887 (*Rolls Series*, XC:1).

William of Malmesbury, *Visio Karoli*, pt. iii of *Ex gestis regum Anglorum*, book ii, 1, ed. D. G. Waitz, in *Scriptores IV, Rerum Germanicarum X*, Hanover, 1852 (*MGH*).

William of Newburgh, The First Four Books of the Historia Rerum Anglicarum of, in *Chronicles of the Reigns of Stephen, Henry II, and Richard I*, vol. I, ed. Richard Howlett, London, 1884 (*Rolls Series*, LXXXII:1).

William the Clerk, *Besant de Dieu*, ed. Ernst Martin, Halle, 1869.

Williams, Robert, ed., *Selections from the Hengwrt MSS*, trans. G. H. Jones, 2 vols., London, 1876, 1892.

Willson, Elizabeth, *The Middle English Legends of Visits to the Other World and Their Relation to the Metrical Romances*, Chicago, 1917.

Wimberly, Lowry Charles, *Folklore in the English and Scottish Ballads*, Chicago [1928].

Windisch, Ernst, *The Debility of the Ultonian Warriors*, see E. Hull, *The Cuchullin Saga in Irish Literature*, pp. 95ff.

Windisch, Ernst, *Irische Texte*, vols. I and II, Leipzig, 1880, 1884; vol. III, 1, 2, Leipzig, 1891; with W. Stokes, vol. IV, 2, Leipzig, 1909.

Withington, Robert, *English Pageantry, An Historical Outline*, 2 vols., Cambridge [Mass.], 1918, 1920.

Wolfram von Eschenbach, Parzival, A Knightly Epic by, trans. Jessie L. Weston, 2 vols., London, 1894.

Wolframs von Eschenbach, Parzival und Titurel, ed. Karl Bartsch, 2nd ed., 3 vols., Leipzig, 1875–1877 (*Deutsche Classiker des Mittelalters*, 9–11).

Wolframs von Eschenbach, Parzival und Titurel, ed. Ernst Martin, 2 vols., Halle a.S., 1900, 1903 (*Germanistische Handbibliothek*, IX, 1, 2).

Wooing of Emer and Cuchullin's Education under Scathach, The, trans. Kuno Meyer, in *The Cuchullin Saga in Irish Literature*, edited by E. Hull, pp. 55ff.

World's Great Classics, The, Oriental Literature, revised ed., vol. I, New York [1900].

Wright, John K., *The Geographical Lore of the Time of the Crusades, A Study in the History of Medieval Science and Tradition in Western Europe,* New York, 1925 (*American Geographical Society, Research Series,* 15).

Wright, John K., *The Leardo Map of the World,* New York, 1928 (*American Geographical Society, Library Series,* 4).

Wright, Thomas, ed., *The Anglo-Latin Satirical Poets and Epigrammatists of the Twelfth Century,* 2 vols., London, 1872 (*Rolls Series,* LIX).

Wright, Thomas, *Saint Patrick's Purgatory; an Essay on the Legends of Purgatory, Hell, and Paradise, current during the Middle Ages,* London, 1844.

Yderroman, Der Altfranzösische, ed. Heinrich Gelzer, Dresden, 1913 (*Gesellschaft für romanische Literatur,* 31).

Ywain and Gawain, ed. Gustav Schleich, Oppeln and Leipzig, 1887.

Zanden, C. M. van der, *Étude sur le Purgatoire de Saint Patrice accompagnée du Texte Latin d'Utrecht et du Texte Anglo-normand de Cambridge,* Amsterdam, 1927.

Zarncke, Friedrich, *Der Priester Johannes, Erste Abhandlung, Koeniglich-saechsische Gesellschaft der Wissenschaften, Abhandlungen, Philologisch-historische Classe,* vol. VII, Leipzig, 1879; *Zweite Abhandlung,* vol. VIII, Leipzig, 1883.

Zend-Avesta, The, Part I, *Vendîdad* etc., trans. James Darmesteter, Oxford, 1880 (*Sacred Books of the East,* IV).

Zend-Avesta, The, Part II: *Yast,* trans. James Darmesteter, Oxford, 1883 (*Sacred Books of the East,* XXIII).

Zend-Avesta, The, Part III: *The Yasna, Visparad, Âfrînagân, Gâhs, and Miscellaneous Fragments,* trans. L. H. Mills, Oxford, 1887 (*Sacred Books of the East,* XXXI).

Zenone da Pistoia, *Pietosa Fonte,* ed. Francesco Zambrini, Bologna, 1874 (*Scelta di Curiosità,* 137).

Zosimus, Narrative of, in *Apocrypha Anecdota,* ed. M. R. James, Cambridge, 1893 (*Texts and Studies,* II, 3).

Zosimus, The Narrative of, trans. W. A. Craigie, in *The Ante-Nicene Fathers,* ed. Allan Menzies, vol. IX, 5th ed., pp. 219ff., New York, 1906.

Zwicker, J., *Fontes historiae religionis Celticae,* vol. III, Berlin and Bonn, 1936.

INDEX

The following index is not complete. It has not seemed worth while to list all the instances of every motif, such as the garden, the fountain, birds, flowers, and the like.